DOYLE BRUNSON'S
SUPER SYSTEM

A COURSE IN POWER POKER

Doyle *"Texas Dolly"* **Brunson**
in collaboration with

Bobby Baldwin
Mike Caro
Joey Hawthorne
David Reese
David Sklansky

Special Writing and Coordination by
Allen Goldberg

This Cardoza edition is printed by
special arrangement with B & G
Publishing Co., Inc in affiliation with
Mike Caro University of Poker Press.

MIKE ♠ CARO
MCU
· UNIVERSITY ·
The Advanced School of Winning!
POKER · GAMING · LIFE STRATEGY

CARDOZA PUBLISHING

Play Poker with Doyle Online!
www.doylesroom.com

Cardoza Publishing is the foremost gaming and gambling publisher in the world with a library of almost 100 up-to-date and easy-to-read books and strategies. These authoritative works are written by the top experts in their fields and with more than 10,000,000 books in print, represent the best-selling and most popular gaming books anywhere.

THIRD EDITION
14th Big Printing

Copyright ©1978 by B & G Publishing Co., Inc under original title:
How I Made Over $1,000,000 Playing Poker.
Copyright ©1979, 1984, 1989, 1994, 2002 by B & G Publishing
All Rights Reserved

Library of Congress Catalog No: 2002104552
ISBN: 1-58042-081-8

Visit our website or write us for a full list of Cardoza books, software and advanced strategies.

CARDOZA PUBLISHING

P.O. Box 98115, Las Vegas, NV 89193
Phone (800)577-WINS
email: cardozabooks@aol.com
www.cardozabooks.com

This book is dedicated to
Louise, Doyla, Pam and Todd

and
a special dedication to
the Binion Family
for their contribution to Poker

Acknowledgements

Many people helped me in creating this book. I want to show my appreciation for their efforts by acknowledging them in alphabetical order:

Bobby Baldwin
Mike Caro
Craig Creel
Richard Englesteen
Eve Firestone
Allan Goldberg
Joey Hawthorne
John Hill
A. D. Hopkins
Marie Kimbrell
John Luckman
Steve Margulies
Bruce McClenachan
Steve McClenachan
Ken Miller
David Nicol
David Reese
"Amarillo Slim" Preston
Victor Resnick
Edwin Silberstang
David Sklansky
Jimmy *"The Greek"* Snyder
Frances Strauss
Carol Shabaz Thompson
Dean Zes

and

Stan Hunt...*for his caricatures.*

D. B.

TABLE OF CONTENTS

FOREWORD

by

JIMMY *"The Greek"* SNYDER

You're an odds-on favorite to be a real big winner at Poker with *"Doy-lee's"* book. (They call him *"Dolly"* now, but I was the first one to call him something other than **Doyle** many years back. I still call him *Doy-lee*.)

I was flattered when he asked me to look at the manuscript of his book and write this **Foreword** if I really thought he had something. He has — a very special something.

At last, there's a course (this one) that will really teach you about the business of playing Poker. It took *Doy-lee* (25 years) most of a lifetime to learn what he's revealed in these pages. Long before he actually won the World Championship of Poker for two years straight (1976 and 1977), he was generally recognized as the best all-around Poker player alive. And, whether he won or lost the actual titles, nobody ...but nobody...ever questioned his right to claim the "title" of the best No-Limit player in the world.

Doy-lee's expert collaborators also know what they're talking about. They should. *Doy-lee* picked them carefully. Very carefully. **They're all Poker** *players* **(as opposed to Poker** *writers***).**

That's the thing that makes this course unique. It was created by **players** — *not* **writers**. (But **don't** misunderstand me by thinking *Doy-lee's* book **isn't** well-written. **It is.**)

The only thing I found wrong with it is that it's **not** a course for a beginner. You **don't** have to be a thoroughly experienced player to get the most out of it, but a rank beginner just wouldn't be able to appreciate its value.

Barring that one criticism, I have nothing but the highest praise for *Doy-lee's* book. It covers everything you'd like to know about Poker — and a lot of things you never thought about.

Doy-lee's book is filled with more than 600 pages of techniques, strategies and original and very creative Poker ideas that could only come from the mind of the master and his five expert collaborators — the very best Poker players on the face of the earth. On top of that, it's got the most complete and most accurate Poker statistics and computations that have ever been in print.

I firmly believe *Doy-lee's* book is a super-favorite to become the all-time Poker classic. It's a monster favorite to become the "Bible" for Poker players.

PREFACE

by

"Amarillo Slim" PRESTON

I was out on my ranch in **Amarillo, Texas** when the phone rang. My wife Helen said *"Slim, it's Doyle"*. I'd had a hard day branding my registered *Maine-Anjous* so I was ready to leave the ranch for some action. I thought *Dolly's* call might be my chance. Maybe there was a big game going somewhere and the current World Champ needed some help.

If he did need some, I knew he would be calling because of our past relationship. *Dolly, Sailor* **Roberts** and myself had started on the road together as youngsters. For over seven years, we played out of the same bankroll — sharing our wins and losses. I doubt if there ever will be three Poker partners with the kind of playing talent we had. We sure did play some jam-up Poker. Any one of us could pinch-hit for the other when he was tired or just not feelin' right. We had been one hell of a team.

We still remained the best of friends even though we dissolved our partnership. And we didn't do too bad going our separate ways. We'll always be proud of the fact that each of us became the World Poker Champ. Out of the first seven *World Series of Poker* champions, between us we won it four times. (I won in 1972, *Sailor* won in 1975 and *Dolly* took it down in 1976 and 1977.)

When I answered the phone, *Dolly* said *"I finished writin' a book, Slim — I wonder if you'd do the Preface for me"*. Now, we're such good friends, I couldn't say "No". But I wasn't too crazy about writing some nice things in "just another Poker book". A few other Poker "writers" asked me for about the same thing and I turned 'em down. I didn't want to be discourteous, but I didn't even want to see their book. What could they have to say? In order to write a great Poker book, a guy's got to be a great Poker player. It's the only way.

So, I said to *Dolly*, *"Sure pal, send it to me. I'll look it over and tell you what I think"*.

I was really surprised when I got the manuscript. I could tell right away it **wasn't** "just another Poker book". This baby really gets into things. *Dolly* writes about the very things he and I used to talk about every night after the Poker games. It's real deep stuff — Poker secrets that very few players in the world know about. I can't begin to tell you how much better this book is than any other Poker book I've ever read. It's like daylight and dark.

My first thought after studying just part of *Dolly's* course was that it's sure going to wise up a lot of Suckers. It's goin' to make a Pro's life a lot tougher — I can tell you that.

My second thought was *maybe* **not**. Someone who's **not** a Pro *might* **not be able to understand some of the things that** *Dolly* writes about. It's a powerful school full of very sophisticated Poker strategies.

But as I read on, I changed my mind about an amateur being able to understand it. Each section is explained very clearly by *Dolly* and his experts. (Where did he find all those guys?) He **didn't** write-down to a grade-school level and you **won't** breeze through it. But, if you give it your careful attention, you'll really learn how to be a consistent winner. You'll learn the things it took me 30 years of playin' to get right. And you'll learn 'em all in a few days.

Because this course is so good, it's worth many times its weight in gold. It could turn any amateur into a winning Pro. It will also make someone who already is a Pro a far better one. It'll make you a winning player at Limit or No-Limit Poker. If you're a Poker player, what more could you ask for?

If we (me, *Dolly* and *Sailor*) could have had this course 15 years ago, we could have saved a lot of sleepless nights scratching a broke rump driving home after a tough game. (Yeah, we had some losers.) If you read it and study it — and then use it like *Dolly* wrote it — you'll save some too.

Amarillo Slim

INTRODUCTION

I thought playing Poker was tough. That was before I started trying to create a Poker course. This is my first Poker book and probably my last one. I wish I had one like it when I started playing. If I did, I would have been flying from game to game or driving the new Lincoln Continental I now own instead of the two-year old Ford I shared with my Road Buddies, *Sailor* **Roberts** and *Amarillo Slim.*

Fourteen months ago, I started what I thought was going to be a three or four week job. After I read the so-called "expert" books on the market today, it made me a little bit sick. Nowhere could I find a book that had been written by a legitimate *World Class* Professional Poker player. So I decided to write the best possible book I could, regardless of time or expense. Believe me, no one will ever go to the trouble of writing a book comparable to this one. I truly believe this course will long outlive me and my collaborators.

Speaking of my expert collaborators, I had a talk with each one of them before we began each section. I told them if they had any reservations about giving up any "trade secrets" **not** to start the job. I would find someone else. Fortunately, each expert liked the idea of doing an authoritative Poker course and agreed to do their very best. As I had picked the top player in the world in each game, I was both grateful to them and relieved I didn't have to take second choice in any game.*

Each section was done individually and completely separate from the rest. (For that reason, certain things are said in one section and repeated in others.) All the experts and myself have basically the same philosophy of play and each stressed many of the same points such as ante structure, aggressiveness, position, etc. Rather than stifle anyone by

---

*I did *not* have a collaborator on the material in this book relating to No-Limit Poker (which includes *Deuce—to—Seven Lowball* and *Hold 'em.*) For over 20 years, No-Limit Poker (particularly No-Limit *Hold 'em*) has been my specialty — so I did it alone.

vii

saying *"we've already said that,"* we made each section complete in itself. So, if some things are said more than once, they are obviously very important in all types of Poker and **should** be stressed. The theme is POWER POKER.

If you're a beginning Poker Player, this book **may** be a little too sophisticated for you. But...if you're one of the millions of players who play regularly, you should easily be able to apply the concepts and strategies that this book has — if you put a little effort into it. We (myself and my experts) are living proof that they work.

No one person can master every game in this book. I recommend that you read the entire book, then pick the game of your choice and *really* **study it**. After you feel you *really* **know** that section...take another section and do the same with it. If you do it that way, you'll be an all–around player...and you'll be able to play any form of Poker in the toughest line-up you could find. **Super/System** is really six or seven courses in one.

You'll find mathematical work in the *Statistics* section of this book that has **never** been done before. Thanks to *"Crazy Mike"* **Caro**, my Draw Poker expert, there are tables and charts that could almost teach you how to play all the games by themselves.

I was also fortunate enough to get **Allan Goldberg**, the best Poker writer in the world to assist me. I read articles he had written and decided then, that when I did my book I was going to get him to help me make it the best Poker book I was capable of creating.

I know, for sure, whoever you are, wherever you are, you're going to learn a lot reading each section. I know I did.

D. B.

MY STORY

MY STORY

in brief

I suppose at some time in our lives we all reflect on the good and the bad that has happened to us and ask ourselves the question: *If we had it to do all over again are there things we would change?* I'm no exception.

There's no one alive who could have had it much tougher than I had. I was in a photo-finish with death. That's as close as you can get to the ultimate *"bad beat"*.

There's also been near-tragedy in my life due to health problems with my wife **Louise** and my oldest daughter, **Doyla**. Additionally, I've been so broke that I couldn't afford bus fare from Las Vegas to my home in Fort Worth...and could barely scrape up the dime to call my wife to send me money for the ticket.

But...there are two sides to the coin that's been flipping my life around.

I finally got to the point where I got my bankroll up to One Hundred Thousand...and I've **never** looked back since. My wife and family live in relative luxury...and they'll **never** have a hungry day as long as they live.

I've made millions playing Poker...lost most of it betting on Sports and Golf — but I've always done "my thing". And...I'm a happy man because of it. The pleasures have definitely outweighed the pain.

Through it all, I've learned that, in Life, a man's **not** beaten even though he's all-in. You **can't** count him out until the fall of the last card.

I've been tested time and again on many "battlefields". I've lost a lot of little skirmishes. . .but I've won the big ones. **That's** what **really** counts.

The adversity I've faced has been a blessing in disguise. It's strengthened my character. I've had to draw on that strength many a time at the Poker table. I'll continue to draw on it for the rest of my years.

I'll need that strength too. You see. . .I'm a gambler. I'll always be one. I couldn't be anything else. So, my life will always be filled with wins. . .and losses. I wouldn't have it any other way. It's exciting. There's almost never a dull moment in my life. And I can't imagine anyone having a better life than the one I have right now. I've got just about everything I want.

Yes. . .the deck's been stacked against me at various times in my life — but I've overcome every *"cold deck"* I've faced. I'm enough of a dreamer to realize it might have been that elusive something a gambler calls luck. But, I'm also enough of a realist to know that in general we make our own luck — through knowledge, skill and experience. And that goes for the game of Poker as well as the game of Life.

In the summer of 1933 I was born in the West Texas town of **Longworth**, a spot on the road consisting of a few houses and a general store. I don't suppose the population ever exceeded 100. We had only two industries in the area — farming and a **U. S. Gypsum** plant. My dad worked for **Planters Gin Co.** and while he didn't make much money there was always food on the table and a little extra for the kids once in a while. We lived in a four-room frame house at the time, with an outhouse at the back. I remember thinking when I was little that if I ever got any money, I'd bring the plumbing indoors. It used to get mighty cold on those prairies during the winter.

There were five of us living at home when I was small: **Dad, Mom**, my sister **Lavada** and my older brother

Lloyd. It was crowded but we didn't mind. There was a lot of warmth...and a lot of love.

My mother is a religious, God-fearing woman who did her best to raise us with a sense of moral values. I suppose a good deal of that has remained with me. She used to tell us that you'll find good in every man if you look hard enough. I've always tried to remember that and act accordingly... although sometimes it's been mighty difficult considering some of the unsavory characters I've come in contact with.

My Dad was perhaps the calmest, most even-tempered individual I've ever been exposed to. Nothing ruffled him. I can't remember ever seeing him get angry. When things went wrong he'd take it in stride, smile and say that setbacks were only a temporary thing. Tomorrow would always be better. Of course we kids would get into a little trouble every once in a while (as all kids do) and he surely would have been justified in whaling the tar out of us. But, he never even raised his voice. Not once. Nor did he ever hit us. He had a capacity for making us know we'd been out of line without raising as much as one finger. He was a truly remarkable man. When the Good Lord made my Dad...HE destroyed the mold.

I attended grammar school in **Longworth** where several grades were held in one room. I recall that my third grade class consisted of only three kids — two boys and a girl. We got a lot of individual attention. That's for sure.

After grammar school and Jr. High I entered **Sweetwater** *High School* with two of my closest friends from **Longworth** — **D. C. Andrews** and **Riley Cross**. We turned out for the Basketball team. It didn't take long to become known as the **Longworth** triple-threat and the three of us took over the varsity team. Why not? We were in prime shape. We were always working out, running and swimming. **D. C., Riley**, and I would run non-stop from **Longworth** to the swimming hole on the **Barclay Ranch** (about eight miles away). Sometimes we'd run from **Sweetwater** back to **Longworth** after school, but the coach didn't take too kindly to that. He gave us a station wagon so we'd be sure to make the practices on time. Sports was my whole life in those days. It was everything.

In addition to Basketball, I also turned out for the Baseball team. . .and at the suggestion of my coach started running Track. I was never much interested in Track, but the Basketball season was over and I needed something to do to keep in shape. . .so I took on the mile run. It seemed like a fair distance and, with all the running I was doing, I felt I could do all right. I honestly didn't realize at the time how well I'd actually do.

In 1950, as a Senior, I entered the *Texas Interscholastic Track Meet* as a mile runner and won it in a time of 4:38. Without really trying, I suddenly found myself the best high school miler in the state of Texas. In the meantime, I had also been chosen as one of the five best high school Basketball players in the state — a rather heady experience for a boy of sixteen.

After that, the scholarship offers started coming in. There must have been a hundred or so all told from various colleges and universities throughout the country. I finally settled on **Hardin-Simmons**, a Baptist-affiliated college in **Abilene** which was primarily known for turning out teachers and coaches. At the time I felt my life's work would be in one of these areas. In my Junior year at **Hardin-Simmons** I was voted the most valuable player in the *Border Conference* and the Pro teams were beginning to show an interest. The **Minneapolis Lakers** (now the **Los Angeles Lakers**) were making overtures and I began to set my sights on a career as a professional Basketball player. **Dell** *Basketball Magazine* picked me as one of the top ten college players in the country. I was riding high. In addition to the Basketball honors, I had run the mile in 4:18.6. That put me in contention for a spot on the National team. I often wonder what would have happened if I had trained as hard for Track as I did for Basketball. I was only eighteen years old at the time. Thinking about it now, I'm sorry I didn't. I think I missed my true calling in Sports. There's no doubt in my mind that a four-minute mile was possible.

The future looked bright indeed. In the summer, I got a job at the **U. S. Gypsum** plant. It wasn't any great shakes as jobs go, but I planned on saving enough to last me through my Senior year. I had been assigned to unload some sheetrock one day and as I was hauling the sheets off and stacking them. . .suddenly. . .the pile began to shift. I tried to stop it with my body, jamming my knee into the lower half of the pile to keep it in place. What a dummy I was. I couldn't stop it. Two thousand pounds of sheetrock crashed on my right leg. It snapped in two places. I remember my first thoughts were, *"My God, I'll never play Basketball again."* My leg was in a cast for two years due to complications. The fractures finally healed. But, when the cast came off, my speed and coordination were gone. So were my hopes for the Pros.

I'd been playing Poker off and on since my high school days. In fact, I still remember my first game. It was five-card Draw and I ended up the big winner. I recall thinking at the time what easy money it was. After I entered **Hardin-Simmons**, I'd play in the usual Saturday night games. In general, I seemed to do pretty well. I got caught once or twice and was disciplined for gambling. . .but, since I was one of the Basketball stars nothing much came of it.

After breaking my leg, Basketball was out of the question and I spent a lot more time playing Poker. I began paying more attention to my studies also. Prior to my injury I felt that Basketball would carry me through school. But, from here on in I'd have to use my brain. My Poker winnings paid for my expenses and in 1954 I graduated with a Bachelor's degree. I stayed on at **Hardin-Simmons** receiving my Master's degree in Administrative Education the following year. With these credentials, I felt sure I'd be offered a job which would lead to a superintendent of schools or at least a principalship. It didn't work out that way. In fact, the top job offered to me was that of a Basketball coach at **Dalhart** (Texas) *High School* at a salary of $4,800 a year.

It didn't make sense. I was making more than that just playing Poker. I used to travel around to the different colleges in Texas setting-up games and making a fair living by my wits. At that time, however, the idea of becoming a Professional gambler had **not** occurred to me even though it was apparent I played better than most.

After graduation, I went to work as a business machines salesman...a profession which could ultimately make me some twenty five or thirty thousand a year — or so I thought. But, it wasn't in the cards. My first day on the job I called on a few prospective accounts. I didn't get much further than the front door and wound up in a Poker game before the day was out. It was a Seven-Stud game where I cleared a month's salary in something less than three hours. *"My God"*, I thought, *"what am I doing trying to sell machines nobody wants to buy from me when I can sit down at a Poker table and make ten times the money in one sixth the time?"* It didn't take me very long to figure out what to do. I quit the company and began my career as a full-time Professional Poker Player. I've never regretted that decision.

The first games I played which amounted to anything were down on **Exchange Street** in **Fort Worth, Texas**. I'd be surprised if you could find a tougher street in the whole world. There were shootings, muggings, robberies, and just about every kind of violence imaginable. The stuff we see on TV today is tame compared to what **Exchange Street** was like almost any hour of the day. But, at the card table, amidst all that violence, everything was as gentlemanly as could be. It was literally two different worlds. My buddy, **Dwayne Hamilton**, and I would frequent a Card Room run by a gangster named **Tincy** whose main claim to fame was having killed half a dozen people. He ran an honest game, though, and **Dwayne** and I did fairly well. No-Limit Hold 'em was our main game. After we accumulated a good sized stake we moved uptown to the three hundred and five hundred buy-in games where we played with Doctors, Lawyers and other Professional people.

For the next five or six years we made the Texas circuit, playing bigger and bigger games throughout the state. Occasionally we'd drop into the big games in Oklahoma and Louisiana. During this period I met **"Amarillo Slim"** and **"Sailor" Roberts** — a couple of the finest Poker hustlers I've ever met. We hit it off from the start and after **Dwayne** moved back to **Fort Worth**...**Sailor, Slim** and I decided to go into business together. We must have hit every town in Texas relieving the locals of their money. It was a sight to see, the three of us taking on all comers. And not just at

Poker. We got to the point where we were gambling on just about every game there was — Golf, Tennis, Basketball, Pool, Sports betting. . .just about everything. As long as we thought we had some sort of an edge. . .we'd bet. And, we made money. Pretty soon we got to know most everybody in the games no matter where we played. You kept running into the same guys all the time — **Jack Straus, Johnny Moss, Bob Hooks** and a lot of others.

As our reputations grew, we were invited to games in private clubs and homes. These were for the most part rich oil and cattlemen who had a hankering to take on young Professionals like us. It was safer playing in these games than playing in back rooms where you took a risk every time you won a fair amount. I've been hijacked a few times and I can tell you it's not a pleasant experience to be looking down at the business end of a shotgun.

Sailor, Slim and I stuck together for six years or so and we had some mighty fine times. Once in a while we were down, but mostly we managed to hold our own better than most. Our partnership finally broke up after our first big trip to Las Vegas. We lost our entire bankroll (close to six figures) and believe me there's nothing more cantankerous than three broke gamblers. We went our separate ways after that, but have remained close friends to this day.

In 1960 I met my wife, **Louise.** She was a Pharmacist in **San Angelo, Texas** and I courted her for about two years. She was something worth winning you see and I can tell you I had an uphill fight persuading my sweetheart that I was her one and only. She was convinced I was married and it took a heap of testimonials to convince her I was single and available. I worked harder for our first date than anything I've ever done in my life. After I asked her to marry me she had to think twice about permanently hitching up with a Professional Gambler. She had a lot of doubts. It wasn't what most girls were doing at the time. I finally convinced her and we were married in August of 1962.

About four months after we were married, I woke up one morning with a sore throat and thought I was coming down with a bad cold. There was a little knot on the side of my neck about the size of a pea. **Louise** insisted I go to a doctor and so for about three weeks I was taking heavy doses of antibiotics every day. That didn't help...and the knot grew to the size of a hen's egg. By that time, I was plenty worried. My brother **Lloyd** had died of cancer a short while before and I couldn't keep that off my mind. We consulted a cancer specialist in **Fort Worth**. He took one look at me and scheduled me for surgery the following Monday. He **didn't** think the tumor was malignant, but said it would have to come out.

I went into the operating room at 6:30 a.m. When I woke up in the recovery room it was dark. Even though I was very groggy, I could tell things weren't going too well for me. Not only was my head and back in bandages, but my entire chest was wrapped in gauze and completely covered with tape. I remember thinking, *"Doyle, there's something awfully wrong"*. **Louise** was there at my side telling me everything was going to be all right, but I knew she was trying to hide something. I was in a lot of pain...and with the drugs they kept feeding me I was fairly stupified for the next few days.

I remained in the hospital for quite a while. My relatives and friends were always coming by to see how I was doing. That was a comfort. Still...nobody had the courage to tell me what the real situation was. The only thing I knew was that I was going to be taken to **Houston** to the *Cancer Center* at **M. D. Anderson** *Hospital* for further study of my condition.

What I had **not** been told was that when the doctors opened me up they found massive cancer spread throughout my body. It had reached close to the base of my brain and my chest and stomach area were riddled with it. Four surgeons had been called in and they all agreed that it was useless to proceed further. The cancer had attacked so much of my body that it was only a matter of a short period of time before I died. I was a big *"dog"* to live longer than four months.

While I suspected the worst, it wasn't until I was taken home for one day (prior to flying to **Houston**) that I really knew I was going to die. Over two hundred people came to our house that day from all over the country. I was really surprised. I didn't think I had that many close friends. From the way everybody was acting it was obvious they came to say goodbye. My friend **Dwayne Hamilton** just broke down and cried.

Louise was pregnant at the time and I thought to myself how sad it was that I'd probably never get to see my baby. By all rights I'd be dead and gone before it arrived.

Louise was thinking the same thing and had made the arrangements for further surgery at **M. D. Anderson**. Though the doctors had told her there was no hope of my living, there might be a slight chance of prolonging my life a few more months by radical neck surgery. With that operation, there'd be the possibility I'd be able to live long enough to see my baby before the cancer reached my brain.

We flew to **Houston** the next day. For the next two and a half weeks, I rested in the hospital to build myself up for the surgery to come. I went into the operating room at 10:30 a.m. I spent eight hours under the knife. At 6:30 p.m., they gave **Louise** the news. I **was** going to make it. But. . .it had been touch and go.

At one point during the operation, my blood pressure dropped to zero. . .but they pulled me through. What was truly incredible was that there was no longer any trace of cancer in my system. The doctors couldn't believe it. The impossible had happened.

The odds against my merely surviving the operation itself were very high. That the cancer, *melanoma* (whose black corruption had been visible to the naked eye a month before) had disappeared was incomprehensible to the staff at the hospital. Five doctors had unanimously agreed that it was a medical impossibility for me to live longer than a few more months — with or without the operation.

For the next two weeks, **Louise** and **Sailor** took turns watching me 24 hours a day since we couldn't afford a private nurse. I had to be observed closely. The tubes that led to my body had to be checked constantly. . .and my vital signs had to be monitored continuously. I don't know when **Louise** and **Sailor** got any sleep.

After leaving the hospital, I recuperated at my sister's. When my strength returned, I reported back to the hospital in **Fort Worth** for a checkup. The doctor who had first operated on me was at a complete loss for an explanation. The only thing he could say was that occasionally spontaneous remissions occur, but in my case he could only believe a miracle had happened. Later we found out that during the operation several friends had spoken to their church pastors about my case and entire congregations were praying for my recovery. Those prayers surely must have been answered.

Louise had always been a religious woman, but this experience (and two others in our lives) reinforced her conviction that there's a higher power that watches over us.

Shortly after my recovery, **Louise** developed *a uterine tumor*. That normally requires extensive surgery and removal of the female organs. She was scheduled for surgery...but the operation wasn't necessary when it was discovered that **her** tumor had **also** disappeared. Another miracle.

In 1975, when my daughter **Doyla** was 12 years old she was found to have a debilitating spinal disorder, *idiopathic scoliosis*. That affliction causes extensive curvature of the spine **or** permanent crippling. Specialists were consulted and radical procedures were recommended — including implantation of a steel rod in her spine or a full body brace. None of that was necessary.

Louise organized a marathon prayer session for **Doyla** which included radio broadcasts and correspondence with the late **Katherine Kuhlman** (the famous faith healer). Within three months, **Doyla's** spine had straightened completely. The doctors acknowledged that her's was *one of only three* known cases of such an occurrence *without* surgical assistance. The third miracle in our family.

Since that time, **Louise** has been extremely active in Christian ministry — heavily involved in work with foreign missions. She spends as much (or more) time as a servant of the Lord as she does in taking care of our family. She's said time and again: *"It's so exciting to be a Christian. It's by far the most exciting part of living."* And, I know, she believes that as strongly as any person on earth.

Fortunately, money was **not** a problem when the mountains of medical bills came pouring in for **Louise** and **Doyla**. I did very well at the Poker table during all those years. When I left the hospital after my operation, I recuperated for a while and then I returned to the Poker circuit with a zest and appreciation for life I had never had before. Each day when I woke up the sky was bluer and the grass was greener. The world was as bright as could be. I was alive. From the first session I started playing again, **I won 54 straight times in a row**. I never booked a loser until the 55th session I played. Never before — or since — have I ever had such a streak. I won enough to completely clear my immense doctor and hospital bills — and had plenty left over to keep my family comfortable for several years.

Before the surgery I would have classified myself as a slightly better-than-average player. However, after that ordeal something happened. Everything seemed to click and I was playing better than I had ever played in my life. My playing became almost instinctive. I was reading my competitors more accurately and I felt a self-assurance I had never experienced. My brush with death had apparently triggered innate abilities that had never surfaced before.

The most important thing of all was that I discovered my true vocation. I had finally dispelled any doubts I had about what my profession in life was going to be. Because of pressure from my family and friends, I had thought about returning to "legitimate" work. But now I knew I never would. I was never going to be a "working stiff" — nor was I ever going to have a boss. I was going to make my way through life *my way*.

During the next few years, I gravitated between **Fort Worth** and **Las Vegas** where more and more of the action was developing. I was still doing most of my playing in Texas, but it was getting difficult to find the really big games there. I was beating them so regularly that they were finally saying: *"we can do without Doyle"*. The action, for me, was really beginning to dry-up.

Also, in 1970 **Congress** passed legislation making it even more difficult for a Poker Professional to make a living. The law which directly affected me was one that made it a federal offense to run a large scale Poker game from which five or more players derived an income — except of course in states where such gambling was legal. The handwriting was on the wall.

So, in 1973, I moved my family — **Louise, Doyla, Pamela** (my youngest daughter who was nine years old at the time and a year younger than **Doyla**) and my little boy **Todd** (who had his fourth birthday on the road) to **Las Vegas** where we established our home. It's a good place to live — good weather, good action and good people.

I'm known as a Professional gambler rather than just a Professional Poker player...and I have to admit that I am. I've been known to bet on just about anything. And because of that...I've surely had my share of losers. If I had stuck to Poker, I'd probably be a far wealthier man today. But...old habits are hard to break. I just like to gamble.

But, it's more than just liking to gamble that's in my blood. I'm very competitive by nature. As long as there's a contest — any kind of contest (even if it's a marble shooting contest) — I want to be a part of it. If I couldn't be an active participant as I am at Poker and Golf (when I'd be betting on myself)...I'd have to bet on one side or the other of a Football team, a prize fight, or whatever.

One of the reasons I feel I've been so successful playing Poker is because of the competitive instincts that are within me. You've got to *play hard* to be a consistent winner at Poker. And I'm able to do that instinctively. I was a very hard competitor as an athlete in High School and College. That competitive spirit remained with me. In fact, I'm sure it has a lot to do with my success at the Poker table.

I've never lost the feeling of exhilaration that comes when you're doing the best you can and gambling real high. There's no feeling quite like it.

Next to Poker, Golf is my favorite game and I'm considered a pretty good player — probably a little better than the next guy. Unfortunately quite a few of those "next guys" have played a shade better than me when we got to betting on the course. I remember going back east with my best friend **Jack Binion** one year and ending up playing Golf with a millionaire. We kept raising the stakes until finally we had $180,000 riding on one hole. He putted out for a par to my bogey and all that money just flew away. And that's just one of several such stories I could tell you. Now, the title of this book is *"How I Made over $1,000,000 Playing Poker"*. The title of my next one is going to be *"How I Lost over $1,000,000 Playing Golf"*. There's definitely a moral in there somewhere.

A lot has been written about my winning the 1976 and 1977 *World Series of Poker* (a total win of some $560,000). You may have read some of the many stories. They were tough games against tough competitors. The best players in the world sat at those tables and the pace was grueling. That kind of playing is **not** something I would care to do every day...but for a sheer gut–level contest it can't be beat. There's a certain pride in knowing that you've taken on the best and come out on the top. But, with this pride also comes the realization that you can **never** afford to become complacent. In both the 1976 and 1977 Series, I made a Full House only when the final card was played. And, perhaps, there's a moral in that too. As I noted, in Poker as in Life, you can't count a man out until the last card falls.

Doyle Brunson's

SUPER/SYSTEM

A Course In Power Poker

Class Begins...

GENERAL POKER STRATEGY

GENERAL POKER STRATEGY

Table of Contents

GENERAL POKER STRATEGY

INTRODUCTION

Poker is a game of people. That's the most important lesson you should learn from my book.

I'll be teaching you guidelines and concepts you'll be able to use with great success, and you'll quickly become a very good player. But, if your ambition is to become a great player, a top-flight Pro, a superstar...you'll need to really understand your opponents. You'll need to get inside your opponent's head and be able to estimate with a high degree of certainty what his check, bet or raise really means...and what hand he's likely to be playing.

Being able to do that accurately **isn't** easy. But you **can** do it if you're alert, observant, disciplined and if you concentrate whenever you play (**whether or not** you're involved in the pot). Using my advice and the advice of my expert collaborators, you'll find that the "task" of unmasking your Poker-faced opponents will become easier and easier.

When you're able to put your opponent on exactly the hand he's playing (because you know him almost as well as he knows himself) you can select the best strategy possible for that particular Poker situation. When you reach that level of skill, you'll be a complete player.

That's what Poker's all about. People...and the strategy you use against them. More than any other game, Poker depends on your understanding your opponent. You've got to know what makes him tick. More importantly, you've got to know what makes him tick **at the moment** you're involved in a pot with him. What's his mood...his feeling? What's his apparent psychological frame of mind **right now**? Is he in the mood to gamble...or is he just sitting there waiting for the *nuts?* Is he a loser and *on tilt* (playing far below his normal capability)...or has he screwed down (despite his being loser) and begun playing his best possible game? Is he a cocky winner who's now playing carelessly and throwing off most of his winnings...or is he a winner who's started to play very *tight* so he can protect his gains?

When you can accurately answer questions like those (and there are many more like them)...and employ the other ideas, principles, rules, techniques and strategies I'll teach you in this book — you'll be one **super-tough** Poker player.

Put all of it together and your playing ability will border on being World-Class.

It takes a lot to play winning Poker at a World-Class level because Poker is such a complex game — more complex than any other game...or any other form of gambling.

For example, the difference between playing good Poker and playing good Blackjack is as vast as the difference between squad tactics and grand strategy in warfare. You can beat a Blackjack game by knowing exactly what to do in every situation...and doing it. That's tactics. But in Poker you may face an identical situation twice against the same opponent, handle it two different ways, and be *right* **both times**. That's strategy.

And that's why there's **never** going to be a computer that will play World-Class Poker. It's a people game.

A computer **could** be programmed to handle the extensive mathematics of a Poker game. But the psychological complexities are another matter. A system figured out by computer can beat Blackjack because **there** the dealer has **no options**. He has to stand on 17, he has to hit 16.

A computer could play fair-to-middling Poker. But no computer could ever stand face-to-face with a table full of **people** it had never met before, and make quality, high-profit decisions based on psychology.

To do that requires perception and judgment. It requires a human mind.

The way I accumulate knowledge of a particular player is by listening to him, and looking at him, instead of talking.

PAY ATTENTION...
and it will pay you

Concentrate on everything when you're playing. Watch and listen...remember you have to do **both**, and relate the two. You **listen** to what your opponent says, but you **watch** what he's doing independently of what he says — because a lot of players talk *loose* and play *tight*, and a little later they'll reverse it on you. So you look at a man every time he's involved in a hand. You judge him **every time**. That's the way you get to know him **and** his moves.

If you aren't learning what you want to know just by watching and listening, create your own opportunity. Try to bluff at him the first good opportunity, and **see** if he'll call you or not — what kind of hand he'll call with, and what kind he'll throw away.

Of course, anybody with a lick of sense is trying to keep you from reading him. But you can **still** figure him because it is very, very difficult for any man to conceal his character.

**A man's *true* feelings
come out in a Poker game.**

You'll see smart lawyers playing Poker and giggling and carrying on like school kids. And a man's hostilities can boil over after a while, too.

Watch a ballgame with a man when he's betting a lot of money on it. You'll learn what kind of temperament he's got, how well he can take disappointment. That's the way it is with Poker.

If you wanted to use Poker just for a test of character, solely to learn about the men you'll have to deal with away from the Poker table, it would be a telling test. As a matter of fact, isn't that what a lot of Friday night Poker games between business acquaintances are really all about? Size them up at the Friday night Poker sessions...and then take advantage of them during the next business week.

This brings us to another subtlety of Poker: Not everybody you're going to play against thinks the way you do. Almost everybody wants to win, but they expect to win in different ways.

PLAY AGGRESSIVELY
it's the winning way

There's a very well-known Poker player, a man who enters the *World Series of Poker* every year, who has a talent for figuring out exactly what your hand is. But when he decides that you're holding a Pair of Jacks (in Hold 'em) and his own hand will **not** beat the Jacks, he'll try to make you throw your hand away.

To me, that's **not** being aggressive...that's being stupid. It works sometimes, but should you jeopardize your money when you think your opponent's got a good hand? Let him win the pot and wait till you think he doesn't have much of anything. That's when you can try to bluff him out of the pot. Or wait until you think you have him beat.

Everybody in Poker thinks he knows what a *tight* player is, but I'm going to define it again because so many people confuse the term "tight" with "solid".

"Tight" means conservative. A *tight* player is a player that is tight pretty much all the time.

> But a "solid" player is a player who's tight about entering a pot in the first place...but after he enters the pot he becomes aggressive.

Most **good** players, by the way, are *solid*.

The opposite of the *tight* player, as you would imagine from the name, is the *loose* player. He'll play most of the pots. Often he'll be drunk. You need patience to play him, and you require a good hand to bet because he'll call you with extremely weak hands.

The perfect opponent to face is the *Calling Station*. He's similar to a loose–drunk player, but he rarely bets. Most of the time, he just checks and calls. And **if you can't beat a man who always checks to you...you can't beat anyone.**

Timid players *don't* **win in high-stakes Poker.**

As you'll learn, I **don't** fit into any of the classic categories. I have the reputation of being a **very** *aggressive* player with a definite tendency to be on the loose side. But, despite my aggressiveness and looseness, I exercise a considerable amount of judgment whenever I play.

TELLS — look for them... and you'll find them

Once you've pegged a player's basic style, **don't** make the mistake of assuming he's going to play that same way every day of his life. Sometimes a player makes a conscious effort to change his manner of play. More often, however, his **current** *mood* affects his play.

Some days people have more of a playing spirit than on other days. If a man **doesn't** feel like playing, and has become involved in a game anyway, he'll throw his hand away very easily. He can be bluffed.

But if you see another guy sitting there chewing gum, and bouncing his leg up and down, you know he's anxious to get into action. He came to play. You have to handle him with caution. It's **not** safe to bluff him, at least not to start with.

Almost all players have *Tells*...those giveaway moves that are almost as revealing, to a rival who has spotted them, as actually showing him your hand.

The most common *Tell* is the pulse in a man's neck. On a lot of people, the pulse in the neck is visible. If so, a man can't hide it, since nobody can control their heartbeat in stress situations. When you see a man's neck just throbbing away, you know he's excited, and usually he's excited **because he is bluffing**.

You may have heard someone ask another player: *"How deep are you?"* That question is sometimes an attempt to establish a Tell. (The question means: How much money do you have in front of you?) It's worth knowing. I don't think a player should be obligated to tell you, even though I have heard it argued both ways.

Questions like that are worth asking for psychological reasons. When a man's under pressure, his voice may break, and then you know something about his current attitude.

> **When I'm playing in a big pot, I *won't* let anyone involve me in conversation.**

Even real Pros are susceptible. Once I had a Tell on *Puggy* **Pearson**. Every time he put his chips in the rack and bet them, he was bluffing. He must have been doing that six months before somebody else discovered it and told him.

Another time, *Amarillo Slim* **Preston** pointed out to me that I was counting my chips off and betting them when I had a hand, and when I was bluffing I would just push them in **without** counting. That's the only *Tell* anyone had on me that I **know** about, but I'm sure there have been others.

All top Professionals have a defense against people using *Tells* against them. Sometimes when I'm bluffing I say some particular thing, like *"gee whiz"*, so that people will connect **that** with bluff.

But the next time I say *"gee whiz"*, I **won't** be bluffing.

With a great deal of experience, you may learn **not** only whether a man is bluffing or has a quality hand, but the actual cards he holds. This is what people mean when they say a particular player can *"put a man on a hand"*. My natural ability along these lines has contributed a lot to my success.

I remember playing in a game where you could almost tell what **Jimmy Cassella** had by the **amount** he would raise. That's the only thing you had to know. With an A-10 in Hold 'em, he'd raise about $100; with an A-J, he'd raise $125, and so forth.

Other players have patterns that, while less pronounced, are definitely visible to a Poker Professional. You take into account the way they are sitting, their previous playing habits, how they bet, and often even the tone of their voices. It's the totality of everything about them rather than any one particular thing.

ESP — it's a Jellyroll

This book will deal scientifically with Tells and with psychology, but sometimes you **don't even know how you know**...only that you're **sure** of what your opponent has.

I believe some good Poker players actually employ a degree of extrasensory perception (ESP). While I've never studied the subject in depth, it seems to me there's too much evidence to ignore that ESP exists or that most people have it to some degree. Everybody has had the experience of riding with someone else in an automobile and thinking of a song, then being surprised to hear his companion start singing that very song.

You can't imagine how often I've called a player's exact hand to myself and been proven right. There's even a plausible, though completely unproven, explanation how a person could know what cards another player is holding. The brain's functions involve electrical impulses. In this electronic age we're becoming more familiar every day with appliances which broadcast, purely as an unintentional by-product, energy impulses which are picked up on dissimilar appliances at considerable distances.

Is it really too unreasonable to suspect that such a highly sophisticated electrical device as the human brain, during the intensity of concentration in a big pot, could broadcast a simple message like a *"Pair of Jacks"* a mere eight feet?

I hope I live to see that question answered, and not merely asked. I like to think of ESP as a *Jellyroll* anyway.

In the meantime, use all the sophisticated techniques and strategies presented in this book in determining whether or not to call, bet or raise. But in the rare situations when all your card knowledge and best judgment leave you in doubt, go **with** your strong feeling...and **not** against it.

SUPERSTITIONS
there are bigger faults

I **don't** believe in the traditional superstitions, but there are a couple that I still honor. Like most Poker players, I don't like to be paid in $50 bills. But there's also a reason for that. It's easy to mistake a $50 bill for a $5 bill.

And I don't eat peanuts at a card table. There's no reason in the world eating peanuts should affect the outcome of the game, but it doesn't cost me anything to observe the taboo against it, so I observe it. That's a *Jellyroll*, too. And...there are bigger faults a player can have.

When I lose a pot, I sometimes get up and walk around the chair. Some Poker players do that to change their luck. I do it just to cool off.

Nor do I like to see women at a Poker table. That's not superstition, either. I was brought up to respect women, and I just **don't** feel comfortable in high-stakes warfare against women.

I've never met a woman who was a really top player. Maybe that's because there aren't a lot of women players. I have, however, seen some who were **pretty** good, even by Professional standards.

I doubt that any of my children will decide to play professionally. It can be a very good life, and it has been for me, but my children haven't come from the background that produces good Poker players. You try to make life a little easier for your kids than it was for you (and rightfully so), but the other side of that coin is that they're not forced to be so competitive when they're young, and are unlikely to develop the instinct it takes to be a good player.

HONOR — a gambler's Ace-in-the-hole

It is good insurance to have the reputation and respect that make it possible for you to borrow money, but borrowing is to be **avoided**. The first time I came to Las Vegas, I lost my entire bankroll of $70,000, and I got up from the Poker table and **didn't** ask anyone for anything. And the men who were at that Poker table will always respect me for that, even though I have loaned money to some of them, and they to me, since.

I was completely broke when I got home to Fort Worth. I got a $20 bill somewhere, and started grinding it out playing two cent Auction Bridge. When I built up a little bankroll, I moved into richer company, and eventually returned to Vegas.

**Don't borrow from anyone
you don't want to loan money to.**

I could've made a faster comeback by borrowing money, but you have to be careful whom you borrow from in the gambling business. And if you make up your mind to use the credit you have, you may not manage your money so well, or the money you borrow.

When you've mismanaged somebody's money, it is hard to compete against him. It's hard even to play in the same game.

Make it a practice **never** to be staked, never to borrow money, if you can help it. And if you can't help borrowing, borrow the **minimum**, and pay it back on the **exact day** you promise. . .or sooner.

You *must* maintain a reputation for honor in the gambling business. Your word must be your bond. It'll be your *Ace-in-the-hole.*

BE AS COMPETITIVE AS YOU CAN BE

Few people realize how intensely competitive you must be to become a good Poker player. I couldn't play Poker just for fun, and I don't think many of the top Professionals could. I've always played to win, and whenever I could discover any bad habits, I've tried to eliminate them just as I would try to eliminate mistakes in a business I might be running.

Use your best game against anybody you play. Many of the top Pros are close friends, but they almost never give each other a break in a game. *Sailor* **Roberts**, for instance, is one of the best friends I've ever had. He helped pick me up when I was young and unknown and broke. But when I play cards with *Sailor*, I do my level best to cut his throat and he tries to cut mine. It's been like that from the time we met. In fact, the first time we played he broke me.

In the trade, this characteristic is called *Alligator Blood*, and it is highly valued and respected. It means **you'll do anything** *within the rules* **to win**. You try to have special moves, such as making a slow, hesitant call in place of a fast call, when a man might bet at you again (after the next card is turned up in Hold 'em). You might set a trap for him by leading him to believe you're betting a hand which is a slight favorite, when you actually have a hand that's practically unbeatable.

I go into a Poker game with the idea of completely destroying it.

Changing gears is one of the most important parts of playing Poker. It means shifting from loose to tight play and vice versa. Don't do it gradually...it works better to switch suddenly. Once they catch on, *change gears* again.

If you're playing with a lineup of people who have played you before, do this even **more often**. When you really **think** they know you, *change gears* several times in one game.

In a No–Limit game, the gear to stay in most of the time is the one that most people at the table are **not** using. In other words:

> **Play** *mostly* **tight in a loose game,**
> **and** *mostly* **loose in a tight game.**

I also vary my play according to how I'm going. If I am losing badly, I play tighter. If I'm winning, I try to play looser. Players are more apt to be intimidated by me when I'm winning.

When I'm playing a No–Limit game like *Hold 'em* or *Deuce-to-Seven Lowball*, if I win a pot, I nearly always play the next pot as well, within reason. Although the cards will break even in the long run, card *rushes* **do** happen. A card rush means more than that you're winning a lot of pots. It also means that you have temporary command of the game. Your momentum is clear to all the players. On occasions like this you're going to make correct decisions and your opponents may make errors because they are psychologically affected by your *rush*. Make the most of these opportunities and give yourself the chance to enjoy them to the fullest.

ART *and* SCIENCE
PLAYING GREAT POKER
TAKES BOTH

Poker is more art than science, and that's what makes it so difficult to master. Knowing **what** to do — the science — is about 10% of the game. Knowing **how** to do it — the art — is the other 90%. You not only have to know when to bet, when to raise, and when to fold. . .you also have to be able to do those things with a certain finesse.

But one has to start with the basics. There are certain things about probabilities that you *absolutely* **must know**.

The first is that the cards break even. If you turn over 13 cards from a deck, then reshuffle, and do this again and again, the **A♠** will show up just as many times (one out of four) if I'm shuffling them or if you're shuffling them yourself.

> **Over a long period of time, the** *worst* **player in the world is going to catch** *just as many* **good cards as the** *best* **player in the world.**

We'll have the same cards to play, but I'll beat him sooner or later because I'm a better player.

That's universally true. It applies to **all forms of Poker**.

But. . .as you'll soon discover. . .there are certain games that involve a lot more skill than others. You have to know what to do with your cards in all types of Poker, but the relative importance of that knowledge varies with the kind of Poker you're playing.

IMPORTANT TIPS

Another thing you should understand is that Poker is set up in a fashion that is not entirely logical. A Royal Flush is the highest hand. But it's just as hard to be dealt **exactly** J◇-9♣-6♠-4♡-2◇ as A♡-K♡-Q♡-J♡-10♡, but the first hand is worthless. A Flush is better than a Straight because it's harder to make than a Straight.

But the ranking of the cards themselves is arbitrary. There's no real reason a King should be worth more than a Deuce. (And that's a very good justification for playing high cards, particularly in games where winning hands often consist of a mere Pair. It's just as easy to make a Pair of Kings as it is to make a Pair of Deuces...but the Kings will get the money.)

In any Poker game you're in...remember that it takes a stronger hand to call a raise than it takes to raise it yourself.

> **Also, remember that in Limit Poker, you must show down the best hand most of the time to win. In No-Limit, on the other hand, you more often than not take a pot without ever showing your hand.**

If you've never had the opportunity to see a real No-Limit game, you'd be very surprised how much bluffing there is. Good No-Limit players bluff four or five times as often as good players in Limit games.

You have to pick your players to bluff. **You can hardly bluff a Sucker at all, whereas any good player can be bluffed.** But always bear in mind the player's mood that particular day...if he's anxious to play, you handle him more cautiously than you would otherwise.

Bluffing is the main reason I believe No-Limit Poker requires more skill than Limit. Bluffing in No-Limit requires real strategy, and the ability to size up your opponents every time you sit down to play.

Yet, paradoxically, Poker becomes easier the higher the stakes of the game, at least in games where Professionals are involved.

Down in the low-Limit games, the Professionals who are involved don't have much money, and what they do have they're trying to keep for a stake and to live on. So they're playing the best Poker they know how to play.

But up in the high-stakes games you encounter big businessmen, bookies, hotel owners, millionaires...and they're playing for entertainment. And they are **not** *playing hard.*

MONEY MANAGEMENT

I've never been as conservative about money management as most successful people are. I don't think your bankroll is the only factor you should consider in deciding whether or not to play in a high-limit game.

If the game cries out to be played in — if it's a good game, you feel good, and if you aren't tired, you should try that game even if it is higher than you normally would play. And you should **stay in it** until the game becomes bad or you grow tired.

Of course, you make that decision within reason. Any time you extend your bankroll so far that if you lost, it would really distress you, you probably **will** lose. It's tough to play your best under that much pressure.

I prefer using judgment on individual games rather than hard rules, but if you want such a rule, I would suggest you **not** play $10 limit until you have at least a $1000 **bankroll** (*not* the *buy-in*).

In No-Limit, you'll usually want a bigger bankroll for a game of the same general size. In a No-Limit game with two Blinds of $5 and $10, I'd say you need at least $2,500.

To play No-Limit $5, $10, $25 and $50 (Four Blinds), you'd need about $10,000.

It's been a long time since I was broke, but the way I always got broke was by playing with desperation money. I let myself get into too much of a hurry, and played in games I didn't have the bankroll for.

If you have a limited bankroll, be very certain to get the maximum amount of gamble you can for your money. That's an important factor to consider in picking your games.

If you have only a small amount of money to invest in a game, and if you have a wide choice of games (like you do in Las Vegas), you may be better off playing a **small** No-Limit game than a high Limit game. If you have $10,000 you can afford to lose in one game, you might be better off risking it in a No-Limit game, simply because if you do get lucky, you can win real big and your bankroll might get healthy **fast**.

When I buy into a No-Limit game, I want to have as many checks in front of me as anybody else at the table, or more. I'm not afraid, and you shouldn't be afraid, of getting drawn out on a hand and going through the whole stack. All your efforts in Poker are directed toward getting in a position to bet the maximum amount you can on the hands that are worth it. When those opportunities do occur, you **don't** want to be limited in the amount of action you can accept.

Always play for Chips, rather than cash.

Chips are easier to win. A $5 chip is the same size as a $500 chip — it's just not the same color. If you bet a man $20,000 in $500 chips, that's only forty chips, two stacks. But if you bet him $20,000 in $100 bills, it would be a big pile of money, and would tend to freeze him up.

The way to get a person to convert to chips is to point out to him that it takes too long to count out the bills. It's the truth, and a legitimate reason to change to chips, though **not really** the reason you're doing it.

It's also to your own advantage to **think of chips as units**, and **not** as money. You may consider your money status before the game and after the game, but while the game is in progress it is **only a game**, and the chips are **just units**. You're trying to win as many units as you can.

This concept is not really unique to Poker, when you think about it. All good businessmen realize that they have to have different standards of what constitutes extravagance in business, and what constitutes extravagance in their lives outside of business. And the standard they set for business is often more liberal. They realize that the house, or the car they buy for their private use has to be paid for out of profits, rather than out of operating capital.

So when they need a new piece of equipment to make a few more dollars of profit, or just to maintain their competitive edge, Poker Professionals don't say to themselves: *"I could buy a new house with this money — what am I doing risking it in a Poker game?"* They realize that it's operating capital, and not profit, and therefore **not really available** to buy that new house or car, anyway.

All I'm telling you to do is apply the same sound principles to the *business* of playing Poker — and that reminds me of a story.

LOWBALL PETE
and his friend SHORTY

This guy named **Lowball Pete** went over to his friend **Shorty's** house and **Pete** said to **Shorty:** *"I've got to have some money, the baby don't have any food, the rent's due and they're going to throw me out of my house."* So **Shorty,** who was a good friend of **Pete's** said *"well I understand, here's $100."* **Pete** said *"thanks* **Shorty***, I'll pay you back as soon as I can."* **Shorty** said: *"well, I know that. Where are you going now?"* And **Pete** said *"I'm going over to Al's house, they have a $200 limit Lowball game going right now."* **Shorty** said: *"well what difference does that make, how are you going to play?"* And **Pete** said *"Oh. . .I've got money for THAT."*

The factor that really determines what kind of game it's going to be is **not** the limit itself, but the **size of the ante in relation to the limit.** If you're playing $10 limit and anteing a dollar, you'll have to play more liberally than if the ante is only a quarter.

This is very **important information** because it's something you can ascertain before you ever sit down and risk any of your money.

That information, and all the other pre-game data you can collect (such as the kind of players your opponents are) should be weighed against the following consideration: *How much do you stand to win in this game?*

Suppose the ante is so high, and the players are such that you'll have to involve $8,000 or $9,000 of your own money to win, but the players have only about $30,000 among them on the table, and you know that they probably won't bring any more money into the game if they lose that. It's pretty hard to get more than about half the money in a game, so $15,000 would be a big win.

To go into that game you'd be risking $8,000 or $9,000 to win a maximum of $15,000, even if you got the best hands of your life and played them *jam-up*. That's probably too much risk for that much money, since there's usually a better game down the street.

I can remember losing $98,000 in a game that didn't warrant losing $10,000. I could have only won $30,000 or $40,000...and to do that, I'd have had to break everybody there.

So this advice amounts to telling you to **do as I say, and** *not* **as I do.** I believe a person should try to learn from watching another man's mistakes. It's so much cheaper than learning from his own.

You have to set a stricter limit on your losses if you're playing Limit Poker than if you're playng No-Limit, because it's harder to win money back in a game where the size of the pot's limited.

In a Limit game, if you find yourself losing consistently over a significant period of time and you feel that the cards have been breaking close to even — the game may be too tough for you. Walk away from it, and don't come back until something has changed to make you more of a favorite — like the absence of a few very good players who were there before, or the feeling that you have improved your own play.

COURAGE
the heart of the matter

I'm asking you to walk a very thin line between wisdom and courage, and keep a tight rein on both. The line gets thinner the more you excel at Poker.

The reason it's so narrow a line is that courage is one of the outstanding characteristics of a really top player. It's important because some people completely break down when they lose a big pot, and they play very badly after that. Whereas other men play just that much harder.

If I could give you a single player to take as a shining example of true courage, it would be *Puggy* **Pearson**. Puggy at his best is really, really good, but he has suffered long losing streaks. Yet even during such dismal streaks, his play doesn't rise and fall with the way he's doing in a particular game. He just keeps trying. Nothing stops him.

One of the elements in a player's courage is the realization that money you have already bet is no longer yours regardless of how much is involved. You no longer own any money you've already put in the pot. It belongs to the pot. Your decision must be based on the **current** situation. If you feel that large bet is **now** necessary to win the pot, then that's what you should do. If you think that there's no way for you to win the pot, then you have to give it up — even if you've already committed a large amount of money. It's a cliche, but true anyway, *don't throw good money after bad.*

Another element which demands courage and judgment is dealing with *implied odds*. It's a concept you'll be dealing with in other sections of this book. It means you have to weigh your bet against **not only** the present size of the pot, but the anticipated size of the pot when all psychological and mathematical factors are evaluated. It takes a lot of courage to risk your money against a profit you can't see. And it takes courage to move all-in with a bluff when you suspect an opponent is weak. They say courage is invisible, but I never knew a top player who didn't have it written all over his face — clear as day.

The important Twins of Poker — PATIENCE and STAYING POWER

Come to the table with enough time to stay and play awhile. While sitting down and trying to destroy a game by firing from the start is my **favorite strategy**, it **doesn't** always work. There are games that demand *staying power*.

Limit games take lots of *patience* because the best hands are usually shown down — that means it's harder to bluff successfully. So you have to wait for the best hand, and you have to recognize the best hand when you get it.

Or suppose you sit down at a game that includes two drunks who are calling every bet. It will be impossible to simply take charge of that game, so you'll have to wait until you get hands that will beat them.

OTHER IMPORTANT QUALITIES FOR SUCCESS — Alertness

Whenever you're in a game...you have to stay alert the **whole** time — concentrate during the entire session. And it can be a very long time indeed.

The ability to stay alert for long sessions can be a major factor contributing to your earning power, and it has been a **key** to my own success. Once, when I was in my middle twenties, I played five days and five nights without any breaks except to go to the bathroom or to eat meals which were brought in. I never left the table for more than five minutes.

> I wouldn't do it again, and I wouldn't recom-
> mend anyone else do it. I never again had the
> stamina I did before that session. But it
> demonstrates how long it's humanly possible
> to stay awake and alert when you have the
> resolve and the courage.

Today, at the age of 44, I suspect I could and would play three days in a game where I could make a great deal of money. But I **don't** like to play that long now, not only because it's grueling and not particularly healthy, but because it's bad policy to play anything but the best you can. (And that's simply not possible much beyond the first day.)

I can play at my best for about 36 hours now, but after that the drop-off becomes noticeable — to me, if not to my opponents. The reason I have more staying power than other players is just discipline.

Discipline

I **don't** drink much, and neither do most good Poker players.

> **And, I NEVER drink when I play.**
> **No** *top* **player drinks while playing.**

Nor do we let our minds dwell on personal problems when we're playing.

You should make a conscious and constant effort to discover any *leaks* in your play and. . .then eliminate them. If you discover you're playing too many pots. . .tighten up. Other times you may need to play **more** pots.

One form of discipline is to learn to play **all** Poker games, profitably. . .even those you **don't** like. Keep yourself alert and conditioned by playing some of the games you're not best at. Besides. . .it'll enable you to give the other guy a little action at **his** game if he wants it.

Try to keep a mental record of the kinds of games in which you do well, as opposed to those in which you don't. (I know, for example, that Limit *Ace–to–Five* is my worst game, because I've won the least money at it.)

Constant self-discipline will pay off in those long, drawn-out sessions because *any bad habits you have* **will become exaggerated as you grow tired**. The fewer bad habits you have, the less risky it is to play longer sessions.

Discipline will also help your general confidence after three or four losing sessions. If I lose a few times, I will re-examine my game and ask, *"Am I playing bad?"* **Sometimes I'll ask somebody else's opinion as well.** If the answer is *"No, you're not playing badly, you're just playing unlucky"*, I can believe the answer because I know I've done everything I could to keep my game at its best. So my confidence is unshaken. I can continue to play the way I know I should.

Maintaining confidence is your strongest defense against *"going bad"*. When you start to *go bad*, or just start to **think** you're *going bad*, you become hesitant. And that oft-quoted rule that *your first instinct is the right one* is more true in Poker than in any other game. When you act hesitantly, you often go against your first (and best) judgment.

> **Allowing your confidence to be shaken can turn a simple losing streak into a terrible case of** *going bad.*

At the same time, you still have to remain open to the idea that you may need to shape up your play. You know about how often you can expect to lose, just on the basis of luck, and if you have a streak of many straight losses, you must admit (to yourself) that something might be wrong. If so, try to correct it.

For instance, if I lost five straight sessions at one of my better forms of Poker, I'd suspect something basic was wrong. If I lost ten straight, there would be **no doubt whatever** that I was doing something wrong, and that luck was **not** the main thing.

You may also be fortunate enough to have the unforgettable experience of *going good*. But that's no more a matter of luck than *going bad*. There are reasons for it.

Controlling Your Emotions

Romantic problems have the biggest effects, of course. I have seen very good, solid players (even by Professional standards) thrown into second childhood by their wives or girl friends. Emotional entanglements affect their judgment at **everything**. And, at the Poker table, of course, it costs them money.

They divert their interest to their love affairs. They **don't** concentrate. They have trouble sitting and they want to get up and walk around. Poker doesn't really interest them.

I'm sure that any kind of trauma involving my wife or children would affect me much the same way. But, I **wouldn't** be playing at such a time.

It's hard to give anybody advice about this, but I believe that if something happens that is so upsetting that it really affects your ability to play, you should consider quitting entirely — at least for a time, until you regain your emotional balance.

I've been fortunate enough not to go through any traumas of that sort, but it seems to me that **taking a long break because of a big problem is a logical extension of the proven practice of taking a short break because of a little problem.** So, you'll be doing yourself a service, if you follow this rule:

Never play when you're upset

It's not my disposition to get upset very easily, but I have saved a great deal of money over the years by quitting whenever I have lost enough money to bother me. And that is an even more important principle in Limit Poker than in No–Limit...because it takes you so much longer to grind it out at Limit.

About once every three or four months something will happen (like a fight at home, or an argument with a friend) that will get me upset. On those days I go see a movie or play golf. I'll pass a game up on those days, regardless of how good it is, because I know I'll probably lose if I play.

Actually
SCHEDULE VACATIONS

And if you're playing Professionally, remember to take some vacations. You've got to give your mind a rest.

Once, my friend Jack Straus had come by a game just to watch me play, and he told me *"Doyle, you're playing terrible."*

I had been under the impression I was playing pretty well, but I hadn't been winning as often as usual. Jack pointed out to me that I had been playing almost every day for a year.

So I went to Hawaii for two weeks, and when I came back I not only played better, but **dramatically** better, than I had before leaving.

Looking back, it's worth noting that even though I do a lot more self-examining than most Poker players, I had failed to recognize how badly my game was off, and **why** it was off, until Jack pointed it out to me.

Because it's so difficult to recognize when you're going stale, I think it's best to take some vacations **even when you think you** *don't* **need them.** Schedule them.

There's such a great difference in the makeup of people that I can't tell you how often you should go. But it seems to me that it would be better to err on the side of too many vacations than too few. They don't have to be lengthy. But there should be three or four days in which you're having fun and **not** thinking about Poker at all. Hunt, fish, or just lie on the beach — you'll be a better player afterward.

The occasional break makes it easier to get a perspective on how you're doing, and what your abilities are. That's very important.

> **Sure, you want to study the emotional makeup of your opponents. But of all the players at the Poker table, the one whose capabilities and limitations are going to affect you** *most*, **is the one sitting in your chair.**

BE VERSATILE

Having recognized those capabilities and limitations, it's best to test them occasionally, not only to see if your assessments are still valid, but also to maintain a reputation of being willing to give action.

I know very well that I play any kind of No-Limit Poker better than almost any kind of Limit Poker. And I know that Hold 'em is my best game, and Ace-to-Five my worst.

But that doesn't mean I won't play anything but No-Limit Hold 'em. I've seen too many players who won't play unless everything is in their favor — won't play unless the game is right, won't play unless it's their game, and then won't bet unless they have the *nuts*.

I reject their philosophy for what I consider the best of reasons. . .**none of those players has any real money**. If you get a reputation for playing only when you have the best of it, you'll get very few people to play against you.

So I end up playing a lot of games in which I'm not a big favorite, just to stimulate action, and keep Poker going.

Even if you lose money by doing that, at least you have put it back into the Poker economy of which you are a part, which isn't the case if you blow it in the casino on Craps or spend it on a trip to Europe — or anything else.

By playing the other man's game, you may get him to agree to play yours in return. By participating in the game of the day, you make it hard for others to shut you out with a game you **don't** play. (If you're an all-around player, you **do** play his game.) Once they've decided that you'll play whatever the game is, most players will go back to lobbying for the game at which they think they're the best. That may well be your own strongest game.

By playing games like High-Low Split, Razz, Seven-Card Stud, and Draw Poker, I may get a weaker player to face me, because I don't have a great reputation at those games.

Finally, by playing **those** games I maintain a reputation as a man who will bet on something at which he has no real advantage. A reputation for giving action.

Don't worry that you might get a reputation for being a Sucker if you follow this advice. That's the best thing that could possibly happen to you. (To have the reputation of being a Sucker, with everybody in the world throwing their money at me trying to win mine, would be my idea of earthly paradise!)

YOUR REPUTATION
can be a two-edged sword

The opposite kind of reputation is, of course, a two-edged sword. It cuts both ways. After winning the World Hold 'em Championship two years in a row, it is understandably hard for me to get a lot of high Hold 'em action.

Ideally, you want a reputation (particularly in Hold 'em) that will make other players just a little afraid of you. Not so afraid they won't play...but afraid enough to respect you.

There isn't really any good way of establishing your credentials as a top Poker player except to get to the top and stay there.

Playing head-up against another good player, for instance, is **not** a realistic test of who's the best player because it happens that some people who are very good at head-up play are not very good in a Ring game...and vice versa.

The perfect test would probably be to have the same **line-up** (set of players), playing against each other five nights a week for a year. There would be no extraneous factors (like the introduction of new players), and almost no amount of luck could keep the best player from winning the most money over a period of a year (providing there was a **real** difference in the quality of play between the best and the second-best player).

TOURNAMENTS
More benefits than meets the eye —
and how to adjust to them

But in the absence of games like that, about the only way for a man to establish a reputation quickly is to enter and win (or perform well in) a Poker tournament.

But, that's **not** the only motivation for entering a tournament. By the time I won the World Hold 'em Championship, the title of champion didn't mean much to me. There are only a very few people who are **good enough** players **themselves** that I value their opinion that **I'm** a good one. Since all of these men are also Professionals, they **know** who is the best player without having to hold a tournament to decide it.

Believe me, the main motivation was the $220,000 it paid me in 1976, the first year I won, and the $340,000 in 1977, the second year. (I also won $90,000 in the *Deuce-to-*

Seven World Championship in 1976 and in 1977 I won $55,000 in the *High-Low Split* World Championship.)

But, you don't have to win the tournament to profit by it...even a winner-take-all tournament. The tournament itself will generate other games which can make the buy-in price of the tournament — even the $10,000 buy-in Hold 'em Championship — a bargain for a good player.

After people start getting eliminated from the Hold 'em Championship, there's a solid week of the best Poker action to be found anywhere. Everybody is still in a mood to gamble, and most of them have the money to do it.

Not only do you get a chance at that money by being at the tournament, but you get to know these people, and because they're from all over the country, you develop contacts that can get you a game almost anywhere.

The contacts and side games at the *World Series of Poker*®* are so valuable that a lot of players who could afford to enter **don't** bother to. They show up for the side games and contacts alone.

I think that's often a mistake. Playing in the tournament itself helps you establish a reputation as an action man who's willing to risk a significant amount of money in a game, even if he **doesn't** have any substantial advantage. And action is the most important aspect of the reputation a Professional Poker player has to maintain.

Furthermore, the people who actually play in the tournaments are the ones who get the chances at the **best** action surrounding the tournaments. If you force another player out of a pot in a tournament, and break him because you're both playing on artificially limited bankrolls, he may get a little sore about it and invite you to try him in a regular game. **There's nothing like playing somebody who is mad at you to increase your earnings for the year.**

---

*The *World Series of Poker*® **is a registered trademark of the HORSESHOE HOTEL-CASINO in Las Vegas, Nevada.**

> This brings up one of the most significant
> points about tournaments — the strategy of
> tournament play differs from the strategy of
> ordinary play.

It took me longer than it should have to learn this. I
played in the Hold 'em Tournament for seven years before I
won it. Of course, I wanted to win the money, but another
way I'd justify entering the tournament year after year —
and it was a legitimate justification rather than a rational-
ization — was on my general principle of investing money
just to promote gambling, and to keep a reputation for being
an *action man*.

Since I felt the need to be there anyway, I kept
pondering how to win. And I noticed that **Johnny Moss**
always seemed to do very well in the tournaments. I've
always been an apostle of **John's** at No-Limit. I used to
observe and watch him in each Poker game I went to, and it
seemed he was **always** there. *Slim, Sailor* and I used to joke
about how crazy we were, wearing our automobiles out
chasing **John** all across Texas. The truth was, **John** was
usually the big winner in the games...with myself a close
second. As the years passed, the margin between us got
closer and closer because I was watching and picking up his
favorite plays as any young apprentice might watch and
learn from the master in his field. Much of my No-Limit
strategy comes from those times.

I have much more respect for **Johnny** than a lot of
younger players do. In his prime, he was the best No-Limit
player I've ever seen, and a lot of people don't believe that
because they're too young to have seen Johnny play at his
best. They fail to take into account the fact that he's some
70 years old now, and that is 20 years past the point at
which most men's play begins to deteriorate. Just because
the years have affected your circulation and the speed at
which you think, and may have softened your ability to play,
does **not** mean you know any less about **how** to play. And
Johnny's success in those tournaments indicated he knew a
great deal about how to play. (He's the only man besides
myself who has won the *World Series* more than once.)

So I studied Johnny's strategy and saw that he **didn't** try to win early in the tournament. He just tried to exist, and to keep from losing his money. Now, as you may remember from the earlier part of this section, this is **exactly the opposite** of my normal strategy in ordinary games. And I had been trying to win the tournament the same way I have always won at ordinary games. That was **wrong** *for tournaments*.

I had been jeopardizing my chips on even-money situations, which can be a very good strategy in the early stage of an *ordinary* Poker game, but is **not** good in a *tournament*, where you **can't** pull another few thousand out of your pocket and buy more chips.

In my new strategy, I tried to avoid playing big pots until the field had been narrowed substantially. Then later, after the field had been cut to a few players, I played more aggressively, and tried to get players to jeopardize all their checks at every opportunity.

Using this strategy designed specifically for tournaments, I've won the World Championship the last two years in a row.

It should go without saying that you should mentally train for a Poker tournament, but there, I said it anyway because it's so important. You wouldn't go into a Basketball or Golf tournament without working on your game first and you should give the same consideration to a Poker tournament. You sit down alone, you concentrate, and when the first tournament hand is dealt...you're playing for keeps.

One of the things I like about the *World Series of Poker* is that it brings out the **finest** in a lot of players. There's a friend of mine who **doesn't** play any good Hold 'em the rest of the year, but always plays pretty well in the *World Series*.

It's been an expensive lesson to him each year, but I keep hoping that the tournament will make him realize he could be playing tough the whole year round.

Tournaments are **not** *always* won by the best player. You have to be good to win, but you can be the very best and **not** win in a tournament.

Every year at the *World Series* we have half-a-dozen or so who always make it to the last couple of tables, but have **never** won and **never** will win. Some are very solid players in ordinary situations, but just not quite good enough to win in a game against four or five of the best. And some are as solid as they come, but just don't have the killer instinct — they fade at the finish.

When you're in a tournament, and it becomes obvious to you that you're probably going to lose, I think it's best to die with a bang, rather than a whimper. Go out playing with courage, instead of playing tight and meekly.

For one thing, it gives you the **better** of those two famous chances — *slim.* and *none* — to stay alive long enough to win. If you play conservatively on a low bankroll, the antes, which increase as the tournament goes on, will eat you up.

If you **do** get eliminated early, you can get into those very rich side-games I mentioned earlier.

BE COMPETITIVE
with Class

When you do get into those side games, I hope you'll remember **not** to kill the goose that laid the golden egg. A lot of people who come to tournaments don't really have much chance of going home winner. They're people who like to play high, largely for the enjoyment, and are willing to pay for the pleasure.

A few years ago there was such a man who played in the *World Series.* He wasn't a good player, but he could afford to lose, and besides that, we all liked him.

But one of the World Class players (a big name player) got that man into a side game and made some kind of Sucker play at him, and the fellow went for it. So instead of just taking his winnings gracefully, our "big name" player (**no** name in **this** book) showed everybody at the *rail* what he had done. Then to make matters worse, one of our local bookmakers made this poor fellow a 100 to 1 shot **not** to win the tournament. (Nobody likes to be a 100 to 1 dog.)

The guy left, and he hasn't been back. Each of the Professionals had invested $10,000 every year for several years, knowing he probably would **not** win it, but did it anyway to stimulate action. And then these two guys (the "big name" and the bookmaker) drove off one of the biggest action men we had ever attracted — just for the sake of a few cruel laughs.

That's not only **bad manners**...it's **bad business**. It's not only conduct unbecoming a gentleman, but especially conduct unbecoming a Professional Poker player. I don't care if you're playing $1 ante or $10,000 buy-in — **don't** ever be guilty of it.

Be highly competitive...but do it with class.

Meet Your Faculty

Seated: **Doyle Brunson**
Standing: *(left to right)* **Bobby Baldwin, Joey Hawthorne, David "Chip" Reese, David Sklansky,** and *"Crazy Mike"* **Caro.**

My Expert Collaborators

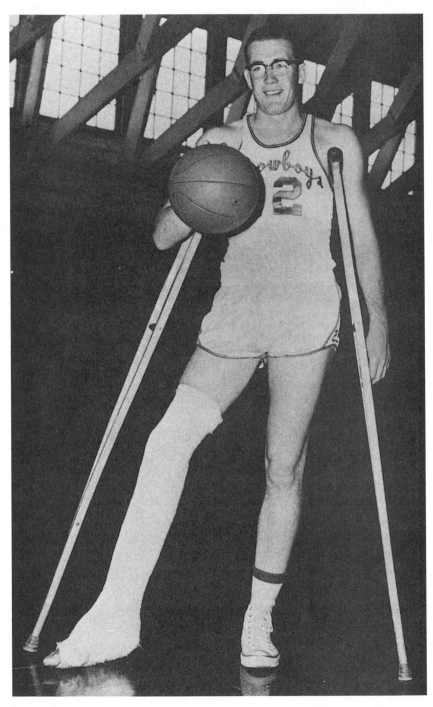

A funny thing happened to me on the way to the Minneapolis Lakers.

When the Lakers were still interested!

My Family — (clockwise) Todd-8, Pam-13, Doyla-14 and my wife Louise.

My wonderful wife of 15 years — Louise. (Note the scar and skin graft on the right side of my neck. This is a result of my cancer surgery.)

Like Father, like Son.

This Publishing business is all right!

The participants of the 1st *World Series of Poker*® — truly a collector's item.

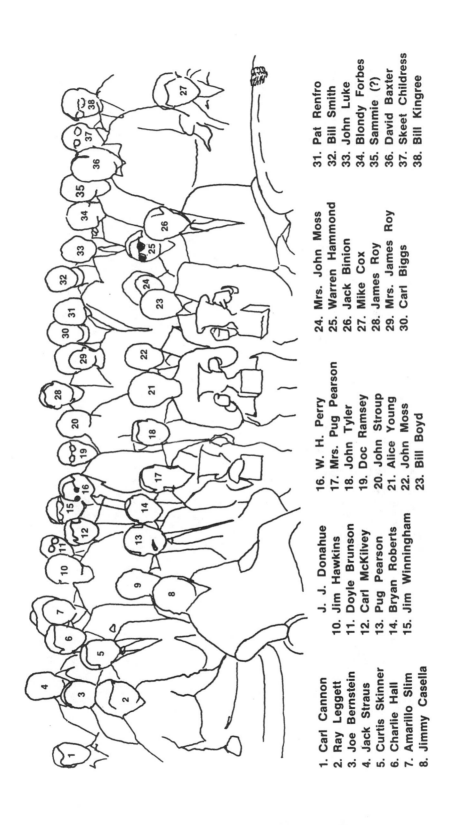

1. Carl Cannon
2. Ray Leggett
3. Joe Bernstein
4. Jack Straus
5. Curtis Skinner
6. Charlie Hall
7. Amarillo Slim
8. Jimmy Casella

J. J. Donahue
10. Jim Hawkins
11. Doyle Brunson
12. Carl McKilvey
13. Pug Pearson
14. Bryan Roberts
15. Jim Winningham

16. W. H. Perry
17. Mrs. Pug Pearson
18. John Tyler
19. Doc Ramsey
20. John Stroup
21. Alice Young
22. John Moss
23. Bill Boyd

24. Mrs. John Moss
25. Warren Hammond
26. Jack Binion
27. Mike Cox
28. James Roy
29. Mrs. James Roy
30. Carl Biggs

31. Pat Renfro
32. Bill Smith
33. John Luke
34. Blondy Forbes
35. Sammie (?)
36. David Baxter
37. Skeet Childress
38. Bill Kingree

The 2nd *World Series* — another collector's item. (Now, there are ten times as many participants.)

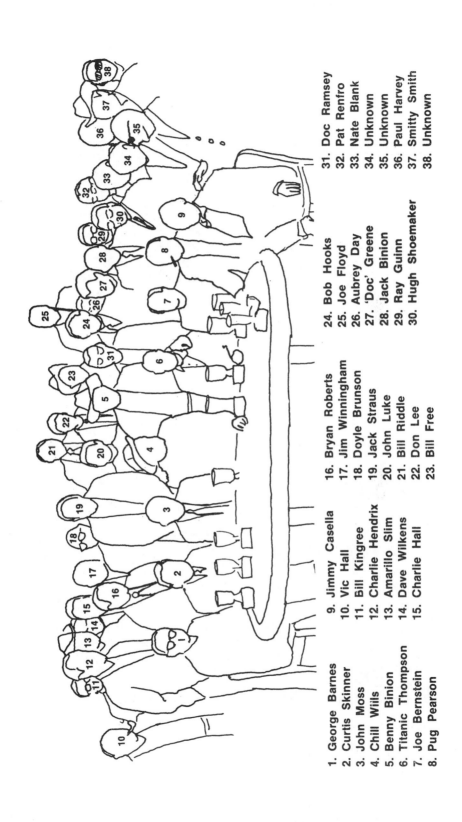

1. George Barnes
2. Curtis Skinner
3. John Moss
4. Chill Wills
5. Benny Binion
6. Titanic Thompson
7. Joe Bernstein
8. Pug Pearson

9. Jimmy Casella
10. Vic Hall
11. Bill Kingree
12. Charlie Hendrix
13. Amarillo Slim
14. Dave Wilkens
15. Charlie Hall

16. Bryan Roberts
17. Jim Winningham
18. Doyle Brunson
19. Jack Straus
20. John Luke
21. Bill Riddle
22. Don Lee
23. Bill Free

24. Bob Hooks
25. Joe Floyd
26. Aubrey Day
27. 'Doc' Greene
28. Jack Binion
29. Ray Guinn
30. Hugh Shoemaker

31. Doc Ramsey
32. Pat Renfro
33. Nate Blank
34. Unknown
35. Unknown
36. Paul Harvey
37. Smitty Smith
38. Unknown

Ten-Deuce does it again! (That's Gary *"Bones"* Berland, the young man who finished second when I won $340,000 in the 1977 World Championship Hold 'em event.)

My best friend, Jack Binion.

(Right)
I can get this playful with Bob Hooks because he's one of my very best friends. James Smith another friend of mine, is standing next to me and The *Grand Old Man* of Poker, John Moss is sitting in front of him.

(Below)
I really can't explain this one. It's for real. I must have been drinking (which I never do) because I actually took *"Insurance"* from my very good friend, Jack Binion.

(Left)
I thought I had more than that. I must have lost a pot. (Bob Hooks can't understand it either.)

(Below)
Golf and Football are not my only losing bets. I've got other losing habits including this one . . . but this time I won.

Benny (right) explains his Golden Rule to Johnny (center) and Slim (left)
"The man who has the Gold makes the rules."

I got raised. Maybe I should've looked before I bet.

The 1977 World Championship Hold 'em prize money - $340,000
"Count it right, Jack!"

SUPER/SYSTEM's POWER COURSE IN

DRAW POKER

by

"Crazy Mike" CARO

DRAW POKER
Table of Contents
Page

SPECIAL NOTE

"Crazy Mike" is quite an individual. His Draw section speaks for itself...but, more than that, I want to point out that Mike is the **only one** of my expert collaborators who actually wrote his own section. Every word you're about to read on Draw Poker was written by "the crazy man."

What's more, **every one** of the mathematical tables on **all** the forms of Poker that you'll find in the *Statistics* section were created, calculated, checked and re-checked...and are all Mike's. That very laborious and complex task was done on his own computer. As you'll discover, there are no statistics on Poker that are more complete or more accurate.

Mike's work extends far beyond the confines of Draw Poker...and **not** merely as a theoretician — because, above all else, Mike is a Player. He's **not** just the best Draw Poker player in the world — he's right up there with the best of them at playing **any form** of Poker.

He's truly multi-talented. Poker teacher, Poker writer, Poker mathematician...and, most of all, Poker Player.

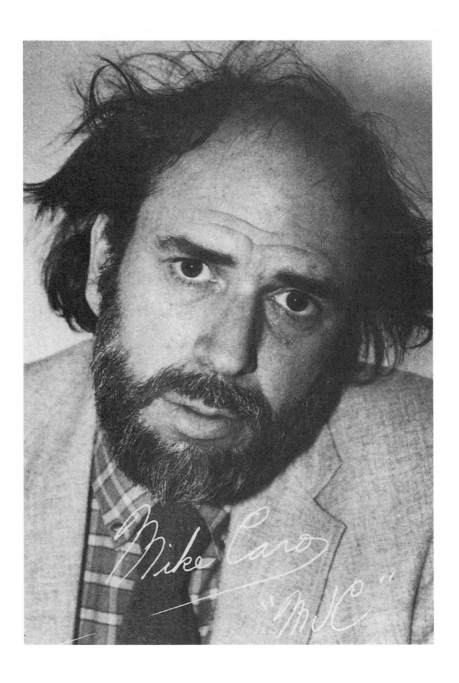

"Crazy Mike" CARO

My Expert Collaborator
on
DRAW POKER

The first time I watched Mike play, I was convinced that not only was he crazy but that he was also weird. Bearded, long haired and balding, he looked like a hippie just down from the Haight. He had gone into a pot with nothing except five garbage cards. He then stood pat on these hideous-looking cards, cackling like a banshee when he laid down his fiasco and lost the pot. A little later he pulled the same stunt, only this time he raked in a four thousand dollar pot on the strength of a natural Flush. He was crazy all right, crazy like a fox.

At thirty-three Mike is the finest five-card Draw Poker player alive and openly admits that his unorthodox, bizarre style of play is only an act calculated to throw his opponents off-guard. And, it's true. When you play "Crazy Mike" you can't read him. Most players I've known — and that includes the **best** — have some Tell on them, some mannerism or mode of play which under certain circumstances can give you a clue as to what 'they may have in their hands. Mike has so **many** strange mannerisms while playing and is so unpredictable that the only thing you know for sure about his game is that you don't know **anything** for sure about his game!

It didn't take me long to realize that Mike was winning much more than he was losing and that aroused my curiosity. Here was this young, wild-looking and crazy-acting hippie relieving some of the best players in the country of their cash. There had to be an answer.

After a particularly hectic game (and every game Mike sits in is hectic simply because he's in it), we were having coffee. His wild-man cover-up was replaced by the quiet low-keyed individual that is the **real** Mike Caro.

"I'm a regular Jeykll and Hyde" he laughed. Soon he became serious, pulling sheet after crumpled sheet of notes from his pockets.

"It's all here" he said. *"The odds, the possibilities, the longshots, the chances, the psychology."* He waved them in front of me. *"You could say this is my Bible."* I looked at his figures — page upon page which represented years of work in analyzing the game.

He stuffed the sheets back into his pockets. *"That's my secret. I have it all here...and here..."* First he tapped his pockets and then his head. *"I defy anyone to find one error! In any given hand I calculate the odds and weigh the psychological factors — and I play accordingly."* He smiled. *"Of course, it helps if everyone thinks I'm a little touched."*

I had to agree. This rather gentle, sensitive man has volunteered hundreds of hours to organizing and leading adult and high school *Great Books* discussion groups. And if that seems unusual for a Professional Poker player, he also enjoys philosophizing on concepts greater than Royal Flushes and he even writes poetry. He's made a living playing Poker for the last seven years, starting with the two–and–four dollar games in Gardena, California. Hardly a day goes by that he doesn't get one or two urgent phone calls from other Professionals seeking advice on some tricky Draw Poker situation.

"I knew right away", Mike told me, *"that I had to play a lot better than average just to beat the 'rent' in Gardena, and so I decided to learn Draw inside–out. That's when I started compiling my figures. I was making a hundred a week then as a sports editor..."* His voice trailed off and he looked at something in the distance above my head as though remembering. Then he snapped back to the present.

"That was a while ago." He grinned and took a gulp of coffee. *"I don't dwell too much in the past. There were some hard times back then."* He grinned again. *"Anyway, how about it Doyle? Ready for a game of Draw?"*

"No thanks", I said. *"I'll stick to Hold 'em."*

Minutes later he said goodbye. I watched him walk from the lounge into the Casino, and the second he set foot on the Card Room floor, a dramatic change came over him. The "crazy man" was on stage again...

DRAW POKER

With the Joker...and without (and other variations)

INTRODUCTION

"Watch closely, Rosemary. Analyze this next play for me." A clamorous blend of laughter, splashing chips and strident voices swallowed my words. **Gardena's** elegant **Eldorado Club** echoed this Saturday night with a Poker frenzy so contagious that even the floormen and the crowd waiting for the next available seats were consumed by it.

"I can't hear you!" she shouted.

"This next hand — watch it carefully. Remember everything you've learned so far, and try to decide what the players have by the way they're acting."

"Okay. You mean this table right here?" She pointed to a small–limit Draw game a few feet from where we stood. I nodded.

The cards were dealt clumsily by a cheerful sixty–year–old woman who stopped twice in the course of distributing the hands to apologize for her ineptness.

"What can you tell me about the dealer? Quick!" I demanded.

"Well, she doesn't know very much about Poker."

"That's certainly true. Would you expect her to bluff this next hand?"

"No! She seems too friendly and nervous."

"Exactly, and there's an even more important reason," I explained. *"She fears the other players might already dislike her*

*because she's so awkward. She won't risk alienating somebody
further by getting caught bluffing. How could the poor woman ever
live down THAT disgrace?"*

"The guy that just opened is weak!" said Rosemary. "He
threw his chips in with too much emphasis, so he has Jacks or
Queens, right?"

"Absolutely! You're a fast learner."

A male in his mid-twenties called, faking a raise. It was
an obvious act. Sheltering his cards in one hand, he kept the
3♡ separated by an index finger. This was not an act because
it wasn't blatant.

"What does the caller have?" I asked.

"Two-Pair, unless he's on the Come.* He's about to draw
one."

"Two-Pair, and they're very small," I said. "He faked the
raise hoping to discourage someone else from raising. Players on the
Come, don't mind other players entering the pot, and they don't feel
intimidated by someone else's raise. If a guy is on the Come in this
situation, he won't bother pretending to be strong."

The Opener drew three and checked blind. The caller
discarded the exposed 3♡, looked at the card he'd drawn,
then glanced immediately to his chips and bet while
shrugging his shoulders.

"He's got a Full House, huh?"

"That's right, and not just any Full House," I added. "We
know it's a small one."

First the Opener looked at two of the three cards he'd
drawn. Carefully he peeked at the third and final card. He
shook his head sadly and raised slowly.

"HE's got a BIGGER Full House!" announced Rosemary,
tugging my shirt to make certain I heard her. She has
developed into a consistent winner using the same statistics
and psychology you will learn in this section. But here was
her first experience at deducing from people's mannerisms
what Poker hands they were holding.

---

*On the Come **means a player is drawing to a Straight or Flush.**

I said, *"He might even have four Jacks or four Queens, don't forget."*

But it turned out that the Opener had Jacks Full over Sevens and the caller had three Fives and two Sixes.

"It's magic!" said Rosemary.

Inexperienced Draw Poker players complain that there aren't enough clues to indicate what hands their opponents hold. Unlike various forms of Stud, no cards are turned face-up by the dealer. There are only two Rounds of betting, one before and one after the draw. Doesn't this minimize the card-reading advantage a good player has against a weak opponent? How can you tell if a player has exactly one Pair before the draw? If a player has drawn one card, how is it possible to know that he's made a Flush? Couldn't he have Two-Pair instead? And, well, what if you need to know whether the raiser has a moderately strong hand like Queens-up, a powerhouse like Aces-full or nothing much at all?

After you *master* the concepts of this section, you will be ready to step into any Draw Poker arena in the world favored to leave with a profit! You will be able to read the hands of weak opponents with "magical" precision! *You will begin to apply the* **most accurate** *statistics ever published on the game!*

Doyle asked me to teach you Draw in my own way. For years I have gathered data, computed probabilities, analyzed Tells, charted strategies and tested new theories. I've logged thousands of pages of notes about plays and about people, and I've worked long hours with a computer. All on this one form of Poker — Draw. When Doyle said he considered me to be the best Draw player in the world, I was flattered. And when he asked me to write this section, I accepted.

The advice I'll give you has been thoroughly tested by Professional players. The strategies are easily learned because they have been tailored to the Poker student. I've tutored aspiring players and from their learning experiences has come the simplified, dynamic system of instructing Draw Poker you'll soon read. Elaborate maneuvers too difficult to remember have been discarded in favor of crisp, clean guidelines which will bring you a maximum profit.

> **In the *Statistics* section, you'll find mathematical tables on Draw Poker which (*along with data on other games*) I've prepared especially for this book. The *more accomplished* you become at Poker, the *more valuable* you'll find those statistics.**

Draw Poker is played in various forms throughout the world. Most of this section is devoted to Draw **with** the Joker, using a 53-card deck. Additionally discussed are Draw **without** the Joker (52-card deck), Draw Open-Blind and High-Back-to-Low. The standard game requires a Pair of Jacks (or better) to open.

FINDING A GAME

If you're in a home game, obviously you **don't** have much choice of opponents. Naturally, if it's **your** home, you should invite weak players willing to part with their money. If you're in a casino, you do have a choice of games. Look for a table with a lot of laughter because people who seem to be having a good time are generally there for "sociable" gambling. Look for that "home-game" atmosphere where no one's taking Poker too seriously. You probably know from experience that home games among friends are the loosest and most beatable.

Even though you're **not** going to find a game in a public casino as carelessly played as the one at Aunt Elsa's with your uncle and three of your brothers, you should still pick the easiest table available. Since the object is to make money, it is worth your time to appraise the various games.

Try to spot players who sit upright and who seem attentive. Avoid them. Select a table where there are distractions — an attractive woman, a boisterous drunk — because they will bother your opponents more than they will hurt you. Players changing seats impulsively are apt to be superstitious. Play in their games. Players exposing cards will be helpful. Choose the table with the biggest pots and the most players per pot. When you see a lot of double and triple antes, the game is apt to be tight. If there are three, four and five players drawing cards most of the time, the game is promising. If you notice a lot of sandbagging (check–raising), some players in the game **may** have developed a degree of sophistication. This is not to your benefit, particularly while you're still learning Draw.

If there's a lot of conversation unrelated to Poker, good — they aren't concentrating. If there are arguments, forget it. Don't even consider sitting in a game where there are persistent squabbles. Sure, the angry player is not as mentally alert as he could be, but he isn't in a gambling mood, either. Distracted players are most advantageous when they're pleasantly sidetracked and eager to fling chips joyously into the pot. Where you find icy silence, you'll probably confront a table full of Rocks trying to take your money. Avoid silence!

All right, picture this. You're in a public casino ready to enter a Jacks-or-better-to-open Draw Poker game where the stakes are $5 before the draw and $10 after (or whatever limit you feel comfortable playing while you're still learning). Presumably no one at the table is uptight, there are no heated arguments and you've observed players joking with each other. A sexy woman sits across the table, flirting with and distracting the guys. **You** are **not** distracted. There are a couple of players who've been drinking, and although they're gambling recklessly they aren't drunk enough to slow down the game. No one here looks like a Professional Poker player. In fact, all seem thoroughly unsophisticated. Here's a table full of happy, superstitious gamblers eager to give you their money.

WHAT HANDS DO YOU PLAY?

Using a regular deck of 52 cards, there are 2,598,960 possible five-card hands. Add a Joker and you have 2,869,685. The difference isn't staggering — 270,725 more hands, an increase of 10.42%. Beware! This assumption that it isn't a significant difference has been the ruin of players who had never before confronted the Joker.

Most of the time in an eight-handed game **someone** *will have* the Joker before the draw. Specifically, there's a 75.5% chance that one of eight players will be dealt the Joker — and that's better than three out of four times. Under formal conditions today, Jacks-or-better is usually played **with** the Joker, and you'd better be aware of what this does.

The Joker is not generally used as a wild card. Its power is limited to serving as an Ace, completing a Straight or completing a Flush (including a Straight-Flush).

Used in that way, the Joker means this:

(1) It is easier to hit Flushes drawing one card. Instead of 4.2 to 1, the odds against making become 3.8 to 1.

(2) Open-end Straights are completed 10.16% more often.

(3) There are important draws you never confront with a 52-card deck. One card to 6♣-7♣-8♣-Joker — 22 cards out of 48 will complete, meaning you'll make a Straight-Flush, a Flush or a Straight 45.8% of the time. Not bad! One card to 7◊-9◊-10◊-Joker — 19 out of 48 will complete, 39.6%. There are 16-way Straights like 10-Jack-Queen-Joker — the odds here are 2 to 1 against making. It's 3 to 1 against completing a 12-way hand like 7-8-10-Joker. Additionally, you'll get hands which include Ace-Joker and allow you to keep the Aces while trying for a

Straight, Flush or Straight-Flush. Here the one-card draw might miss and still provide you with Aces-up or three Aces. At worst you'll retain the original Pair of Aces.

(4) There are 2.4 times as many ways to be dealt three Aces as any other specific kind of Trips.

(5) You will be dealt a Pair of Aces 53.6% more often than a Pair of Kings, Sixes or any other kind of Pair.

(6) You will confront players who habitually play two-card draws to hands like 5♡-8♡-Joker (called a *Cat-hop*).

This is an example of a 22-way hand. Four cards will give you a Straight-Flush, six cards will make a Flush and twelve cards will make a Straight:

But, if you hold **this** 22-way hand...

you have a better chance to beat an Opener who drew three. That's because the A♢, A♠ and A♡ are not needed to make a Straight. So in addition to the 22 cards that complete a Straight, a Flush or a Straight-Flush, you have three cards that will give you a possibly winning Pair of Aces.

What you see here is a 19-way hand. Three cards will make a Straight-Flush, seven will provide you with a Flush and nine will give you a Straight:

Here are three different types of 16-way hands. First, a hand with three cards that will complete a Straight-Flush, seven that will make a Flush and six that will make a Straight. If you hold the hand in the middle, there are 16 cards that will give you a Straight. The last example allows two cards to make the Straight-Flush, eight to make a Flush and six to make a Straight:

This 13-way hand affords you two chances to make the Straight-Flush, eight chances to catch a Flush and three cards to complete the Straight:

Here's an example of a 12-way Straight:

When you draw one to a Flush using a 53–card deck (including the Joker), there are 10 cards that will complete your hand:

This is a Country Straight draw. Nine cards will complete it, including the Joker:

This Inside Straight draw can be completed by five cards, including the Joker:

Basically Draw Poker is a **game of Aces**. This is true even using a 52-card deck. **When the Joker is** *included*, **any devised strategy which** *discounts* **the importance of Aces** *will fail*. Assume you play a Pair of Aces and your opponent plays a Pair of Kings. One of the biggest mistakes a mortal can make is to think this is a close contest. If both you and your opponent draw three, you'll win four out of five times. But it's much, much worse moneywise for your opponent than just 4 to 1 against. If neither of you helps (which will happen almost half the time), you win — and you might even catch a high-kicker, bet and get called if your image is healthy. If you help and he doesn't, you win. If you both make Two-Pair, you almost certainly win extra chips. If you make three Aces and he makes three Kings, there's going to be action after the draw, and you're going to love it!

There's the small chance that you'll both make Full Houses or better. Most of the time **you** make big money when it happens. The guy with the Pair of Kings has to hope he helps (which he will 29% of the time) and has to hope that you won't (and you **won't** help two-thirds of the time **if** your Aces **do not** include the Joker). Or he might hope he makes three Kings while you make Aces-up. That's a lot of hoping. But he'll keep right on doing it forever — we hope!

Study the distribution charts on Draw in the Appendix. You'll develop a feel for how often various hands can be expected. Also, examine the following table just for fun. In an eight-handed $5 Draw game, an average of 48 hands are played every hour, including the times that nobody opens. On that basis, the following list shows how long on average it takes for you to be dealt various hands before the draw. The assumption is that your luck is normal. You might be dealt five Aces pat the first hand you play, but the odds against it are almost three million to one (2,869,684 to 1, to be exact). To look at it another way, if you sit in an eight-handed $5 Draw game and play six hours each day, five days each week, you can expect to see five Aces pat every 38 years.

HAND DEALT PAT	EXPECTANCY, ONCE IN. . .
Five Aces	59,785 hours
Royal Flush	2,491 hours
Any Straight-Flush	293 hours
Four-of-a-kind	72 hours
Full House	13 hours, 41 minutes
Flush	7 hours, 40 minutes
Straight	2 hours, 55 minutes
Any complete hand (including Four-of-a-kind)	1 hour, 46 minutes
Three-of-a-kind	57 minutes
Two-Pair	26 minutes
One Pair (of Openers)	8 minutes, 49 seconds
Jacks (or better)	5 minutes, 35 seconds

Now that you have some idea what hands can be expected, you are ready to consider which hands to play.

Again, this is a **game of Aces**. If you have a Pair of Aces dealt to you, even if you're in first position with seven players still to act, you are even–money to have the best hand going! This is a fact which startles many seasoned Professionals. It means you can always open on Aces and anticipate a profit. Of course, you should **not** open if you've **seen** someone's Pat Flush or if you have a Tell on a player that lets you know you're beat. Incidentally, you can expect a Pair of Aces on the average of every 26 minutes. Because of this frequency, it is certain that **Aces**, *played well,* **will be the biggest money-maker in your Draw Poker arsenal.** Occasionally you may choose to pass Aces...and, if the pot is opened by another player, you can either call or raise. But it is essential to remember that, without Tells to the contrary, **it is** *always safe* **to open with Aces!**

Since the assumption is that you've decided on a $5 Draw game with a $1 ante, take a look at the *Opening Strategy Table,* MINIMUM OPENING REQUIREMENTS FOR MEDIUM ANTE GAMES. The single-ante Round of the $5 Draw game is structurally identical to the $10 Draw game chosen in the example. The ratio of total–ante to opening-bet, eight-handed, is 1.6 to 1.

Why is this ratio important? The question every good Poker player asks himself before putting his money in the pot is: *"How much can I win and what will it cost me?"* Obviously, the larger the total of antes is in proportion to the opening–bet, the more favorable the pot odds. The more you stand to gain, the less certain you need to be of winning the pot. Therefore, if the ante is large and the bet small by comparison, you can open on weaker hands. You can afford to lose more often because the times you do win will compensate. Also, you can theorize that other players tend to open weaker, so you can call and raise with less strength. This is why it's important to weigh what is in the pot against the amount you're betting.

Study the *OPENING STRATEGY* tables. You'll see the difference in recommended Openers between the games defined as small, medium and large ante. Minimum to open does not mean you must open, only that if you do open you can expect a profit.

PLAYING STRATEGY
(Opening, Calling, Raising)

A skilled Draw player takes many things into consideration when deciding whether or not to open. How many Jacks, Queens, Kings and Aces are in his hand? Has any player still to act indicated an interest in opening? Have any **key** cards been exposed by other players? Does anyone appear to have passed with the intention of raising? Is the hand strong enough to call a raise? Is it strong enough to re-raise? How many players are yet to act? What is the size of the ante relative to the size of an opening bet? Is it a tight game, making it less likely that someone will open? Is it a loose game, making it probable that players will call on Shorts (a Pair less than Jacks)?

The following is a **general opening guide** based on data gathered in **Gardena** card clubs during actual play.

MINIMUM OPENING REQUIREMENTS FOR SMALL ANTE SITUATIONS
$2 DRAW

(The opening bet is $2, the bet after the draw is $4 and the ante is 25¢.)

Position	Minimum to Open
1st *(Under gun)*	Aces *(but **not** with Two-Pair less than Aces-up)*
2nd	Aces *(but **not** with Two-Pair less than Aces-up)*
3rd	Aces *(but **not** with Two-Pair less than Queens-up)*
4th	Aces *(but **not** with Two-Pair less than Tens-up)*
5th	Kings-with-an-Ace *(or better)*
6th	Kings *(or better)*
7th	Queens *(or better)*
8th *(Dealer)*	Jacks *(or better)*

MINIMUM OPENING REQUIREMENTS FOR MEDIUM ANTE SITUATIONS
$10 DRAW

(The opening bet is $10, the bet after the draw is $20 and the ante is $2.)

Position	Minimum to Open
1st *(Under gun)*	Aces *(but **not** with Two-Pair less than Kings-up)*
2nd	Aces *(but **not** with Two-Pair less than Queens-up)*
3rd	Aces *(but **not** with Two-Pair less than Jacks-up)*
4th	Aces *(but **not** with Two-Pair less than Tens-up)*
5th	Kings *(or better)*
6th	Kings *(or better)*
7th	Jacks-with-an-Ace *(or better)*
8th *(Dealer)*	Jacks *(or better)*

MINIMUM OPENING REQUIREMENTS FOR LARGE ANTE SITUATIONS $5 DRAW (Double-ante)*

(The opening bet is $5, the bet after the draw is $10 and the ante is $2.)

Position	Minimum to Open
1st *(Under gun)*	**Kings** *(or better)*
2nd	**Queens-with-an-Ace** *(or better)*
3rd	**Queens** *(or better)*
4th	**Jacks** *(or better)*
5th	**Jacks** *(or better)*
6th	**Jacks** *(or better)*
7th	**Jacks** *(or better)*
8th *(Dealer)*	**Jacks** *(or better)*

Note that even though a Pair of Aces is a safe opening hand in any position, Two (small) Pair is **not** a good opener in the early positions. The reason is that you'll usually have to throw Two-Pair away if you get raised. If the raiser is **not** a frequent bluffer and if his *minimum raising requirements* are Aces-up (which is the normal minimum raising hand for over half of your opponents), you cannot call on Tens and Sevens. The odds against you making a Full House are 11 to 1 and the *pot-odds* (the total dollars already in the pot weighed against the amount of your call) are **not** nearly this great.

You have a vulnerable hand when you open early with Two (small) Pair. Besides, if you do get a caller who has, say, a Pair of Aces, his chances of improving to a hand that will beat your Tens-up are about one in three. Your chances of improving are only one in twelve. Even if you have the best hand going, you are in a defensive position after the draw, and this runs contrary to the approach suggested in this section: Be aggressive, intimidate! Often your caller will

*This situation occurs *only* in the $5-Draw after everyone has passed on the first (single-ante) round. Another $1 is anted by each player making the total anted by all eight players $16. Since the opening bet remains $5, the Opener initially gets 16 to 5 or 3.2 to 1.

have Two-Pair bigger than yours even before drawing. The median (half higher and half lower) Two-Pair is Jacks-up.

Even in the early positions it is safe to open on Aces-up. That's because you have the option of throwing away the small Pair and drawing three to Aces, when you call a raiser. If you elect to draw one to Aces-up, the chances against making a Full House are reduced to 8.6 to 1, down from 11 to 1. The fifth Ace (Joker) **does** make a difference!

You now know you can open with Aces and that Two (small) Pair is a dangerous Opener because you generally **can't** call a raise. But can you call a raise with Aces? Despite mathematical calculations which show that you **shouldn't** call if the raiser is thought to have Trips (or better), data recorded during thousands of hours of actual play proves that your wisest strategy is to call the raiser most of the time with Aces. Even raisers whose minimum requirements seem to be Three-of-a-kind, frequently decide to take shots with Two-Pair and with Come (incomplete) hands. Sometimes they are just plain bluffing. Your image should be strong enough that, if you make three Aces, you can check into their Trips after the draw, lure a bet and then raise. This sort of psycho-strategy is explained later.

Additionally, you should usually **know** when a raiser is really strong (also explained later) and be quick to throw your Aces away. And, of course, against a player who really **does** only raise with Three-of-a-kind (or better) and who **never** varies his play and never bluffs, you **must pass** Aces when raised. Since you should generally throw away Jacks, Queens, Kings and Two-Pair (less than Aces-up) against a legitimate raiser, you can scarcely afford to routinely dump Aces, too. Your image would be so tight and your opening game so predictable that your profits would dwindle.

If you're now familiar with the table of Opening Requirements for medium-ante games like $5 Draw, you know you can open with Aces in any position, you can open reluctantly with Two (larger) Pair in the first four positions (the earlier the position, the larger the Two-Pair need to be), you can open with Kings (or better) in 5th and 6th positions, and you can open with Jacks (or better) in 7th and 8th (though in 7th it is advisable to have an Ace with the Jacks).

If the pot is opened already, what should you call with? Here's a mistake that almost every Professional Draw player I know makes. If it's opened early by a player whose minium-to-open is Aces, they **call** with Aces. **That's wrong!** Totally, inexcusably wrong both mathematically and practically. If the Rock in 2nd position opens, throw your Aces away! This will give you an advantage over most Professionals who suicidally insist on playing Aces in such circumstances. You **should** call with Aces if the Opener seems weak (explained later) or if it's an Opener who is likely to play Jacks, Queens or Kings from the early positions. You can call with Aces against an Opener whose position is middle to late. You can even play Aces against an Aces-or-better Opener who never bluffs.

Seldom call three or more players
with a small Two-Pair.

You should **not** call an Opener with Jacks, Queens or Kings. And if you make this a hard and fast rule — **never, never call with Jacks, Queens, Kings** — your game will scarcely suffer. If you're more into flexibility, you can **consider** calling with Kings against the dealer who's the Opener, particularly if you hold an Ace. You can call with Kings if a double-ante $5 Draw ($16 total ante eight-handed and a $5 opening bet) pot has been opened, and you should **raise** with Kings when you **know** the Opener is weak.

You usually **shouldn't** call with a four-Flush, single-ante, against one player. The exception would be if your four-Flush is Ace-high and there are four (or more) players who might still come into the pot. You can profitably play an Ace-high four-Flush against two or more players, but it **must be** Ace-high. You can play a 12-way Straight against the Opener if any players are still to act. You can profitably call with a 12-way Straight against two or more players. You can always call with 16-way, 19-way and 22-way hands (described earlier in this section). In fact, you can *often* **raise** with 16, 19 and 22-way hands. There is also a 13-way Straight-Flush (6♡-7♡-9♡-10♡), which should be played a little more liberally than a 12-way Straight.

What hands should you raise with? It's been suggested that, in terms of mathematics, you should raise whenever you have a 2 to 1 advantage over your opponent. This is a myth. The bad reasoning is that when you raise in Limit Draw, you're trying to get one extra bet from your opponent. But if he has you beat, he will re-raise and you must call. Thus, if you raise with a hand that is a 2 to 1 favorite, you can afford to call and lose the one-in-three times he has you beat, because the two-in-three times you have the best hand he will call and lose.

This theory of raising used by many Professional Draw players is garbage! Obviously your opponent **isn't** going to re-raise every time he has you beat because he doesn't **know** he has you beat. There are a lot of considerations that help decide whether or not to raise. If the Opener is very weak, he might **not** even call your raise — something you may or may not desire. Are the players you'll be raising timid or aggressive — will they be likely to get the most out of strong hands by re-raising? Could you get players in behind you by just calling? Would a raise more liberal than mathematically warranted help your table image? How anxious does the Opener seem for your call?

In general, I find that a 3 to 2 advantage over your opponent is about right against one player. Against more than one player, you don't even need that much of an edge. If the Opener has Aces (or better), Kings-up is a reasonable raising hand. Unfortunately, players who will not open early on less than Aces often choose **not** to open on Two-Pair. If you're considering raising this sort of Rock, you'd better have at least three Sixes.

Occasionally you'll play with someone who only opens with Aces in early positions, electing to sandbag Two-Pair or better. In that case, you can raise on any Two-Pair because you **know** the Opener has **exactly** Aces. If the Opener will open on anything — Jacks, Two-Pair, etc. — your minimum raising requirement is a Pair of Aces. By the way, if your opponent has Jacks, you're better off with Aces than with Two (very small) Pair. That's because you're much more likely to improve Aces than Two-Pair. If your opponent has opened with Kings (or better) raise with Jacks-up, minimum. Using these simple guidelines, it won't take long for you to have a perfect feel for raising.

With what should you call a raise *Cold? Calling a raise cold* means you're coming in for both the bet and the raise without having any of your money invested in the pot, except for your ante (before the draw). Professionals tend to make another big mistake here. They assume they need the edge against the raiser before calling. If they reason that the raiser has a 51% chance of having them beat, they pass. Wrong, wrong, awful!

If you're playing $5 Draw, there's $8 in antes to begin with. It's opened for $5, that's $13. The raiser puts in $10, and the total is $23. Your turn. If you call it's going to cost you $10. Clearly you don't have to be holding the best hand 50% of the time to play. You're getting $23 to $10 (2.3 to 1) and there's an overwhelming likelihood that the Opener will call making it $28 against your $10.

There's a small chance the Opener will re-raise, your main worry at this point. Let's say 2nd position opens, 3rd position raises and you're in 7th with three Sixes. You know that the raiser has Aces-up (or better). This being the case, his median hand is three Nines. You are holding three Sixes and your opponent has an estimated average of three Nines. Call! You're going to have him beat two out of five times and **that's enough** if you have pot odds of 2.3 to 1, even considering you may lose some ground on the after-draw betting.

Roughly — and varying with the playing habits of your opponents — you can call an Aces-up-or-better raise *Cold* with three Fives, minimum. Your discards should **both** *be higher* than the small Trips (your Fives) making it more likely you have your opponent beat. For a Trips-or-better raiser, use three Nines as minimum to *Cold Call*. If the raiser requires Tens-up (or better), you can call with a minimum of Aces-up (his median hand is three Deuces). If you deduce that the raiser is likely to have Aces (or better), Sevens-up **should** be enough for a *Cold Call*, but considerably more caution is due because you'll probably have to throw your hand away if you're re-raised. The odds against filling Two (small) Pair, remember, are 11 to 1. It's best **not** to call **this** raise *Cold* with less than Kings-up.

When should you re-raise? Consider it whenever your hand is stronger than one allowing you to call a raise *Cold*. This doesn't mean you should always re-raise simply because your hand is strong enough. Sometimes call and see what develops on the draw. Maybe you'll learn that yours was the best hand all along. If so, you can bet or raise after the draw with the near certainty of getting called because you didn't reveal the strength of your hand earlier. Remember, we're talking about a game where the bets after the draw are **twice** the size of the Opening-Round limits. If you discover yours is **not** the best hand, you have paid less for a chance at improving.

One of my *favorite* plays goes like this:

A player who has just sat down opens in 5th position. I am unfamiliar with his playing habits and, unfortunately, his opening mannerisms have given me no firm indication of what hand he holds. Probably he's got more than Jacks or Queens because he has not thrown his chips in forcefully. The player in 6th raises, and I'm not sure what he has either, although it's likely he has Trips or better. I'm holding **3-Aces** in 7th.

Naturally, I can consider re-raising, but a simple call is the superior play here. Why?

Let's look at two things that might happen.

First. The Opener draws three; the raiser draws two. Now I draw one, **knowing** that mine is the best hand going. After the draw, it's check, bet. Now, it's my turn.

"You're betting into me?" I say as if in disbelief. *"What if I make a Full House, Aces-full say? Then you'll be sorry. Except I can't make Aces-full because I don't have any Aces, but I can make. . ."* I look quickly at the card I've drawn. *"Yes, it's true! The miracle of the century, Straight-Flush!"* Now, I raise.

The Opener says, *"If HE wasn't behind me, I WOULD call you,"* and throws his hand away. The reason he says this is to avoid an embarrassed ego in the event the original raiser calls and catches me bluffing.

Naturally, the probable Trips **will** call unless he was bluffing with a small Pair and an Ace kicker or a *Cat-hop*. He may even call with a lone Pair since my seemingly inane patter has so confused him that he wishes his mother would make the decision for him. Of course, he might have made a Full House or four Kings, but he's very likely to just call even with these hands figuring that I either made a Straight-Flush or I have nothing.

That's the point! I still have the 3-Aces I went into the hand with, but my verbal maneuvers might keep this player (I'm having a bit of trouble reading him) from re-raising with a Full House if he improved after the draw. Maybe it won't work. Maybe it will only work one time in twenty. But when it does, **preventing his re-raise** will save me money because mathematically my opponent has the best of it if he fills-up and re-raises.

Unless I have an absolute *Tell* making it safe for me to throw my hand away when re-raised, game strategy dictates that I must call *most of the time.*

All the playful talking I employ at the Poker table is **calculated** to have a **predictable** psychological effect on my opponents. It is **not** meaningless! The most probable outcome of the betting sequence described is that I win with 3-Aces against, say, three Sevens.

A re-raise **before the draw** would have shown a smaller profit.

Second. Suppose the Opener stands pat after having timidly decided to just call the raise. The raiser is pat also. I now draw two cards to the three Aces, affording the maximum chance at improving. Alas, no help! Opener checks, raiser bets. I start to raise, then re-examine my cards.

"No!" I say dramatically as if some revolutionary surge of discipline has just taken me by surprise. "I made Fours and Threes and I'm STILL not calling! If I didn't keep the Ace kicker I might even have made a Full House. Then you would have been in trouble!" I toss my hand defiantly into the discards.

Here, the impression is that I've made a wild and reckless call against a raise with a Pair of Fours and an Ace, and, had it not been for the fact that there were **two** Pat hands against me, I would have called or even raised! And the players at the table won't doubt me for a moment because they've **seen** me do the most bizarre things ever encountered at a Draw Poker table, over and over, endlessly, without regard to the odds against me, with no reverence for the holy Poker chip — or so they think. Meanwhile, I've just paid the minimum price to lose on 3–Aces.

What if you have 3–Aces including the Joker with the option of breaking Trips, while retaining Ace–Joker and trying for a Straight–Flush?

Here's what your hand looks like. . .

You open in 4th position and 5th position raises. All others pass. Unless there are some Tells which demand another strategy, there is **only one way** you should play this hand. Call. Request one card and **do not discard** immediately. While the card that's just been dealt to you remains on the table, pretend to be distracted. If the raiser is pat, throw away the **A♣** and go for the Royal Flush (your best chance to beat a Pat hand). Otherwise discard the **K◇** retaining the 3–Aces, and try to check–raise after the draw. This wait–and–see drawing maneuver applies to many hands which include the Joker.

Why am I teaching you all these things? Doyle didn't know I was **this** crazy!

Remember, there are situations where it is more profitable to call a raise *Cold* than to re–raise, even though the strength of your hand seems to justify the latter.

Now you have a general notion what the values of the hands are and what hands to play. *Don't forget,* **it's a game of Aces.** *In a $5 Draw game with a $1 ante, a Pair of Aces is so* *powerful that* **even if the Opener spreads Kings–up on the table, you should still call!**

Aces are larger than life and greater than mountains!

DRAWING

Which cards should you throw away? How many should you draw? Most decisions of this kind will seem obvious. Here are some rules:

(1) Seldom keep an Ace kicker to a Pair of Jacks, Queens or Kings. An astonishing thing from a mathematical viewpoint is that your chances of improvement are very slightly better if you **do** keep an Ace kicker. But this tiny difference is overshadowed by the increased difficulty you will have beating Three–of–a–kind. If you **know** your opponent has Kings–up, then keep the Ace kicker with your Jacks. If your opponent stands pat, you have a slightly better chance of making a Full House or better keeping the Ace kicker. (This surprises a lot of knowledgeable players.) Otherwise, do **not** keep the Ace.

(2) Keep a King kicker with your Aces whenever you feel that your **lone** opponent has Aces also. You can also keep a Queen kicker in such circumstances. Against two (or more) opponents always draw three.

(3) You should usually draw one to an Ace–Joker four–Flush.

(4) If you have Ace–Joker, King, Jack, Seven of mixed suits, your best chance of improvement is to draw three. Against Trips, draw one.

(5) If you have Ace–Joker and one suited card that makes a Straight–Flush possible, drawing two provides your best chance of improvement. If you have **A♠-Joker-5♠-3♡-9♣**, draw two (to the **A♠-Joker-5♠**) because that'll give you your best chance for improvement. **Don't** draw one to

the Straight (A♠-Joker-5♠-3♡) *unless* you're sure you must beat Trips.

(6) Draw two to Three-of-a-kind *unless* you have a specific reason to draw one. You may keep a kicker to disguise your hand or because certain cards have been exposed and you're keeping a "live" card. If you do keep a kicker, the Ace is usually the best. Chances of making a Full House or Four-of-a-kind are just as good keeping an Ace kicker as drawing two, in fact, slightly better. However, your chances of making Four-of-a-kind **exactly** are only half as good. If, for strategic reasons, you decide to keep a kicker other than an Ace, keep the **lower card** since your opponents are more likely to be using higher cards in their hands.

(7) If you have a choice of drawing one card to either a *Country Straight* or to a Flush, draw to the Flush. If the choice is between a 12-way Straight and a Flush, the 12-way is **usually** better.

(8) In general, do **not** split Two-Pair and draw three. If you have called an Opener who draws one, your best bet is to draw one also, even though he probably has your small Two-Pair bettered. The reason is: There is a high enough probability of him having Ace-Joker with a Straight or Flush combination and you'll have him beat **or** that he's disguising big Trips and you'll **need** a Full House. If you **know** that your opponent has 3-Sixes, then you *should* **split** Two (small) Pair of, say, Sevens and Threes and draw to the Pair of Sevens.

You should usually draw one card to this hand, discarding the 7♠:

If you hold this hand, your best chance of improvement is to draw three to the Ace–Joker, but against Trips, draw one to the Straight:

OR

If this is your hand, drawing two and discarding the 3♡–9♣ will give you the best chance to improve. Against Trips, draw one to the Straight:

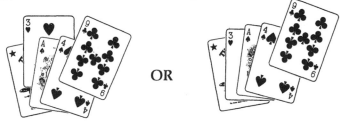

OR

If you hold this, throw the 9♠ away and try for the Flush:

Here you should usually draw two, but if you keep a kicker for strategic reasons, the Three (smaller card) is better:

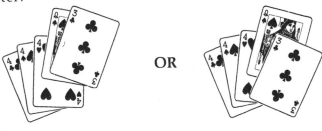

OR

TABLE IMAGE

Even when you've acquired experience and know with confidence which hands to play and how to draw to your hands, you **won't** win much without a good image. You can develop an image that permits you to get away with a lot of bluffs, but this is a big mistake in Limit Draw Poker where players call much more often than they should. To make your profit by a bluff strategy, you might first appear tight. This will get your opponents to call less often (some of them — others won't pay attention). Since **bad** Draw players have the habit of calling too frequently anyway, you would have to force them to call a smaller, more realistic percent of the time. In other words, the first thing you'll do is make your opponents play better! If you're persistent enough, eventually your opponents will lay down hands more often than they should and your bluffs will be profitable. Unfortunately, you're fighting against the current. The **main flaw** in the game the majority of people play is that **they call too much**. You should reinforce this weakness — that's where the money is.

In attempting to take advantage of most players' habit of calling too frequently, you should try to get as many calls as possible. This should be easy, since your opponents will seem almost eager to cooperate with your efforts.

A book devoted almost entirely to Draw Poker stresses the importance of a reckless image and states that I have *"the BEST wild image of them all."* I go out of my way to act crazy and bizarre at the table. Sometimes I'll sit in a game and announce, *"Just consider this a Poker exhibition. I'm going to do the strangest things ever seen in the history of Gardena!* Maybe you'll beat me, but if I get lucky, watch out!"* Off and on, I continue this nonsense patter. I try to convince them that I bluff 40% of the time (sometimes I use 50%) and that they should call but they won't know when. (Of course, the

---

*In Gardena, California, where I often play, I'm known as *"MJC"* (the initials I use for the *Call-Board* in order to get seated). Elsewhere, I'm known as *"Crazy Mike."*

object is to get called almost all the time without bluffing much. This inane chatter *"Call me, I'm bluffing — no wait, DON'T call me I'm NOT bluffing — well, I mean, I haven't looked yet but I'm probably not bluffing!"* so totally confuses players that they nearly always call. To supplement this verbal barrage, I fidget, bite my fingernails, force a giggle, swallow nervously, tap the table, breathe hard and do almost anything I can think of that will encourage the call.

There is a theory here which is very important:

> The average person you play against is **not** a skilled player. He's come for entertainment — gambling. Often he seeks to escape the pain of disciplined living. He walked into the club with the intention of throwing chips into the pot, hoping his luck would be good. He doesn't have a specific game plan and he hasn't analyzed Tells — he has no theories on reading people. He will call or won't call purely on instinct. But, remember, he sat in the game with the hope of putting chips in the pot. **The more things you do, the more likely it is that one of them will trip his calling mechanism.** He's just looking for reasons to call.

> Provide them. He is not thinking rationally, he has gambling fever, he is hiding from the real world outside. He will call **because** you were counting your chips, **because** you swallowed hard, **because** you shrugged your shoulders. It doesn't matter to him that these are not rational reasons to call. It just matters that you've provided him with an excuse to put money in the pot. *That's why it's* **silly** *to base your game plan on* **bluffing**. These fellows want to call — let them! When you locate your opponent's number one weakness, move in for the kill, capitalize. Sure, some Draw Professionals have been able to win by swimming up-stream (by using a game plan centering on bluffs). But you'll *win* **more** following the advice in this section.

If you're **not** the talkative sort, and if you don't like the idea of wiggling around in your seat, there are still plenty of ways you can appear so "crazy" they have to call you. I carry around a fancy pocket notebook that is embossed *"Mike Caro Playbook"* on the front cover and *"How to Bluff Constantly and Win"* on the back. Of course, when I ostentatiously display this notebook, people are skeptical and think it's just a gimmick. But they call anyway...just in case.

Here are a few of the ploys I use to make players think I left my mind in the glove compartment — and tend to make them call and call and call:

(1) You're in 2nd position with garbage (9◇-7♣-5♠-4◇-2♡). The guy in 5th opens, 6th calls, 1st calls — and then **you** call! (You might even emphasize your call with, *"This pot's too big to stay out of!"*) The player in 1st position draws one, you stand pat and everyone gives you a startled stare because you haven't check–raised before the draw. The Opener (5th position) draws two and 6th draws three. Now the Opener checks (the Opener is always first to act after the draw). The other two guys check also. Now it's up to you.

The Opener has his chips in his hand, because he's very anxious to call the bet they **all** expect you to make. And 6th is just hoping the Opener **doesn't** call so **he** can be the lucky one. Perhaps 1st position has made a Flush and is eagerly anticipating your bet so **he** *can raise.*

But you disappoint everyone by simply spreading your hand. There's a long stunned silence as they all gaze at your cards. Then the best hand takes the pot mumbling some questions about why you didn't bet.

If it's a $5 Draw game, you've just **given away $5** *without* **any chance of winning the pot.** Your play was so bizarre that no one could possibly forget it — and they'll keep talking about it all night.

That's **not much** of a price for the calls you'll get later. It's much more effective and a lot cheaper than the common form of "advertisement" where you raise and follow through after the draw by betting, getting called and losing $20 (*$10 before and $10 after the draw*).

(2) Suppose you've opened with a Pat Ace–Joker Flush. You have one caller who draws three. After the draw, you bet and he raises. **Don't** even consider calling an unsophisticated player in this situation, and here's the reason:

Unsophisticated Draw players **don't** expect you to **ever** throw away a Pat hand because they, themselves, have never done it. If you're raised, they think, you may not like it but you'll call anyway. A Pat hand is surely a calling hand, isn't it?

Since they expect you to call their raise if you do have a legitimate Pat hand, it would seem stupid to them to raise unless they have your Pat hand beat. Sure they like to gamble, but the opportunity to gamble is already afforded them when you bet. All they have to do is call and **gamble** that you're bluffing!

It **doesn't matter** that your opponent's chances against making a Full House or better drawing three (when you hold Ace–Joker) are about 80 to 1, **because a Full House (or better) is** *exactly* **what he has!**

Throw your cards away without hesitation. Even good players incorrectly take their time about passing in this situation. The hesitation makes them look like they've discarded a good hand — and that makes them appear tight.

"Loose and crazy" is the image you should strive for! Even Professionals sometimes compound the error here by defiantly spreading face–up the hand they're passing. This may be food for their egos, but, pretty soon, that guy who never used to bluff them is stealing one time in twenty and that's still not frequently enough to justify a call. But it means a whole pot lost now and then that would have been saved had they not done the ego bit.

How **should** you respond? You should throw your hand away **immediately**. You might say: *"I was only fooling!"* or *"Every time I try to bluff, someone calls!"* But the best line of all is: *"You never would have called if you hadn't improved!"*

For those of you who think it doesn't matter much **what** you say in a Poker game, let's examine what happens now. First of all, your opponent thinks he's made a good play because, after all, he's stacking the chips! But now you've challenged him by suggesting he wouldn't have called if he hadn't helped. Invariably his response will be something like: *"I would have called you anyway! I knew you were bluffing!"*

Now...how do you like this bit of super-psychology? Not only have you correctly laid down a Pat Flush and saved money, you have done it instantly making the other players suspect you were bluffing...but, you've accomplished more than that. You've got the raiser's ego involved and caused him to announce aloud to the table that you're a bluffer while the echo of his own words reinforces that fact in his mind!

Without even *running a play*, you have established a reckless image that will bring you call after call in the next few hours!

(3) If you open late and a caller backs–in and draws one, obviously *on the Come,* consider splitting Openers by placing all five cards face–up on the table and drawing five. Now check blind. If the Come–hand misses and does **not** pair, he will usually try to bluff. You can call profitably with any Pair or just an Ace–King high (and nothing else)! The small average loss you can anticipate overall is offset by the crazy image you're creating.

(4) Draw five if you've called with a Pair of Aces and the Opener turns out to be· Pat. The 2% chance you're giving up of making a Full House or better is a small sacrifice for this kind of advertising.

(5) Split openers against a lot of callers and draw one to garbage. Check your one–card draw blind. Generally, no one will bet and they'll wait for you to look and see if you made your hand.

Suppose you split Jacks. You now turn your other four cards face–up on the table — J–8–6–3 (mixed suits). *"Let me look and see,"* you say, peeking carefully at the card you drew. *"Nope, I missed,"* you sigh sadly. This will receive a lot of comments questioning what you were drawing to and some whispers about how crazy you are. Sit back and wait for the hands now — **a lot of chips will come with them!**

"Crazy Mike" Caro believes this is the most **profitable** hand you can play in Draw Poker! (The profit comes later.)

PSYCHOLOGY — PSYCHO-STRATEGY

Now you're beginning to see the importance of having a reckless image and using psychology in Draw Poker — a game where, unlike Stud, exposed cards are **not** the key to your strategy.

Sandbagging is one finesse that has built-in psychological impact. Anytime you pass a hand, let another player open, then raise, you appear intimidating. If you can blend your crazy and bizarre image with the threat of offense, you'll instill a fun-and-fear attitude in your opponents. You'll control the game.

Take a look at the *SANDBAGGING REQUIREMENTS* (on Page 84). Note that the tables suggest hands which give you the option to sandbag. You need not — and should not — sandbag every time you get the chance. If you have a good image, confuse your opponents further by mixing up your play.

The important concept behind this sandbagging advice is Count cards. These are Jacks, Queens, Kings and Aces. The reason that inclusion of these cards in your hand makes sandbagging less desirable is that they limit your opponents' ability to open. If you have an Ace and a King, it is 40% **less** *likely* that another player will have Aces for Openers and 50% **less** *likely* that any player will have a Pair of Kings. The fewer the *Count* cards in your hand, the safer it is for you to sandbag.

Attempts have been made to set simple standards about sandbagging. The *Fox-Sathmary Count System* published in a book by John Fox gives numerical values to Jacks (½ point), Queens (¾ point), Kings (1 point) and Aces (1½ points), then attempts to provide position-by-position guidance on whether or not to sandbag.

The system is crippled because it doesn't take into consideration the fact that each additional card of the same kind, Jacks or higher, has a diminishing power to limit an opponents' chances of opening. A crude explanation of the intricate mathematics is this:

There are six kinds of Pairs of Kings your opponent might have — **K♡-K♢, K♡-K♣, K♡-K♠, K♢-K♣, K♢-K♠** and **K♠-K♣** Say you have the K♢ in your hand. Now there are only three combinations of Kings remaining with which your opponents can open. The first King cuts in half his chances of having a Pair of Kings. If you have two Kings, Diamonds and Hearts, you've eliminated only two more combinations (of the three that remain). The second King must be worth only ⅔ of what the first King is worth. If you have three Kings, the third one denies an opponent his last chance of having a Pair of Kings and is valued only ⅓ as highly as the first King in terms of preventing Openers. The fourth King has no value.

Additionally, the *Fox-Sathmary* system counts three points for the Joker. This makes it **much less** *desirable* to sandbag three Aces (including the Joker) than three Aces (excluding the Joker). It should seem obvious that the reverse is true...you'd rather sandbag when you have the Joker as one of the three Aces, thereby **limiting the chances** that any player has a Pat hand.

The value the system gives to the Joker is roughly twice what is mathematically justified. Many players, using the published *Count System* just discussed, are hurting their game substantially. Often, they would be better off using their best judgment.

Even the Sandbagging tables published here are not perfect. Let no one tell you that his automatic sandbagging advice is going to be optimum. However, the *SAND-BAGGING REQUIREMENTS* tables in this section will give you a good grasp of the subject whenever you're in doubt.

There are numerous factors to consider when deciding whether your hand should be sandbagged. Is the game composed of players who open liberally? Will your table image improve if you sandbag? How large are the antes relative to the size of the opening bet? How many cards higher than Tens are in your hand? Are there indications that players to your left plan to open? How likely is it that yours will be the winning hand after the draw? If you open and are raised, is your hand strong enough to re-raise? How many players have not yet acted behind you?

SANDBAGGING REQUIREMENTS
53-card Jacks (or better)

Here's a general sandbagging guide based on data gathered in **Gardena** Card Clubs during actual play.

Definitions *(for use of the tables):*

NO-COUNT: No Jacks, Queens, Kings or Aces *(including Joker)*.

LOW-COUNT: One Jack, Queen or King; Pair of Jacks; Pair of Queens.

MEDIUM-COUNT: One Ace *(or Joker)*; two face-cards *of different kinds*; 3 or 4 Jacks; 3 or 4 Queens; 2, 3 or 4 Kings.

HIGH-COUNT: Two *or more* Aces *(including Ace-Joker)*; One Ace *(or Joker)* PLUS a face-card; three *or more* face-cards *(of at least two different kinds)*.

PROFITABLE SANDBAGGING SITUATIONS IN SMALL ANTE GAMES
$2 DRAW

(The opening bet is $2, the bet after the draw is $4 and the ante is 25¢.)

Position	Option to Sandbag
1st *(Under gun)*	Anything.
2nd	Anything *except* Pat hands with High-Count.
3rd	Aces *(with no face-cards)*; any Two-Pair *(except Aces-over-faces)*; Three-of-a-kind with Medium-Count *(or less)*; Pat hands with Medium-Count *(or less)*.
4th	Two-Pair with Medium-Count *(or less)*; Three-of-a-kind with Medium-Count *(or less)*; Pat hands with Low-Count *(or No-Count)*.
5th	Two-Pair with Low-Count *(or No-Count)*; Three-of-a-kind with Low-Count *(or No-Count)*; Pat hands with No-Count.
6th	Two-Pair with No-Count.
7th	Do *not* sandbag.

PROFITABLE SANDBAGGING SITUATIONS IN MEDIUM ANTE GAMES
$10 DRAW

(The opening bet is $10, the bet after the draw is $20 and the ante is $2.)

Position	Option to Sandbag
1st *(Under gun)*	Anything *except* Pat hands with High-Count.
2nd	Aces *(with no face-cards)*; any Two-Pair *(except Aces-over-faces)*; Three-of-a-kind with Medium-Count *(or less)*; Pat hands with Medium-Count *(or less)*.

PROFITABLE SANDBAGGING SITUATIONS IN MEDIUM ANTE GAMES
$10 DRAW (cont.)

3rd	Aces *(with* no *face-cards)*; any Two-Pair *(except Aces-over-faces)*; Three-of-a-kind with Medium-Count *(or less)*; Pat hands with a Low-Count.
4th	Two-Pair *less than* Jacks-up; Three-of-a-kind with Low-Count; Pat hands with No-Count.
5th	Two-Pair with Low-Count *(or No-Count)*; Three-of-a-kind with No-Count; Pat hands with No-Count.
6th	Do *not* sandbag.
7th	Do *not* sandbag.

PROFITABLE SANDBAGGING SITUATIONS IN LARGE ANTE GAMES
$5 DRAW *(double-ante)*

(The opening bet is $5, the bet after the draw is $10 and the ante is $2.)

All positions: Rarely, *if ever,* **sandbag.**

The really important things you should know about sandbagging are:

(1) The *fewer* the Count cards in your hand the *more likely* it is that someone else will open.

(2) Two *(small)* Pair is generally sandbagged on a wait-and-see basis, with the intention of calling, raising or passing.

(3) Big hands *can* be sandbagged late. (Note that you have the *option* to sandbag Sevens-Full-Over-Fours as late as 5th position in a game like $5 Draw, $1 ante.)

(4) You should give consideration to opening with Pat hands where there is a good chance you'll be raised — then you can re-raise.

(5) The *more liberally* players in your game tend to open, the *more safely* you can sandbag.

(6) Occasionally checking and then raising a *weak late* Opener with Aces will aid your image.

By the way, I'm **not** questioning the Draw Poker mastery of either John Fox or Art Sathmary, who are responsible for devising the Point-Count system discussed. They're **both** superb players and close friends of mine. **Neither uses that** *Count System* **in his own play, only as an instructional guide for beginners.** Many of my theoretical concepts about Draw Poker psychology were formulated during daily jogs with John, and our exchanges of information have created similarities in our game styles. Art (known as *ASQ* in **Gardena**) has recorded volumes of data about profits and losses for specific hands in recurring situations. Sharing Poker knowledge with him has been rewarding. Also, my research into dusty corners of Poker theory has afforded me the privilege of working closely with other notable and intelligent superstars of Draw, including Steve Steinkamp, Victor Resnick, Steve Margulies and Rick Greider.

Some plays incorporate logic, mathematics and psychology. An example: You have sandbagged Sixes and Threes in 3rd position. The dealer opens. You're reasonably sure he's weak, but you have no overwhelming Tell. You call and draw one. The Opener draws three. You **do** have the best hand going. You shuffle your cards without looking at the one you caught. You do this conspicuously, appearing to be *on the Come*. The Opener checks blind. You bet and continue shuffling. You have put yourself in the position of getting a call without having to fear a raise if he makes Trips. He feels you're trying for a Flush and **won't** raise with less than a complete hand. He will call hoping you missed. (This is an implied either/or situation — to be discussed shortly. Either you made the *Come* hand or you didn't.)

Another example is this: Suppose you have made a Full House and you're convinced your opponent has made

Three-of-a-kind. Since you drew two cards, he's a little hesitant about betting. The last thing you want him to do is show his hand down without betting. You act fast by making it safe for him to bet. How? You grab enough chips to call and hold them threateningly in your hand. You might say, "I don't think you have ANYTHING and I'm probably going to call!" That's all the encouragement he'll need. Expect his chips to come flying at you rather defiantly. He isn't sure whether or not you really intend to call. He **wants** your call because you've practically told him you can't beat Three-of-a-kind. Alas, it **doesn't** occur to him that you might raise...until it's too late.

EITHER/OR SITUATIONS

What you've just read is an example of an either/or situation. You have implied that you're **either** going to call a player **or** you're going to throw your hand away. This is one of my **most effective** psychological concepts. The reason it works is that unsophisticated minds, given a choice of two things, will waste all their reasoning power pondering which is their better option. You have, in effect, eased their mental burden by summarizing the decision they must make — leaving out the third possibility, the truth (that you were about to raise).

Here's a situation: The Opener has drawn three, probably to a Pair of Aces. You're the raiser with three Jacks and have drawn two without helping. The Opener checks to you blind. There's no question you're going to bet, but you want to make the bet as profitable as possible. Suppose this guy's hard to read and you're worried about him making three Aces and raising you. Is there a way **you can get the call and** *not* **be raised** if he's made three Aces?

Yes, by using the either/or concept. I would do something frenzied like look at my card and suddenly sit up straight, exclaiming, "I don't believe it! I apologize, I was really trying to bluff you before the draw, but not anymore! This is the ultimate miracle — Straight-Flush! I think it's a Straight-Flush UNLESS that's a Club. I'll look again. Now I'm not sure — I GUESS it's a Straight-Flush! Maybe not!"

Now the Opener doesn't know what to think. He's surprised to hear you drew two cards to a Straight-Flush, but not **too** surprised since you have such a crazy image. Now he has a decision to make — **either** you made the miracle **or** you have nothing. He'll call because making a two-card Straight-Flush seems so unlikely. He **won't** raise with three Aces because he figures you'll simply pass if you missed and you'll re-raise if you connected.

Instead of claiming to have made a Straight-Flush, you might announce that you either kept a kicker and filled-up or else you didn't help at all — *either/or*. Give them a choice.

Let's apply the either/or concept to a three-card draw. The Opener has drawn one and your three-card catch gives you Aces-up. He checks. You're going to bet, but you would just as soon **not** have to call a raise in the unlikely event he's filled. A good line would be, *"This is really strange! I went in with a Pair of Shorts and, guess what! I made four of 'em! I might be lying — it's possible I just have a Pair of Nines still, but I THINK I'm telling the truth. Your best bet is to call and see for yourself."* Which is **exactly** what's going to happen. After all, you **either** have Four-of-a-kind **or** you can't even beat a Pair of Openers!

A common opportunity to use an either/or approach is when the Opener has rapped pat and you've made a small Flush. Since the median Pat hand (including Four-of-a-kind) is a King-high Straight, you have an advantage. He bets and you'd be quick to raise except that his re-raise (on an Ace-King Flush, for instance) would put you in a difficult situation. You could probably *soup* (throw away) your hand, but you'd just as soon he *not* re-raise, thank you. A good thing to do here is exclaim: *"I'm going to call with Aces-up, unless, wait a minute, sports fans. It's the biggy! I raise!"* From his point of view you have **either** Aces-full, which beats even a smaller Full House. . .**or** you have Aces-up, in which case his Six-high Straight wins. He'll just call unless he has Aces-full beat.

If the Opener seems to have opened weak in 6th position and you've called in 7th on an Ace-King four-Flush, there's an opportunity which sometimes arises when the Opener draws three. If you **pair Aces,** you can spread your four suited cards face-up and bet after he checks. The implication here is that you **either** made your Flush **or** you didn't. The Opener certainly doesn't have to be afraid you're betting Two-Pair. If your image is right, he'll almost always call here with a Pair of Jacks and you'll win with your Aces.

Either/or is an effective way of screening the truth from an opponent — the result always surprises him.

MORE STRATEGY and PSYCHOLOGY

You must learn to lay down big hands. If you feel your opponent is *on the Come*, three Aces is **not** much better for you than a Pair of Jacks. If you **wouldn't** *call* with the Jacks, you **shouldn't** *call* with three Aces. Whenever you lay down big hands, attempt to make the other players think you had nothing.

You can raise two (or more) players when you have a 19-way or 22-way Straight-Flush. This is because the odds against making these hands are only 1.5 to 1 and 1.2 to 1, respectively, and you can anticipate getting better odds than that for your money if the players call your raise. (And they **do** call, because your game plan enables you to get the greatest number of calls possible.) Occasionally, you may want to raise with a 16-way hand. Raising *on the Come* enhances your image.

"Don't bet into one-card draws," is a bit of homespun advice that collapses under scientific examination. If you've opened in 3rd position with Aces-up and 4th position calls and draws one, your best strategy is usually a bet. Sure, he **may** be flushing. But if he's a tight player, he frequently **won't** play four-Flushes under the circumstances and chances are he has Two-Pair smaller than yours. Even if he will play Come hands, you should bet if your image is wild enough to insure that any Two-Pair will call you. This is because, all things considered, he will have **completed** a Come hand or made a Full House less than one time for

every three times he will call with Two-Pair. Mathematically, you should bet. If you get raised, you can throw your hand away. It is often profitable to bet Aces–up or Three–of–a–kind into **two** one-card draws!

Against unsophisticated players who have backed in, clearly *on the Come*, when you're the Opener and have drawn three: Bet, if you make a Full House. If they complete their Come hand, they will raise (figuring you for Trips). If the situation is the same except that you've drawn one, check and then raise. You usually **won't** get raised if you do bet, so there's no chance for a re-raise. If you draw two and fill-up, use your best judgment.

When a game is short-handed (less than eight players), you can sandbag **more** *frequently* because the total amount of antes you stand to lose is smaller. (Even if you do open, you can't consider the ante **yours** unless you win the pot. It's a mistake to think you lose the whole ante if you pass Trips and no one opens.)

Just because your best strategy is to strive to get called doesn't mean you can't bluff successfully. Opportunities do present themselves. Some players are so unobservant that even your loose image will not affect them. Occasionally, bluff these types. The rest of the table will take this as further evidence that you're wild and unpredictable. Whether you get away with a bluff or not, show your hand whenever possible. This is good for your image. An opportunity to bluff is when one (or more) Come hands are last to act. The player with a Pair is then reluctant to call because he doesn't know if the Come hands connected.

The best time to bluff is just after a player sitting next to you has made some friendly gesture. He may have bought you coffee, told you a joke or sought your Poker advice. Bluff immediately — the next hand if possible! He'll never expect it! He'll never see it coming! And the worst that can happen is he'll call. Then you can praise him for his insight, making him feel proud. Since your image, though wild, is playful rather than belligerent, you can bluff without making your opponent(s) angry. Not even after you've just accepted a free cup of coffee! Rick Greider (a close friend of mine and **a Grand Master** at the art of stealing pots in Draw Poker) even recommends that **you** buy your opponent's coffee, pat him affectionately on the shoulder. . .and **immediately** bluff him.

Don't try to discourage a bet you intend to call. If an on-the-Come player starts to bet into you after the draw, you should only reach for your chips if you intend to pass. If you're going to call his bet, the only effect reaching for your chips will have is to make him think twice about bluffing. You may prevent his bluff, but that's something you **don't** want to do. Obviously he's still going to bet if he made his hand.

READING PLAYERS

Since Draw **doesn't** provide visual clues like Stud (where the cards are dealt face-up), you've got only your opponents to "tell" you what cards they hold. And they do "tell" you, with a precision and persistence unequaled in any other form of Poker.

You will be playing against mostly unskilled gamblers. Their minds are not particularly sharp and often they haven't lived life very successfully. They're financially troubled or psychologically battered. Maybe they think they've come for the entertainment of gambling or to make a little money. But you might as well know the truth, sad as it is — they've come to escape the pain. It's not enough to know **how** a person acts when he's bluffing. When you understand **why** he acts that way, you'll be able to read him even in unfamiliar situations.

Thoreau said, *"the mass of men lead lives of quiet desperation."* Most people are prevented from living life as they want. In childhood, they're required to do chores they hate. They grow up having to conform at school. As adults they must shake hands they don't want to shake, socialize with people they dislike, pretend they're feeling "fine" when they're feeling miserable and "act" in control of situations where, in truth, they feel frightened and unsure. These people — the majority of folks you meet every day — are actors. They present themselves to you as people different than they really are.

Deep within themselves they **know** they are **not** the same person they pretend to be. On an unconscious level, they think, *"Hey, I'm so phony that if I don't ACT to disguise my (Poker) hand, people will see right through me!"*

And that's why the majority of these pitiful people are going to **give you** their money by **always acting weak when they're strong and strong when they're weak.**

Let's look at how it works. If a simple-minded player to your left is staring conspicuously at his cards before the draw, he's **never** going to open. He's thinking, *"Oh gosh! Again I have nothing. Well maybe if I just keep staring at these stupid cards it will look like I'm interested in this worthless hand. Maybe that will keep 'Crazy Mike' from opening."*

What if he has something like three Tens? Then he closes his hand immediately, stares around the room like he's watching butterflies dance and shows disinterest. He's **acting** like he has nothing, which **means** he has something, which **means** he's going to open, which **means** you ought to check your Full House and make him happy. Your subsequent raise might annoy him briefly.

If he's ostentatiously reaching for his chips before it's his turn, he **won't** open.

When a player opens by throwing the chips in a little more aggressively than is his usual manner, **he's weak.** He wants to **seem** strong and he figures that extra little show of force will do the trick. You know better.

Sliding the chips in quietly and unannounced is a manner of opening that indicates strength. The player doesn't want to do anything to let you know he's strong.

Voice *Tells* are abundant. A player who chirps *"open"* when he throws his chips in...is weak. He is trying to conceal weakness with a voice he hopes will seem optimistic and confident.

A player who announces his opening in a tone of voice with which he might as well be saying, *"My best friend just died,"* has got the goods! He's **acting** like opening is such sadness. He's pretending to be weak.

Similarly a sigh shows strength. Anytime a simplistic player goes out of his way to **act** dejected, watch out!

The classic recurring *Tell* is the player who is dealt a Pat Full House, sighs, murmurs a dismal, *"I'll try it,"* puts his chips in the pot reluctantly and shakes his head sadly. The Pat Straight you were excited about a few seconds ago has suddenly become worthless! Pass.

You're the Opener and have one caller. You draw three. If the caller then asks for one card in a **discouraged** voice, he surely has Two-Pair and, having just now learned he had the best hand all along, is trying to disguise it. If you make Kings-up, bet.

Occasionally, you'll find a player who **acts** *strong* when he **is** *strong* or **acts** *weak* when he **is** *weak.* Fortunately, this tendency is consistent — so if you've seen it once, you'll know what it means next time around.

This act-strong-when-weak/act-weak-when-strong syndrome is the most important tool you'll use in learning to read your Draw Poker opponents. You are now not only able to get into a game and document that it works, you know why it works.

Here are some other *Tells* **of importance:**

If a player *on the Come* bets into you and then looks back quickly and inconspicuously, he made his hand. He's just double-checking. If, however, he makes an **act** out of staring at his hand just when you begin to call, he's **missed** the Straight or Flush. As a last desperate move, he's trying to convince you that the garbage in his hand is really grand and awesome.

Players have a habit of shuffling through their cards after drawing one when they're *on the Come.* That's because they want the added excitement of not knowing the location of the card drawn. They then look at one card, Heart. Another, Heart — but *"was that a NEW one? Did I make it? I'll look at the next card. Heart! Heart, Heart — I've got a Flush!"* Generally a player going through this procedure is

Flushing. He likes this suspense because it's an all-or-nothing situation: either he's made his hand or he holds nothing. You'll **seldom** see a player do it with Two-Pair.

Incidentally, if a player shuffles and then starts looking at his cards one-by-one but stops before getting to the last card, he's *usually* **missed**. He's looked at, say, a Heart, another Heart and then, alas, a Spade. There's no reason for him to look at the other two cards because the Spade is the stranger. If he bets now, you'd better call him because he's probably bluffing. Even if he knows the Heart is a new one, he'll look at the rest of his hand just to make sure. An exception is when he catches the Joker. He knows **that's** a new card and he may quit shuffling as soon as he sees it. In general, though, you'll make a profit calling if he **doesn't** look at his fifth card.

A player *on the Come* who has just vocally complained about having missed 63 Flushes in a row is *almost* **never** going to bluff. Why should he? He wants you to know how bad his luck is running by saying, *"See what I mean? That's 64 I missed in a row! I've never seen that happen to anyone else!"*

Which brings us to another concept which you should learn if you want to know what goes on in the inscrutable minds of your opponents. In Poker, exaggeration is a form of sympathy-seeking. The odds against missing 64 four-Flushes in a row are over three million to one. *"Six times in a row that guy drew one card to Two (small) Pair and made a Full House against me!"* (2,985,983 to 1.) *"I haven't made a 16-way Straight the last twenty-four times I drew to 'em!"* (16,833 to 1.) *"How could I win when that lady got dealt six Pat hands in a row?"* (379,000,000,000 to 1.) *"Listen to this, this REALLY happened. . ."* Listen and sympathize, but **don't** challenge these fabrications. They're **not** telling you what actually happened. They're telling you how bad they feel, how sorry they are for themselves. Be friendly, share in their sorrow — and bluff them at the first opportunity. (You'll find some more "sad stories" at the end of this section.)

If the Opener draws three and checks into you without hesitation, he **hasn't** helped. Why? Because unsophisticated players need time to think when they help a hand. They **don't** have a preplanned attack. They **haven't** analyzed the game the way you will. If they draw three and make Aces-up, this thought circles their mind: *"Hmm, well, this looks pretty good. I wonder if I should bet and try to get a call or check real sneaky and see if 'Crazy Mike' will bet. Aces-up is probably the best hand, but you never know. I guess I'd be safer if I checked."* (That thought process requires several seconds.) You can **always bet** Two-Pair into a three-card draw **when the check is immediate.**

Players who **deliberately** *expose* the Joker and bet are apt to be bluffing. The Joker is a threatening card and they're pretending to be strong.

Players who are bluffing often refuse to make eye contact for fear you can see right through their phony act. Some, though, having been told this, make such blatant eye contact that it's an absolute cinch they're bluffing.

MATHEMATICS
OF INTEREST

There are two very common hustle propositions in Draw Poker.

(1) The hustler offers you 100 to 1 that you won't have a pinochle (the **Q♠-J◊**) in your hand. (Sometimes the offer is only 50 to 1.) The **correct** *odds* are 136.8 to 1.

(2) The hustler offers you 50 to 1 that you won't get a Pat Seven (or better) Low hand. (The Ace is Low and Straights and Flushes are **not** disqualified from being used as Low hands in Ace-to-Five Lowball.) The **correct** *odds* here are 93.2 to 1.

Earlier you learned that if a player will open on anything, Jacks (or better), his median hand (half higher, half lower) is a Pair of Aces. Here is a table of medians.

TABLE OF MEDIANS

If the hand held is. . .   then. . .   The median hands is. . .

Any Five cards . . . . Pair of Deuces

One Pair *(at least)* . . . . .Pair of Tens

Jacks *(or better)* . . . . .Pair of Aces

Aces *(or better)*. . . . . Tens-up

Two-Pair *(exactly)* . . . . .Jacks-up

Two-Pair *(or better)* . . . . Aces-up

Jacks-up *(or better)* 3-Threes

Aces-up *(or better)*. . . . . 3 Nines

Three-of-a-kind 3-Nines

Three-of-a-kind *(or better)* 3-Kings

Three Sixes *(or better)*. 3-Aces

Three Jacks *(or better)*. . . . . Seven-high Straight

Three Aces *(or better)* . . . . Ten-high Straight

Five-high Straight *(or better)*. . . . . King-high Straight

Any Flush *(or better)* . . . . Ace-high Flush

Any Full House *(or better)*. . . . . Tens-full

Aces-full *(or better)*. 4-Fives

If you have a Pat Flush, 59.8% of the time it will be Ace-high. With the inclusion of the Joker, Ace-high Flushes are **far more** *common* than with a 52-card deck. If you have a Flush that's **not** Ace-high (say, a **K♡-Q♡-J♡-10♡-8♡**), expect to **lose** to a Pat Flush of unknown strength three out of five times. Because some players are selective about what kind of four-Flushes they draw to, about two out of three *on the Come* Flushes made will be Ace-high.

Here's a list of odds against making various hands you'll be drawing to.

ODDS AGAINST
IMPROVING VARIOUS HANDS

Attempt	*Odds against*
Inside Straight *(4-5-6-8)*	8.6 to 1
8-way Straight *(7-9-J-Joker)*	5 to 1
Country Straight *(5-6-7-8)*	4.3 to 1
Four-Flush	3.8 to 1
12-way Straight *(6-7-9-Joker)*	3 to 1
13-way Straight-Flush *(3-4-5-7 suited)*	2.7 to 1
16-way Straight *(10-J-Q-Joker)*	2 to 1
16-way Straight-Flush *(5-6-7-8 suited)*	2 to 1
19-way Straight-Flush *(7-9-10-Joker suited)*	1.5 to 1
22-way Straight-Flush *(4-5-6-Joker suited)*	1.2 to 1
Full House *(drawing one to less than Aces-up)*	11 to 1
Full House *(drawing one to Aces-up)*	8.6 to 1
Full House or better *(drawing one to Trips with an Ace kicker)*	8.6 to 1
Full House or better *[drawing one to (small) Trips with a non-Ace kicker — example 6-6-6-5]*	11 to 1
Full House or better *[drawing three to Kings (discards: 4-3-2)]*	76 to 1
Three-of-a-kind or better *[drawing three to Kings (discards: 4-3-2)]*	6.6 to 1
Two-Pair or better *[drawing three to Kings (discards: 4-3-2)]*	2.4 to 1
Full House or better *(drawing three to Aces)*	47 to 1
Three Aces or better *(drawing three to Aces)*	4.5 to 1
Aces-up or better *(drawing three to Aces)*	2 to 1
Full House or better *[drawing two to Trips (smaller than Aces) without discarding an Ace]*	9.4 to 1
Full House or better *(drawing two to 3-Aces)*	6.1 to 1

Earlier you learned that you can sandbag profitably in deeper (later) positions than most players suspect. The following table shows what percent of the time you can expect a pot to be opened when you pass in various positions. The first percentage given is an approximation. It is based on data gathered during **actual play** and takes into consideration what hands players tend to open with. Additionally, the first figure accounts for *bunching* — **the fact that if players already have passed, there is a higher-than-usual likelihood of Jacks, Queens, Kings and Aces being present in the hands of players still to act. That means more Openers in the late positions.** The second column of percentages is the **actual** mathematical probability of one of the remaining players opening [assuming all players will open with Jacks (or better)]. The second column **ignores** the *bunching factor.*

CHANCE OF POT BEING OPENED WHEN YOU PASS IN VARIOUS POSITIONS

Players still to act	(Players selective; bunching considered) Will open, actual	(Open on anything; no bunching factor) Will open, mathematical
8	81%	86.9%
7	77%	83.1%
6	74%	78.2%
5	71%	71.9%
4	65%	63.7%
3	55%	53.3%
2	42%	39.8%
1	25%	22.4%

It's interesting to note that, in an eight-handed game, if you pass in 5th position (three players still to act) with average count, the odds are 11 to 9 **in your favor** that the pot will be opened. In a $5 Draw game, you can expect four out of five pots to be opened by someone.

Knowledge of the mathematics involved in Draw Poker can have benefits beyond the obvious.

I accepted Rosemary as a Poker student because she learned quickly and because she had excellent insight and was able to read people. Using the same advice contained in this section, she grew from an **unskilled** *pleasure player* to an

accomplished *Professional* within weeks. After a lot of homework, she decided it was time to make her first serious attempt at beating Draw Poker. To celebrate the occasion we decided to give her three new initials to put on the board, *NGL* — the consonants in "angel". When the floorman called *NGL* for the game of her choice, she took her seat with confidence. An hour later she was winning two hundred dollars, and she got up from the table to talk with me.

"I can't believe it!" she said. *"Everything you taught me really works! I keep catching this guy bluffing and he's really getting mad. He says I can't play Poker, that I should cash-in while I still have some chips left."*

"What did you say?"

"Nothing, should I say something?"

"Sure, don't let him intimidate you."

"What should I say to him?"

"I don't know, Rosemary. You're smart. You'll think of something." I walked away and she returned to her game.

Twenty minutes later she was involved in a pot with the same guy who had been critical of her play. She called the Opener with a 16-way Straight. Our "villain" backed-in *on the Come* and drew one. The Opener drew three. Rosemary drew one. She missed her Straight but paired Sixes. The Opener checked, Rosemary checked, and "Ignoramus" began to shuffle through his cards, looking them over one at a time. Upon encountering the third card he stopped, hesitated and then threw his chips in with extra emphasis. (You'll recognize this as a bluff from the earlier discussion.) The Opener passed. Rosemary called with her Sixes and won.

"That's the worst call I ever seen!" the guy whined. *"I been playin' cards thirty years and I ain't never run into nothin' bad as that! You ain't got no business playin' Poker!"*

By that time, I was standing behind Rosemary, and I was smiling sadistically.

"I might've had anything." the guy persisted. *"Do you know how many hands there are in this game?"*

She began to giggle.

"Go ahead and tell him," I urged.

"There are exactly two million, eight hundred sixty-nine thousand, six hundred eighty-five possible hands," she said as she raked in the chips.*

It pays to know your mathematics!

You already know the odds against making various Come hands.

Here are some stats on two-card and three-card draws:

If you draw three to Ace-Joker, you will improve about 36.8% of the time, depending on how many Straight or Flush cards you discarded. If you draw two to Ace-Joker-King *suited* (throwing away, say, a Nine and Six *offsuit*), you will improve 37.85% of the time. This comparison demonstrates that if you hold **A♣-Joker-K♣-8♠-7◊** you are more likely to make Aces-up or better keeping the **K♣**. However, by drawing three, your chances of making trip Aces or better are improved from 3.68 to 1 against (21.37%) to 3.59 to 1 against (21.79%). The chance of beating a small Pat Straight, though, is much greater if you draw two. The entire breakdown is included in the *Poker Statistics* section.

A few months ago I showed those same figures as a favor to a fellow Professional Draw player. His name is Mike Caro. Until I began playing in Gardena, California, I had never encountered **another** Mike Caro. Sure, I'd sometimes tried to imagine what one might be like, but I'd never actually seen one. Then I began to answer telephone pages at card clubs only to discover that the folks on the other end would rather **not** speak to me! Once I got a long-distance call from Mike's mother.

"How is he?" she asked.

"Fine," said I. *"He misses you."*

There was even a confusion at a local bank about our

Rosemary **is a real, live girl. Her last name is Dufault. She's a** *true* **Professional...that is, she plays Draw Poker ("the** *Mike Caro* **way"). It's her** *major* **source of income. While not yet a World-Class Draw Poker player...she's surely on her way to becoming one. At the very least, she's probably the very** *best* **woman Draw Poker** *player* **alive.**

checking accounts. It's 28.6 to 1 against holding Trips or better before the draw, **but what are the chances of** *two* **Mike Caro's both being Professional Poker players in Gardena?** In order to establish a separate identity, I have always preferred to be called *MJC* or *"Crazy Mike"* around the Poker tables. All this leaves us with the obvious, though obscure, philosophical question: **Since there's only** *one* **of me, why are there** *two* **of him?**

If you draw two to 3–Kings, discarding a Five and a Three, the odds are 8.64 to 1 against improving. When you draw two to 3–Aces, the price against helping is 6.09 to 1. Against making five Aces, the **best** *possible* hand, it's only 1127 to 1 — **not** as difficult as most players think. Drawing three to a Pair smaller than Aces will give you Two-Pair (or better) 29.4% of the time, and the odds against improving are 2.4 to 1.

An often–asked question is whether you'll improve more frequently by keeping the Ace kicker to a set of Trips. It's 8.72 to 1 against improving if you discard the Ace. Keeping the Ace will give you a **better** shot, 8.6 to 1 against. The chances of making a Full House (or better) compute to 10.28% drawing two, 10.42% drawing one. But, before you conclude that it's always better to keep an Ace kicker to Trips, be warned that **insufficiently** *shuffled* cards make it more likely that you will catch a *cold* Pair drawing two. Also, a one–card draw provides you with *only* **half** as good an opportunity to make Four-of-a-kind.

SEATING POSITION

There are two types of players you prefer to have seated at your right (in front of you).

First, loose players who habitually draw to *Shorts* and *Cat–hops*. Since you play an aggressive game, raising more than your share of pots, it is important to have that Pair of Sixes call **before** you raise. Unfortunately, only a **few** players are suicidal enough to *Cold call* a raise with a small Pair.

Second, you want intelligent players who raise liberally on your right. Most of your profit comes from the weak players, and you certainly **don't** want some knowledgeable competitor re-raising you with Kings and Sevens right after **you** have smartly raised a weak Opener with your Fours and Threes. Position yourself at the table so that you act **after** other strong players.

Tight, predictable players belong on your left (behind you). They pose no threat. Those who open with any Jacks-or-better hand but who seldom play Shorts also belong on your left. Their presence behind you allows later and more effective sandbagging. Naturally anyone with a recurring opening Tell should be on your left, also allowing you to sandbag in later positions — even 7th!

Sit next to players who constantly expose cards.

You'll encounter players who change seats for purely superstitious reasons. As laughable as this may seem to many Professionals, these seat-changing luck-seekers are helping their chances. They tend to reposition themselves only when they're luck is poor. More often than not they are running bad partially because of their unfavorable seating position. A change, even when there is no strategic motive, is apt to be beneficial.

Unless you're in an unusually good position, **you** should give consideration to changing seats if you've been losing. That's because other players tend to react to your bad fortune by becoming less fearful and more aggressive. In effect, they begin to play better. Change seats. If you win a pot or two in the new seat, impress this fact vocally on the opposition ("*I knew this was going to be a lucky seat! You Turkeys are in trouble now!*") Players can be easily intimidated when they feel your luck has changed for the better.

Earlier you learned the importance of **table** selection. Choosing the right **seat** will add enormously to your Draw Poker profits.

ILLUSIONS

Since the main fault of recreational Draw players is that they call too much, naturally you want to exploit this weakness. Previously I explained how simply calling with nothing, rapping pat and spreading the hand without betting creates a bizarre image. This sort of "insane" maneuver is highly cost-effective in bringing a deluge of calls when you do have the best hand.

Sometimes I even give away "prize" money:

"Look, I'm really getting bored. I haven't had a Pair in three hands, so here's what I'm going to do. Show me the Six of Spades and I'll give you ten dollars."

Someone exposes the Six of Spades and collects the $10.

"On this next hand," I sometimes announce, *"Anyone who has a Pair gets a free ante."*

That costs me about three antes on average, but once I had to ante for all seven opponents. No matter, they're more than willing to give it back in multiple doses for these reasons:

(1) They think they must call anyone too crazy to care about money;

(2) They feel obligated to give me action in return;

(3) They can now freely yield to their gambling compulsions without embarrassment, since playing a Pair of Fours seems like a trivial sin by comparison to my deeds;

(4) They can call me without any damage to their egos because the atmosphere is fun and frivolous.

Frequently it is not necessary to make any other advertising plays all night after doing something as blatantly senseless as splitting openers, trying for garbage and checking — or giving away a few dollars for no apparent reason.

Your "insane" facade can be maintained by confusing patter. Anything you say can influence your opponents now, because they've witnessed your "economically suicidal" behavior. If you must *soup* Aces-up to a raiser, make them think that you had Jacks.

But **don't** say, *"Take it, I just had a Pair of Jacks."* This makes them think: Well, maybe he did have just a Pair of Jacks. But probably he really laid down something better and is trying to advertise himself as a loose and losing player.

Remember, unsophisticated thinkers tend to reason things out in an either/or fashion (as discussed earlier). Either he had Jacks or he's lying and trying to talk loose.

Isn't it much better psychologically if you say, *"I'll throw away my three Jacks"*? Now they reason: He never would have laid down three Jacks, so he must have only had two of them. You have now implanted in the simplistic mind of the opposition the notion that you had opened weak without actually saying it, thus denying them their right to be suspicious!

Don't say, *"I always play Shorts."* Someone's natural reaction is: Sure, and I always eat ants for breakfast!

Say, apologetically, *"I DON'T really play that many Shorts. Lots of people play them every time."* Now they think **either** you are being truthful and you play Shorts selectively **or** you're lying and you play every Pair of Shorts you can get your hands on! The truth, that you **never** *play* Shorts does not occur to them.

Don't say, *"I just played a Cat-hop!"*

Say, *"That's the LAST Cat-hop I'm going to play tonignt!"* leaving your listeners with the dilemma: Is he or isn't he going to stop playing so many Cat-hops? **Either** you are going to stop **or** you're planning to go right on drawing two to Flushes without regard for probabilities. The fact that you have not played one single Cat-hop all night will not be discovered because you have caused them to waste their limited mental energy on a fallacious **either/or** choice.

Don't say, "I *always* bluff!"

Say, "*I don't see why YOU GUYS say I'm always bluffing. I bet as many real hands as anyone else. And lots of times I miss a Flush and just throw my hand away.*" Now they think: **either** he's telling the truth, he only bluffs most of the time but not always **or** he's lying and, like everyone says, he always bluffs. Sounds to me like he's a compulsive bluffer pretending to have a little discipline. Anyway, I'm sure not going to let him talk me out of calling!

While most players are swept into the illusion, a few are perceptive enough to understand your tactics. These people take great pride in laying down hands against you whenever they feel they're being conned into calling.

One play I've used successfully against such players goes like this: The target opens in a late position. I back in with 9-8-7-6-2, (mixed-suits) and draw one. Of course this one-card draw to a *Country Straight* does **not** afford me favorable odds under normal conditions. The Opener draws, perhaps, three. Maybe two, maybe one. As long as he doesn't rap pat, this play is still operational. Now he checks. I spread 9-8-7-6 on the table and begin to vocalize.

"*You ought to call me! There's a good chance I haven't looked, and even if I HAVE peeked, I'm probably bluffing — unless I'm not, in which case it would be a bad call. I really don't know how to advise you.*"

Normally this confusing monologue gets a call. But here the player prides himself on his perception. He is adamantly unwilling to be hustled. He will usually throw his hand away for two reasons. One, he feels he is too smart to be lured into calling. Two, he knows I play a mathematically sound game and would not have backed in on an Open-end Straight. That latter being the case, my remaining card must be the Joker! Naturally this play works better when you **know** the Joker is **not** in the Opener's hand. Additionally, you're going to connect almost 19% of the time, and then you can reverse your tactics and try for a call.

WITHOUT THE JOKER

Now that you understand Draw with the Joker, adjusting to a 52-card Joker-less deck is going to be easy. This is a rare game.

Expect fewer pots to be opened. The odds against you having openers are 3.85 to 1 (instead of 3.46 to 1 with the Joker included). Sandbag less. Three Aces will be dealt only 41.67% as often. Pat hands are harder to come by, the odds against are 131 to 1 (including Four-of-a-kind). With the Joker it is 84 to 1. You can raise and re-raise more liberally with Trips. If you keep a kicker to Trips, an Ace is **not** recommended since it is of no more value than any other kicker — and frequently your opponent has Aces.

Come hands are less desirable. The odds against making a Flush are now 4.22 to 1 — **not** 3.8 to 1 as with the 53-card deck. You'll only connect with an Open-end Straight 17.02% of the time (4.88 to 1 against). The chances against making an Open-end Straight-Flush are 2.13 to 1. There are no 13-way, 16-way, 19-way or 22-way hands, and **many of the complexities** *which worked in your favor with the Joker included* **no longer exist**.

While it is more difficult to connect on Come hands using the 52-card deck, it is actually easier to make a Full House drawing one to Two-Pair. Instead of 11 to 1 against, it's now 10.75 to 1 against.

For more detailed information, see the statistical tables in the *Statistics* section.

OPEN BLIND

Here the player to the left of the dealer opens **before** *looking at his cards.* Most of the sophisticated information and techniques found previously in this section **will** be of value. **Stay out of** *Open-Blind games* **until you've mastered Jacks-or-better.**

If you're in 2nd through 8th position, the pot has already been opened when the action gets to you. In the early and middle positions you require **about** the same playing hands you did in Jacks-or-better. Since the opener did not know what he held when he put the first bet in, the customary and **correct strategy is to raise** *rather than call.* If you have Aces in 3rd and 2nd folded, raise. If you hold Eights in 7th and 2nd through 6th have passed, raise. Occasionally choose to simply call, extracting maximum pot-odds for a 16-way Straight — or purely to confuse the opposition. But basically *Open Blind* **is a game for raisers.** It's loosely structured, so **don't** play too timidly.

If the action comes around to you and no one has called or raised, you need these minimums:

MINIMUM PLAYING
REQUIREMENTS FOR OPEN BLIND

Your Position	Minimum to play *(If no other player has called or raised the blind)*
8th *(Dealer)*	**Any Pair or an Ace with a Face Card** *(Pairs smaller than Fives should be played cautiously and sometimes discarded.)*
7th	**Pair of Eights**
6th	**Pair of Jacks**
5th	**Pair of Kings**
4th	**Pair of Aces or any Two-Pair**
3rd	**Pair of Aces or selected Two-Pair**
2nd	**Pair of Aces or selected Two-Pair**

Even though you have a bet in already, **don't** call routinely when you're in the Blind (1st position). You need Aces to call a **tight** *early raiser,* Kings to call a *middle–position raiser,* Jacks to call a *7th position raiser,* and **one** Ace to call the dealer if he tends to raise liberally. **That's right, against the dealer (when just the two of you are in the pot) you can often call his raise, draw four and make money!**

Here's a guide for use if the pot has already been raised. . .

MINIMUM RE-RAISING
REQUIREMENTS FOR OPEN-BLIND

Position of 1st Raiser	Minimum to re-raise
8th (Dealer)	Pair of Kings
7th	Sixes-up
6th	Jacks-up
5th	Kings-up
4th	Aces-up
3rd	Aces-up
2nd	Aces-up

Of course, you will make more money if you adjust these requirements to individual game conditions, taking into account how loose or tight the other players are.

Unless you're in the Blind and a late position raises, you need *almost* as strong a hand to Cold Call as you do to re-raise.

> After the draw you can bet more frequently and on weaker hands than you could in Jacks-or-better. That's because you'll get calls from Pairs less than Jacks which almost never happens in Jacks-or-better.

> *Come hands* less than 16-way Straights are seldom profitable. Since pots are almost always raised — and if you don't raise someone else probably will — the amount it will cost you to play is at least two betting units. Thus the ante becomes smaller by comparison and it's difficult to get correct pot odds for your four-Flush.

You'll want to use all the player-reading skills you've developed. Frequently, players **don't** know the value of their own hands. They may try to act strong to conceal a hand they think is weak. In fact, the hand may be relatively strong. This often happens when the dealer attacks the Blind. No one else is in the pot, so he raises with a Pair of Jacks. Figuring the Blind has a weak hand, he throws his chips in with extra emphasis. The fact that he's a 3 to 1 favorite to have the best hand before the draw is **NOT going to help you read him,** *because he doesn't know he's a favorite.* Be **careful** you **don't** misinterpret his mannerisms and re-raise with a Pair of Eights.

HIGH-BACK-TO-LOW

The rules of this game are simple. It's Jacks-or-better and if no one opens, instead of anteing and re-dealing, it becomes Lowball (Ace-to-Five). The 1st position must now open Blind for Low and it's up to 2nd position to play or throw his hand away.

This once-popular game is **rarely** played today.

If you've read this section on Jacks-or-better and the section on Lowball, you're pretty well equipped to play.

Note that the low hands, when it does go Low (about one time in four), are *better than normal.* **This is because the absence of high hands makes the presence of small cards more probable.** *In spite of this,* **you can play pretty much the same hands you would in normal Ace-to-Five Lowball. The reason is that, even though some of your opponents may hold better-than-usual low cards, the frustration players feel in having most hands opened High when they hold dynamite low hands causes them to play more liberally than they should. This means extra profit when you win on the low-side.**

The only real problem you'll confront is whether to open High or check for Low with hands that seem marginal.

The biggest mistake made in High-Back-to-Low is by players who think they must open

when they're holding cards that can't be played Low but stand to win High. For some reason they forget about sandbagging Three-of-a-kind. In early positions, even if they habitually sandbag in Jacks-or-better, they will open with Pat Nine-high Straights. They reason that it will be a losing hand for Lowball. But they *DON'T have to* play Low! They can check, and raise if opened for High, pass if it goes Low.

PROBLEM HAND PLAYING ADVICE

Here's a list of High-Back-to-Low *problem* hands and advice on how to play them.

HAND	ADVICE
Bicycle *(A-2-3-4-5)* & Six-high Straights *(same for Flushes)*	Always sandbag High and hope it goes Low.
Pat Seven-high Straights *(no Joker, same for Flushes)*	Sandbag for High through 6th position. Plays either High or Low for profit. In 7th and 8th, open High.
Pat Eight-high Straights *(same for Flushes)*	Sandbag for High through 5th position. Basic profit is for High.
Nine-high Straights	Choose your best Jacks-or-better High strategy.
Ace-Joker combinations with one-card draw to Seven *(or less)*	Check for Low.
Ace-Joker combinations with one-card draw to Eight	*Sandbag High (generally just call if opened)* through 6th position. Will show small profit Low. In 7th and 8th positions, open High.

Most players open in the Blind position for High with a Pair of Jacks, fearing that they'll have to open if it goes Low. You're better off passing and hoping someone else opens High. Then you can throw your hand away.

REASONING

In spite of all your preparation, you'll occasionally run into situations you haven't foreseen. A sharp mind will take home the most money.

There's a favorite Poker problem I devised to test people on their Poker reasoning potential. *Only* **one person** has ever given me the answer **without** *hesitation*.

This is the problem:

You are in 1st position and have sandbagged three Jacks, an Ace and a Queen. The player in 2nd position opens. Everyone else passes. You raise. The Opener calls the raise and is all-in (he has no more chips so no betting can take place after the draw). You're about to ask for cards when the Opener spreads his hand on the table apprehensively.

"I wonder if I have you beat going!" he sighs.

You look at two Kings, two Queens and a Jack. You hope he doesn't figure you for Trips because, based on past experience, you know he usually throws away his smaller Pair and draws three against what he thinks is Three-of-a-kind. *How many should you draw and, specifically, why?*

DRAW POKER LOGIC PROBLEM

Your opponent spreads this hand face-up on the table. He is all-in (so there can be no betting after the draw). He has a tendency to split Two-Pair and take three anytime he suspects an opponent might have Trips.

This is your hand, and you're first to draw.

How many cards should you draw? Why? (The correct answer can be found on page 124 of this section.)

THE ARENA

Although it is commonly believed that Draw Poker existed legally in Milwaukee 80,000 years ago, some scholars remain skeptical.

We do know for certain that today Draw is played throughout the world. Particularly popular in the United States and Canada, it's a game you should consider dealing at home-style Poker parties (that are "Dealer's Choice" games) because it offers a great positional advantage to the dealer. Card Clubs abound in California where the only kinds of Poker allowed are five-card Draw and five-card Ace-to-Five Lowball.

My favorite Poker arena is Gardena, California, which advertises itself as "the Poker capital of the world."

Well, that might be a pretentious claim when you consider that the largest bet allowed by the city government until 1977 was $20! Today the largest legal game is $40 per bet before the draw, $80 after — and **no limit** on the number of raises. Still, that's a long way from one thousand and two thousand Seven-Card Stud sometimes played at the **Dunes** in Las Vegas.

Games have been devised which circumvent this $40-$80 limit without violating the law. Draw is occasionally played with a $20 Blind (1st position opens without looking at his cards), a $40 raise Blind (2nd position raises without looking) and a $60 re-raise Blind (3rd position is obligated to put in three bets). From there, the bets and raises are in increments of $60. Though the structure of games vary depending on what the players agree to and on what the *house* will allow, the Draw game just described is the biggest you're likely to see played in Gardena. The smallest is the $1 Draw with bets of $2 on the final round. $5 Draw ($10 on the second betting round) is now the most widely played game.

Gardena is in Los Angeles County, pretty much squeezed between L.A.'s southern suburbs. Though Draw is commonly played throughout the state, Gardena is the only place in the Metropolitan Los Angeles area where you can play. And the Clubs here are impressive, six multi-million dollar facilities devoted exclusively to Poker and Pan [the latter (Rummy-type game) only legalized recently]. Each Club, by agreement with the city, has **exactly** 35 tables. That's a lot of tables when you consider most of the casinos in Las Vegas have fewer than 10. Of course, the gambling in Vegas is much more diversified and there's a lot more money floating around. But Gardena's Card Clubs exist because of Poker. Gardena **is** Poker — Roulette, Craps, Blackjack and Slot Machines are **not** allowed. It is a place sometimes sedate, sometimes overflowing with excitement, and there's plenty of money to be made there.

The fact that each Club has exactly 35 tables brings up some other truths about Gardena. Rules are standardized, and that's good. Booklets are given out free by each Club. But the 35-table limit and the standardized rules are evidence that the Clubs here have tried to co-exist without the "brutality" of overt competition.

Years ago, the Clubs competed vigorously for each other's customers. But no more! The bad fact for you is that the minimum amount of *rent* (collection) the Clubs must charge for the seat you occupy is fixed by the city council. In the $5 Draw, the collection is $2.50 per **half hour**. No Club can charge **less** (though they are allowed to charge more).

This strategy of the Clubs to avoid price wars with each other has resulted in the situation today where the rent is

$16 per seat, per hour, in the $40-$80 Blind. In an eight-handed game, that's $128-an-hour for the table. Doyle tells me that at the **Dunes** the maximum table collection is $75-an-hour, even if they're playing one and two thousand! Also, **don't** expect free food, drinks or entertainment in Gardena. Incentives of this sort are illegal.

When you examine the whole picture, though, you come up with a Gardena that has the finest Card Clubs in California with good service and standardized rules — a place where you can definitely be a winner.

GARDENA RULES (JACKS-OR-BETTER)

The value of the hands in Jacks-or-better to open is the same as in the normal High Poker: Five Aces, Straight-Flush, Four-of-a-kind. Full House, Flush, Straight, Three-of-a-kind, Two Pair, One Pair, no Pair. Five Aces is possible because of the inclusion of the Joker, which can only be used as an Ace or to complete a Straight or Flush.

Players take turns dealing. This means **you** must deal, so if you're totally inexperienced, practice your shuffling before entering a Card Club. Each player receives five cards, one at a time, face down. Action then begins with the player to the dealer's left (1st position). If he has a Pair of Jacks or some better hand than that, he may choose to open. If he has less than a Pair of Jacks, he must pass. Other players in turn have their options. Each may open or, if it's already opened, call, raise or throw his hand away.

Checking and raising (sandbagging) is permissible. When it's your turn and you **can't** open, **don't** discard your hand. If someone else opens and the action returns to you, you can then call, raise or pass. After the Opening Round of betting, players draw cards in an attempt to improve their hands. Draws of any number of cards from one to five are permitted. You may, of course, take no cards (stand pat).

Before receiving cards you must discard the number you are drawing, insuring that your hand consists of five cards at all times.

Following the draw there is another Round of betting. In Gardena this second Round generally consists of limits twice the size of the first-round bets. The best hand, among those who have called the last bet, wins.

Here are some rules taken from Gardena's standardized rulebook which you should know:

*You need **exactly** five cards after the draw or your hand is *dead*. If you have four cards, even if they're all Queens, you cannot win.

*You must call *time* if you're not prepared to act when the action reaches you. If three or more players act behind you, you have forfeited your right to act. [If it is opened and **three players to your left** (behind you) pass before you call *time*, you can't play.] The use of the term *time* is second nature to Gardena Poker players, and local businessmen **are** familiar with its meaning, too. It's **not** uncommon to stand in a check-out line at a supermarket and hear someone call *"time"* while fumbling for the correct change. *"Wait a minute"*, is an expression virtually unknown to Gardena.

*You can draw as many as five cards.

*You **must** *protect* **your hand** at all times. (If a guy walks up, grabs your hand and throws it in the discards, don't bother complaining to the floorman. Your hand is *dead*, you should've held on tighter.)

*If you drop a card on the floor, pick it up and play it. If your card is **dealt** off the table, it's a *dead* card but you'll receive a replacement.

*If you're dealing, *burn* before distributing the cards requested by players drawing to their hands. If you, as dealer, give the *burn* card to yourself, your hand is *dead*.

*You *cannot* **overcall** your hand. (If your opponent throws his hand away when you say *"Aces-up"*, you must produce Aces-up *or better*. Otherwise he wins.) This rule **doesn't** apply until the last person has acted after the draw. Before that, overcalling your hand is just "table talk."

*Verbal raising or calling is **not** binding. Chips in the pot denote action.

*All players at the table have the right to see any called hands. Anyone at the table has the right to see the Opener's hand.

*Money and chips cannot be removed from the table until you quit the game and cash in.

*The buy-in is ten times the minimum bet (which is a *full* buy). In the $1 Draw, $10. In the $20 Draw, $200. If you lose this buy-in, you are entitled to buy for less (a *short* buy), but only once after each time you make a *full* buy.

*You must put your initials on the Board in order to get seated when no openings are available. (There is generally a boardman whose job it is to keep initials on a blackboard. If you have very common initials, you might try using three letters instead of the usual two. I'm known in Gardena as *MJC*.)

*You need Jacks-or-better to open. You *split* Openers by turning your discards face-up beneath a chip and announcing *"splitting"*. **You must** *turn your discards face-up and* **declare** *that you're splitting* **or you can't win the pot.** (An example: You have two Queens and a Club Flush you can draw to by discarding the Q♦ When it is your draw, turn the Q♦ face-up **under** *a chip,* **say** *you're splitting* and ask for one card.) Many, many pots have been lost by players new to Gardena who split incorrectly. Additionally, **you must** *not* **retain Openers** when you declare you're splitting. If you have A♡, Joker, J♡, J♠ and 6♡, you may wish to break this hand (Aces-up) and draw to the Ace-Joker Flush. But be careful you **don't** *declare you're splitting* and turn the J♠ face-up. You didn't split Openers. You still have the Ace-Joker in your hand, a Pair of Aces. Careful! If you make the Flush, though, no one will ever know you split falsely, since you could have caught the Ace or Joker.

*The Joker is used as an Ace or to complete a Straight or a Flush. [There is no such thing as a "double Ace" Flush. If you have **A♣, Joker, K♣, 7♣, 3♣**, your Flush is A–K–Q–7–3 (since you'd be using the Joker as the **highest** card you can — namely the Queen) and your hand will **not** beat an A–K–Q–9–8 Flush even though you have Ace–Joker.]

*If after the draw a player calls the Opener with no one left to act and it turns out that he **cannot beat** a Pair of Jacks, he gets the money back that he called with. This confusing rule is intended to protect a player who, being last to act, misreads his hand and calls the Opener with only two Sixes. Apparently the thought here is that since the caller couldn't win, he shouldn't lose the last dollar(s) he wagered.

Those are basically the rules to watch for in Gardena. If you thought that last one was strange, try this: Under *"General House Rules"*, **number 34** states, *"No going the overs permitted."* That's the entire rule. I think I know what it means, but if you're not privy to Gardena slang the rulebook will leave you wondering. From time to time I've tried to get a concise clarification, asking numerous floormen and Card Room managers. Opinion varies. Some think it means no gambling beyond the stated table limits — and that's the most likely interpretation of the rule. One manager told me it meant that you can't play for the antes if you have other chips in front of you. Another opinion was that the rule forbids taking money out of the pot by mutual consent in order to buy jewelry (frequently sold around the Clubs).

In my office is a sign that reads, *"No going the overs permitted!"* This crazy fantasy tickles my mind: I'm sitting innocently at the **Rainbow Club**, stacking up mountains of chips, when a whole herd of Gardena policemen thunders up to my Poker table. Fifteen minutes later I'm locked in a holding cell charged with 43 counts of *"going the overs"*. Have I finally won too much money?

Days pass. My every attempt to communicate with my captors is met with a snarl or a snicker. What is *"going the overs?"* I ponder.

When a guard stalks past my cage on the fifth day, I plead, *"Isn't there anything around here I could eat? Maybe some bread crust or a raisin? It's been five days and you haven't fed me. All the other prisoners get to eat!"*

"Stop whining!" the guard barks bitterly.

"It doesn't seem fair," I argue. *"You won't let me make a phone call, and my lawyer doesn't know I'm here. Besides, I'm thirsty!"*

"Why didn't you think of that before you went the overs?" He vanishes down a narrow hallway.

> Gardena is the *best place* in the universe to practice the concepts you've learned in this section. Maybe it is the Draw Poker capital of the world. But if you feel like *going the overs,* do it in Vegas.

There are six clubs — the **Gardena, Normandie, Eldorado, Horseshoe, Monterey** and **Rainbow.** The **Gardena Club** caters mostly to small limits, while the largest Draw games in town are found at the **Horseshoe, Rainbow** and **Eldorado** Clubs. Game sizes:

$1 Draw. The ante is a quarter, the bet before the draw is $1, and it's $2 after the draw. If the pot is **un**opened, players ante another quarter and the bets are $2 before the draw, $4 after. The $2-$4 remains effective until someone wins the pot. There are no additional antes. This is the smallest Draw game, played by the weakest players. **The ratio of total antes to opening bet in an eight-handed game is 2 to 1, which means it's structured for *loose* play.**

$2 Draw. Quarter ante, $2 before the draw, $4 after. If the pot isn't opened, players ante another quarter and the game is $3 and $6. If it's still **un**opened, a third quarter is anted and the betting is $4 and $8. This is the **tightest** *structured game* in town with a ratio of ante to opening bet of 1 to 1. It's a game where a few very tight players **(Rocks)** eke out small livings without knowing anything about dynamic strategies like those you have already learned.

$3 Draw. Half-dollar ante, $3 before the draw, $6 after. If passed around, another quarter is anted and the game becomes $4 and $8. If still not opened, a final quarter is anted making the total antes $1 per player and it's then $5 and $10. The ratio of total ante to opening bet in an eight-handed game, without additional antes, is 1.33 to 1. You will not find many sophisticated players in this game.

$5 Draw. Dollar ante, $5 before the draw, $10 after. If no one opens, another dollar is anted by each player and the stakes **remain the same** ($5 and $10). If still **not** opened, a third dollar is anted and the game becomes $10 and $20. The ratio of ante to opening bet, eight-handed, single-ante, is 1.6 to 1. There are numerous players who make a living exclusively in the $5 draw. **Choose your table** *wisely.*

$10 Draw. Many professionals are found in this game. You can expect to find one or more in every game this large. **This is no place for an** *inexperienced* **player.** The ante is $2 with a bet of $10 before the draw and $20 after. If not opened, players ante another dollar, and the game is **either** $15 before the draw and $20 after the draw **or** $15 before and $30 after **depending on what the players agree to.** There is another $1 ante if, the pot is still not opened. The bet then is **either** $20 before and $20 after **or** $20 before and $40 after. Look for the betting standards to become uniform over the next year, probably with the bet after the draw always doubling the wager before the draw. The ratio (ante to opening bet) is 1.6 to 1, same as with $5 Draw, single ante.

$15 Draw. An **uncommon** game which is actually a $10 draw with the assumption that everyone passed the first time around, so you begin with a $3 ante. With eight players, that's $24 in antes with an opening bet of $15 — a ratio of 1.6 to 1, just like the $5 Draw and the $10 Draw.

$20 Draw. With a $5 ante, this game was very popular for years at the **Horseshoe Club**. It was discontinued in 1975 because of a municipal ordinance which stated that the sum of all antes in a given hand could not exceed $20. That restriction was recently rescinded (in 1977) and the game has been revived and is now going every day. Before the draw, the bet is $20. After the draw, it's $40. The ratio (eight-handed) of total antes to opening bet is 2 to 1 — a **liberal** (loose) game.

Open Blind games. (Also called *"California Draw"*). Here Jacks–or–better is **not** an opening requirement. The player to the left of the dealer opens blind. **Sometimes** the game is structured so that not only does first position open blind, but **second position** *raises* **blind.** And **occasionally** this is carried through third position and becomes open blind, raise blind, **re-raise blind.** This type of Poker, with much more liberal playing requirements than Jacks–or–better, has been discussed earlier in this section.

High-Back-to-Low. This is a Jacks–or–better game. Instead of anteing a second time, it becomes Lowball when no one opens for High. Some hints on strategy have already been provided.

This course, like all the courses in **Super/System**, has stressed *Power Poker.*

You should probably choose a standard Jacks–or–better game until you acquire skill and confidence. Initially, your best bet is the $5 Draw (or a smaller game).

Whatever size, whatever variation of Draw Poker you choose, you won't be wasting your time mastering the concepts presented in this section. It's a prestige game with bigger limits available once you advance beyond the basics. Let me know how you do.

A FINAL EXCLUSIVE

It's the pain of losing that causes most unskilled Draw players to imagine that their luck is supernaturally bad. Earlier I gave you some examples of Gardena exaggerations and the odds against their occurrence. That was just an appetizer, Jacks–or–better fans, because here — for the first time in the history of Poker — is the complete...

TABLE OF SAD STORIES
(A cherished collection
of actual bad-luck claims
gathered in Gardena, 1973-78)

Miserable misfortune	Odds against
"I sat there 19 hours and didn't get one single Pat hand!"	48,305 to 1
"I ain't held the Joker in two hours!"	13,530 to 1 (if he NEVER drew cards)
"Maybe I should start keeping a kicker. I always draw-down to Trips, but I didn't help in 96 times so far this month!"	33,500 to 1 (depending on how often he threw away an Ace and assuming he meant Trips — Deuces through Kings)
"I've been sitting here an hour-and-a-half so far and I haven't seen so much as a Pair!"	10,522,652,460, 000,000,000,000 to 1
"That old woman drew to 14 Flushes against me and didn't miss a one!"	3,446,492,384 to 1
"That's four times in a row that some idiot drew three to a Pair of Shorts and beat me out of a Pat Flush!"	35,000,000 to 1 (depending on how many times the "idiot" discarded an Ace)
"So why do they call this game Jacks-or-better? That's 150 hands I played today — and I haven't had a Pair of Jacks or better!"	33,329,993,880, 000,000 to 1
"I only made one Flush in 65 tries!"	229,940 to 1
"I'm zero for 30 this year on 16-way Straights!"	191,750 to 1

"I was sitting next to this dude who didn't believe I'm so unlucky like I say I am. So we kept track. He just couldn't believe it! We drew to ten Flushes apiece. He made every one and I didn't hit any!"

67,141,150 to 1

"Other folks have all the luck. This guy sits down, gets eleven straight Pat hands and leaves the table!"

1,686,574,119,000,000,000,000 to 1

"Can you believe that? She gets two Full Houses and now a Straight-Flush! I've been playing in Gardena 10 hours a day, every day for sixteen years, and I never had a Pat Straight-Flush!"

203,909,594,800,000,000,000,000,000,000,000,000,000,000,000,000,000,000,000,000,000,000,000,000,000 to 1

The answer to the problem on Page 113 is:

You should draw none! Since the Opener has a Jack, you **can't** make Four-of-a-kind. If you draw one, there's a **chance** the Opener will think you're disguising Trips and will draw-down to his Pair of Kings. If he draws three to Kings, he has a better chance of beating your 3-Jacks than if he draws one. If you draw two, he will certainly figure you for Trips and draw three. After all, you raised. If you stand Pat, though, he will be forced to take his best shot at beating a Pat hand, which is to draw one, hoping to make a Full House.

A **key point** here: If you draw, you can't effectively help your hand if he draws one also. And if he draws three, he's cutting into your win-probability.

The reason you can't help if he draws one is that Jacks-Full is no better than three Jacks against his Full-House. If his one-card draw gives him a Full-House, it will be Queens-Full minimum. That beats Jacks-Full, and you can't make 4-Jacks, since he holds a Jack. It doesn't matter whether you keep the Ace kicker, the Queen kicker or draw two because you can't make any meaningful improvement against his one-card draw. And it's mathematically to your advantage for him to draw one.

Stand Pat.

If the analysis seems complicated, it's because the logic is difficult. But, don't worry about it.

In case you're curious about who solved that problem without hesitation, it was Doyle Brunson.

SUPER/SYSTEM's
POWER POKER COURSE
IN

SEVEN-STUD

SEVEN-CARD STUD

Table of Contents

DAVID "Chip" REESE

My Expert Collaborator
on
SEVEN-CARD STUD

It was in the Card Room in the **Flamingo Hotel–Casino** in **Las Vegas** in 1974 when I first saw *Chip* at a Poker table. He looked like some kid right out of college (which he was). Like all of the local Pros, I looked his bankroll over and "licked my chops". We (the local Pros) are used to seeing young, bright looking "home town champions". Little did I realize as I drooled over the prospect of winning his money, I was looking at one of the two finest young (under 30) **all-around** Poker players in the world. (Bobby Baldwin is the other one.)

That night, and the many nights that followed, *Chip* won my respect grudgingly and then my admiration as I watched him consistently beat the top players in town (which means the top players in the world).

Although we're still fierce competitors at the Poker table, we're very friendly when we're not trying to win each other's money. As I got to know him better, I found out he graduated from **Dartmouth College** in New Hampshire. *Chip* was rarely penalized for missing classes because many of his professors owed him money from the daily fraternity Poker games. Those fraternity games were his "basic training" and almost all the gambling students on campus owed him money since there was no one who had anywhere near the Poker talent he did. Proof of this is the fact that the card room in his fraternity *Beta Theta Pi* was dedicated the **David E. Reese** *Memorial Card Room* when he graduated.

Deciding not to go on to graduate school, *Chip* worked for a year as a Manufacturer's Representative and left a $25,000 a year job to come West.

He was living in Arizona when his friend (and now partner) Danny Robison came to Vegas for a weekend. Between them, they had $800 and started playing in the low-limit Seven-Card Stud games. They doubled their bankroll the first day and have continued to win to the point where they're already a legend in Vegas.

Chip reminds me of the saying: *"Gamblers are like little boys, the only thing that changes is the price of their toys."* It seems as though he's always playing for "fun" as I've seen him literally pour black ($100) chips into the pot when he's playing with the "big boys". But, I know he's dead serious every time he plays.

In addition to being a fundamentally sound player, he has the best natural instincts about what to do in difficult situations of any card player I've ever sat at a table with.

Although he's a super all-around card player, at his specialty — Seven-Card Stud, *Chip* appears to be on a different plateau from everyone else. And...by everyone else, I mean the best Seven-Stud players in the world. Without a doubt...*Chip's* the best Seven-Card Stud player I've ever played with.

SEVEN-CARD STUD

Down the River

INTRODUCTION
a lasting lesson

When I was 18 years old, I was playing in a Seven-Card Stud game one night in my home town of Sweetwater, Texas. I had been playing conservatively, rationally and intelligently — attempting to use my abilities to grind out a nice win for myself against players I was pretty sure I could beat.

Unfortunately, the story does **not** have a happy ending, and I learned a lesson that night that I have tried not to forget since — in my later years as a sometime gambler in college and a full-time gambler in Las Vegas, where night after night I play against the best Poker players in the world.

There was the inevitable drunk in that particular game, who seemed to be pouring White Russians down his throat at the same rate he was showering the pots with white chips. As I say, I was taking advantage of — and creating — the most favorable situations imaginable for myself.

But, after four cards, the drunk found himself with four Diamonds, and I found myself with two Aces. I was only a slight favorite mathematically to win the hand, but the drunk's annoying demeanor helped convince me I was going to win a real big pot.

We raised each other 36 times, until I had all my chips in the center. Then...the drunk caught his fifth Diamond.

I was broke. The drunk, naturally, went broke, too, but that didn't help me much as I was sitting on the sidelines waiting for another game.

The point indelibly etched in my memory was that I had used very poor judgment. If my opponent had been about equal (in ability) to me, than my play would have been completely justifiable. But I had foolishly risked my bankroll against a drunk when I was only an 11 to 10 favorite, rather than waiting for one of the many occasions that would arise when I would be a 4 to 1 or 5 to 1 favorite against him. I learned then and there that the mathematically correct play is **not** always the best play.

THE ANTE
and other considerations

When you approach a game of Seven-Card Stud, you have to decide what sort of ante structure suits your style of play. By that, I mean a low–ante or a high–ante. For simplicity, we'll discuss the ante structure in terms of a $10 and $20 Limit Seven-Stud game — one with an ante of $1, and the other an ante of $4. Basically, there are three factors you should think about in considering the ante structure:

(1) What type of players are there in this particular game? Are they players who like to play every pot? Are they there because they need the money or are they pleasure players? If you feel most of them are *loose and fast* players, you should try for a **low–ante**. If the majority of the players tend to be *tight or conservative* you want the **high–ante** game.

(2) The second thing you should consider is your own style of play. Are you the tight–type of player who'll wait for the quality hands or are you the type of player who enjoys action and plays lots of pots. Obviously, if you're the tight–type...the lower the ante — the better. If you're a liberal player, you **must have** the high–ante structure to be à consistent winner.

(3) The third factor to consider is whether you want the high-card or the low-card to make the first bet *(bring it in)*. In Las Vegas, in most Seven-Card Stud games, the low-card is **forced** to bring it in. (For example, in a $10 and $20 game with a $1 ante, the low-card *brings it in for* $2. In the same game with a $4 ante, the low-card *brings it in for* $5 — and because the ante's so high, the low-card's "forced" to get involved in the pot.) A liberal player prefers the low-card to bring it in while the tight player prefers the high-card to bring it in (because he doesn't want to put any money in the pot unnecessarily). Over any period of time, this element is very important to the game.

If you feel you know your own style of play and can correctly appraise the styles of others, then it's simple enough to determine what type of ante structure will be favorable for you in every game. If possible, you should attempt to get your opponents to establish an ante structure that's to your advantage.

STARTING HANDS

As you might suspect, the types of hands you'll be playing are also predicated on the ante structure. The starting hands in themselves are:

(1) Premium Pairs and Trips

(2) Drawing hands

(3) Small Pairs [The Pairs in (1) and (3) can be either concealed or split.]

(A) An example of a split Pair is:

(B) An example of a concealed Pair is:

A Pair of Tens or better are what I refer to as the *premium* hands.* The reason I refer to them as *premium* hands is that they may stand up as winners by themselves. It **isn't** hard to recall the number of times I've started out with a four-Flush or a four-Straight and been unable to beat two Queens after all the cards were out. You should get one of these *premium* hands about 7% of the time. Three-of-a-kind on the first three cards *(rolled–up Trips)*, is of course the very best of the *premium* hands.

The drawing hands can be classified in two categories: the three-Flushes and the three-Straights. Obviously, it's preferable to have the three-Flush since a Flush is a higher-ranking hand. Also, the higher the cards you have (in your three-Flush) the better off you'll be. An A♡-K♡-10♡ is superior to the 8♡-6♡-3♡ because another Ace, King or Ten will give you a *premium* hand. In the same way, a three-Straight of K-Q-J is preferable to that of 9-8-7. Also, your chances of making a Heart Flush when your first four cards are Hearts is about 47%, while your chances of making a Straight with a four-Straight in four cards is about 43% (.4716 vs. .4288).

Small Pairs are Nines down to Deuces, and, again, the higher the better. However, one important factor in determining the actual value of the small Pairs is your additional card *(kicker or sidecard)*. On many occasions, a Pair of Deuces with an Ace is much more valuable than a Pair of Sevens with a Four (as you'll learn about later).

---

*The reason I use Tens or better is because to make a Straight, you must have a Ten or Five. If I have two Tens, my opponents' chances of making a Straight are reduced considerably.

The concealed Pairs are Pairs in the hole. They're **more valuable** than split Pairs since you can get more value out of them when you make Trips (because of the deception factor).

Another significant factor is your position in relation to the player bringing it in. I call the early positions those of the players forced to act first, second, third or fourth, while the late positions are those of the fifth, sixth, seventh and eighth players to act. Naturally, the later your position, the more advantageous.

So with an appreciation of the types of starting hands and an understanding of what is meant by position, we can discuss when and how to play the various types of hands from various positions.

The structure I'll be discussing is a medium–ante $10 and $20 game, where each player antes $2 and the **low-card** brings it in for $4.

How to play the
PREMIUM HANDS

Let's start with the *premium* **Pairs,** either concealed or split. I'd play these hands from any position, with three exceptions. If I have two concealed Tens, and an opponent in an early position has raised the pot with a Jack showing (*representing* two Jacks) and another opponent has re-raised the Jack with a Queen–up, the chances are pretty good that I do **not** have the best hand. In this, or a similar instance, (when I have two Queens vs. a raise from a King and a re-raise from an Ace), I would fold. But otherwise I would play my *premium* hand through until the end, with just two other exceptions.

If I started with two Aces in the hole, and by the sixth card one of my opponents has a four-Straight or a four-Flush on the Board, it's highly probable that I'd be drawing *dead* (no chance to win the pot)...and I'd be forced to throw away my hand. The other case is if my opponent pairs his first up card *(door card)*. For example, if that opponent started with an Eight up and then paired it right away, it **isn't** certain that he would have three Eights, but he could possibly have Two-Pair or a powerful drawing hand, and I'd be a decided underdog or just a small favorite.

Since you only get the premium hands about 7% of the time, you **shouldn't** waste the opportunities they present. These hands create your **best** money-making possibilities. It's important **not** to waste them.

> On Third St., with a Pair of Tens through Aces, your *primary objective* is to eliminate as many players as possible from the pot. When you have a *premium* hand that might stand up by itself, you want to narrow the field so that you give yourself a good chance to win *without* any improvement.

For example, let's say you have two Aces with a Nine kicker. In the early positions, **raise** — you force people behind you to put more money in the pot and consequently you know they must have some sort of hand. By raising it from any position, when there are players behind you, you will eliminate as many of them as possible. No one will be able to come in without some kind of starting hand.

When you're in an early position and the pot has already been raised in front of you, you should **re-raise** with your two Aces because the only way anybody could have you beat at this point is to have two Aces with a higher kicker (a freak) or rolled-up Trips (a longshot).

If you have a **smaller** *premium* Pair, and there are two or more up-cards higher than your premium Pair, try to just call and see what develops. By raising with two or more higher up-cards behind you, you might be setting a trap for yourself. That's the last thing you want to do.

The *general rule for raising with a premium Pair* **in the first three cards is, go ahead and raise with it when there's only one (or no) higher up-cards behind you, call when there are two or more.**

If you do raise with your premium Pair and a higher card re-raises you, it's up to you to evaluate the play, asking yourself: *"Would this player re-raise me knowing that I have two Jacks, without two Queens himself?"* If your opponent is the type of player who **wouldn't** make this play **without** two Queens, you're better off throwing the hand away. You've invested one full-bet already, and if you continue to play the pot knowing you have the worst hand, it's **not** worthwhile to chase your money when you only had to put one-bet in to begin with — **unless** you have an Ace or King kicker.

Once you've raised (with what you consider the best hand), you've done your job of trying to eliminate players. If you're re-raised by a bigger card, you can go ahead and call. Let your opponent take the lead and wait until a later round, when the larger bets start, before you decide whether to force the issue yourself.

On Fourth St., one of your primary objectives, assuming you still feel you have the best hand, is to eliminate players again (or at least try).

Many beginning players with a marginal edge instinctively try to keep as many players **in the pot** as possible. This is totally wrong, and the sooner you understand this super-valuable concept, the better off you and your Seven-Stud bankroll will be.

One of the most important principles in Seven-Card Stud is that when you think you have the best hand, you want to get players out of the pot — rather than trying to get extra money in the pot *(unless you have a really strong hand).* **Here's a good example:**

YOU

Player *A*

Player *B*

For purposes of discussion, we'll assume there are three remaining players as in the above illustration. You have a split Pair of Aces with an Eight kicker, and have caught the 9♣ on Fourth St. The original raiser (Player B) started with the J♠ and caught the 10♣. The other player A, who started with the 6♡ has picked up the Q♣. You must now attempt to eliminate him (A) so that he doesn't stay around to pick up a fourth Heart and present the threat of a Flush.

If you bet the Ace, the man with the 6♡-Q♣ might call, assuming the man with the J♠-10♣ would be afraid to raise it. He would usually be right in this assumption.

The proper play is to check the Ace (since you're first to act because you have the high Board). The player (A) with the drawing hand will check also. The player with the J♠-10♣ most likely will bet, figuring that your Ace represents part of a drawing hand. Then you raise, to force the player with the 6♡-Q♣ to put in a double-bet — merely trying to make a four-Flush. He probably **won't** call, realizing he's a heavy underdog, so you've accomplished your purpose.

You now have two Aces in a head-up situation, against another player who probably has two Jacks (plus you've knocked out the player with the 6♡-Q♣ to put some *dead* money in the pot).

Sometimes, however, depending on your Board, it **isn't** practical to try to further eliminate any players. Using the same hypothetical hand, let's say you've caught the K◊ to go with your A♡, while the other two players have both picked up a Ten on Fourth St. If you check this new hand hoping for the same play as when your Board was Ace-Nine. . .you probably **won't** get it. The Jack-Ten would probably be afraid to bet, feeling that he could have the 2nd best hand. Then everybody would get a *free* card — which is exactly what you **don't** want to happen.

So if your Board on Fourth St. is impressive enough (say, A-K) to discourage anyone else from betting, your **best strategy** is to **bet** your hand and hope that the Q-6 folds. If he doesn't fold, he's still **not** a favorite to make a Flush, and you've succeeded in getting more money in the pot.

Another aspect of premium Pair play on Fourth St. — assuming you still have the best hand — is to add deception to what you do. Assume now that you are head–up and have caught the 4♢ to go with the A♡, while your opponent has caught the same Ten to go with his original Jack. In this case, you probably would **not** want to bet out strongly on Fourth St. because you'd be letting the J-10 know that you must have two Aces to be betting into his Board. So you check (for deceptive purposes).

If he checks, too, it is still **not** that bad. Although you've given him a *free* card, you're putting some doubt into his mind as to whether you have two Aces or not. You put yourself in a position where you might pick up a double–bet on Fifth St., or influence him to call you down (to the River) **without** improving his two Jacks — because he has some doubts that you have two Aces. If he checks it back to you on Fourth St. there's a good chance that he did **not** start out with two Jacks, and that the Ten did **not** help his hand. The most logical possibility is that he raised coming–in with a three–Flush. If this is the case, you haven't made the best play, but you're still a comfortable favorite against his hand.

If he bets, he has now committed himself to playing the pot by becoming the aggressor. Rather than re-raising on Fourth St., and thus letting him **know** you have two Aces, you just call — unless you feel that one extra bet (your re-raise) on Fourth will psychologically commit him to the pot.

It's **important** to try **to eliminate** players on Fifth St. Your strategy with a good hand on Fifth should be to **never permit anybody** *to get a free card.* A single bet on Fifth St. will eliminate many hangers-on.

One way to eliminate players on Fifth St. (which should take care of many problems on Sixth St.) is to **raise** when you feel pretty certain you do **not** have the best hand.

For example, you have two Aces, which you've represented all the way, and one of your opponents has made an open Pair. He **hasn't** paired his *door card* (which was a Queen), but he has caught two Sevens. The chances are pretty good that he has Two-Pair.

He bets, and you must act **before** the players behind you, whom you feel have some kind of a hand like an inside-Straight draw or a Flush draw although you're really not sure.

At any rate, you feel pretty certain that the players behind you **don't** have you beat, while you're still aware that you'll have to make Two-Pair to win the pot. When the player with the two Sevens bets, you **must** *raise*, driving everybody else out. Although you still have only your two original Aces, it's possible that you could have made anything — Aces up or a concealed Three-of-a-kind. Not too many opponents will think that you're raising against an open Pair with only a Pair of Aces.

If you succeed in driving out all the opponents other than the one with the Two-Pair, then you've created another positive situation — the likelihood of a *free card* on Sixth St. (if you fail to improve).

The man with the Two-Pair will likely check, and you go ahead and check if you've missed or you bet yourself if you have now been fortunate enough to make Aces-up.

The importance of this sort of play can't be emphasized enough. It's a very strong maneuver. Many times you'll lose a pot by merely calling on Fifth St., letting in a straggler who might end up making a small Three-of-a-

kind or be successful with an inside-Straight draw.

Also, by raising on Fifth St. with good possibilities in the draw, you have achieved what Seven-Card Stud is all about: *getting in an extra bet when you should.*

By Sixth St., if you still feel that your two Aces are the best hand, you should try to eliminate any remaining stragglers. Against certain hands (four-Straights and four-Flushes) you **won't be able to do this**...so your best strategy is to continue betting and make them pay to draw out.

Occasionally, there will be stragglers in the pot with weak hands — such as a busted three-Flush and a small Pair. You have to try to get them out, because there's the chance that they might make two small Pairs or Trips on the last card and beat you. There's already enough of their money in the pot as far as you are concerned.

Remember, you're only going to get so many hands each session...and so you **must** *maximize the profit* from each of them. Figuring out ways to get double-bets out of your opponent(s) on Fifth St. and Sixth St. is the best way to achieve this end.

The ideal premium hand is *rolled-up* Trips, a hand with an excellent chance of standing-up by itself against other premium hands that your opponents will be playing very strongly.

Rolled-Up Trips

Hole-Cards   *Up-Card*

My main objective with a Set of rolled-up Trips is **not** to eliminate players. I've been in many games with players who raise the pot on Third St., watch everybody else throw their hands away and then complain about how unlucky they are. The man who basically **wasted** this hand (by raising) should not be complaining. He should realize that **he's** at fault for driving his opponents out in a situation where he might have won a large pot.

Your primary concern with this hand (rolled-up Trips) is the quality of your up-card and whether it will scare other players out of the pot. As a general rule, in an early position, **never** raise the pot, no matter what happens on Third St., because you **don't** want to tip the strength of your hand. If you happen to get the Trips beat...you just get them beat. But, as I say, you'll win many more pots than you'll lose with them...and you want to try to win as big a pot as possible.

By calling in the early rounds and giving others a chance to get in cheaply and develop some kind of hand, you increase your opportunities to win a big pot.

After you've gotten a little money in on Third St. and Fourth St., and your opponents are involved, you can begin to play your hand according to its true strength. That means ...play it *fast*. People tend to go farther in Seven-Card Stud once they've got a little money in the pot.

So, generally speaking, you should wait until Fifth or Sixth St. to raise — because by then you can be pretty sure that they'll be going down the river (to the end) with you.

The **only exception** to the rule about **not** raising on Third St. is if you're in a late position with the biggest card up and would normally try to steal the pot without a hand. You must hope that somebody has a hand behind you. It looks too suspicious if you limp-in (without raising) in Sixth position with an Ace-up and there are only one or two people behind you.

Your opponents know that you would raise it with an Ace-up anyway, even if you didn't have a hand, and they will be wary of falling into a trap.

How to play
DRAWING HANDS

Generally speaking, how you play your drawing hands depends upon two considerations — your position and your door-card.

A good example would be a three-Flush in Hearts with the 6♡ showing and you simply call the first bet. You aren't giving away your hand because you could have anything. You want to get as many people into the pot as possible. By raising it you would decrease your money odds on the hand, and it's likely you will have to make the Flush to win.

But remember, a drawing hand is **not** a premium hand, and should not be considered as such. If two big cards ahead of you raise, you would not call the raise unless you have two big cards yourself in the hole (as in the following example).

**This hand is always playable...
even if the pot's double-raised in
front of you.**

Hole-Cards   **Up-Card**

If the pot is raised twice behind you, you automatically throw your hand away...if you have a three-Flush — but **don't** have two big cards in the hole.

However, if part of your three-Flush is a *premium* card, a Queen, for example, you have to consider the question, *"What are my chances of winning this pot if I do NOT make the hand I'm drawing to?"* If the Queen is the highest card showing, go ahead and raise because it's possible that no one behind you will have a hand and you're likely to steal the ante. Additionally, you've also succeeded in creating an element of deception — the illusion that you might have two Queens. Also, if your Queen-up is part of a three-Straight instead of a three–Flush, you have two other *premium* cards to Pair. The final factor: if your Queen is the highest up–card, it's very unlikely that there'll be more than one raise behind you. That eliminates the possibility of your having to face a double–raise in back of you.

RAISER   **YOU**

*Marginally   should NOT
playable   be played*

You should **throw away** a three–Flush containing small cards if you're going to be in a head–up situation with a man who has raised. If your three–Flush has one card above the raiser's door card, then it is a close decision (as in the above example).

Another time when you do **not** want to draw to a small Flush is when, in a seven–handed game, you see two of your suit out in other hands. In this case, you must **have** big cards in your hand to add to the possible winning hands you can make.

If you have a three–Straight–Flush (such as A♡-K♡-Q♡ down to a Q♡-J♡-10♡) another interesting possibility presents itself. In this instance, raise **only** when there's one card (or no cards) behind you higher than your up–card. For example, if you have the Q♡ up and there's only one Ace or King behind you...go ahead and raise. You might pick up the antes, and you don't figure to get raised twice. By raising immediately, you also put yourself in the excellent position of catching a Heart on Fourth St. — with nobody suspecting that you have a four–Flush. This play is very rare among average Seven–Card Stud players, but has been a winning one for me over the long run.

On Fourth St., say your three-Flush is still a three-Flush — you've busted out. The **major rule** to follow here is: **if the pot had NOT been raised or raised only one time...you should pass.** If somebody bets into you, throw your hand away. You **deviate** from this rule **only** when you've had to put in two or more bets on Third St. In that case, you can take another card if it **doesn't** seem likely that you'll again have to face the prospect of more than one bet.

If on Fourth St., you have not completely busted out, it means you've made a three-Straight or a Pair in addition to your three-Flush. If you've made a big Pair, you can begin to play your hand by the guidelines for *premium* Pairs. But if you've made a small Pair and suspect a double-raise...throw your hand away.

The best possibility, of course, is that you make a four-Flush. Even if you do, you'll make your Flush less than half (47.16%) of the time. Before you get excited at the prospect of 3 to 1 or 4 to 1 odds on an almost 50-50 proposition, you must ask yourself if your opponents have a pretty good idea as to the quality of your hand.

If you came in for two raises with nothing more than your ante invested, and in your own mind you feel that your opponent(s) have guessed you have a four-Flush, you must proceed to bet, because the likelihood of any continued deception is small. Or, if your opponent bets, you should go ahead and raise him.

However, if you merely called in an early position (a position in which you could have had a small Pair instead of a three-Flush) and in a head-up situation, your opponent bets, do **not** raise. Just call behind him in a late position — for two reasons: despite the promising possibilities — you're still a small underdog. By **not** raising you create some deception because many players think they have a license to steal money with a four-Flush after four cards. They **don't** use good sense and they *overplay* their hand. You must proceed cautiously but confidently, because you know that you'll be playing this hand until the end unless your opponent makes something extremely threatening like Two-Pair or Three-of-a-kind in-sight on Sixth St.

I **don't** recommend, if big cards are raising, playing a three-Straight in a double-raised pot, unless you've got all big cards — such as J♡-Q◇-K◇ with a two-Flush in your three-Straight. I would throw a small three-Straight away unless my cards are bigger than the cards they're raising with. But I'd call with three starting cards like the J♡-Q◇-K◇. I might not only catch another Straight card, but I could catch a Jack, Queen or King — or another Diamond — which gives me a lot of flexibility at this point. The following illustration is two examples of the points I just made.

AGAINST A DOUBLE-RAISE

Playable	*NOT Playable*
BIG 3-Straight/2-Flush	**small 3-Straight/2-Flush**

There's another three-Straight situation — a three gutshot Straight like a 6-7-9. The only time I would play a split Straight draw like that would be when everybody had small up-cards. If the highest card is a Seven and I have a Nine, I'll take a card if I'm fairly certain I'm **not** going to be raised.

A gut shot Straight that is a pretty good hand is a 9-10-Q...**if everybody else has smaller cards**. If I feel I won't be raised, I'll put the minimum bet in and draw to it. I might catch a Jack right in the middle, and if I do I've got a powerful hand. But there's a big difference between playing a 6-7-9 and a 9-10-Q. A 9-10-Q is obviously a better hand because you've got **three** big cards you can catch to make a decent Pair — depending upon what the other people have. (And if you've got a two-Flush with your split Straight draw, it's even stronger, because you have a chance to make a Flush.)

Before you draw to a small Straight, you should check to see how many of your cards are *dead*. If, for example, you have a 7-6-5, the most important cards are Eights and Fours with Nines and Threes of secondary importance. If you see three or more of these 16 cards, you should not draw to your hand.

The best possible hand you could make is the four-Straight on four. In this instance, you're going to complete your Straight 42.88% of the time. But once again, it is pretty likely you'll be going the distance on the hand, so keep calling — **no raising** (unless you make your hand) — so you can keep as many players in the pot as possible to enhance your pot odds.

Two other possibilities are that you may catch a card which gives you an inside Straight draw (for example, a 7-6-5-3 or a 9-7-6-5), or you may make a small Pair. These hands **should be discarded** if the pot was **not** raised on Third St. and the action on Fourth St. may result in your being put in the middle. **Don't** get strung out with these marginal draws, especially if you have very little invested. There'll be better spots for your money.

If there are bigger cards in your Straight draw, and you're not certain you're up against a premium Pair, you can take a card in these marginal situations. But only do it if you're sure it will cost you only one bet.

Naturally, if you catch a complete blank, you'll pass if there's a bet.

Another situation you want to avoid is when you start with a three-Straight, two-Flush hand, and catch a third Flush card on Fourth St. You've got a three-Straight, three-Flush hand, and you're in what's called a *whipsaw*. The criterion that should be used in this situation is — how big are the cards?

Let's say you have a three-Straight and a three-Flush on the fifth card and you think your opponent has only a Pair of Tens. Now, you **don't** even have a Pair, but...you've got a J-Q-K with your Straight and Flush draw. In this case, you're justified in taking another card because **not** only can you improve the Straight or Flush draw, you can also make a

Pair that could win the pot for you. You have to let the size of your cards determine whether you play or not when you get in a *whipsaw* situation.

By Fifth St., you have to assume that if you make your drawing hand, you'll win the pot. Your prime objective on Fifth St., as it was on Fourth St., is to keep as many players in the pot as possible.

If you're in an early position and the aggressor bets, do **not** raise with a four-Flush on Five because you want to insure that you'll continue to get good money odds for as long as possible. There are, of course, some situations where raising with a drawing hand in a late position is justified. For example, on Fifth St., there are four players in the hand and you have a four-Flush in last position. The first player bets his Ace (representing a Pair of Aces) and the original raiser calls with a King (so you give him credit for a Pair of Kings). The third player calls, and you feel sure that he's coming in with a four-Straight. In this instance, you should raise... even though you have the third best hand.

On Fifth St., with two cards to come, you'll make your Flush 34.97% of the time (1.86 to 1 against), but you'll be getting 3 to 1 on your money. The Ace could re-raise trying to eliminate players (as discussed earlier), but the chances are that the four-Straight will stay, along with the player with two Kings, who is, by now, very deeply involved. Even should the two Kings fold, you'd still be getting 2 to 1.

The principle here is: **If you are less than a 2 to 1 underdog to win the hand and you're getting 3 to 1 on your money...you can raise and take that kind of gamble all day — because you'll be getting the best of it.**

The play of
SPLIT PAIRS

This discussion assumes that your split Pair is **smaller** than the *premium* Pairs. For medium split Pairs (Sevens, Eights and Nines) follow the general rules as applied to *premium* Pairs. Say, for example, your split Pair is Nines. If there's only one (or no) cards behind you higher than Nines...go ahead and raise. Try to eliminate players with your two Nines. With these marginal Pairs, you're always happy to win the pot as early as possible. If the pot is re-raised behind you...go ahead and play. But, if it is re-raised **twice**...throw your hand away (when it gets back to you).

If there are two or more cards behind you higher than a Nine...**don't** raise. You should call and see what happens. The reasoning behind this, once again, is the same as was discussed for the premium hands. Don't trap yourself unnecessarily.

The only exception to the above rule would come when you had your two Nines accompanied by an Ace kicker. Then it's advisable to raise despite the two high cards because of your Ace. Even if one of the players behind you has a larger Pair, you've got the possibility of catching an Ace (or a Nine) which will give you an excellent hand.

If you've seen either of your two other (split Pair) cards exposed, your hand should be thrown away...unless you think it's the best hand at that point.

What you always try to do with a split Pair on Third St. is win the pot immediately. You take one shot, as in the case of raising with the two Nines. If it develops that your medium or small split Pair is probably **not** the best hand, then it should be easy to get away from it.

One of the most important things I've learned about split Pairs is the value your kicker or sidecard has. If a Ten raises the pot and you've got two Fours and a Jack, your hand is a fair one because your Jack is an overcard. But if you've got two Fours with a Nine kicker, your hand **doesn't** have much value because even if you catch a Nine and make Two-Pair...you'll often lose to your opponent's Tens-up.

> **I will *not* call a raise from a high card with a
> small or medium split Pair *unless* my sidecard
> is higher than the raiser's door card.**

You can be pretty sure you do **not** have the best hand if the original bettor continues to lead. So play your split Pair as slowly as possible — just check and call until Fifth St. If you **don't** improve your hand by then, it's time to throw it away.

On Fourth St., if the original bettor bets, and you've put in one raise (or more) on Third St., be very wary of the fact that you might have to put in two bets this time instead of one. If a Jack bets after catching a Queen, and the player behind you now has the 6♡-7♡, and you have your original two Nines...you'll more than likely be taking the worst of it. The man with the 6♡-7♡ *might* **raise** after you call. In that case, you could be facing a second raise from the Q-J. It has to be stressed that you must use foresight in this situation and throw your hand away on Fourth St. if you fail to improve.

If you do improve on Fourth St. — making Two-Pair that are split — you are obviously in a much more favorable situation. If the pot is head-up, you have a number of different ways to play the hand. If the player with the Q-J bets, you probably have to figure him for one Pair, and you've got the best hand. Many people say that Fourth St. is the time to show the strength of your hand...but I disagree.

If you have Two-Pair on Fourth St. (Nines and Sixes, for example), you'll probably be better off **not** raising until Sixth Street. Your sole concern is to avoid falling into any Traps. By raising on Fourth St. — with a 9-6 against a Q-J — your opponent is aware that you have a weak Board and is subject to re-raise it. You have suddenly invested a great deal of money in the hand and have almost forced yourself to play until the end.

Even if you raise on Fourth St. and the man with the Q-J **doesn't** re-raise, he has a pretty good idea of what you have. Then, on Fifth St., he might improve — catching a Queen or a Jack, while you **don't** improve. In this case, there's an excellent chance that he has two Queens and two Jacks or three Jacks...and that puts you in a very bad situation.

Another **major** *disadvantage* of raising on Fourth St. is that you might be fortunate enough to make a Full House on Fifth St. If you've already revealed the strength of your hand to your opponent, he'll suddenly find it very easy to fold two Jacks. But, if you take a wait-and-see approach, he'll probably go all the way with you. And that's all to your advantage.

Another possibility is that you catch a Nine on Fourth St. — giving you three Nines (which is pretty likely to stand up). Now, your primary concern becomes getting maximum value out of the hand.

At this point, you have to hope that your opponents think you started out with a drawing hand and paired your up-card. However, they'll be aware of the possibility that you have three Nines.

You quickly have to evaluate the caliber of your opponent. If he happens to be the type of player who generally throws away his hand when you Pair your up-card, you should definitely check (if he has a powerful *front*). If he has a weak *front*, you must bet and hope that he has enough to call. Checking to a weak hand in this situation virtually announces that you have three Nines. When you do check, he'll either sense that you're trying to trap him (which you are) or he'll believe that you can't beat two Jacks.

If you check and your opponent checks, you have lost nothing since he probably would have thrown away his hand if you bet. But if he bets, you should only call because many players will bet into an open Pair on Fourth St. to see what you'll do. If you check-raise, he'll probably throw away his hand and you will have lost the chance to win several extra bets.

But, if you just call after checking, it's possible that he won't figure you for Trips. By this play, you may create the impression that you started with a three-Flush or three-Straight and that's an impression that you hope your opponent will retain until you choose to change it.

If you happen to catch a card (on Fifth St.) that's the same suit as your original up-card, you can go ahead and bet — representing a four-Flush. It's unlikely he'll throw away his two Jacks. If you **don't** catch a card of the same suit as your first up-card...check again. It should then appear to your opponent that you've missed a second try at a four-Flush.

It's more than likely that he'll bet again. Now, you put in your first raise — after waiting a full Round until Fifth St. It's almost too late for him to throw his hand away. You've successfully baited the Trap and he's fallen into it. You've played the hand perfectly, and if he beats you, you've played unlucky, **not** badly.

GETTING FREE CARDS

One of the greatest assets of a Seven-Card Stud player is his ability to get free cards. This talent is utilized when you have the worst hand on Fourth or Fifth St., but a hand that still has a large potential for improvement. In these cases, you want to get more cards as cheaply as possible.

YOU   **OPPONENT**

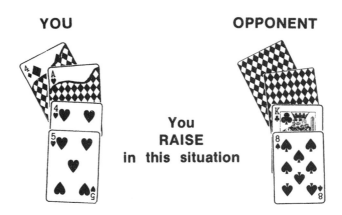

You
RAISE
in this situation

Suppose you have a split Pair (as in the above example). The 4♡ is your up-card and the 4◇-A♡ are down-cards. Your opponent, who has originally raised you with the K♣ up, catches the 8♠ while you catch the 5♡. On Fourth St., your opponent bets. You should raise. You've raised, of course, knowing that you probably have the worst hand.

On Fifth St., in the event that neither of you improve visibly, your opponent will likely check to you, assuming he remains high. You check right behind him.

In reality, you've put in a smaller bet on Fourth St. to **save** a larger bet on Fifth St. Your opponent would probably have bet on Fifth St., if you hadn't raised on Fourth.

If on Fifth St., however, you catch another Heart and your opponent does **not** improve...you bet — *representing* the Flush. He will possibly throw his hand away. But, even if he doesn't, you still have a four-Flush, two Fours and an Ace kicker, which is a strong drawing hand.

If you happen to get lucky and catch a Four on Fifth St., which would make you high, you can go ahead and bet because you've *represented* a Flush and will possibly get some extra value out of pairing your up-card.

If you catch an Ace on Fifth St., you'll have made Aces-up. Or, if you catch a Five, you've made Two small Pair which probably is the best hand — if your opponent doesn't improve in-sight.

Suppose you've got the **10♠-J♠** up...and the **10♣-Q♠** in the hole. Your opponent started with a King-up and caught a Baby on Fourth St.

Now, if you catch a King or an Ace, you'll be high — but it won't wreck your *play* because you'll have a chance to make a Straight. You **want** to make this *play* when you've got the type of cards that if you do fall high...your hand has improved.

The whole *key* to this *play* is to make sure that the card that will make you high has improved your hand.

Just to make the *play* crystal clear — whatever card your opponent has that makes him high — you have to be sure that if you do catch a card higher than his card, that the card you catch will improve your hand.

YOU   OPPONENT

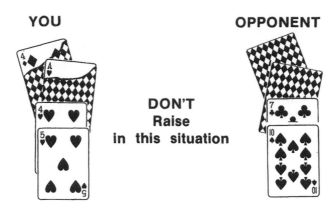

DON'T
Raise
in this situation

Once again (as above) suppose you had the 4♡-5♡, but this time your opponent has raised it with a Seven-up (the highest card out) and you feel fairly certain he has two Sevens. On Fourth St., you catch the 5♡ and he catches a Ten. Now he has 10-7 showing, and you have 5♡-4♡ showing with the 4◊ and the A♡ in the hole.

In this case, you **don't** raise because on Fifth St. you could possibly catch a Jack, Queen or King to fall high. You **wouldn't** be able to get a free card because you'd have to bet first.

Playing
CONCEALED PAIRS

The most important factor in playing your concealed Pairs in the early positions depends on what your up-card is and what you hope to *represent*.

If you have the highest card showing around the table, for instance an Ace with two concealed Deuces, you should go ahead and raise, *representing* two Aces. You can either win the pot right away or you can improve your two Deuces along the way and make the best hand. You should *always* **raise** when you have the highest up-card and a concealed Pair...just to see what happens.

On Third St., in this instance, it's unlikely you'll get raised more than once because the Ace is a powerful card. If you have the highest card, which **isn't** an Ace, the only circumstance in which you're likely to get raised more than once is when **two** of your opponents have concealed Pairs also higher than your up-card. If you do get raised twice...you have to give up the hand.

If you have a small card up, such as a Six, to go with your two Deuces, it's best to only call. Again, you **don't** figure to have the best hand. You're just trying to make concealed Trips as cheaply as possible.

If the pot is raised ahead of you and you have a concealed Pair **lower** than the up-card of the raiser, **don't** call the raise when there are two or more players behind you with up-cards higher than your Pair. If an Ace raises and you have two concealed Jacks, you'll probably be chasing two better hands if two players — one with a Queen and one with a King — trail in behind you.

As a general rule:

> **You should proceed cautiously — even with a** *premium* **Pair — whenever you're in a pot where two or more people have up-cards** *higher* **than your Pair. This is true** *even if only one of them has raised.*

Here's another guideline I have:

> **As long as my opponent has an up-card higher than my** *split* **Pair (say, Eights)...I'd rather have a lower** *concealed* **Pair (say, Deuces).**

For example, if I have an Eight-up and my opponent has a Ten-up there's a good chance that he's got two Tens — especially if he's the aggressor in the pot. In that particular case, a Pair of Eights or a Pair of Deuces is almost the same thing because I have the worst hand.

I play my split Pairs and concealed Pairs according to what my opponent's up-card is. If he has an Ace-up, I have to worry about a Pair of Aces. In that case, I'd rather have any Pair in the hole rather than a split Pair of Kings. Either way I have the worst hand. Even if we both make Two-Pair, I'm going to lose the pot to his Aces-up.

However, with a concealed Pair, the hand can become more powerful because when I catch Trips he won't be able to read me for that hand.

But if my split Pair is higher than my opponent's up-card it represents a more powerful *front* than a concealed Pair and I'll be able to take the lead with my hand from the beginning. The **disadvantage** of split Pairs is that when you make Trips, by pairing your *door card*, your opponent can readily see your strength.

As additional requirements, you should also look for a **small edge** with the concealed Pair — such as a two-Flush or a two-Straight. It gives you an opportunity, however small, to make some kind of hand if you don't help your original concealed Pair.

Your chances of making Three-of-a-kind (exactly) starting with a concealed Pair is about 1 in 10 (if you take all seven cards).

Generally speaking, whether your Pair is concealed or split, if you're in a position of weakness — by that I mean, when you're **not** the aggressor in the pot — if you **don't** improve your hand by Fifth St. — you should throw it away there. By Fifth St., you should have the best hand (or the best draw, if that's the type of hand you have). That's what you always want. You **don't** want to be chasing on the expensive streets (where the betting doubles). It's **not** worth involving yourself too deeply if you suspect you have the second or third best hand. There is no such thing as a *Place Ticket* to be cashed in Seven-Card Stud.

As in the case of all the other starting hands, many different situations can develop with your concealed Pairs on Fourth St. and Fifth St.

First of all, you can catch a *Blank* on Fourth St. (for example, starting with two concealed Fours and a Nine and then catching a Ten). Again, you must still apply the same rules as you would for split Pairs or for partial improvement of drawing hands. If the original aggressor bets and you feel the pot will **not** be raised behind you. . .go ahead and call. If you **don't** improve your hand by Fifth St. — throw it away.

A second possibility would be pairing your up-card, giving you two Tens on the Board and two Fours in the hole. At this time, you should lead aggressively with your hand and hope that the original bettor will throw his hand away — fearing that you have Trips. You want him to pass because you're **not** a big favorite to win the hand. When one or more people call, you still have the chance to make a Full House (or your Two–Pair might stand up).

If you do get called, continue to bet until an opponent makes an open Pair or some sort of other threatening Board.

The third, and best, possibility is making concealed Trips by catching a Four on Fourth St. You'd then follow the guidelines for playing rolled–up Trips (as discussed earlier).

If your opponent is a good player, this time you'll be able to take advantage of the **free card** *play*, as discussed earlier. This play is even more advanced and your opponent **must** be a sophisticated player.

You have the three Fours, with the Ten of the same suit as your first up-card. Your opponent, who now has a K-Q up bets. You raise. You're hoping he's familiar, in a limited way, with your **free card** *play* as discussed in the split Pairs section. If he re-raises on Fourth St. — just call. Then, it's almost certain that you'll get a double-bet on Fifth St.

It's a good play, regardless of which way it's being used. If you're just trying to get a free card, it accomplishes that objective against an average player. If it's being used against a good player, it accomplishes the purpose of getting extra bets in.

By Fifth St., your concealed Pair has often taken on the value of a split Pair, in the sense that you can apply the same rules for betting, calling and folding.

If you make (concealed) Trips on Fifth St., you have two alternatives. The larger betting Rounds have now started. You may be willing to let some weak hands catch-up a little and wait until Sixth St. to pop it. Your other choice, which you'd probably use when your opponents had strong Boards, is to raise it immediately and see if your opponents want to play a big pot. Stringing other players along or taking the lead yourself is simply a judgment decision based upon your evaluation of how you can best take advantage of the opposition.

The general rule to follow is to get as much money in the pot as possible **without** giving anybody free cards.

There is, in addition to the *premium* hands, drawing hands, split Pairs and concealed Pairs, a hand familiar to everybody: **garbage** — which is something similar to Q♡-7♣-2◇. While this hand has no chance to win in showdowns, it can play a role as a part of the important play of stealing the ante.

ANTE STEALING

Stealing the ante is a worthless maneuver in low-ante structure games. In high-ante structure games...it is a necessity.

The first reason for that fact being true is that you must keep winning small pots to prevent the antes from draining you. The second reason is, not surprisingly, tied to the idea of getting value on your hands.

You have to get caught stealing occasionally, and when you do, you put it into other players' minds that you'll occasionally bet **without** a hand. When you eventually have a hand, you're much more likely to get paid off. But even when you **are** stealing the ante, you have things to think about.

First, you **must** be in a late position. If no one has entered the pot ahead of you and your up-card is higher than any of the up-cards of the few remaining players behind you...**go ahead and raise it** in hopes that you'll get the pot.

If you have a Nine up in Sixth position with a King in the hole, and a player behind you has a King showing, you can try to pick-up the antes.

You should also be aware when an opponent may be trying to steal the antes. For example, you have a split Pair of Fives, with a Queen and you're in last position. Normally, if a player with a Queen-up raises the pot, you probably would **not** call because of the chance that you're up against two Queens. But if the raiser was in the *steal* (next-to-last) *position*, you might re-raise him (re-steal) because your sidecard indicates that there's a fairly good chance that he does **not** have the hand he's representing.

In trying to represent a hand, you're risking the possibility he might have two Queens (or some other playable hand). But, if he catches you (re-stealing), he'll more than likely come in with a marginal hand against you later.

When you do happen to get a good hand against his slightly inferior hand, your opponent may remember you're a player who tries to steal antes, and he may give you more action than his hand warrants. Your image as a player who'll bet **without** a hand will get you that loose action.

Although you **don't** bluff a lot in a regular game, you **do** want to bluff **just enough** so that people will pay you off and help you to get value out of your marginal hands.

> **That's what makes the difference between** *winning and losing* **Seven-Card Stud players.**
> **Winning players get the most value out of their hands.**

If a person thinks you never bluff — well, why should you ever bet one Pair on the end for value? They're **not** going to call you *unless* **you're beat.** You've got to let them know that the possibility exists — even if it's remote — that you **might** be bluffing.

However, if you try to steal the ante and get re-raised. . .give it up. Under **no** conditions should you chase your money by calling. **Stealing the ante is a** *one-shot play.* You might make something on Fourth St. that would enable you to win the hand. . .but do **not** invest any **extra** bets. Just throw away your hand and wait for the next one.

SIXTH STREET PLAY

By the sixth card, it's not really necessary to discuss the distinction between premium hands, drawing hands, concealed Pairs, and split Pairs, because **by Sixth St., anybody that is left in the pot with any kind of a hand will have enough money in the pot to justify taking the seventh card.**

So the important thing on Sixth St. is to decide whether or not you have the best hand. There is very little concern with eliminating players, and what you want to do with the best hand is to try and get double bets in.

The main device used to get an extra bet in a pot is to check-raise. There are two reasons why you want to check-raise:

(1) **You've got the best hand and you're trying to win an extra bet;**

(2) **You think your opponent might be so weak that you can make him throw his hand away. The latter doesn't happen very often.**

If you're playing $10 and $20 and you've got three rolled-up Sixes — you don't want to check-raise after four cards because you don't want to scare your opponent. You want to wait until he has committed himself on Fifth St., when it's a $20 bet. **Once a person commits himself in Five,**

he generally goes all the way. So you have to ask yourself on Fifth or Sixth St., or whenever you decide the time is right, *"What does my opponent· have?"* You've got to try and determine what he has and what he thinks you have considering the way you have put deception in your hand — by the **impression** you tried to create. Knowing your opponents and their reactions will help you to make the proper plays in different situations.

Every single pot is a separate money transaction. You have to get the most or lose the least in every hand that comes up. **Getting extra bets and saving money is the name of the game.**

The significant thing about getting the double bets in is this: it must be done against a **fairly sharp player** who likes to get value out of his hands.

I'll give you an example. A player with a Jack-up raised it originally, and you re-raised with an Ace. Your opponent knows you don't necessarily have to have two Aces, but could have anything.

On Fourth St., you catch the 10♡ to go with the A♡, while your opponent catches nothing. You continue to bet on Fifth St. after catching an offsuit Deuce, while your opponent once again catches nothing.

On Sixth St., you catch an off-Trey, so your Board is A♡-10♡-2◊-3♣. In fact, you have an Ace and a Ten in the hole making Aces-up. Against a quality player, whose Board is now J-6-2-Q, you can make your best play (check-raise) if you feel his hand is two Jacks or better.

If you really know your player, you can sometimes check your hand, even though you've taken the lead all the way. By doing so, you can make him believe that you might have been betting a four-Flush, since your first two up-cards were Hearts, and you've busted off twice in a row — and are now hoping for a free card.

If your opponent is an aggressive player, he might bet his two Jacks — and certainly will bet a hand like Jacks-up. He feels he has to bet out, getting as much value as he can out of the hand, thinking that you might possibly have a four-Flush. He would know that you're more than a 4 to 1 underdog to make the Flush.

By checking, you're representing a busted four-Flush, so you raise back after he bets. Then bet out on Seventh St. trying to get that extra bet.

The key aspect of this particular example is your thorough knowledge of the opponent, because it's not worth checking if he has one Pair and would say, "*Well, maybe I'm up against two Aces and maybe I'm not.*" Then check right behind you.

Another technique on Sixth St. is **raising to get a free card**. In this instance, you're facing an opponent you know fairly well. You know he's pretty aggressive, and capable of bluffing. You have re-raised the pot with an Ace-up and an Ace in the hole. Your opponent started with the 10♡, caught the 6♡ on Fourth St., and the J♣ on Fifth St. But he's been calling you all the way.

Your hand on Sixth St. is two Aces and four Clubs — A♣, 7♣ in the hole, A♠, 5◊, 9♣ and 6♣ up — while your opponent has made two Jacks in-sight, having caught the J♠ on Sixth St.

You feel fairly certain that he has Jacks and Tens, but there is the outside possibility that he has a four-Flush and is going to try to steal the pot. But you think the **best** he could have is the Jacks and Tens.

So when he bets on the sixth card, you raise him. He isn't likely to re-raise with Jacks and Tens, so he just calls and checks on the end. Now on the seventh card, you have a strong drawing hand against Jacks and Tens. **You don't have much the worst of it.** If you improve at all, you figure to win the hand.

So by raising on Sixth St. you've put the **same amount** in the pot you would have anyway, because if he bets out at the end with two Jacks showing, you would have called him, just in case he had busted out with a four-Flush and was trying to steal the pot. If you improve down the river, you bet out. (You've gained an extra bet on Sixth St.)

Once he checks to you on Seventh St., you check right behind him if you **haven't** improved. If he has two-Pair, he wins, of course, but **you haven't put any extra money in the pot** and you had that chance to win the **extra bet.**

SEVENTH STREET PLAY

After the seventh card you have **all** your cards, but playing it correctly is still a necessity. You must remember the **axiom** of successful Seven-Card Stud play: **Get the most value you can out of your hand.**

The three factors in getting value are:

(1) Betting for value.

(2) Raising for value.

(3) Calling for value.

Betting For Value

Suppose you've taken the lead all the way with two Aces until the seventh card, but that is **all** you end up with. You have to think about what you're going to do.

You know that going into the last card, two Aces was almost certainly the best hand, but without improving you want to know if **now** you will be checking and calling, checking and throwing your hand away, betting and getting called, or calling a raise if you do decide to bet.

Once more, the important thing to know — after the cards are out and you have a hand of one Pair — is **how your opponent typically plays** on Seventh St.

If your oponent is the type of player who **will call with one Pair**, you have to feel **obligated to** go ahead and **bet** the hand yourself. For example, you **should bet** if you started with an Ace, raised the pot, and bet the whole way, and he has been calling you with a King-up (and a likely Pair of Kings). Ask yourself if **he would call with a Pair of Kings** in the hope that you were bluffing?

If you believe the answer is **yes**, you should **definitely** go ahead and **bet**. Of course if the answer is **no**, then there would be **absolutely no reason to bet the one Pair**. The only way you would get called by such a person is if he had you beat.

If you make Aces-up, you have to do just as much thinking as you would with only a Pair of Aces. Ask yourself, *"If I check, is my oponent the type of player who would bet Two-Pair?"* If so, **checking** is the **right** thing to do. If he's the type of player who would call you with one Pair, then **betting** is the **right** thing to do.

However, if your opponent is the type who would not call with one Pair, but would bet with Two-Pair, then there is no reason even to bet Aces-up. That's because, in order for him to put any more money in the pot on Seventh St., he would have to make Two-Pair. It would be the **wrong** thing to do to bet Aces-up and win only one bet when he's not going to call you with one Pair anyway. If he makes Two-Pair, he figures to bet on the end and then your check-raise enables you to win **two bets** at the end. **You have gotten extra value on the hand.**

Raising For Value

Suppose you're in the pot with two Queens and your opponent has been representing two Kings while betting all the way, and then he bets at the end.

You look at your seventh card and you have made Two-Pair. You also know that your opponent is somebody who would bet one Pair on the end for value.

Well, you think that he had two Kings on Sixth St., and whether he made three Kings or Kings-up or failed to improve, he would be betting regardless. You have to appreciate the fact that Queens-up could easily be the best hand, but you wonder if it is worth the risk to put in an extra bet (raise).

The first thing you have to consider before raising with Queens-up at the end is whether this particular opponent would think you to be capable of bluffing **without** a hand. If you **don't** think he would, then you just go ahead and **make a flat call.**

The second thing to consider before raising is, what does my Board (Q-6-10-2 offsuit) represent. **If the Board is not too powerful, then it would be pointless to raise.** But if that same Board contained **three Clubs, you can go ahead and raise,** because it **isn't** very **likely that you will be re-raised** unless your opponent has a Full House and isn't afraid of a Flush.

If your opponent is the type of player who would bet one Pair at the end for value, and he has all dead cards and is unlikely to have made Two-Pair, **go ahead and raise.** Now, I am assuming he thinks you are capable of making a bluffing play, but all you are really trying to do is get him to put in an **extra bet.** That is, in fact, **all it can cost you. If he re-raises, you throw away your hand without being concerned that you are throwing away the best.**

It's also possible to get even **triple bets** at the end, and it's against the kind of **aggressive** player who wouldn't call with one Pair but would bet with Two-Pair.

For instance, you have two concealed Pair, Aces-up on Sixth St. and have been betting since Third St. Your opponent has a Board of **10♡, 6♡, 2♣, and 3♣,** and you're pretty sure that he's been going for a Flush the whole way.

At the end you catch another Ace to make Aces-Full, and think, maybe you should check-raise. **Most average and even many good players check-raise with Aces-Full.** But by check-raising, you are making the sort of play that **indicates** you have a big hand. And your opponent, who has finally made his Flush, is likely only to call your bet.

But if you **lead** with a bet, it is **almost a certainty that your opponent will raise** you with a Flush. **By leading, there are any number of things that could happen to make it the right play.** Your opponent could have a Pair with his Flush draw, miss the Flush but make Two-Pair, and call you anyway. Or he could have **K♡-Q♡** in the hole as part of his

Flush draw, again miss the Flush, but catch a King to make two Kings, and call you in hopes you are bluffing.

The **best** possibility is for him to **make the Flush** and you will win a **minimum of one bet**—he might just call—**or** a **maximum of three bets** if he calls your re-raise.

If you are able to predict what your opponent will do in typical situations, you should be able to make raising for value a very profitable play. We call it Power Poker.

Calling For Value

Often you feel that you've had the best hand all the way through, and your opponent (who is **high, but has been checking**), suddenly **bets into you at the end.** If he has shown himself in the past to be a player who will bluff in that situation, **it is to your advantage to call.**

There are many times when you bet all the way with the best hand but fail to improve with any of your last four cards. You feel unlucky not to have helped, and are worried that your opponent drew out on you. But **you are making a common mistake if you throw your hand away when he bets.**

In Limit Seven-Card Stud, the pot is usually so large by Seventh St. that it isn't worthwhile to try and guess when to call and when to throw away — even if the pot is only head-up. If you even rarely make the wrong decision you are costing yourself money. So, if you feel you have the best hand or just **might** have the best hand, go ahead and call, assuming you don't face the threat of a raise by a third player in the pot. **Don't play any guessing games, on Seventh St. for any reason.**

For example, in a $2 ante Seven-Stud game with seven players, there is $14 in the pot to begin with. The low cards bring it in for $4 making a total of $18. Even in a head-up situation, after a raise to $10 and a call with the other players folding, there is $38 in the pot after Third St., $58 after Fourth St., $98 after Fifth St., $138 after Sixth St. and the final $20 bet at the end to make a total of $158. If you don't call that bet with $20, there is a chance you have thrown away $158. You can't afford to be wrong more than once out of nine times.

In the long run, you can do nothing but make money by calling that bet; you're mathematically better off.

Besides the basic logic of this play, there is **another** reason to call for value: **You must prevent players from bluffing you.** If there is such a thing as a defensive call, this is it.

Aside from playing good, solid Seven-Card Stud with a full knowledge of the technical aspects of the game, **the thing that separates the good players from the average players is getting the** *ultimate* **value out of their hands.** Over the course of many sessions, you are going to get **your share** of hands and everybody else is going to get **their share** of hands. By understanding when to bet, raise, and call for value, you are way ahead of the game. When your Full House beats another player's Ace-King Flush, you are going to win a lot of his money. Your goal is to lose **less than he does** when **his** Full House beats **your** Ace-King Flush.

OTHER VALUE PLAYS

In addition to the basic idea of when to bet what hands against whom, there are several other value plays.

One of these involves calling without a hand. This play is rare, but it does come up enough to make it worthwhile to understand. It can win you a lot of money.

Once I saw three top–notch players in a big Limit game, and Player *A* had been losing heavily and was now playing crazily. Player *C* was very conservative and Player *B* was an expert at getting the full worth from his hands.

A was playing almost every pot, including this one, so· you couldn't assume he was at the top of his form, while *B* and *C* were both going for Flushes. On Sixth St., *C* made open Eights, the best hand on the Board, but checked without looking on Seventh St.

A, whose Board was Ace-King-Queen-Seven with three Clubs, came out betting and B looked down to see that he had missed his Flush and ended up with a Pair of Deuces.

But B, fully aware that A was throwing his chips around foolishly, thought he might have A beat, but was of course 100% certain that he didn't have C's two Eights beat. And like any solid player will, he (B) was trying to think how he could win the pot without the best hand.

So B thought, "If I raise this pot now, even if C made another Pair, he probably won't call. But as goofy as A is playing, he might be goofy enough to call if he has as much as a Pair of Three's. The best way to win this pot is to just call and hope that two Deuces has A beat." So B just called.

C squeezed his hand and threw it away (since he didn't help his Pair of Eights). Sure enough, A didn't have a Pair. So B won a pretty decent-sized pot. C immediately went through the roof when the winning hand was shown down after he had thrown away his two Eights, because he wasn't willing to believe that B could make such a sophisticated and well thought out move.

C's first reaction was that A and B were playing partners in order to cheat him out of the pot. But B pointed out, and rightly so, that if he had been trying to run C out of the pot, he would have raised it—not just called. C finally had to concede that B had made a powerful play.

B's play was doubly ingenious because it is possible that C might have seen through a raise, because there is a lot of raising in Seven-Card Stud just to get other people out. C just thought that bettors and raisers can bluff, but callers never can.

That was a case where a *caller* **was bluffing.**

Another value play is raising without a hand—the simple bluff—but in Limit Seven-Card Stud it should be exercised with **caution**. It isn't a play to be used very often, and once you try it against one player and get caught, it is very hard to ever use against that same player again.

There are specific opponents, who bet for value at the end and, if they get raised, meekly throw their hand away and think they are being very clever by saving one extra bet. This is the sort of opponent a good player can take advantage of—the one who will invest one final bet to win one other final bet, but will not invest a second bet to win the whole pot.

I pointed out before how unprofitable it is in the long run to try to guess each particular hand, but there are still players, and **good** players, I should add, who nevertheless manage to **out-think themselves** when given the chance.

As I say, the value play of **raising without a hand** has to be made **only in the most favorable circumstances,** but it is often possible to use it against the same player repeatedly. Just don't try it twice if you've been called once.

A value play that should also be used with extreme caution is saving bets at the end of the hand. I don't want to contradict myself after explaining what a smart percentage play it is to almost always call the last bet or face losing the pot, but if you become a very adept Seven-Card Stud player, and play with the **same people** over and over, you reach a point with certain players where you know their habits so well it is almost as if they are **playing with all their cards turned face-up** on the table.

If you can analyze these players and all their plays—to the extent that you can be sure you are doing the right thing 99 times out of 100—then try to save bets. The best example of this comes after you have been betting one Pair all the way, failed to improve, checked on Seventh St. and then watched the Rock bet out. Don't call.

It's pretty sweet when you find a player like this—you just hope he never runs out of money. But you have to know when he will call you with Two-Pair, when you can bet and when you can check-raise. You have to know whether he will come out bluffing with one Pair or a busted Flush and when to throw your hand away when he bets. Be very certain you are doing the right thing when you start trying to make delicate laydowns on marginal hands.

POSTSCRIPT

Seven-Stud is probably more widely played than all other forms of Poker combined. Because of that, there are literally millions of players who think they know the game. But, I wonder how many of them will still think so after they read this section? And, I also wonder if they'll be able to appreciate the very high level of sophisticated ideas it contains?

I made a special effort to make the Seven-Stud section as concise as possible — without eliminating any important playing strategy or technique. What you have is the meat...and no fat. And that meat is "Filet Mignon".

SUPER/SYSTEM's
POWER POKER COURSE
IN

LOWBALL

LOWBALL

Table of Contents

JOEY *"Howard Hughes"* HAWTHORNE

My Expert Collaborator
on
LOWBALL

The first thing that strikes you about Joey Hawthorne is his self-assurance. He's cool, calm and collected. He has the look and air of a successful businessman and indeed, that's just what he is.

Joey is a Poker player with a plan. Poker playing is a means to an end. As he has discussed with me many times, Joey has watched with dismay almost all the successful card players destroy all or most of their money at some point in their life...either due to bad habits, personal problems, or the one thing nobody can control — time and age. So, Joey's plan has been to invest his money as he has made it in real estate, construction, buildings, etc. He keeps a working bankroll and never touches the money he has invested.

For that reason, Joey really plays hard to win. And play he does. He's an acknowledged master of Ace-to-Five Lowball and is one of the most formidable opponents I've ever played against. Win or lose, his reserve doesn't crack. His discipline at the table is really amazing and while he may get upset, he **never** gets "mad" at his money.

Joey approaches everything he does with an eye to the ultimate potential. Take his car. Most of us would be satisfied with a **Lincoln** or **Cadillac**. Not Joey. He drives a **Rolls Royce**. *"It's simple"*, he told me. *"Most people think I'm just trying to impress everyone. The reality is that the Rolls is a good investment. That car is worth $5,000 more than I paid for it a year and a half ago."* This philosophy dictates everything he does — including Poker. Joey doesn't get into anything unless it makes good business sense.

Joey started playing penny–ante at the age of nine and at sixteen he was taking on the Professionals in **Gardena**. By twenty–one he was self–supporting and had developed his plan for the future.

For four years he did nothing but play Ace–to–Five to accumulate enough money to begin his "Master Plan". While his family is very wealthy and has business interests all over Southern California, Joey states with pride how he **never** took any money from them and got started entirely **on his own**. He's truly a self–made man.

Joey specializes in Lowball. . .but he's an all–around card player. He says he's **not** interested in being known as the best all–around player in the world, but the Lowball players in the western part of America won't dispute the fact he is the premier player at that game.

There's no doubt in my mind that Joey will reach all of his particular goals. Determination alone would probably get him there even if he wasn't as talented as he is. Joey, the specialist. The specialist with a plan.

LOWBALL

Ace-to-Five
Deuce-to-Seven
Seven-Card Razz

INTRODUCTION

The first Lowball game was almost certainly played as a joke. Some guy was probably losing real bad and said, *"It's a shame there ain't a game where the WORST hand wins, 'cause I'd have all the money before daybreak!"*

Naturally everyone agreed to give it a try. Well, you can bet your house that the game they played that night was High-Poker stood on its ears, with 7-5-4-3-2 the best (worst) hand you could come up with — and that Straights and Flushes couldn't win beans in a showdown. That's the kind of Lowball I still prefer today, Texas-style Deuce-to-Seven. Later on I'll explain how you can make big money playing No-Limit Deuce-to-Seven.

First we'll take a look at Lowball in general and at a very popular form of Low Poker — Ace-to-Five. Last I'll say a little about Seven-Card Razz.

If you've never played any sort of Lowball before, the first thing you're going to notice is that it is truly an **action game**. Lowball players (particularly **bad** Lowball players) can find so many hands to play that I sometimes wonder why they even waste their time **looking** before charging into the pot with their chips. With Hold 'em, a Sucker who plays almost every pot is noticed by everyone. In Lowball you can play every single pot for an hour and they'll think you're just one of the boys!

I've seen players jump double-raises to draw three cards to a Seven in limit Ace-to-Five Lowball! Some Lowball players will not only draw one card at a *rough* hand every chance they get, they'll draw two and three and, if they feel **lucky, real lucky**, they'll draw four or five.

Yes! I **have played** against gamblers who yielded to the urge to call a raise, throw their whole hand away and take five! Sure, we're talking about the exception. There **are** players who play **too tight**. But in almost every game, you're going to be against at least one (and often seven!) opponents who **think they're playing Bingo**, who feel that **luck** is the **only** consideration and who are blissfully unaware of the skill factors you're about to learn. After all, when you turn the original idea of Poker upside-down and try for your **worst** hands, there's a lot more *tickets* that seem attractive — to the Sucker!

Low Poker is exciting to people who have the **urge to gamble**. Its seeming simplicity and the fact that they can **often** go into a pot with by far the worst hand and end up stacking the chips are what appeals to them. One of the sorriest things that can happen to a High-Poker player is to have one of his day-in-and-day-out pigeons disappear into a Lowball game and never return. Even though there's a great deal of skill involved in Lowball, the novice suffers the **illusion** that it's only a crap shoot.

So, very frequently a big loser drifts over from Draw Poker to Ace-to-Five or from Seven-Stud to Seven-Razz and you just never see him again. It's Lowball oblivion! They just play night after night at this "no-skill" game, hour after hour until eventually, and quietly, they go busted...

It's been said that *"Lowball is not a game, it's a disease."* And it **is** a disease for a lot of people. You see old ladies sitting in the same seat for twenty hours, scarcely able to pull themselves from the table long enough to go to the John.

If you play by some relatively conservative standards and if you can keep your emotions in check, you can beat the average Lowball game just by playing steady. But you **won't** win anywhere near the most money **available**, and you **won't** beat other strong players. In this section you **will** learn how to get the maximum profit out of your game and how to not only beat the Suckers but how to beat the Pros as well.

Besides the fact that the typical *Lowball Personality* seems to be gamble and luck oriented, many Lowball addicts seem grumpy when compared to High players. I think this irritability comes after years and years of drawing to the *nuts* and coming out with *garbage*. If you're looking for a game to inflict the maximum amount of psychological agony on yourself, Lowball will do the trick. It's the most frustrating game in the world. The reason I'm telling you this is so that you can keep your emotions controlled and **not** *go on tilt*.

It's just **not enough** to play a **disciplined game 85%** of the time and a terrible game 15% of the time. You're dealing in small percentage gains, pot after pot, over a long period of time. **That's** how you make your profit at Low Poker. Bits and pieces. It all mounts up month by month, but **you can** *steam* **it off in one night**. If losing a big pot is going to bother you emotionally, if getting drawn out on four hands in a row is apt to put you *on tilt* or if sitting for a long time and not getting the hands you're looking for will cause you to play inferior hands — **Lowball is not your kind of Poker!**

LOWBALL — *in general*

Forms of Low Poker seem to increase yearly in popularity. In California, where the only two kinds of **legal** Poker are five-card Draw High and five-card Draw Lowball, the Low end now accounts for most of the games. That's right, in California and in many areas of the country, Low Poker has replaced High Poker as the people's choice. Deuce-to-Seven is hugely popular down South. Seven-Card Stud low (called Razz) is increasing in popularity in Las Vegas. Many home games which start out as dealer's choice end up almost entirely Lowball by the time the game breaks up.

No, I don't think Lowball is going to replace High altogether. Because **High games tend to be a lot more challenging** than Low games, there will probably never be a time when true Poker enthusiasts will desert Hold 'em or Seven-Stud or Draw. I'm emphasizing the growing popularity of Lowball only to impress you with the fact that many, many players are willing to *throw off* **a lot of money** treating Lowball as purely a popular game of luck, and there's plenty of opportunity for you to cash-in on their costly Lowball habits.

Just manage your money well, expect a lot of short-term fluctuations (the ups and downs here are greater than in any other kind of Poker) and **stay off** *tilt*. If you can do that, I can show you how to win...

> *Tight but aggressive* — **that's the kind of Lowball player you should strive to be. If you keep that concept in mind, you'll be able to understand why very tight players at almost any form of Lowball are only able to eke out small wins at best and why super loose players slowly go busted. You need to be selective about which hands to play, choosing only those which will be immediately profitable** *(or which are marginal and will bring you profit by enhancing your image on following hands)*. **But when you** *do* **enter a pot, be prepared to put in the** *maximum amount of action* **dictated by the strength of your hand and other game factors.**

Others will judge you as an **action player** *not* by the **number of pots** you play *but* **by the aggressiveness** with which you play your hands.

This generally applies to all forms of Poker, but particularly to Lowball where players are so preoccupied with their own fortunes that you can slip out of pots almost unnoticed. What they **do** remember is how many bets you fling at them when they're involved in a pot with you.

Another way to state this concept is:

Gamble a lot, but only in the right spots.

Not only must you be selective about which hands you give action with, you should be careful **which players** you give action to. You'll find players who gamble much more than is justified mathematically. If you just stick completely to your predetermined game plan, they're very apt to become irritated and stop throwing money your way. But if they see that you're at least splashing **some** extra chips into their pots, they'll appreciate the fact that you're gambling with them. Scarcely ever do they realize that you're slowly but surely taking away hunks of their bankroll by **not** gambling quite as much as they are.

On the other hand, when you're up against the common ordinary variety of Lowball *Rock*, tighten up on the number of bets you put in the pot. They figure to have much better than average hands when they do play against you.

There are a great many *Hard Rocks* who seem to have split personalities. The great majority of the time they just keep grinding away, playing their stable everyday game. Well, suddenly something happens. They lose a few pots to a Sucker who drew three cards...or they start off with A-2-3-4 in Seven-Card Razz against an opponent who has King-Queen showing and end up with a Full House (having to play a Pair for Low) against a Ten. That does the trick! Soon they're playing as bad and as loose as the worst Sucker in the game.

When a *Hard Rock* goes *on tilt*, it's just awesome! And conservative players are much more likely to break down emotionally against *live ones*. After all, it's the *live* players who most often make a totally ridiculous play and draw out on the *Rock*.

Lowball is just that sort of game. It's easy to start playing bad, even though you know better. Above all other things I can teach you about Low Poker, this is the most valuable:

Keep control of your emotions!

This does **not** mean you should be inflexible in your standards. One of the biggest secrets a true Professional Low player has is his ability to adapt *(change gears)* from game to game and from hand to hand.

So. . .

> **Be flexible, but make sure your flexibility is governed by your intellect and *not* by your emotions!**

There are two basic reasons you will occasionally want to vary your play from the minimum standards you will soon learn in this section:

(1) **To adapt to game conditions;**

(2) **To put your opponents off-guard (and to increase your profit expectancy on future plays).**

Now let's get into the particular strategies that will enable you to win in specific kinds of Lowball games.

FOCUSING ON
ACE-to-FIVE

Ace-to-Five Lowball is a five-card game which allows you to draw any number of cards you choose to improve your hand. Usually it's played with a Joker in the deck, and the Joker is used as whatever card will make the best possible hand you could have.

Two uncommon variations of Ace-to-Five are:

(1) **Without the Joker (52-card deck) and**

(2) **a game where Straights and Flushes have high value.**

In the popular form of Ace-to-Five that I'll be discussing, Straights and Flushes are **not** considered High hands. All the Pairs of hands you see here have identical values and would tie if held in the same showdown.

ACE-to-FIVE

(California-style with the Joker)

The hands in columns *A* and *B* have the same value

<u>*A*</u>   <u>*B*</u>

The **Ace** is the **lowest** card you can get.

Basically Ace-to-Five is played eight-handed and these are the three most usual variations:

Blind. The player in first position (to the left of the dealer) puts in a bet before he gets his cards. Usually, because there's an ante, in addition to the Blind, it becomes impossible to just sit back and wait for the nuts. This is the most popular form of Limit Ace-to-Five Lowball. Sometimes the bet after the draw is twice the limit before the draw, but often it's played Straight-Limit — the bet **before** *and* **after** the draw being **equal**. Straight-Limit is the more popular form of the game in northern California.

Gardena Card Clubs have games which are usually two-bet (the double-limit after the draw variety). Some of the games are more than just one Blind. **Raise-Blind** is a popular game. First position opens Blind, and second position raises before getting any cards. That really stimulates action. But, when you play in a game like that, be prepared for some pretty big fluctuations because you have far less control over your Lowball destiny than with a single-Blind game where you can be a lot more selective about which hands you play.

Occasionally games are played with **three** Blinds, and if you're really interested in a crap shoot where your Lowball skill must take a long time to overshadow the luck factor, there was a game running recently in **Gardena** that was **four** Blinds! First position bet $20, second position raised to $40, third position made it $60 and fourth position called those three raises and raised $20 more (for a total of $80) before getting any cards. Bets from that point on were just by increments of $20, so you could afford to play very, very loose Poker. In any of these Blind games it's customary that the Blind is *live*. That means if the Blind bet is only called (and **not** raised), the **Blind himself** has the option of raising.

Straddle. Nobody antes in this variation. There are usually three positions that are required to put in chips. First position usually invests one chip, second position two chips and third position three chips. Then, the betting and raising will usually be by three-chip units. Very often the Dealer is one of the three positions who puts in a small amount (often called **incorrectly** the *ante*). Then first position puts in the medium amount and second position the full Blind.

Pass-Out. Here there is no Blind. It's a straight-ante game. If you pass before the draw, you must throw your cards away.

There are also various rules which make one Ace-to-Five game different from another. In some games, you can check-and-raise, but in most limit forms of Ace-to-Five, sandbagging is **not** permitted after the draw. And, before the draw, sandbagging is impossible since either there's already a Blind in the pot or (in Pass-Out) you must bet or throw your hand away. Sandbagging is usually reserved for No-Limit Lowball — especially Deuce-to-Seven.

A very common Ace-to-Five provision is that you **must bet a** *Seven*. As objectional as this concept may at first seem to serious Poker enthusiasts, I really think that in limit-play this rule **stimulates the action** and is, therefore, **desirable**. There are two interpretations of this rule:

(1) If you check a Seven (or better), and someone else bets and you call with what turns out to be the better hand, you win the pot but you **lose the action**. In other words, you must give back your opponent's last bet. There are very rare occasions when even a good player will — if this is the rule — deliberately check a Seven that seems **almost** *hopeless* and then call because the pot is big enough to justify it. Their reasoning is that if they **do** bet the Seven, they are looking at an almost-certain raise.

(2) If you check a Seven, you lose the **whole** pot. Obviously, if this is the governing rule, you just don't ever check a Seven unless your hand is so hopeless that you're flat out surrendering your investment in the pot.

Another uncommon option for Ace-to-Five is where you **cannot** check and raise, but you **can** check **any** hand including Sevens, Sixes and Bicycles. Here, you can check the stone-cold *nuts* right into an unwary opponent...and you can **just call** him if he bets.

Sometimes, there's a limit on the number of raises allowed. In other games you can trap a player in the middle of a three-handed pot and raise indefinitely. Some games set a limit on the number of raises, if there are three or more active players, but allow as many raises as you're willing to go if you're head-up.

> **The many combinations of the rules you just discussed make it impossible for me to give you exact advice for every possible contingency. But you'll be able to play** *no matter what* **the rules and standards are by following the advice presented here and adjusting to the game structure using my advice.**

Let's agree on this structure. The game is $20 Blind, $40 after the draw with an ante of $2. That means first position opens for $20 before getting any cards and every one of the eight players must ante. The chips in the pot (before there's any action) total $36. You bet and raise by increments of $20 before the draw and $40 after the draw.

There's no limit on raises and if you check a *Seven* after the draw, you **lose** *only* the **action** (after the draw). You're playing with a 53-card deck, Aces are low, Straights and Flushes do **not** count against you, you can draw as many cards as you want or stand pat and the Joker is used as the lowest possible card in your hand. ·

GRUMPY and the KID

That last (Joker) rule reminds me of the time I was in a No-Limit Ace-to-Five game and a player new to town sat down. We had to explain the rules to him. Low hand wins, Ace is Low, you can draw as many as you want, you can't check a Seven, and so on...

"How do you use the Joker?" he wanted to know.

A guy named Grumpy was growing real impatient with this novice and snapped, *"Use it for anything you want, Son! The Joker's anything you want it to be. Now will somebody DEAL for Godsake?"*

Well, a few hands later Grumpy and this new kid got involved in a small pot. The kid bet and Grumpy called. *"Whatcha got, boy?"*

The kid laid down Joker-7-6-5-4 and announced: *"Eight-high Straight"*, obviously more familiar with High Poker than Low and conditioned to thinking of the Joker fitting at the **upper** end. *"You guys SAID that it doesn't count against me to have a Straight,"* the kid said nervously, spreading his cards on the table.

"It DON'T count against you, kid," said Grumpy, eager to take advantage of the fact that the kid had misinterpreted his hand, *"but I got myself a better Eight."* He spread 8-7-6-3-2.

Even though I was feeling sorry for the kid, I didn't say anything because it was considered bad ethics at **that** game to butt in on someone else's pot.

I guess the kid figured it out for himself shortly after Grumpy dragged in the chips because you could see his face redden. But he just sat there and waited.

I could nearly read his thoughts, and it didn't take me the least bit by surprise when it happened...

There was just a small amount of money in before the draw. Grumpy and the kid were going at each other again. The kid had opened, called a small raise and had drawn one. Grumpy was pat. The kid checked. Grumpy put an Eight in the *window* before betting. It was something he liked to do to entice a call and I knew he **had** the Eight and probably a pretty good one. Since it was illegal for the kid to have checked a Seven, Grumpy moved all-in with his chips.

"I don't have that much money," the kid protested.

"Well, just call what you got then. I have a Jack in my hand, so you BETTER call."

So the kid called what he had in front of him, about four hundred dollars worth which was **ten times** the amount of the pot before the draw.

"You'll need an Eight–Four to beat me, Son," Grumpy said, showing down his 8–5–3–2–A. *"You shouldn't have listened to my Poker talk. I never would have bet so much on a Jack."*

"Well, I happen to HAVE an Eight–Four," said the kid. Immediately Grumpy's rare smile wilted.

Then the kid spread Joker–4–3–2–A.

"Ha–ha!" laughed Grumpy. *"I get my money back! The boy's got a Wheel. You can't check a Wheel, sonny, I told you that! I get my money back!"* He grabbed for his $400.

The kid stopped him *"You DON'T get ANYTHING back,"* he said. *"A while ago I had Seven, Six, Five, Four and the Joker which I thought was an Eight-high Straight. You took the pot with an Eight. But really I had a SEVEN didn't I?"*

"Well, it's not my fault if a guy's stupid enough to use the Joker for an Eight. You want to call the Joker an Eight, kid, that's just dandy with me."

"Okay, then, I'm calling the Joker an Eight. I just checked an Eight–Four and you bet an Eight–Five. I'm taking the pot!"

Well, Grumpy tried to argue himself out of it, but we other players just didn't want to **hear** it. The kid took the pot, and rightly so.

By most standards, the Joker in Lowball is your **lowest** possible card — **not** whatever you want it to be.

Anyhow, the game we're using for an example is $20 Blind, $40 after the draw and a $2 ante.

DERIVATION
of the
PLAYING STANDARDS

Before I discuss these playing standards, you should know about the trouble I went to in making sure they are the **best guidelines ever published.** First, my expert *Joey Hawthorne* and I spent days going over actual game situations and pooling our years of playing experience. We came up with a set of guidelines that would make **any** Lowball addict envious. But I didn't figure even **that** was enough. We talked to a lot of Professionals and a couple of mathematicians. And then my Draw expert, *"Crazy Mike"* put me in touch with a noted mathematician, *Dean Zes,* who has probably done more work on the minimum standards of *Ace-to-Five* than anyone else. I got what I wanted and more!

But still we weren't done with it! There was another all-day conference with *Joey* and my other experts and bit by bit, taking into consideration the playing habits of the average opponents, the effect my recommended aggressive strategy has upon other player's emotions and just plain super-power Poker theory, we had our final guidelines as the sun was rising.

Well, you just **aren't** ever **going to find** any **better advice** than the standards given throughout this section. I think that we've taken the world's best mathematical work and welded it to the soundest actual playing advice available, and fine-tuned it into the high-powered overkill guidelines you're now going to deal with.

MINIMUM RAISING REQUIREMENTS

What follows is a list of minimum hands you must hold in order to enter a pot in this game, depending on what position you're in and **assuming** no one else, except the Blind, is already in the pot.

MIMINUM TO RAISE THE BLIND

Your Position	Minimum Pat hand **without** the Joker	Minimum Pat hand **with** the Joker	Minimum draw **without** the Joker	Minimum draw **with** the Joker
2	9-7-6-4-3	9-8-5-4-Joker	7-4-3-2	7-6-5-Joker
3	9-8-4-3-2	9-8-6-5-Joker	7-5-4-3	8-5-4-Joker
4	9-8-5-4-3	9-8-7-6-Joker	7-6-5-4	8-6-5-Joker
5	9-8-6-5-4	10-9-5-4-Joker	8-5-4-3	{ 8-7-5-Joker 3-2-Joker* }
6	9-8-7-6-5	10-9-6-5-Joker	8-6-5-4	{ 8-7-6-Joker 5-4-Joker* }
7	10-9-5-4-3	10-9-8-5-Joker	{ 9-7-6-5 3-2-A* }	{ 9-8-7-Joker 6-5-Joker* }
8	10-9-8-7-6	J-10-9-6-Joker	{ 10-8-2-A 7-6-5* }	{ 10-9-5-Joker 8-7-Joker* }

These are two-card draws.

Now...notice that you **don't** just come barging into the pot in 2nd position with a straight Nine. That's a big mistake a lot of Lowball players make — raising it up with 9-8-7-6-5. Sure, you can play 9-7-6-4-3, but that's the **minimum** hand, the one on the fence where it's roughly break-even. (You could either play it **Pat** against one opponent **or** *break* and **draw** to the Seven.)

If you have the Joker you can play a *rougher* hand (9-8-5-4-Joker). That's because the Joker makes it less likely that others will have good playing hands. And, even though it's very unlikely you would want to *break* this Nine and try for the Eight, you have three extra cards that make the Eight when you hold the Joker than when you don't.

If you're next to the Blind *(under the gun)* in 2nd position, 7-6-5-4 is **not** a playable hand with the double bet after the draw. Ninety percent of the players I know **do** come in with a *rough* one-card Seven *under the gun* — and they lose a lot of money for that reason. You can see that the earliest position you can safely come in with a Straight–Seven draw (**without** the Joker) is 4th, with two players between you and the Blind (to your right) having already passed. (We're talking about an eight-handed game, remember.) **Any sort of one-card Seven is playable if you have the Joker.**

It's in the late positions where most players really hurt their game — either by playing much too loose or by letting money-winning opportunities slip by.

If you're the dealer and no one else is in the pot except the Blind, go ahead and *pop it* with 10-9-8-7-6. Even though this is a **marginal** hand...you'll just break about even in the long run and the result is good for your image. Players will give you more action on following hands.

That's why I'm telling you to *always* **play your marginal hands**.

You can also raise the Blind with one card to a good 10-8. And, if you have the Joker, one card to a *smooth* 10-9 will be enough. Notice that you **can play** two-card draws under **selective** conditions. **Without** the Joker, you should **never** play a two-card draw until the 7th position, and even then it should be perfect — A-2-3 (ABC). As the dealer, it's okay to raise the Blind with **any** two-card draw to a Seven (or better) even if you **don't** hold the Joker.

If you **have** the Joker, your two-card drawing standards are considerably relaxed. You can play 4-3-Joker in 5th position, 5-4-Joker in 6th, 6-5-Joker in 7th and 8-7-Joker in 8th. (You probably suspect that wherever possible I've tailored these guidelines so that they are more easily remembered — and you're right!)

Now you're probably wondering: *How flexible are these standards?*

The answer is: If you stick to them absolutely without ever varying your game, you'll show a nice profit. You'll *grind out* a living. But I didn't market this book just so you could *grind out* a living. I want you to do big things with your Poker game.

Sure, you should be flexible.

But that's not all. If you're going to play Lowball **for all it's worth, you MUST be flexible.**

For example, if you're in 6th position with a two-card draw to a 7-6-5 and both 7th and 8th indicate they're about to throw their cards away, raise it! You only need what you would have required had you been in the dealer seat. If the game is very tight, you can loosen up your 5th position requirements and make the first raise with a one-card draw to **any** Eight. If both the dealer and the Blind tend to be tighter than normal, you can raise in 7th with two cards to **any** Seven.

In a $20 before-the-draw, $40 after-the-draw game with a $2 ante...

You can play this hand from 2nd position...

but you *cannot* **play this hand...**

You can play this hand in 3rd position if *only the Blind* **is active...**

but you *cannot* **play this hand...**

You can play this hand in 4th position if *only the Blind* **is active...**

but you *cannot* **play this hand...**

You can play this hand in 5th position if *only the Blind* is active...

but you *cannot* play this hand...

That 9◇ may look tempting, but remember one-card to a Nine *isn't* playable in 5th position. Against any player but the Blind, you'll have to *draw first*.

You can play this hand in 6th position if *only the Blind* is active...

but you *cannot* play this hand...

You can play this hand in 7th position if *only the Blind* is active...

but you *cannot* play this hand...

You can play this hand in 8th position if *only the Blind* is active...

but you *cannot* play this hand...

Comparing the Pat hand you **can** play when you hold the Joker in 2nd position with the hand you need if you **don't** have the Joker will give you some idea of that card's value.

Looking at the examples for the 3rd position, you can appreciate how much more potent a Pat Nine is than a Pat Ten. And only a **good** 9-8 is even playable in this position.

Although you can begin playing **any** one-card draw to a Seven as early as 4th position, a one-card draw to 8-7-2-A (played by the vast majority of Lowball enthusiasts) is **financially disastrous!**

From 5th position, 2-A-Joker is playable, but not 3-2-A.

A Straight-Nine is playable from 6th position if no other player has come in before you. But a big mistake many players make here is raising with *rough* Pat Tens. The *Minimum Requirements* table allows you to play 10-9-6-5-Joker here, but **only** because you have the **option** of playing the 6-5-Joker if necessary **and** because the presence of the Joker makes it more difficult for others to hold good cards in the 7th, 8th and Blind positions.

You can begin to be pretty aggressive with two-card draws in 7th position, since there's just the dealer and the Blind left to punish you. But, remember, there's a **big difference** between two-cards to 3-2-A **(playable)** and two-cards to 7-6-5 **(definitely** *not* **playable).**

Raising the Blind when you're the dealer and no one else has played requires the **most judgment** of any of the positional plays. You can use a lot of flexibility here. If the player in the Blind is very conservative, you can **almost** raise and rap pat on **anything.** And **anything** means **nothing.** What's more, against certain very conservative players, you can *always* **raise** and stand pat because they'll **never** call after the draw **unless** they make a Nine or better. Many players, though, lose bundles of cash trying to "rob" the Blind at every opportunity. Against a reasonable player, you cannot **routinely** raise and stand pat on a Queen or draw one to a Jack. **You cannot draw three cards EVER**...and two to a Nine is *almost* **always** a loser. Under average conditions, a Straight-Ten is your **minimum** raising-the-Blind hand when you do **not** hold the Joker...a *rough* (but **not** *the roughest*) Jack when you **do** hold the Joker.

Adjust to the habits of the player in the Blind. He's the **only** one you have to worry about when you're the dealer and no one else has played. You can really **focus** on him, and him alone.

Play your players!

What I've just suggested should give you good information on which hands to play when no one else has already entered the pot. But, there's probably a big question in your mind...

Should you raise or just call?

Raise. *Almost* **always raise if you're the first player in the pot** *against the Blind.*

Here's three good reasons:

(1) The game (with the antes **plus** the Blind) is structured for action, and players almost always bring it in with a raise. When you *slow-play* a big hand, others are **suspicious** *and* **reluctant to give you action.** If they **do** raise and you re-raise, the betting generally ends there.

(2) Playing marginal hands by just calling runs **contrary** to the aggressive image you should present. And when you just call with big hands, you seldom make as much money as you would if you raised to begin with. Players **expect** you to put in the first raise. It **doesn't** scare them out of pots any more than a plain old call.

(3) Just calling and later re-raising **irritates** the other players for no real reason in limit Ace-to-Five. They may retaliate and stop giving you action.

Occasionally you might just call for the sake of variety. But, in general, **if you're the first player to put money in the pot...RAISE!**

THE IMPORTANCE
of the JOKER

You probably noticed from the *MINIMUM TO RAISE THE BLIND* table how much more liberally you can play if you hold the Joker than if you don't.

There are two really important reasons you'd rather draw at hands with the Joker.

(1) If you have it...your opponent won't.

(2) Your chances of making a hand are significantly improved...when you have the Joker.

The first reason needs little explanation. Not only are your opponent's chances of holding a Pat hand reduced because you have the Joker, the chances of him having a real good drawing hand are also drastically cut. So, at the same time, he **can't** have the benefits associated with drawing to a hand with the Joker. You **do** have them.

Take a quick scan of the Ace-to-Five tables in the *APPENDIX* and you can learn some valuable facts.

There are more Pat Bicycles (5-4-3-2-A) **with** the Joker than **without**. About 24% of **all** Pat Eights (or better) **include** the Joker. [When you have the Joker you're **reducing** your opponents chances of having a Pat Eight (or better) by about one-sixth.]

If you draw one card to a *Wheel* and you hold the Joker, you'll make it 16.7% of the time. But, **without** the Joker in your hand, you'll only make it 10.4% of the time. The figures for drawing one card to a Six are 25% with the Joker and 18.8% without.

> **As you draw to** *rougher* **hands,** *the importance of the Joker* **diminishes** *sharply* **— so much so that if you're drawing to a Ten-high and hold the Joker you'll make it 58% of the time, but even** *without* **the Joker, you'll connect 52% of the time.**

Draw two to a Bicycle, though, and you'll really feel the impact of the Joker. It's **exactly** *twice as hard* (46 to 1) to make a *Wheel* if you **don't** have the Joker as it is if you do have the Joker (22.5 to 1). (If you're not real familiar with how odds work, I assure you 22.5 to 1 — one chance in 23.5 — is **exactly** *half of* 46 to 1 — one chance in 47.)

It's about 6 to 1 against making a Seven if you draw two to 7-6-Joker, but it's about 9 to 1 against making a Seven drawing to 7-2-A.

You'll make a Bicycle 16.7% of the time drawing to this hand...

but only 10.4% drawing to this hand...

If you draw two cards to this...

but if you draw two cards to this...

it's **46 to 1 against making a Wheel.**

the odds are only **22.5 to 1 against making a** *Wheel.*

It's **6 to 1 against making this Seven...**

but **9 to 1 against making this Seven...**

A really telling test of the strength of the Joker is this: Player *A* draws one card to 4-3-2-A, throwing away a

King, while his opponent *B* draws one card at Joker–3–2–A, throwing away a Queen.

Well, if you think this is a close contest, you better figure it again. Hand *B* wins (of those that are not tied) 57% of the time. That means *A* only wins 43%. And you probably thought it was just a small edge.

A LOWBALL
PROPOSITION

To dramatize this difference, here's a proposition you can make:

Give the Sucker Hand *A* and you take Hand *B*:

Hand *A* (Sucker's)   **Hand *B* (Yours)**

You each discard one. Now you lay him 2 to 1 that you can win five hands in a row **before he can**. (Ties **don't** count.) The deck (consisting of the 43 remaining cards) is shuffled each time before you can draw one card each. You can lay 2 to 1 without worrying about it because you're actually around a 4 to 1 favorite to be **first** to win five times in a row.

> The last word here is that, when you're playing Ace-to-Five with the usual 53-card deck, you better be sure to give the Joker some respect!

How to Play
WHEN SOMEONE ELSE
HAS ALREADY RAISED

Here you **don't** have to deal with a chart, because there's a rule of thumb you can apply if you're familiar with the *minimum requirements* for being the first in the pot.

You need roughly the same minimum hand as the first raiser.

If he raised early and you're sitting **just** to his left, **tighten up** a little because not only does he **probably** have the best hand, there are many players yet to worry about. (You can call even though he probably has the best hand...because the pot is laying you **much more than even money**.)

If he raised early, no one else played, and you're in a late position, you can **relax** your standards a bit and play hands slightly worse than his probable minimum. That's because there'll very likely be just the two of you competing for the pot.

Now **there's** an **important** concept:

> **Often you** *don't* **need to be the odds-on favorite against one opponent, because you can** *both be money favorites.*

Your strategy, for instance, when 3rd position opens is: If you have roughly what his minimum hand should be, you should play. If there are a lot of players still to act, be slightly more conservative, and if there are few players left to act, play a bit more liberally.

When there are two (or more) active players in front of you, you've got to use a lot of judgment. All sorts of factors are involved here — the mathematically proper hand with which the first raiser should have played (see the minimum suggestions for first player in), what kind of players the callers are and the temperaments of all those involved in the pot (is anyone on tilt?). You're going to have to incorporate much of the advice in this section in making *play* or *no play* decisions against **two** *or more* players.

The really big thing to keep in mind is this:

> When there are no active players except you and the Blind, the most important consideration is *your position*.

> When there are already *other* active players in the pot, the most important consideration is the *position* of the *first raiser*. (We assume that it was brought in for a raise, which is standard. You should *call* for one bet with about the same hands you would have called with for two bets.)

> You set *your* standards by *his* standards.

And, unless other players are completely oblivious to what's going on, they'll also make some attempt to play or not play according to the position of the first raiser.

Here are some situations which arise again and again in actual play when there's already one or more active players in the pot. But first let me warn you that these are assumed to be players with just **average** playing habits. You **must** observe your opponents and make profitable adjustments.

What to do in SOME COMMON SITUATIONS

(1) You hold this hand in 7th position...

It's raised in 2nd position, 3rd position calls and 6th position re-raises.

You should pass. A Pat Eight is just **not** a winner against two strong positions and a **very** *strong* re-raiser. There's a very high probability that position Six already has a Pat hand better than yours.

Position Three is **almost certainly drawing,** and a very good rule is:

> **Any player who** *flat* **calls the first raiser is probably drawing.**

But even so, 2nd position also **might** very well have a Pat hand better than yours already. And even if they each draw a card, you're not much of a money favorite. You're going to wind up winning about your share of the time, and your hand will be very vulnerable when bet into by one of the draws. Additionally, you have to be wary of more raises before the draw.

(2) You hold this hand in 3rd position...

Position Two brings it in for a raise.

Just call. **Don't** re-raise because you will show more of a profit if you can get others in this pot. Besides, if 2nd position is pat and if no one else plays, you'll take a beating head-up. If he draws one, you **are** a nice favorite, but **not good enough.** By just calling you disguise your hand, and this very often works to your benefit.

(3) You hold this hand in 8th (dealer) position...

The first raise is in 3rd position, 4th, 5th and 7th positions all call.

Re-raise. The three callers are almost surely **all** drawing, and there's a good chance position Three will also draw. Even if he's Pat, you're getting far the best of this situation moneywise if you put in another bet.

(4) You hold this hand in 4th position...

The first raise comes from 2nd position and 3rd position folds. **Re-raise.** Although there's **more than just a slight chance** the first raiser has a better Pat hand and although you'll be **vulnerable** *after the draw*, you don't want a lot of players drawing to beat you.

(5) You hold this hand in 7th position...

It is raised in 4th position and 5th position calls.

Pass. Barring special Tells, and unless you're in the Blind or the Dealer position, *never* **play a straight Nine against a raiser** *and* **a caller**. Period.

RAISING
WITH A PAT 'SEVEN'
How many is right?

How many raises should you put in with a *rough* Pat Seven? Against **some** players you can raise ten or more times because they give excessive action. Against tight players, four bets is usually right.

There's a big difference between the roughest and the smoothest Seven. The odds against getting **any Seven or better** Pat are **93.2 to 1**. The odds against getting a **7-4 or better** Pat are **238 to 1**. Naturally, you can put in more bets with a smooth Seven.

LET'S BURY THIS THEORY

There's a theory that ought to be put to rest. The theory is that if you have perfect drawing cards like 4-3-2-Joker against three or more opponents, you can almost raise forever. I don't know how that bit of advice got started, but you hear it said so often that it deserves special comment.

I guess the reason people think you can play super one-card Joker draws so aggressively is that there's almost a 42% chance of them making an Eight or better. And even if it's just an Eight that they make, their's is going to be an 8-4 and that sure beats a heck of a lot of hands, they figure. Besides, all the callers are probably drawing — and that means 4-3-2-Joker is a pretty decent favorite against the other draws.

Well, that's a good reason to justify the first **re-raise** and **maybe one more** after that. But when you and the original Opener keep raising back at each other — even assuming the others are going to call a double-raise indefinitely — there comes a time when an Eight's **no longer**

good if you make one — you need a Seven. A few raises more and you need a Six. Well, that's all right, you've still got a 25% shot at making **that** hand. But eventually you **need the Bicycle** *just to tie*. You can't keep raising forever! You've got to stop sometime. But here's the most crucial reason why you should back off:

With four players in the pot there are less desirable cards left in the deck than normally. The deck is *poor*. It's going to be much harder than usual for you to make the hands you're after — and if the first raiser is Pat (and he **definitely is** after a lot of raises **when you hold the Joker**) you **must** make a hand.

That's another reason why you can play a rough Pat Seven very aggressively against four or more players. Here you should usually put in five or more bets before stopping, just **because** the deck is *poor*.

What to do
WHEN YOU'RE THE BLIND

Probably more money is lost trying to defend the Blind than anywhere else. You see players calling in the Blind and drawing four cards against a 2nd position raise. You see players who **never** lay down hands in the Blind against a single raise. It takes **two raises** to get **them** out, and then they sometimes call if they have reasonable two-card draws or a rough one-card try.

Forget it! There's no quicker way to go busted.

Here is a chart that tells you **when** to call and on **what** you should call with in the Blind...

MINIMUM REQUIREMENTS TO CALL A RAISE WHEN YOU'RE THE BLIND
(against one player)

Raiser's Position	Minimum 1-card draw **without** the Joker	Minimum 1-card draw **with** the Joker	Minimum 2-card draw **without** the Joker	Minimum 2-card draw **with** the Joker
2	8-5-4-3	9-7-5-Joker	4-3-2	7-4-Joker
3	8-6-4-3	9-7-6-Joker	5-4-3	7-5-Joker
4	8-6-5-4	9-8-3-Joker	6-4-3	7-6-Joker
5	8-7-5-4	9-8-4-Joker	6-5-4	8-3-Joker
6	8-7-6-5	9-8-5-Joker	7-4-3	8-4-Joker
7	9-7-6-5	9-8-6-Joker	7-5-4	8-5-Joker
8	9-8-6-5	10-8-7-Joker	7-6-5	8-6-Joker

If it's raised in an early position, it is **not** correct to call with a one-card draw to **any** *rough* Eight. Sure, against some players you can call profitably with a one card try with an 8-7-6-5, but against certain *Hard Rocks*, you might have to be drawing at a **perfect** Eight or better.

Notice that the span of one-card draws to Nines (under the minimum one-card draw **with** the Joker column) **doesn't** seem to change much whether the raiser is in position Two or position Seven. But, in fact, there's a great difference in the frequency with which you'll be dealt a one-card draw to 9-7-5-Joker (or better) and the times you'll get a one-card try at 9-8-6-Joker (or better).

Now take a look at those two-card draws. You see that the minimum two-card tries **without** the Joker are a little more rigid than what you'd be drawing to if you threw away the highest card of your minimum one-card draw without the Joker (and drew two). This holds true comparing the one-card Joker tries with the two-card Joker draws.

Naturally, this will bring about some sticky dilemmas. Do you draw one or two when you seem to have about the borderline hand in each category?

Well, that's not much of a dilemma at all. Since this chart pits you against a single opponent, you're *usually* **better off** drawing one. When there's **more than** one opponent, you should give consideration to drawing two, but *only because* **rough hands are** *less* **desirable as the number of players increases.** So **when there are a lot of active players,** *don't* **draw at rough hands.**

The great **disadvantage** of being the Blind is that you have to **draw first** and then **act first** when it's time to bet. That's why defending the Blind is **not** as good a practice as most people think.

I'm sure you noticed that there were no Pat hands on the *Minimum to Call a Raise When You're the Blind* chart. Well, I didn't forget. Here's something you should know:

> **It is almost never proper to** *just* **call with a Pat hand in the Blind.**

If you have a borderline Pat **playing** hand, you should usually raise. Otherwise you'll have to check weakly after the draw. Besides, tricky players will often rap Pat behind you, and you're going to have trouble calling their subsequent bet unless you **know** they're likely to steal the pot with this sort of maneuver.

You'll look a lot more aggressive and help your table-image considerably if you re-raise with any **playable** Pat hand as the Blind (especially against one opponent).

And that leads us right on to the next chart. What hands should you re-raise one player with if you're the Blind?

MINIMUM REQUIREMENTS TO
RE-RAISE WHEN YOU'RE THE BLIND
(against one player)

Raiser's Position	Minimum Pat hand **without** the Joker	Minimum Pat hand **with** the Joker	Minimum draw **without** the Joker	Minimum draw **with** the Joker
2	9-8-5-4-3	9-8-6-A-Joker	4-3-2-A	6-4-3-Joker
3	9-8-6-3-2	9-8-6-5-Joker	5-4-3-A	6-5-4-Joker
4	9-8-6-5-4	9-8-7-A-Joker	6-3-2-A	7-3-2-Joker
5	9-8-7-3-2	9-8-7-3-Joker	6-4-3-A	7-4-3-Joker
6	9-8-7-4-3	9-8-7-5-Joker	6-5-4-A	7-5-4-Joker
7	9-8-7-5-4	10-8-7-6-Joker	7-4-3-A	7-6-5-Joker
8	9-8-7-6-3	10-9-7-6-Joker	7-5-4-A	8-4-3-Joker

There are only slight differences between the Pat hands you can re-raise with if an early position raises, and those you can re-raise with if a late position raises. On most of the borderline drawing hands, you have an **option** of just **calling**. Naturally, you **might** just call no matter what the strength of your hand if this strategy figures to make you more profit after the draw. (But remember, your aggressive stature will be enhanced **whenever** you raise.)

Notice that the one-card draws you can re-raise with are **considerably** *stronger* than the ones you can call with.

A really sticky problem is what to do with a Pat Ten in the Blind if 7th or 8th position raises. Your hand is seldom worth a re-raise, but if you simply call and rap Pat you'll look very weak and vulnerable.

The solution seems to be to **never** re-raise with a *rough* Pat Ten. If you have a perfectly Straight-Ten, it may *not* **even be playable** against normal competition in late positions. Give consideration to discarding the Ten and drawing to the Nine (but **not** a totally Straight-Nine).

This **unusual strategy** is an **exception** to this general rule:

Almost **never break a Ten to draw to a Nine,** *and almost* **never break a Nine to draw to an Eight.**

Against **more than one opponent**, you **need stronger Pat** hands.

Let's look at some common game situations...

The first raise comes from 2nd position, and you're holding this hand in the Blind...

Pass. Even though you have the Joker, this is **not** a playable one-card draw, and the Pat Ten is a loser.

You hold this hand in the Blind. The raise was in 3rd position and 5th position re-raised...

Call. This suggests a bit of advanced strategy we haven't yet discussed. Even though your hand seems strong enough to put in another raise, you'll sometimes get **maximum value** by just calling. If you put in a third raise, it might drive out the original raiser (and you **don't** want that to happen). What's more, you'll have identified your draw as being really strong. Your best money-winning option is to *slow-play* this one.

You're in the Blind with this hand. The dealer has raised you...

Call. You can play **any** two-card draw to a Seven.

You have this hand in the Blind and 6th position raises you. . .

You *may* **re-raise** (but you don't *have* to). The chart suggests this will sometimes bring the maximum profit. But a word of caution here. Re-raising just one opponent when you're drawing can be bad practice. If he's Pat **he** often has a **big advantage**. If he draws one to a good hand, **your advantage is small**. But. . .Always raise two or more opponents when you're drawing to a quality hand like a *smooth* **Seven with the Joker (or any better draw than that).**

HOW TO DRAW
when you must

This is your hand. . .

You put in the first raise from 3rd position. Everyone has folded except the Blind, and he has re-raised. You called.

The Blind has already drawn one. Should you stand Pat or draw one also?

The answer is an emphatic — **Stand Pat!**

And this hand points to a basic concept which you **must know** if you're going to get the most out of your Lowball game.

> *When a lone opponent has drawn one-card,* **DON'T break a Nine or a Ten if you are apt to be drawing the worst.**

It's debatable whether you should stand on a 10-8-6-5-4 if your opponent figures to be drawing **only** *slightly* better, but **under most conditions** (against the better draw), **you should rap Pat**. And you should **always** rap Pat with a Nine if your opponent's draw is likely to be better than yours.

Conversely, if you figure to be drawing better than your opponent, you should almost always break.

> **You should** *never* **rap Pat with a 10-7 if your opponent is drawing to an Eight.**

The principle behind these concepts is: When you rap Pat with a Nine against a one-card draw, you're the favorite. (Even if he's drawing to a 6-4 with a Joker and your hand is a 9-7-6-5-4, you'll end up with the best hand 51% of the time.) With a Ten, you're the underdog (and that's why you **should** *consider* **breaking** when your one-card draw is *almost* **as good** as the other guy's). Often, particularly in straight-limit games (or if your opponent's all in), you'll end up with a higher profit expectancy if you stay Pat than if you draw.

If you have this hand...

and an opponent has drawn one card in front of you, you should draw one also! This follows the rule of breaking the Nine when you figure to being drawing best. Yes, you *will win* **more pots** if you rap Pat, but you *won't win* **as much money** because you can't bet, raise or call as liberally after the draw, and you can't win the really big action. After the draw, remember, the bets are twice what they were before the draw.

When it's a straight-limit game, you **should** think about standing Pat on the 9-3-2-A-Joker. Of course, in No-Limit and Pot-Limit games, you will **always** *draw*.

When you have to choose between rapping Pat and drawing two, use this rule:

> *Stay Pat* **if indications are that you have the best hand going against one opponent. If he draws,** *always* **stay Pat.**

Against two or more opponents, draw two to 10-9-3-2-A.

Yes, there are situations where **one** card to the 9-3-2-A is more profitable than **two** to the Wheel, but wherever that's true, the option to stand Pat prevails. In other words, your choice is between rapping Pat (with the 10-9-3-2-A) and drawing two (to the 3-2-A). The one-card option with this hand (drawing to the 9-3-2-A) doesn't figure to be important.

But if this is your hand...

you sure have a dilemma. If one player has drawn a card to a hand that is smoother than your 8-6, standing Pat is your best option. If you're against one opponent who raps Pat, you're usually better off drawing one. And against a lot of players where there's a Pat hand and **several** *smooth* draws, you can consider drawing two, especially when you're last to act. If it is a Straight–Limit game, the one-card draw would be appropriate **even** against that many players showing strength.

A small edge that is seldom considered, even by experienced Lowball players is the kind of cards you discard. If you have this two card draw...

you'll win more pots than if you have this two-card draw...

That's because (with the first hand) you're more likely to catch a Jack or a Ten and possibly win...and you're less likely to pair (because you're discarding a Three and a Deuce).

You can argue that a Pat 8-4-3-2-A is just about as good as a Pat 7-6-5-4-3 in early positions. Since the hands have almost identical strengths (you get a Pat straight Seven or better 1.06% of the time and a Pat 8-4 or better 1.13% of the time), many experts **favor** the 8-4 because it allows them to check after the draw **without** losing the action (if they subsequently call and win). That's a good argument, but a lot of players have extended this concept to mean that a one-card draw to an 8-4 is better than a one-card draw to a straight Seven.

No way! True, if you make the Seven, you'll have almost as good a hand as if you make the 8-4, but here's the difference...Suppose the 7-6-5-4 catches the 3rd best card he can catch, a Three. He now has 7-6-5-4-3. Suppose you draw to 8-4-3-2 and catch the third best card you can catch, a Six. You can see that there's quite a difference between these hands. The first (7-6-5-4-3) is the 21st ranking hand. The second (8-6-4-3-2) ranks 30th. Only when the first hand catches his **third best** card and the 8-4 catches his **best** card can these hands be construed as approximately equal in strength.

Even though these two Pat hands are about equal...

this is a much better drawing hand...

than this...

ACTION AFTER THE DRAW

One of the profitable things you should learn to do in Lowball games is: **DON'T call when you know you're beat.** Obviously, you've got to **CALL most of the time when** your opponent bets into you, just because the size of the pot almost always dictates this strategy in limit Lowball. If you make an Eight and an average opponent bets his one-card draw into you, you're usually going to have to call.

You'll even need to call on Face-cards (and on small Pairs) against opponents who bet every time they pair-up. But here's two recurring cases where you can **save that bet** after the draw (particularly when it's a double-bet like the Blind game we're discussing):

(1) A Rock in 3rd position opened with a raise. Position Five re-raised and position Six called. You called in 7th position with a one-card draw to a Bicycle. The original raiser called and drew one. Fifth position stood Pat, then 6th Position and you drew one. After the draw, the Rock in 3rd position (the original raiser), who drew one, bets. The Pat hand called, 6th position dropped. You look — you caught an Eight, giving you 8-5-3-2-A.

Almost every player I know makes this call, and it's wrong! A Hard Rock with a line of players to act behind him just **will** *not* **ever** bet unless he has a Seven (or better) — and then the rules **demand** that he bet. He isn't going to swing into the Pat re-raiser unless he has something. **Pass. Save a bet.**

(2) You stood Pat with 7-6-3-2-A. After the draw, you bet into a line of players and a Rock raises. **Pass again. Save another bet.** Unsophisticated Rocks are just **NOT going to raise you** after the draw **with worse than a 7-5** when you're in a strong position.

WHEN and WHAT TO BLUFF

With what hands should you bluff? Bluff with your biggest Pairs. And the more players and the more money in the pot, the bigger your Pairs must be. Of course, you have to keep an eye out for players who will just **never call without some sort** of hand and you should *bluff* **more frequently** against them.

It's interesting that the easier a player is to bluff, the **less** you should *Value Bet* against him. *Value Betting* **is betting marginal hands** when you feel that, although you have no great advantage, your **opponent's call will lose** *more often* **than it wins**. But a player who can readily be bluffed is likely to throw away the marginally bad hands that you're trying to get a call from.

If you drew cards, you should Value Bet this hand into a one-card draw who checked into you...

Many players lose money by just showing-down that hand head-up.

There are even situations where you can Value Bet a Jack-high. The hands which should almost never be bet, either for *value* or as a *bluff*, are Queen-high, King-high and a Pair of Aces. That's because they're ideal checking hands, not bad enough to bluff and not nearly good enough for you to want a call.

When **all** your opponents have drawn and you're last to act...if they check to you, **that's** the time to Value Bet. They've **already surrendered** their **opportunities to bluff** on their worst hands, and **they** *probably* **have hands they'll** *reluctantly* **call with**. Definitely bet **any** Nine.

And a very important concept here is: **DON'T bluff at the end of the line when checked into after the draw.** When players check to you, they are usually showing an interest in calling. In Limit Ace-to-Five, **BLUFF when you're FIRST to act or not at all!**

Particularly in games like Raise-Blind where there are antes, two Blinds and a **lot of action** before the draw, pots frequently get so big that you **bet** after the draw **hoping NOT to get called**. The reason is that you're betting a marginal winning hand, trying to get *value*. The caller will only win, let's say, 30% of the time. That means you're going to show a profit **on the last bet**, but 30% of the time · he will win **not only that last bet**, but the **entire pot.** Clearly you'll be happier if he **doesn't** call.

Players who have just a hazy notion of how *Value Betting* works think they can bet 10-8-7-6-2 for value Pat or if they drew one.

Not true!

> **You need substantially** *stronger* **Pat hands to Value Bet than identical hands made via a one-card draw.** *(The example below explains this.)*

If a one-card draw checks, you **can** bet this hand for value **if you drew one also**...

But...you **cannot** bet it for value **if you had it Pat.**

If you drew a card, your opponent can call on a Jack, a Queen, a King and on a small Pair thinking you might have paired big. **If you stood Pat, he** *cannot* **make these calls.**

When you're first to act, weigh the chances that your opponent might bluff into you when deciding whether or not to Value Bet. If he's a frequent bluffer, your best option is usually to check and be prepared to call with a marginal hand.

If your opponent **doesn't** seem to be drawing super smooth, you can value bet more hands when you're first to act. That's because you **don't** fear a raise.

Because Rocks know that few players bluff into Pat hands, you can often get away with "firing" a one or a two-card bust into a Rock who didn't draw.

Many players select 7-5-4-3-2 as the minimum hand they'll raise with after the draw. While this isn't a particularly bad strategy, there are times when you shouldn't even raise with a Straight Six (like against a one-card draw who swings into you following a hot raising war, as explained shortly). But you can sometimes raise with a Straight Seven (or even a rougher hand) when the bettor **doesn't** figure to be drawing very smooth.

The rule is:

> **Whenever your opponent is probably** *not* **drawing to the** *nuts* * **you can raise more loosely after the draw because you don't fear a re-raise.**

Some players **rarely** *bet* Eights after the draw under **any** conditions. Others **will** *bet* Eights much more often **if it was an Eight they were drawing at**. This is bad policy for them, since the limited amount of action they put in before the draw frequently makes them seem *rough* (and vulnerable).

The average player is **much more likely to bet** in this situation...

Drew to: Caught:

than in this situation...

Drew to: Caught:

---

*For example, when you've raised it to three bets before the draw and he called your last bet.

In the first example, the player is apt to bet because he **caught the hand he was drawing at**. In the second situation, the player caught **outside** and will usually check.

Occasionally, you can bluff by raising. In very liberal *Limit* games, especially in Open-Blind-Raise-Blind, you can sometimes raise after the draw with a Pair of Eights because there's a chance your opponent is bluffing with a Pair of Sixes. If so, he will **not** call your raise.

If you've drawn two, you can bet medium hands more favorably than if you've drawn one because your opponents will tend to think you either made a bust or a monster.

It's just terrible to bluff with a Pair against two players who drew and checked into you after the draw. I've seen so many players use this suicidal bit of strategy. When they check they're surrendering their right to bluff, **so they** *don't* **have** *really bad* **hands**, and they're giving up their right to bet their Eights (and better) if they connected, **so they** *don't* **have** *really good* **hands, either**. What they usually have is something in between — **calling** hands. Why some players persist in trying to bluff out calling hands remains a puzzle in my mind.

If there's a **lot of action before the draw** and you have a Pat 6-5-4-3-2, you've got to be **leary if your opponent** *swings* after the draw. He was drawing to the absolute nuts, probably with the Joker. **Do** *not* **raise**. A typical player **wouldn't** bet worse than a Seven (although he **should** bet an 8-4 rather than check and call with it) and that leaves him **more chances of having you beat than of you having him beat**. Besides, if he does have the best hand, he's going to raise again and, unless you make a brilliant laydown, you laid him 2 to 1 odds by raising.

That ought to handle most of the after-draw betting situations you're likely to run into.

GENERAL CONCEPTS

Now that you have a feel for the types of hands you should play in a $20 Blind game ($40 after the draw, $2 ante), here's a pretty package of advice that will really bring you into the big money...

First, find yourself a good game.

The more you can hear that clatter of chips going into the pot, the better it's going to be for your pocketbook.

There may be exceptions. Years ago I ran across a game with four southern gentlemen sitting at a table — and all of them real friendly.

They were just smiling **so** warm and waving for me to get into the game. Pretty big game, too. Well, I just stood awhile and watched a hand. On the first deal the nice gentleman next to the Blind raised, the next nice gentleman made it three bets and the third gentleman called. The Blind called and the original raiser put in another raise. Well, it got to be so many bets I quit counting. Then came the draw, and all four of them were **still** in it! The Blind drew two, the first raiser stood Pat and the other players drew two apiece.

The Blind checked. The original raiser (Pat) bet and **everyone** called. The Pat hand had a 10-8. It won! Everyone was just laughing and giggling, so I took my bankroll out of my pocket and sat down.

I took the Blind and **suddenly** everyone passed! They had quieted down and the game had become serious.

I said, *"See you later, boys. I'm just in town to visit my sick uncle and he really needs me."*

That just emphasizes something that applies to any sort of Poker game you're thinking about investing your money in. **Be** *extra* **cautious if you** *don't know* **your players.**

Even if you can't find a super-loose game every night, there are ways to make the game you're playing in a lot more lucrative. Remember, **give action to those who are providing you with action** — only **stop** a bet or so **short.**

Here are some of my general thoughts and ideas about Ace-to-Five Lowball:

(1) **Don't** *Snow*.

Running a bluff with a Pat hand in Lowball **isn't** as strategically sound as it is in High Draw Poker because your opponents can make too many calling hands. If you do *Snow* in Limit Ace-to-Five, do it for *commercial* reasons. It's an advertising play. Don't kid yourself into thinking you've accomplished a great Poker finesse if you succeed in taking a pot with a Snow hand. For the record, the best five-card hands you can Snow with in Ace-to-Five are 8-8-8-8-7 and 8-8-8-8-Joker. Your opponents must either have a Seven (or better) or a Nine (or worse).

(2) **Don't** feel emotionally outraged when you see a Sucker winning pot after pot.

Players drawing two-cards hand after hand and ending up with the money stand out in your mind. Look around you. There are probably two to six other players in the same game playing just as foolishly and losing their bankrolls.

(3) If you must lay-down a big hand, **call more** in the pots that immediately follow (to catch bluffs).

Lowball players seldom make big lay-downs. If **you** do, others will take this as evidence that you're vulnerable after the draw, and they'll be inspired to take shots at you. Calling with a Pair of Sixes and showing the hand will generally put a stop to their untimely bluffs and return them to their usual predictable modes.

(4) *Loose* gamblers tend toward the upper limits.

The *highest* **limit game played in a casino is usually** *easier* **to beat than the** *next-to-highest* **limit.** This is especially true in limit Lowball where you get a concentration of gamblers who **would** play bigger **if they could**, but are forced to play the **highest, limit available**. This smaller limit may make them impatient and cause them to throw off even more money than they normally would in a bigger game.

(5) Never put in so much action that you must break a hand head-up.

Many players have an 8-4 Pat and they keep raising another player almost forever. Then the opponent raps pat and they think, *"Well, this Eight ·isn't any good — I think I'll draw one."* But they put **themselves** in that position. They found out they had to break the Eight, but it just wasn't worth finding out. **They should have stopped a lot earlier and died with the hand.**

(6) **Don't** get bullheaded and try to force an opponent to break a good Nine when you have a Pat Straight Nine.

My expert *Joey Hawthorne* calls this common mistake **attacking the** *"imaginary"* **Nine.** There just aren't that many breaking hands your opponent can have.

(7) **Beware** of the *Slow-Play.*

Any player who just calls the Blind or who flat-calls the first raiser and later makes it three or four bets is strong. **Real** strong! I only recommend that **you** *slow-play* under very selective circumstances. One situation would be if you have a Pat Bicycle in 3rd position and 2nd position has already raised. Here you're much better off just calling and letting others in the pot. And you'll want to **flat call with a one-card draw to a** *Joker-Wheel* behind a 2nd position raiser — again, it's the more the merrier. But slow-playing roughish hands is for the birds (that is *pigeons*).

(8) When an early position draws two, he **very likely** has the Joker.

(9) You can be a favorite against each opponent individually **without** being a money-favorite in the pot.

This is a very important concept which is difficult for most people to understand. If I have a 9-7-5-3-Joker and you have a *smooth* one-card draw, I'm the favorite. If four people have one-card draws against me, I'm a favorite against each one of them to end up with the better hand, but I **won't** win my proper share of the time (once in five).

That's because although I'll **beat most** of them, I **won't** very often **beat all of them** *at once.* I might beat three of them and lose to only one. But the nature of the game is that **only** the first place finisher takes any money. If I could make individual side bets with each player, then I'd make a profit.

(10) Seating **is** important. Select a seat where you can act **behind** players who **habitually** draw two cards and play *rough* Pat Tens. You want to raise **after** they're **in the pot**...*not* chase them out.

When you're the dealer, it's good to have a player on your left who's timid and easy to rob in the Blind. Additionally it'll be easier to *bet through* him when a timid player's **between** you and the Blind (when you're in 7th position). If a player seldom challenges the Blind, sit immediately to his left and pick-up some *Walks*.

HOW TO USE PSYCHOLOGY
at LOW POKER

It's harder to read players in Low Poker than in High Poker because players can get enthusiastic about the dangdest hands. And lots of players **don't** really know what a good hand is in various situations, so if they **don't** know what they've got...how can you?

The psychology you'll want to know regarding Ace-to-Five is divided into two parts:

(1) Reading players and

(2) Influencing players

Influencing your opponents is important because you can get them to play looser and give you a lot more of their money than they normally would. Here's how you can do it...

Whenever you see a player make a winning two-card draw when he had no business even playing the hand, **don't** grumble or ridicule him. **Don't** tell him he's playing bad. Be friendly and **encourage** loose play.

Playing break-even hands will suggest to your freely gambling opponents that you're one of the boys, willing to splash chips with the best of them. **Play your break-even hands** because they **aren't really** break-even. They contribute to your profit when you hold big winning tickets.

It's *bad* **to show a** *good* **lay-down.** When you get raised and must lay-down a Pat 8-4, do so **quietly** and pretend to have nothing.

You won't be playing **nearly** as many hands as the losers. But the fact that you **do** *play* marginal hands, coupled with the fact that you give action when you have a good hand (particularly against gamblers), will convince others that you are loose.

You might want to talk about Horses or Craps or Bingo at the card table to make your opponents feel you have the gambling spirit — the Lowball Spirit.

Encourage players to *Kill* the pot. *Killing* is putting in an amount double the Blind before getting your cards. Naturally, this is a losing gamble. But if a lot of players are doing it, *join in* **occasionally.**

Reading your opponents **isn't** especially easy in Ace-to-Five Lowball, but certain Rocks are so predictable in early positions that you *always* **know** what they have — a Pat Eight (or better) or a one-card draw to a smooth Seven (or better).

One thing you should especially be leary of is phony hesitation. When a player hesitates on the draw, then raps pat and **then** bets out — **Beware!** I mean, double and triple beware!

Particularly in small games, a player who *raps Pat* **adamantly** has an Eight, Nine or Ten (depending on his position) and *almost* **NEVER** a Seven (or better).

Whereas most players are pretty predictable (when they're **not** *on tilt*), good players are likely to make unorthodox plays and fool you. Do **not** *routinely* lay-down a

Straight Seven against a strong player who raises you after the draw.

When you're involved in a *raising war* and your opponent has only looked at four cards, keep raising with your Pat Seven or Eight until he looks at the fifth card. Then, if he continues to raise, **stop**...unless you have a 6-4 or a Bicycle.

OTHER FORMS
of
ACE-to-FIVE

The most usual variations of Ace-to-Five you'll run into are *Straddle, Straight-Limit, Pass-Out* (no Blind), *Raise-Blind,* and *Gardena-type Razz.*

Straddle is usually with three staggered Blinds, larger as the position moves left. There is customarily **no** ante. These are **not all** *full Blinds* and, usually, **only** the largest Blind has a full-bet in. This is **not** *nearly as loose* a game as *Open-Blind-Raise-Blind-Re-Raise-Blind,* where there are also three Blinds. Your playing minimums can be nearly the same as those used in the $20 Blind. Don't get carried away when you're in one of the smaller Blinds. It **may be** tempting to play loose, but it's usually **not** worth it. Those first two Straddle positions are just there to tempt you. There are **only a few** hands you can play that you wouldn't have played without those token Blinds.

I've already talked a little about Straight-Limit. The main difference between this and double-limit (after the draw) is that **you can play** *Pat hands* a bit **more** *aggressively* while your drawing hands should be played a little **more** *conservatively.* That is because the single-bet after the draw doesn't allow you to gain much ground against *rough* Pat hands when you do draw out on them.

Pass-Out is such a **rare form** of Lowball that it hardly deserves mention. There's **no** *Blind*, and you must either throw in a bet before the draw or throw your cards away. Your minimum standards must be **a lot more conservative**, both on Pat hands and on drawing hands.

Raise Blind games are the ones with the **most action**. They offer the most potential profit. . .although you've got to expect a lot of bankroll fluctuations along the road. A general rule is to *play Pat hands* a lot **more liberally**. Most of the action will be before the draw and the pot will usually be big enough after the draw that you'll usually be forced to call. In the big Blind you can always call one more bet and draw at **any** Nine. A Pat Ten is always playable for one more bet. **The MAIN MISTAKE is playing too many hands in the** *small* **Blind.**

Gardena Razz **should** *not* **be confused with** *Seven-Card Razz*. The first is a *winner-leave-it-in* game where the player who won the last pot *kills it* for double the amount of the Blind. This is **really a** *loser-leave-it-in* game because it's the losers (who play the most hands and therefore win the most pots). Therefore, they do the most killing. **The BIG ERROR most players make here is defending the** *Razz* **(their** *kill***) too often.** One good thing about the game is that players do **not** think of it as a tightly structured game. When players gamble it up at this game, it's a *Rocks paradise*.

You can see that there's more to Ace-to-Five than just — *"Don't draw to Eights and NEVER draw two"* — the advice you hear from those who think it's mostly luck.

DEUCE-to-SEVEN the ORIGINAL game of LOWBALL

Now let's look at the **original** game of Lowball, where the *worst* **High hand really does win**. In *Deuce-to-Seven*, Straights and Flushes count **against** you. . .and an Ace is **always** considered **high** — it can **never** be used as a *"One"*.

It's been my experience that *Ace–to–Five* **Limit** players have less trouble converting to No-Limit *Deuce–to–Seven* **than vice versa.**

You might choose to take a look at the comparison charts of the two games in the *Appendix.* Here's just a brief idea of how they stack up against each other:

Brief comparison of
DEUCE-to-SEVEN with ACE-to-FIVE

Rank of Hand	Deuce-to-Seven	Ace-to-Five
1	7-5-4-3-2	5-4-3-2-A
10	8-7-4-3-2	7-5-4-3-A
25	9-7-5-3-2	8-5-4-3-A
50	9-8-7-6-2	8-7-6-4-A
75	10-8-6-5-2	9-7-4-3-2
100	10-9-7-4-3	9-8-5-4-2

Well, that gives you an idea of how the **ranks** of the hands compare, but there's another important consideration. How often do you get these hands Pat? Here the comparison becomes more complicated because *Ace–to–Five* is played (generally) with the Joker and *Deuce–to–Seven* is **never** played with the Joker. Beyond that, there are Flushes which are disqualified from being counted as legitimate *Deuce–to–Seven* winners.

You'll get a Pat Bicycle, the best possible *Ace–to–Five* hand, once every 1,246 deals (**with** the Joker in the deck). In *Deuce–to–Seven*, your best hand is 7-5-4-3-2 **offsuit,** and every 2,548 hands you can expect to hold it Pat. This comparison illustrates that it is **much** *harder* to get a quality Pat hand in *Kansas City Lowball* than it is in *Ace–to–Five*.

Also more difficult to make are your drawing hands in *Deuce–to–Seven.* When you draw at the perfect *Ace–to–Five* hand (a Bicycle with the Joker), it's only 5 to 1 against making it. It's almost 11 to 1 against making a perfect 7-5-4-3-2 in *Deuce-to-Seven* when you draw at 7-4-3-2.

Important Considerations in drawing to a hand in DEUCE-*to*-SEVEN

Deuce-to-Seven is much more complicated than other Lowball games because:

(1) It's No-Limit. Instead of having the amount of your bet established beforehand, you have to weigh many psychological and mathematical factors in deciding how much to bet — or even **whether** to bet, raise or call.

(2) Straights and Flushes are high hands and count against you. Many seemingly attractive drawing hands are losers for just that reason.

If you draw one card to a 7-6-3-2 offsuit, the odds are 4.9 to 1 against making a Seven. Now that's a **good** one-card draw. If you draw to **7♣-6♣-5♣-4♣**, it's 14.7 to 1 against making a Seven — and that's a *very* **bad** draw. Similarly, if you draw at 8-5-3-2 offsuit, you have about one chance in four of making the Eight, but if you draw to **8♠-7♠-6♠-5♠**, you only have about a 1 in 8 chance of making the hand you're after.

A SAMPLE of DEUCE-*to*-SEVEN DRAWING PROBABILITIES

The following examples will give you an idea of the probabilities of making some typical hands:

Therefore, A–5–4–3–2 is **not** a *Wheel* **nor** is it a Straight. It's Ace–Five high. It will beat A–7–6–4–3 and 6–5–4–3–3... but will lose to K–9–6–5–2.

A *Wheel* — the **very best** hand in *Deuce-to-Seven* is a 7–5–4–3–2 (with at least one different suit) — hence the name.

Here are some examples:

this hand...   beats this hand...

(King–High)   *(Ace–High)*

and...

this hand...   beats this hand...

(Pair of Threes)   *(Pair of Aces)*

and...

this hand...   beats this hand...

(Jack–High)   *(Club Flush)*

and...

this hand... beats this hand...

(An Eight–Seven) *(A Seven–High Straight)*

and...

this hand... beats this hand...

(Ace–High — NOT a Straight) *(Pair of Deuces)*

Deuce-to-Seven, or *Kansas City Lowball* as it's called, is almost always played No-Limit (table stakes). It's a high-priced gambling game where strong players have made fortunes and weak players have lost cars, homes, businesses and families.

No-Limit *Deuce-to-Seven* is a game of brilliance and brutality, where the psychological warfare becomes so intense at times that you can almost hear Confederate cannons booming in your ears.

Yes, its popularity is mostly in the southern part of the United States. *Ace-to-Five* is the dominant form of Lowball in other parts of the country. The games have many similarities, and much of the advice you've learned while reading the *Ace-to-Five* part of this section will be useful. The main difference is that *Ace-to-Five* is usually played with a **Limit** and *Deuce-to-Seven* is almost always played **No-Limit.**

It's only 4.9 to 1 against making a Seven when you draw to this hand...

But it's 14.7 to 1 against making a Seven when you draw to this hand...

Drawing to this hand, you have about a 1 in 4 chance of making an Eight...

But you'll only make this Eight about 1 of 8 tries...

Any real quality drawing hand must *include* **a** *Deuce* **or a** *Three* **with** *no possibility* **of making a Straight or a Flush.**

IMPORTANT DRAWING CONSIDERATIONS

The best possible drawing hand is 7-4-3-2 offsuit. A pretty good drawing hand is 5-4-3-2 — and it is **not** an open-end Straight draw. Aces are **always** high, remember, so 5-4-3-2-A beats any Pair. Most players don't like to draw a 5-4-3-2...but I do.

In low-ante games, you *almost* **never** draw two cards. I say *almost* because, as with every rule, there are exceptions. If the players are very loose and have a lot of money on the table, you can think about drawing two cards from a late position. The more money your opponents have in front of them, the more you can capitalize if you do connect on a longshot draw.

But, you **never** draw two cards from an **early** position because there isn't enough money in the pot to justify it — and you have to worry about a raise. I have a rule about two-card draws that has helped me a lot. The rule is:

Any two-card draw *must have* **a Deuce in it.**

Not only does this limit or eliminate your chances of making a Straight, you're holding the **most desirable card** your opponents could have in making their quality hands.

Another consideration is when you have small card *duplication*. For example, 7-7-3-2-2 would be an enticing two-card draw. It takes two good cards out of the deck which your opponents could use and it reduces the possibility of your pairing on the draw.

Another example of this concept would be a hand consisting of 7-3-2-2-2. Now **THAT'S the** *best possible* **two-card draw.** It's difficult for your opponent to have any quality Low hand without a Deuce in it — and there's only one Deuce left in the deck.

Now that wasn't difficult to reason out, was it? But I've seen top players make **bad** two-card draws for years (and, in reality, **almost all** two-card draws are **bad**). All the good players know **not** to draw one card to a Straight. But any time they draw to three small cards (3's through 7's) **without** a Deuce, they'll have a Straight draw whenever the first card drawn hits inside. For example, if I draw at 6-4-3 and the first card I look at is a Five, I now have a hand even a beginner wouldn't draw one card to. A Seven or a Deuce would make those four cards (6-5-4-3) a Straight. And the best possible hand I could make (when I looked at my fifth card) would be 8-6-5-4-3 — the ninth best hand in Deuce-to-Seven.

Why draw to "trouble" hands?

The ANTE (including the Blind) and its effect on your strategy

As I've stated repeatedly throughout this book, the ante determines a great deal as to how you should play. If the minimum buy-in is $1000 in Deuce-to-Seven No-Limit, any ante **less than** 3% per hand is considered a **low-ante** game. That 3% includes the antes from each player and the *Blind's* bet. So if the sum of the antes **plus** the Blind is **less than** $30 in a $1000 buy-in game, you're dealing with a low ante. For example, a $2 ante with a $10 Blind, eight-handed, would equal 2.6% of the $1000 buy-in. That's a low-ante game. If the antes **plus** the Blind are in the 3% to 6% range, you're dealing with a medium-ante situation. I would consider anything about 6% (or more) to be a high-ante game.

In low-ante games, the strategy is simple — play tight. The tighter you play, the more successful you'll be because you **can afford to wait** for *quality* hands.

The quality hands I'm speaking of are *smooth* (small) Nines, any Eights or any Sevens. You should try to make these hands (draw at them) at a **minimum risk**, jeopardizing as few chips as possible. Let your opponents play the Tens and *rough* Nines — these are the hands you love them to play against you in the **big** pots.

Of course, the occasion will arise when you'll have to play those hands, too (Tens and *rough* Nines)...but when you do play them, act *defensively* and try to *win small pots* (by **not** getting a lot of your money involved). Your big-pot combat should be reserved for the times when you have high-quality hands.

> In *low ante* **games, more money is lost**
> **with** *rough* **Pat Nines**
> **than with any other hand.**

For that reason, *rough* Nines should be played with **extra caution.** Remember...

> *Low-Ante* **games are structured**
> **for Sevens and Eights.**

When dealing with medium-ante games, you **can't be** quite so selective about which hands you play...and in high-ante games, you've got to come out swinging with some pretty *rough* hands. Still, the following concept prevails no matter what the ante structure...

> **Attempt to win** *small* **pots**
> **with your** *rough* **hands, and**
> **try to play the** *big* **pots**
> **with your** *quality* **hands.**

In low-ante games, your **main strategy** is to wait for the really high-class hands. In high-ante, the strategy changes. The ante and pot odds justify playing weaker hands and **much more** *judgment* **is required.**

I'm not going to be quite as specific about high-ante *Deuce-to-Seven* for a very specific reason. It is:

> High-ante No-Limit Lowball demands so
> much more psychology and judgment than
> low-ante games that it's hard to set any
> absolute standards.

Nevertheless, here are a few more of my thoughts.

The VITAL IMPORTANCE
of
POSITION

Position is vital in every game. No-Limit Lowball is no
exception. In fact:

> Position is *more important* in No-Limit Low-
> ball than any other Poker game with the
> exception of No-Limit Hold 'em.

When your opponent must act first, your hand becomes
much more flexible and it's possible to play marginal hands
(such as a one-card draw to a Nine or a rough Ten).
Remember, when you play these marginal hands, you're
trying to win **small** pots. The reason you play them is that
even with the low-ante, the pot odds justify a (weak) call in
the **late positions**. Almost all top Deuce-to-Seven players
are very solid (tight) from the early positions.

> **Always respect the player**
> **who raises the Blind**
> **from an *early* position.**

It's safe to assume that an early-position raiser either
has a Pat hand or is drawing to a quality hand.

If all the players in the early seats pass and the pot is opened (for a raise) by a player in a middle position, you can rightly be suspicious about how good his hand is. That's why you should always evaluate your hand according to the position of the first raiser.

Play a very solid game from *early* positions.

There are *"trouble"* hands which should be **avoided** from an early position. Your **Pat Tens should be** *two-way hands* **if you enter the pot early.** By that I mean, if you get re-raised you should have a *quality* one-card draw to fall back on. For example, a 10-8-4-3-2 is a playable two-way hand from an early seat because you can throw away the Ten and still have an excellent drawing hand. But 10-9-8-4-3 should usually be thrown away in an early position because, if you get re-raised, you **don't** have a *quality* hand to draw to.

You can play this hand
from an early position... but **not** this hand...

A standard rule is...

**Seldom draw at open-end Straights
from any position,
and NEVER from an early position.**

A good draw with a possible Inside-Straight (such as 8-6-5-4) is **marginal** from the early seats and should be played only on your own judgment, considering the caliber of the players in the game and the amount of money you think you can win if you make your hand. **Those should also be your considerations before calling ANY** *re-raise.*

SNOWING
when and how to do it

In most Deuce-to-Seven games I hesitate to *represent* having a hand when all I hold is garbage (a *SNOW* hand). But...when the ante is high enough, when my position is favorable and when I hold a handful of small *duplication* (matching) cards, it's usually a winning play. However, you should...

NEVER *Snow* **from an early position.**

Obviously, when you *SNOW*, you're going to have to bet your hand, so it's **much better to act last.**

If you act first, there are these disadvantages:

(1) You're jeopardizing your money because your opponent has not yet shown weakness (by checking).

(2) It's an abnormal play because the Pat hand usually checks to the drawing hand. Good players will be suspicious and are likely to call.

However, when you bet from a late position, after it's been checked to you, you can be betting for any of these reasons:

(1) You have a quality hand;

(2) You're trying to *sell* a fair hand;

(3) You're *protecting* your hand (betting a weak hand to keep someone from calling with a rougher hand).

(4) You're *Snowing.*

Your opponents, being aware that there are many reasons you might bet legitimately, are more likely to pass when you *Snow* from last position.

MY FAVORITE SNOW HAND

There is one hand I have *never* **failed** *to Snow with* in 25 years of playing Deuce-to-Seven — and it will be a sorry day in my life if I ever decline to *Snow* with it. That hand is 4-Deuces before the draw — the **strongest** *Snowing* hand you can have. Obviously, it's hard to catch 4-Deuces, but if you play for enough years, you'll get your share. (It's 54,145 to 1 against getting 4-Deuces pat.) Naturally you'd rather hold 4-Deuces with a Seven than with a King, but when you're going to have to wait around another 54,000 hands for the next try...it's tough to be selective.

I've held them four times and played them exactly the same way each time. I've raised or re-raised regardless of my position before the draw, stood pat and bet all my chips when it was my turn to act.

Once after having rapped Pat with my ultimate Snow hand in a late position, the player in front of me bet. Fortunately we both had a lot of chips. I moved-in, knowing the best possible hand he could hold was 8-6-5-4-3, which would be a tough call for him if he had it. It so happened my opponent was bluffing and couldn't call, but it still shows the importance of having a Deuce in your hand in *Kansas City* Lowball.

SOME STRATEGY PLAYS
I've used with great success

As I said earlier, judgment is the most important thing in high-ante Poker. Being able to release your hand with a lot of money in the pot is mandatory.

If you have a talent for "feeling" weakness, and the courage to back that feeling, there are numerous opportunities for *making plays* in No-Limit that simply **don't** exist in

Limit play. For instance, I've been very successful betting into Pat hands after drawing one. If I correctly decide that my opponent's hand is weak, I usually **won't** get called because most players refuse to lose much money with *rough* Pat hands.

Another successful bluff I've used over the years is to make a **large** raise after a bet and a call. Usually, only the original bettor can *snap you off* because if the caller had a quality hand, he **himself** would've raised.

One of my pet plays has always been to draw two, check after the draw and, if my opponent bets, move–in or make a substantial raise. I use this maneuver against a sophisticated player who will interpret my actions as meaning I'm probably very strong — therefore his calling requirements will be much more rigid.

**As in all forms of Poker,
the aggressor definitely has the advantage**

When you get caught bluffing, you obviously feel bad. But to win in high-ante No-Limit games, a player has to have the courage to do quite a lot of bluffing.

WHEN TO *IGNORE* THE STATISTICS

Statistics and percentages **don't** always dictate the right play in No-Limit Lowball. For example, I had an argument with two of my collaborators about a Deuce-to-Seven situation. Joey Hawthorne, Mike Caro and I were talking about whether it was the correct play to bluff into two players after they drew two in late positions and I drew one in an early position. Both Mike and Joey said the percentages favor me bluffing if I make a high Pair in this situation. Mike says both my opponents will pair about 16% of the time and Joey said the first two-card draw must make a Ten or better to call because of the man behind him. It's been my experience that you'll get called well over half the time in that situation. Unlike Limit Lowball, when you're only betting a small percentage of the pot and hoping you **won't** be called. . .in No-Limit you're typically betting about the size of the pot. So. . .if you get called (or raised) over half the time, it's a losing play. So as I jokingly told my two experts in disagreeing with them, *"the hell with y'all, it's my book anyway."*

MORE IMPORTANT CONCEPTS

Joey speaks about *"going through the middle-man"*. It's a concept you should be aware of at all times, whether you **are** the middle-man **or** on either side of him. When I say the *middle-man*, I mean the player who is to the left of the original bettor in a three-way pot. **There is more strategy involved here than anywhere else in No-Limit Lowball.** If all three are good players, there's psychological warfare going on. Each player knows what the others are thinking and vice versa. If the first player draws, the second player (the middle man) stays pat and the third player draws one, then the player in first position almost always bets *(shoots through)* the Pat hand. This puts a lot of pressure on the Pat hand in the middle. He has to hope player number three misses his hand even if player number one **is** bluffing.

For that reason:

> **Almost** *never* **stand pat between two players** *unless* **you have a hand you expect to call with.**

Otherwise, *break off* your Pat hand and draw *smooth*.

When each sophisticated player knows the way his opponent is thinking, you can imagine the psychological guessing game that often occurs in sticky situations.

Even in high-ante games, I **don't** like to play a lot of big pots with Pat Jacks and Tens, especially from early positions. I'm assuming all the players have sufficient chips in front of them. I'd rather *break* a rough hand if I have a quality draw. Then I can try to win a lot of money **comfortably** rather than be in a constant strain with a rough Pat hand.

Naturally, the amount of money your opponent has remaining in front of him determines how you should play a two-way hand. If you can get most of his money in before the draw, you should be reluctant to break. Certainly the **type** of drawing hand you hold has a great deal to do with whether you should or shouldn't break. A 10-7-6-5-4 would have to be played pat or thrown away (because you'd have a Straight-draw if you broke the Ten). But if you held 10-7-6-5-2, you quite possibly would want to draw down, particularly if you were against more than one opponent.

No-Limit Lowball might just be the only game where it's possible to be a *Calling Station* and still be a winning player. I've known players who habitually check their marginal hands and call instead of betting for value. It's a defensive and careful style of play and, while I **don't** recommend it, it seems to work fairly well for them. Their thinking is (and it has some value) that most players will bet the majority of hands they would call with. With that in mind, plus the additional chances of catching bluffs, they have developed an **unspectacular** *but safe* manner of play.

Back in Ace-to-Five I talked about the frustration associated with Lowball. Well that goes double, maybe triple, for No-Limit *Deuce-to-Seven*. The tension can be so heavy at times, you expect to see your opponents crack under the strain. I don't know if any Deuce-to-Seven players have been sent off to the "funny farm" lately, but it wouldn't surprise me to learn that there were some.

STORIES TO REMEMBER

I was in a game once and this player named *Pasquale* was involved in a hand against *"Puggy" Pearson*. It was the high-tension point of the evening, a big pot, a *monster* pot. Pasquale moved in with all his chips and Puggy called.

"*One cavity!*" announced *Pasquale* (meaning there was only one card that stood between his and a perfect hand). He spread 7-6-4-3-2 on the table.

"*NO cavities,*" cackled *Puggy*, almost sadistically, as he laid down his perfect 7-5-4-3-2.

I tell you, *Deuce-to-Seven* can be **brutal**. It's a game where you need that *killer* instinct.

And you can just about take that literally, because I've had two players drop dead on me right at the table. One had just suffered a twenty thousand dollar *beat* with a 7-6-4-3-2. And the other one, a few years later, had the *nuts* (7-5-4-3-2), but he never got to rake in the chips. (He actually dropped dead from the excitement of holding "the name of the game".)

Now maybe you believe what I'm telling you about the aggravation, the excitement and the brutality of Lowball.

SEVEN-CARD LOW (RAZZ)

Razz is a Seven-Card Stud game where the best five-card Low hand wins. It's played on the *Ace-to-Five* scale with the Ace being Low and Straights and Flushes having no value beyond their spots.

Some super Rocks refuse to enter a pot with three cards worse than 7-6-5. While this **isn't** a terrible starting strategy, a quick check of the charts in the *Appendix* shows that they're only going to be playing one out of ten hands.

This game is usually played eight–handed and the **highest** up–card must bet (bring it in). This is a rule which was devised to stimulate action — and it does.

> **The first and most important thing you should know about Razz is that the value of your starting hand depends** *principally* **on what cards other players have showing.**

Say you're playing $100 and $200 Razz. Everyone antes $15. The high card brings it in for $25, the first raise on the intial Round of betting must make it $75 *to go* and any raises beyond that are $100 (until Fifth St.). Second round (your fourth card) betting is by units of $100, and starting with the fifth card all bets are $200.

In the following examples, the cards you see are the first up–cards of your opponents. The card's above **YOU** are your hole–cards.

EXAMPLE 1

If you have this hand, you should **play it** as indicated in the diagram of Example 1.

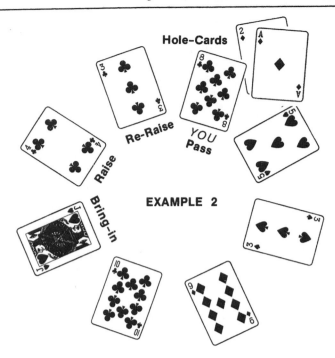

In this case, you have a better hand than in the previous example...but too many of the cards you need are exposed.

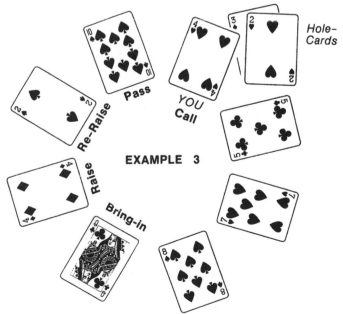

Here, you should just call. There are two reasons why a raise is **not** desirable. One, you're identifying your hand as strong and speculating about only a small gain. Two, you're going to lay down more hands on Fourth, Fifth and Sixth Streets than your less-disciplined opponents. Therefore all the money you've forced into the pot early will **often** be forfeited by you, but *not* often by your opponents.

Naturally, if you play a moderately bad card like a Nine on the first Round of betting, it's much better to have it buried than exposed. If you were forced to bring it in with a King-up for $25 and an exposed Three made it $75 and an Eight called. . .pass. It's *not* **nearly worth it even with perfect cards in the hole.**

Even against one player showing a Five who has a last late shot at your $25 plus $120 (eight $15) antes, you just **cannot** call. Although your cards might be better than his, the fact that your bad card is exposed will mean you're going to have to throw away too many hands before the action gets very far.

If you have 10-2-A and all the players behind you have up-cards higher than Tens you have a **very desirable** playing hand — in fact, the very best starting hand (compared to your opponents).

With a little experience, it'll quickly be apparent which cards you can start with. Your standards should be *pretty conservative*. **Certainly you should** *not* **play 8-7-6 when there are two Threes and an Ace still to act behind you.**

Here are some tips about the more intricate aspects of Razz:

(1) Generally the higher an opponent's up-card, the more likely he is to be "perfect" in the hole.

When players come in with an Eight up against a strong Board and then catch a Seven, you can be pretty sure it **didn't** pair them.

(2) If there's a lot of action on the three-card starting hands and your opponent catches a Seven on the Turn, that's

bad news for you. He almost certainly **doesn't** have a Seven in the hole.

(3) The **minimum** hand that you should be willing to play against a strong Board is three (cards) to a Seven.

(4) The **minimum** you should play as the first raiser against a *weak-to-normal* Board should be 8-6-3.

(5) If you're trailing after four cards (in a head-up situation) and don't gain on Fifth St., you should *usually* **pass.**

(6) Unless you can *read* your opponent, you should generally call on the end when the action gets that far. That's providing you have **some chance** at the pot and if your opponent occasionally makes desperation bluffs.

(7) If you're "perfect" on Fourth St. (and you figure your opponent is too), you can still call on Fifth St. even if he catches good and you don't.

(8) However, if you and an opponent have three Babies and a garbage card after four (cards) and he catches a Six (on Fifth St.) and you get a face-card, you should *almost* **always** pass.

(9) After five (cards), a *smooth* four-card *Come* hand against a rough complete Nine is the favorite. (Unless the exposed cards in other hands dictate otherwise.)

(10) You should *value bet* on the end into a player who has a Ten showing. You're almost sure to get called. Especially, bet a 9-7 into a Board with a 10-8 showing, because you'll **usually** get called (if he has a Ten) and are **unlikely** to get raised (if he has an Eight).

(11) Except against very good players, allow yourself to be "trapped". That is, if a player checks to you, **assume** he's showing **real** weakness and bet whenever you think you have the better hand. It's **unlikely** that bad players will raise.

(12) A **made** Eight on Fifth is a favorite over any four-card drawing hand (no matter how *smooth* it is). But if your opponent checks to you (with what looks like a **made** Eight) he probably **doesn't** have it — so you *should* **bet**. Conversely, if *he* **bets**, you should assume that he

actually **does** have the Eight and therefore you should merely call.

(13) However, with a *smooth* four-card *Come* hand (on Fifth St.), you can bet into an opponent who you think has a *rough* Nine **made** (say a 9–8). If you think his Nine is *smooth* (say a 9–6) **don't** bet. (Even if you had an A–2–3–4–K, you would **not** be a favorite over a made 9–6.)

(14) If you're in a three (or more) handed pot, you should bet a *Come* hand such as A–2–3–4–K against a made 8–7 if you think you can keep a **third** player (with a worse hand than yours) in the pot.

(15) This is *really* **crucial:** Know what your hole-cards are and **never look back except for "show". You've got enough to think about without having to double-check (your hole-cards). What's more, you might give away your hand to other astute players.**

Here are some examples of the things I discussed:

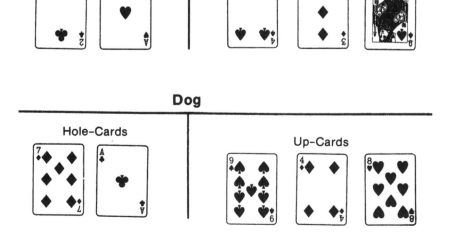

Favorite

Hole-Cards | Up-Cards

Dog

Hole-Cards | Up-Cards

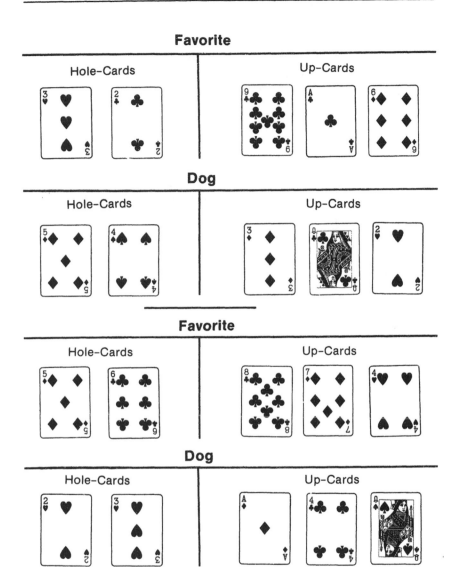

Favorite

Hole-Cards	Up-Cards

Dog

Hole-Cards	Up-Cards

Favorite

Hole-Cards	Up-Cards

Dog

Hole-Cards	Up-Cards

IMPORTANT NOTES

Seating is important in Razz, even though the same player will **not** act first on each betting round. That's because you want to sit behind players who call frequently so they can get their money in **before** you raise.

It's important to remember as many exposed cards as you can because **that** is the **key** that turns an ordinary Razz player into a super-sharp competitor. If you're starting with 7-6-5 and see a lot of Sevens and Sixes, that's so much better than looking at Aces, Deuces, Treys and Fours — the cards you need.

A FINAL REMINDER

Here's just a last word about Lowball in general, because I'm afraid you won't remember what I stressed in the beginning. You're dealing with a game where luck will **appear to be** the dominant factor. You'll get drawn out on repeatedly in any form of Lowball. You'll feel something gnawing away inside you everytime a Sucker "steals" **your** pot with a stupid play.

But stay on top of it. Keep cool. Play according to what you now know and **not** according to what your emotions dictate. . .and you'll be a consistent winner at Lowball.

SUPER/SYSTEM's
POWER POKER COURSE
IN

HIGH-LOW
SPLIT

HIGH-LOW SPLIT

Table of Contents

David Sklansky

DAVID "*Einstein*" SKLANSKY

My Expert Collaborator
on
HIGH-LOW SPLIT

"*Those who can...do. Those who can't...teach.*" We've all heard that one. And, like most generalizations, there's some truth in it. But, only the very naive would take that statement to be entirely true...because there are many teachers who could easily "do". They don't "do" because teaching is what they find most fulfilling. And that's true. Absolutely true. I know. Because David Sklansky (my expert collaborator on High-Low Split) will probably soon be living proof of a doer who'd be happier teaching. If he can ever push himself far enough away from the Poker table, we'll probably be able to find him teaching mathematics in the Graduate School of some University. (His Dad was a mathematics Professor and is now a computer expert.)

David's already in the semi-retirement phase of his Poker career. (Only a Poker player — and a few other individuals — can consider retiring at 29!) When David's not playing Poker...he writes about it (and about the mathematical aspects of gambling in general). He's already written one 64-page book on Limit Hold 'em. (It's highly recommended and available from **B & G Publishing Co., Inc., 1718-S Industrial Road, Las Vegas, Nevada 89102** for the outrageous price of $2.) He's also working on another book dealing with the theoretical considerations that apply to all forms of Poker.

David first started to play Poker when he was in college and continued as an amateur while he was working as an actuary in New Jersey. (His home town is Teaneck.) It didn't take him long to rebel against being bossed around. So he decided to pit his Poker talent against the amateurs and Pros in Gardena and Las Vegas. He's been doing it successfully for several years now. His only significant source of income is from his gambling. (In addition to Poker, David has made about half of his income from Blackjack — another game that he's done some high-level work on. He plays it as well as...or better than...anyone in the world — as many Pit Bosses well know. Unfortunately for David, there aren't many casinos left that'll still let him play.)

I first met David a few years ago when I was playing High-Low at the **Flamingo** (in Las Vegas). It was a $300 and $600 game with a $50 ante (which is an abnormally high ante). It was a very loose game and most of the guys were terrible players. It was a new game for them and they were playing all kinds of **very strange** hands. David walked in and began to watch the game. One of the players who knew David from back East was involved in a pot. When the pot was over, he asked David how he would've played the hand. David said *"I really don't know. I never played a hand like THAT!"*

David considers himself a solid player rather than a tight or conservative one. I'll go along with that. It's an apt description of his playing style. I know. He was the last player I had to overcome in winning the $10,000 Buy-In High-Low Split World Championship Tournament in the 1977 *World Series of Poker.*®

HIGH-LOW SPLIT

Vegas Style

INTRODUCTION

The form of High-Low Split you're going to learn how to play in this section is (Seven-Card Stud) *Cards Speak* (for themselves). This is the version of the game that's played in the **(public)** Poker Rooms in the Las Vegas casinos. It's quite a different game than the form of High-Low Split that's commonly played in a home **(private)** game. That game is most often played with a *declaration.**

One of the reasons why the game is played without a *declare* in casinos is that it would be very trying for the dealers (and card room managers) to settle an argument revolving around exactly how a player declared. Another is that the game is much harder and more confusing to deal than *Cards Speak*. Also, partners — in a game with a *declare* — are a difficult combination to overcome.

Being a simpler version of the game, *Cards Speak* is a much faster game than *Declare*. However, it's this very simplicity that lends itself quite well to casino-play...and, to the analytically-and-scientifically minded player. In fact, that's the thrust of this entire section. So, if you're more of a mathematically-oriented player than a psychologically-oriented one...this is the game for you.

But...more than that, this game — when played *by the book* **(this book)** — allows you to have greater control of your bankroll than any other form of Poker. There are many reasons why this is so. The first...and most impor-

---

*At the end of the *Cards Speak* **section, there's a** *brief overview* **of HIGH-LOW DECLARE. (***David Sklansky***, my expert High-Low collaborator, is currently working on a full-length book dealing exclusively with the sophisticated and subtle techniques and strategies of High-Low Declare. His book will be published by** *B & G Publishing Co., Inc.***)**

tant...reason is that there are (probably) more Suckers at High-Low Split than at any other form of Poker. If we define a *Sucker* as a player who'll play in a game (**any game**) when there's little or no chance for him to win...then it can be accurately said there are Suckers galore at High-Low Split.

Above all else, High-Low Split has a **Trap** that simply doesn't exist in any other form of Poker...and it's that **Trap** that most players fall into. And because they do, they're Suckers whenever they play the game.

Oh yes...the **Trap!** What is it? It's the lure of **at least** half the pot that bad players constantly grasp for...but rarely acquire. They'd do as well grabbing a handful of water. Pot after pot will slip through their fingers. Once in a while, they'll come up with something. But those times will be rare.

> **That consuming thought of** *"at least I'll get my money back"* **is easily the biggest weakness a High-Low player can have. It's a** *leak* **of major proportions...and one that doesn't only exist in bad players. Even very good players at other forms of Poker have this common failing.**

Always remember...when you deviate too greatly from the things you'll learn in this section...you'll be heading straight for the **Trap**. Don't be tempted to pursue a bad hand because you think you'll be able to *escape* with half the pot. More often than not, you'll find that *escape hatch* closed. And, as you'll later learn, what's even worse is that those times you do *escape* will be more illusion than real...and, you'll be tempted to try it again in another *bad spot*. It may even work the next time...and once more you'll breathe a sigh of relief. But...continue to put your money in the **pot** when the percentages are **against** getting any of it out and you'll discover High-Low Split is just not the game for you.

That's true with any form of gambling. Whenever you're taking the worst of it, you **may** get lucky...once in a while. But, more often than not...you'll get "unlucky". And then you'll moan the loser's lament: *"I just can't get a break."* More importantly, by continuing to take the worst of it, you'll notice something happening to your bankroll. It will begin to shrink.

So don't be tempted by the half of the pot you think will be yours. If you don't have a legitimate claim to it...it'll only be a *mirage*. And it'll offer you nothing but *false hope*.

That temptation — which bad players find so hard to resist (and which makes them the Suckers they are) — is exactly what will make you a **consistent** winner at the game...**as long as you resist it**. Having the discipline to avoid the **Trap** is probably even more important than having a technical mastery of the game. Your self–discipline will keep you out of a lot of trouble. And it'll help you keep a tight rein on your bankroll — which will show very little in the way of fluctuations...certainly nothing major. Exercise the right controls...handle yourself, your cards and your money in the machine-like way described in this section... and you'll **never** personally experience the peaks and valleys so common to players who have no *controls*.

Throughout my experiences, I've discovered that most Poker players are continually looking for an excuse to get in the pot. And High–Low Split offers the average player more opportunities to get in the pot **and play** than any other form of Poker. They want to play...and they'll do almost anything to justify playing. They'll play hands that have almost no chance of winning...because they don't know any better. High–Low Split is that kind of game. It's full of **Traps.**

In Limit Hold 'em, for example, even a Sucker would rarely get in the pot with a Queen-Five offsuit. Or, in Ace-to-Five, he'd probably know better than to open the pot in an early position with a two-card draw to an Eight. These examples may seem far-fetched...but similar plays in High–Low Split are **not** uncommon. I've seen players —good ones, in fact — start with a Pair of Kings in High–Low Split *in a multi-way* pot. Now...that's a bad play. But they do it.

Because so many players make so many mistakes at High–Low Split...you should find the game very, very profitable. It generally has more weak players than any other game. If I had "X" amount of dollars to win (and that's **all** I could win), I'd rather play against weak players at High-

Low Split than Hold 'em...even though Hold 'em is my best game. This is because your chances of losing playing High-Low Split against bad players...well, you're just hardly ever going to lose.

THE ANTE AND BETTING STRUCTURE

I rarely play in a game with limits as low as $100 and $200. But...since most of you probably won't be playing in games with limits that "high", I'm going to use that game as the standard around which the discussion in this section will be based. As such, it'll be simple to make an arithmetical adjustment from that game to any other game you may play that has a different limit and ante structure.

Generally, the ante's about 15% of the lower limit. Sometimes it's a little less (10%)...and occasionally it's higher (25%). But, usually, it's $15 in the $100 and $200 High-Low Split game played in Vegas.

In that game, in order to force the action, the first high card *brings it in for* (a **compulsory** bet of) $25. (This is the **only** time the high card **must** act first. After this, the **low** hand is considered "High" and **must** act first — check or bet.) The first raiser (optionally) makes it $75 *to go*. From then on, all other bets and raises are in increments of $100 up to and including *Fourth Street* (the fourth card). Starting with *Fifth Street* (until all the cards are out), all bets and raises are $200. As long as there are more than two players in the pot there's a limit of one bet and (usually) three raises on each round of betting. (The limit on the number of raises prevents partners from putting another player *in the middle*.) However, when the action's head-up, there's **no limit** on raises —the two players involved can continue raising each other until one of them is all-in.

GENERAL STRATEGY EARLY IN THE HAND

You can consider that $15 ante normal. If the ante was $10, you could also consider it normal...that is, **not** really low. So with a $10 ante, your *game plan* (strategy) would be basically unchanged.

However, if the ante was $25 in the $100 and $200 game...then you'd have to make some strategy adjustments. You'd have to start coming in more and play more aggressively (looser). You'd also have to try to steal more antes...a strategy you wouldn't be as much concerned about in a low ante game. Of course, you shouldn't interpret this to mean that you'd indiscriminately take a shot at the antes. Never do that. Only go after the antes when you're in the *steal position* or when you've got a *legitimately playable* hand (both to be defined later). You've got to have some *Outs* when you're *on the steal* and get caught. Don't try to steal with a *garbage* hand when you're out of position.

What's more...once you get *picked off*, you must be able to *put on the brakes*. That's another big weakness in most High-Low Split players (and Poker players in general) —they don't know when to quit. It's a lot of people's downfall. Especially in High-Low Split. Don't get *tied-on* to a hand in the early stages. If you're going to get off a hand (get out of the pot)...**do it early**.

You should also realize that as the ante gets higher, your ability to steal antes and the psychological aspects of the game become more and more important. Correspondingly, your technical knowledge of the game — that is, what to do against fairly well-known hands — becomes less and less important as the ante increases.

As you can see, ante-stealing is more of an art than it is a science. But, there are guidelines you can use until you've perfected your personal art of ante-stealing. For example, let's say you have a *Baby* (a Five or lower) as your first up-card and it's the next-to-last Baby-card in-sight. You're in an excellent position to steal (actually called the *steal position*) because there's **only one** Baby-card behind you that you have to worry about. But, any time there's **more than** one Baby-card behind you, you must have a legitimate hand to play. It's usually **not** worth going after the antes then because the chance that you'll get called is too great.

Most of your ante-stealing situations will require a lot of judgment and a certain "feel" — both of which you acquire mainly through experience. That's why there's so much "art" to it. But, as you gain experience, you'll be able to search your memory-bank and you'll recall that a certain play worked in a similar situation. So you'll use that play again. And you'll wind up with the antes again. As in all judgment situations, your own experience will be a far superior guideline than any hard-and-fast rule.

Ante-stealing and other bluffing situations will be discussed again later when I'll give you additional guidelines you can use. I'll also show you (with specific examples) how to use the guidelines and how to get a "feel" for a particular situation so you can exercise good judgment even with limited experience. But, you should realize that any type of bluffing (or semi-bluffing) you'll do will only be a minor part of your overall strategy. As is true with any form of **Limit** Poker, whatever bluffing you do must be done with discretion...and cautiously. So now, I'll get on with what will be your main strategy and primary goal.

YOUR MAIN STRATEGY

Your main strategy at High-Low will depend to a large degree on your ability to *put your opponent(s) on* a particular hand. That is, you'll have to make an educated guess about the quality of hand your opponent is likely to have. What will help you determine that factor (with a reasonable degree of accuracy) is your *line* on his play — which you'll adjust based on the position he's in.

For example, if you know that he's a solid player (by having **carefully** observed his play) and he gets in the pot in an early position, then you can safely assume he's in there with a pretty decent starting hand. But, if that same player comes in the pot raising from the steal position, you'll then make a different assessment of the kind of hand he's likely to have. In the first case, you wouldn't get in the pot with anything but a **very strong** hand because you'd know he's probably got a very strong hand also. In the second case, you'd probably loosen up your standards because you'd know he's a good enough player to be taking advantage of his (steal) position. But, even though you "know" what he's doing (ante-stealing), there'll be times when you'll just have to let him grab the antes simply because your hand at the time is just **not** playable (under **any** circumstances). However, there'll be other times when you'll "know" he's on the steal and you might try to re-steal the pot from him. Of course, re-stealing is a higher level of art than simply taking advantage of the steal position. So, whenever you play at that level of sophistication, you'll really have to "know your man" and your hand will have to have some *Outs*.

On the other hand, if you're in the pot with someone who you know is a bad (weak) player, then you make the appropriate strategy adjustment. In this case, you can relax your standards somewhat and still be in there with a starting hand that's probably better than his. Or, even if you think this particular (bad) player started with a decent hand, but you know that he'll **routinely call** on Fourth St. if he catches a "Paint" (picture card) and you catch a good card. . .then, you can give him a play on Third St. even if you suspect your hand is marginal (let's say a 6-7-9) and is probably worse than his.

The reason you can give him a play ("gamble" with him) is because you wouldn't be giving up that much. In fact, if he's the type of player I've defined — one who'll **routinely call** on Fourth St. when he catches a Paint **and you catch good**. . .then you actually have the best of him — even though he may have started with a better hand than yours. Here's why:

A player who does that as a matter of course is violating a rule of High-Low Split that you must observe automatically (in **almost** all cases). In fact, it's a rule you must be a slave to. The rule is:

THE *PAINT* RULE

Whenever you catch a Paint *(especially a King or Queen)* **on Fourth St. — and you started with just an** *average* **three-card hand — then that hand is no longer playable and you automatically get out of the pot.**

Strict observance of the **PAINT RULE** will go a long way towards making you a consistent winner at High–Low Split. It would be nice if I could say there are no exceptions to that rule. But there are, of course. Naturally, if you started with a 3♠-4♠-5♠ and caught a K♠ on Fourth St., you'd continue to play. That hand is an exception...and definitely worth playing.

But it's **not** the exceptions you should be concerned with. They'll take care of themselves because the correct play will be as obvious as the example above. It's the average and marginal hands that you won't even consider continuing to play if you catch a Paint on Fourth St. In such a case, you'll just **automatically** throw your hand away.

Conversely, because so many players violate that rule...it gives you the opportunity to convert hands that are only marginally profitable into substantial winners. Here's why: again we'll assume you've played a marginal hand (such as a 6-7-9). In general, with that hand, you'd prefer to have the Nine concealed. But, if you're in the pot with a player who consistently breaks the rule you've just learned, you'd be better off having the Nine in-sight. The reason is that the Sucker would be even more tempted to continue to play against you when he catches a Paint on Fourth St. and you catch good. When he's able to see your Nine, he'll **incorrectly** figure that he's not very far behind you when he catches a King or Queen since both of you now have a *bad one*. Little does he know that the King or Queen that he caught is not merely bad...in High–Low Split **it's a disaster**.

What's more, if you're in a pot with a Sucker who

continually violates the **PAINT RULE**. . .and you have a very good hand such as four low cards on Fourth St. — then he has really fallen into the Trap. Whether your hand is four separate low cards or three low cards and a Pair. . .it doesn't make any difference. If he continues to come (call your bet) after catching a Paint. . .you've snared him. And he's going to have a tough time getting loose.

He may escape (win one-way). . .but the chance that **you'll** get *scooped* (lose both-ways) is very, very slight. And the chance that you'll scoop him is quite good. (I'll soon discuss the concept of *playing to scoop* — which will be your primary goal at High-Low Split.)

In the situation above, because you're practically a sure-winner one-way (either high or low) you're *freerolling*. That is, you have a "free" chance to win both-ends of the pot and (practically) no chance to lose both ways. As you'll later see, in some cases you'll have the *nuts* (an absolute cinch hand) one-way **and** a chance to win the other way. Such a case is a **pure** freeroll. And, because there are so many Suckers at High-Low — players who haven't the vaguest idea about the things you're now learning — you'll find yourself freerolling many a time.

How sweet it is to (constantly) be in a situation where you can win but you can't lose. That's the way it is in High-Low Split, when you're in a good game with two or three Suckers across the table from you. In such a game, you'll be **constantly** freerolling. . .and it's about 7 to 1 or 8 to 1 **against** your having a losing session — even if you play as little as four hours. You've got to like those odds.

There's another decision you must make (related to your overall strategy) that's quite important. It'll be discussed in great detail later. However, for now, I'll just say you must put your **playable** hands into two separate categories:

(1) Those hands that are best (most profitably) played head-up — and

(2) Those hands that you'd like to play with as many players as you can get.

The concept just noted is one of the **keys** to being a winning High-Low Split player. Its importance **cannot** be overemphasized. So...you'll have to keep this concept ever-present in your mind.

Of course, you'll be shown how to categorize the different types of hands. But, first, you must have a clear understanding of what will be your **primary goal** at High-Low Split. Everything else follows from that.

YOUR PRIMARY GOAL

In almost everything that's ever been written on this game *(Cards Speak)*, the basic rule that's most often discussed is to "play for Low." That rule is **almost** correct. But to help you reach your ultimate goal every time you're in a pot...it doesn't quite get there. It's incomplete.

The reason why that rule's so often recommended is because a low hand can work into a high hand quite easily. It's not so easy (and very unlikely) that a high hand will ever work into a low hand. (There are a few exceptions.)

Most (starting) high hands are immediately thrown away because they're **only** one-way hands. And, in High-Low Split, you try **not** to play one-way hands. So that rule's not bad — up to a point.

But, what many players don't realize is that there are also many low hands that are pretty much one-way hands. They have to be thrown away just as quickly as the (one-way) high hands. For example, you'll later learn that hands such as a 7-3-2 — a hand that most people would play without hesitation — is the type of low hand that you'd only play about half the time. Here's why:

Let's say you played that particular hand (7-3-2) and you're in the pot with a solid player. If you catch an Eight on Fourth St. and he catches good...then there's almost nothing he could have that would **not** be a better hand than yours. To go even further, look at the examples on the following page.

	YOU		**OPPONENT**	
Example	_Hole-Cards_	_Up-Cards_	_Hole-Cards_	_Up-Cards_
A.	7♡-3♣	2♡-6♣-K♢	?-?	A♠-A♡-8♠
B.	6♣-6♡	3♡-3♠-Q♢	?-?	8♡-6♡-5♠

Most people with the hands you have above would continue to play them against what they see in their opponent's hand — even though they caught that bad one (the King and Queen) on Fifth St. Their justification for continuing to play those hands is that they think they'll be able to escape with them. In example "A," it appears that you have a good **escape** for the low-end...and in example "B,"· you can escape with the high-end.

It's true. You **can** escape with those hands — so their thinking appears correct.

> **The flaw in their thinking is that they** _won't escape often enough_ **to make those hands profitably playable. That is, the times they do escape and win half the pot will not be enough to overcome the losses they'll incur when they fail to escape and get scooped.**

I'll soon show you how to **specifically** avoid the Trap that most High-Low Split players fall into. But, for now, it's enough that you have the following **general** rule indelibly etched in your mind:

> **When the best you can (reasonably) hope for is to win** _only_ **one half the pot...then your hand must be** _extremely strong_ **in that direction.**

It'll be a very costly mistake to think that a hand which is pretty strong — but only in one-direction — is worth playing. It's not. Once you've given up on half the pot...your hand **must be** _real_ strong for the other half. You'll now be learning **exactly** how strong your hand must be (at the various stages of play). And that's something very few players even consider —much less know how to determine.

However, before I show you how to do that, I want to make a brief but very important comment about what your primary goal should be whenever you play High-Low Split. Here it is:

Your primary goal at High-Low is to win the WHOLE pot.

"Who didn't know that?" you might say. Well...a lot of people don't know it. Because if they did, they wouldn't be in the pot so often trying to escape with half of it. They don't know how much **more profitable** it is to win the **whole** pot. A simple example will show you what I mean. Let's say you're in a three-handed pot and each player has $600 in the pot when it's over. If all you do is split the pot, you wind up with a $300 profit (half of the $600 that one of the players lost). That's really not much when compared to the $1,200 you'd win if you won the **whole** pot. As you can see, it's not twice as good...it's four times as good. And, when the action's only head-up, a split merely means that you get your money back (with the exception of the very small profit you make from splitting the antes). But, when you win the **whole** pot head-up, it's the difference between winning practically nothing and winning everything.

So that's what you should be constantly thinking about whenever you get involved in a High-Low Split pot: **winning it all.** And you should be constantly saying to yourself: *"I want the WHOLE thing."*

Conversely, the **worst** thing that could happen is for you to **lose** the whole pot. That's a disaster. So you must always try to avoid getting yourself into a position where that can happen. You can't always avoid it because sometimes your hand won't let you. For example, your first four cards could be a 3♠-4♠-5♠-6♠ and you'd be tied-on to that hand. Your next three cards could be J♡-Q♣-K♢. If the cards fell that way, you'd almost surely wind-up getting scooped. There's nothing you can do about situations like that. You're helpless. The best you could hope to do is save the last bet.

But, the above example is an extreme case. In most cases, there **are** ways for you to avoid getting scooped. It's **not** easy to do. But it **can** be done.

The times when you'll be most concerned about getting scooped are when you're involved in a head-up pot. (In a multi-way pot, it's **not** likely you'll get very involved without a hand bordering on the nuts for, at least, one-end of the pot.)

To illustrate how you can avoid getting scooped, I'll use the example "A" I previously noted. In that example, when the action got to Fifth St., you had 7♡-3♣-2♡-6♣-K◇. Your opponent had ?-?-A♠-A♡-8♠. Unless a "miracle" occurred and you caught a Four **and** a Five on the last two cards. . .you're almost "dead" to get the whole pot. So, for all practical purposes, you'd have to restrict your chances of getting anything at all out of the pot to your chances of winning one-end of it. In this case, it's clear that your best chance to escape is by winning the low-end. (A high hand of Trips or Two-Pair would be a King-low.) But do you have a 75% chance to escape? No. . .you don't. But, that's what you need to **profitably** continue to play your hand.

You'll be able to see why you need a 75% chance to escape with the simple explanation that follows. (Normal betting — that is, only one bet with each turn of the cards — is assumed.)

In the $100-$200 game, there'd be about $400 in the pot prior to Fifth St. Your opponent is going to have to put in another $600 to get back only $200 (half of the $400 pot that existed prior to Fifth St.). In effect, you're laying 3 to 1. And when you're doing that. . .you must have at least 75% the best of it to make it profitable.

That's what gets a lot of players confused. . .and what causes them to make the bad plays they do. It's also what makes the times they do escape more illusion than real. For example, if they escape two times out of three, they'll psychologically say to themselves *"well, obviously I'm doing the right thing because I'm escaping two times out of three."* But they're deceiving themselves. Because two out of three is just not good enough. In that situation...you must be able to escape at least three times out of four.

The **ESCAPE TABLE** below will give you the guidelines you need in order to determine whether or not it's profitable for you to continue playing a particular hand at the various stages of play.

ESCAPE TABLE

Stage of Play "Street"	Percentage Needed To Escape Profitably*
Fourth	87%
Fifth	75%
Sixth	50%
Seventh	25%

Determining whether or not you have the percentage needed to escape profitably on a particular "Street" is mostly a matter of judgment. Admittedly, it's not easy to do in the "heat of battle." You just have to use good ol' common (card) sense. For example, let's say that you have 7◊-3◊-4◊ -6♣ on Fourth St. and your opponent has ?-?-3♠-3♣. Well, there's no question that your chance to escape (win **at least** one-end) is better than 87%. More than that, your hand has excellent scooping possibilities. So it's definitely worth putting your money in the pot. But, what do you do when it's not that clear-cut — especially when you could **incorrectly** continue to play a hand that should be thrown away. A good example is *"A"* discussed earlier.

---

*These percentages can be slightly less (about 67% — on Fifth St., for example) if you may not have to call the last bet because you *bust out* on the last card (*down the river*). Also, if you have a small chance to scoop, the above percentages can be less by double your scoop-chances. For example, if you have a 10% chance to scoop on Fifth St....then you can subtract 20% (double your scoop-chance) from the 75% you need to escape profitably — dropping that percentage to 55%.

With that hand (7♡-3♣-2♡-6♣-K◇) vs. an opponent with ?-?-A♠-A♡-8♠ you should be able to quickly (intuitively) realize that you **don't** have a 75% chance to escape...so you **don't** put any more money in the pot. Your thinking might go like this:

> "I don't even have to think about winning the high-end. That half's gone for all practical purposes. So, what are the chances I can escape with the low-end? Well, if I make my Seven, I'll most probably win it...although he has a chance to beat my Seven since he's probably got two Babies in the hole. But, what if I don't make a Seven? What if I make an Eight (or worse)? In that case, if he makes an Eight he's likely to beat me on the low-side, too, because my Eight's going to be pretty rough. So...it surely doesn't look like I have a 75% chance to escape. My chances appear to be a lot worse than that. So I think I'll just pass this one."

And while you're throwing away your hand, you get physically (and mentally) ready for the next pot. What's more, instead of feeling bad about having just lost a (small) pot...you begin to feel real good because you were able to (with the help of the **ESCAPE TABLE**) avoid the Trap that most High-Low Split players fall into.

As you gain more and more experience, your judgment (intuition) will become better and better. And as it does, your use of the **ESCAPE TABLE** will become more and more accurate.

I don't want to bog you down with a lot of mathematics, but there's another interesting concept I think you should at least know about. It has to do with the chances of scoop vs. scoop — when two opposing hands both have a chance to win it all. This discussion is going to get technical — and may only be of interest to the mathematicians among you — but, for the sake of completeness, here goes:

HOW TO FIGURE THE CHANCES OF SCOOP vs. SCOOP*

When two opposing hands both have a possibility of scooping, you're really **only** interested in which hand has the best chance of **winning it all.** You're **not** interested in the chances of a split. If one hand has a 20% chance of scooping and the other hand has a 10% chance of scooping — and the rest of the time it's a split — then the 20% hand is a 2 to 1 favorite over the 10% hand.

To show you how to figure which hand is the **favorite** to scoop, I'll use the following two hands as an example:

"NINES"	"EIGHT"
5-6-7-2-9-9	4-3-2-A-8-4

(No flush possible with either hand.)

I'll refer to one of the above hands as "Nines" (since it's a winner going down the river on the high-side with a Pair of Nines)...and the other hand will be referred to as "Eight" (since it has an Eight-low already made).

To figure the chances a hand has to scoop, you must name each (good) card one hand can catch to give it a possible scoop. Then, when you determine how many of those cards there are, you multiply that number by the number of (bad) cards the other hand can possibly catch to make the scoop "stick."

Taking the Nines first...it'll scoop if it improves its Low to a Seven-low — provided the Eight does not improve in either direction. Therefore, the possible scooping cards that will give the Nines a Seven-low are an Ace, Three or Four. There are 3-Aces left, 3-Threes and 2-Fours. Any one of those cards will be a scoop for the Nines if the Eight catches any bad card: one of 4-Kings, 4-Queens, 4-Jacks, 4-Tens or

---

*You might be interested in knowing that you can count on one hand the number of people who know how to make this calculation.

2-Nines (a total of 18 cards). This is shown in the table below.

SCOOPING POSSIBILITIES FOR "NINES"

Good Cards for Nines		Bad Cards for Eight		Total Scoops Possible
3-Aces	×	18	4-K's	=	54
3-Treys	×	18	4-Q's / 4-J's	=	54
2-Fours	×	18	4-10's / 2-9's	=	36

The Nines can scoop in this number of possible ways......... **144**

The Eight will scoop if it improves its High (to Two-Pair, Trips or a Straight) — provided the Nines do not improve its Low (to a Seven-low...**not** an Eight-low). A further provision that must exist for the Eight to scoop if it improves its High is that the Nines cannot simultaneously improve its High to a better High than the Eight. Therefore, the Eight can possibly scoop if it catches one of 3-Aces, 2-Deuces, 3-Threes, 2-Fours, 3-Fives or 3-Eights. Any one of those cards will be a scoop for the Eight if the Nines catch a bad card as seen below.

SCOOPING POSSIBILITIES FOR "EIGHT"

Good Cards for Eight		Bad Cards for Nines*		Total Scoops Possible
3-Aces	×	27 { 4-K's, 4-Q's, 4-J's, 4-10's / 3-7's, 3-6's, 3-5's, 2-2's }	=	81
2-Deuces	×	16 { 4-K's, 4-Q's, 4-J's, 4-10's }	=	32
3-Treys	×	16 { 4-K's, 4-Q's, 4-J's, 4-10's }	=	48
2-Fours	×	27 { 4-K's, 4-Q's, 4-J's, 4-10's / 3-7's, 3-6's, 3-5's, 2-2's }	=	54
3-Fives	×	36 { 4-K's, 4-Q's, 4-J's, 4-10's / 2-9's, 3-7's, 3-6's, 2-5's / 2-4's, 3-3's, 2-2's, 3-A's }	=	108
3-Eights	×	16 { 4-K's, 4-Q's, 4-J's, 4-10's }	=	48

The Eight can scoop in this number of possible ways **371**

---

*An Eight is a good card for the Nines since it'll make a Straight (giving the Nines the nuts for High).

As you can see from the numbers above (Total Scoops Possible), in a scoop vs. scoop — the Eight is a 371 to 144 favorite (or about 2½ to 1).*

You might also be interested in knowing there will be a decision (split or scoop) 1560 times. This is always the number on Sixth St. (assuming no other cards have been seen). That number is arrived at as follows: the total number of cards left is 40; after the first hand catches a card, there are 39 left; 40 × 39 = 1560 decisions.

Of the total (1560) decisions, there will be 515 scoops (371 for the Eight plus 144 for the Nines). So there'll be a scoop about one third of the time. [The Eight will scoop 23.8% of the time (371/1560) and the Nines will scoop 9.2% of the time (144/1560).]

I hope all the previous Math was not too technical and was easily understood. Nevertheless, was it an exercise in futility? Was it of any practical value? Just how much of that stuff can actually be done right at the playing table?

Those are good questions. I'll have to respond to them in two ways. First, if you just glanced at the calculations and didn't go over them **carefully**. . .then it won't be of much value to you. But, if you **studied** the example. . .and, more importantly, make up numerous examples of your own and work them out exactly as shown — then the example will be of great value to you.

The more (home) work you do in figuring out similar problems, the better your judgment (or feel or intuition) will be when you're in a pot and might have to make a big decision. For example, let's say you have the Eight (the exact hand previously discussed) and your opponent has (exactly) the Nines. While you may not know exactly how much better your hand is. . .because of the many examples you've worked on at home, you might see certain similarities and be

---

*An interesting note to this example is that the Eight *automatically gets at least* a split if it improves (even slightly) in either direction. But, the Nines have *no automatic win*. If it just improves *slightly*. . .it can still get scooped. This interesting fact is a good indication of why the results are what they are: that is, the Eight will scoop about 2½ times as often as the Nines.

able to make a very good educated guess that you're about a 2 to 1 or 3 to 1 favorite. [(Of course, you'd never know exactly the true *price* (odds) because his hole cards would be unknown. But, if his *Board* (up-cards) with the Nines was 7-2-9-9, it would be reasonable for you to assume he had two Babies in the hole. Making that assumption, you'd be able to put him on a hand very close to the one he actually has. You'd then know you're something of a favorite. At the very least, you'd know you're **not** a *dog*.)]

Knowing these odds (even approximately) would be of great value to you if an opponent with the Nines was under the impression that he actually had the better hand (to scoop). If he actually thought that, he just might keep on raising you. And you'd be more than willing to get into a "raising war" with him.

Interestingly, the "raising war" is a distinct possibility. The reason is because the example you've just seen is an **exception** to a **general** rule of High-Low Split. That rule is:

> **In a scoop vs. scoop situation, the high hand is** *generally* **in a better position to scoop than the low hand.**

In other words, what the above rule means is the hand in the lead on the high-end usually has an easier time catching-up on the low-end than vice versa. (It's usually more difficult for the better low hand to improve the high part of its hand.)

Before getting into a general and specific discussion of the starting hands you should play (and not play), there's another very important concept you should know about. It's the *protection* concept.

> **Simply stated** *protection* **is having a hand that protects you from being scooped. That is, having a hand that's** *almost certain to get at least* **one-end of the pot.**

Having a protected hand doesn't mean you'll have the absolute nuts for one-end of the pot (although sometimes you will). It means you have a hand that's **almost a cinch** to win one-way (at least) while giving you a freeroll to get the other half. For example, let's say you start with two Aces and a Three. On Fourth St., you catch a Seven. Your opponent has a Five-King (offsuit) in-sight. At that point you'd be practically freerolling. Because, how's he going to beat those two Aces? Dismissing the unlikely possibility of making him a Straight or Flush...he's got to make Two-Pair or Trips. Either one of those hands will give him a King-low — a low hand you're almost certainly going to beat.

Even if his two hole cards are, let's say, a Deuce and a Trey...you'd be in great shape. Two Aces with a Three and a Seven against a 2-3-5-K is just a monster favorite. There's very little chance the A-A-3-7 can get scooped. You may not know which way you're freerolling, but you're almost certainly freerolling in one direction.

If you constantly play hands that are **not** likely to get scooped...then you'll almost always be in a "can win-can't lose" situation. As I said before: *"how sweet it is."* You'll be constantly freerolling. And, when you're constantly up against a hand you can scoop...well, eventually you **will** scoop it.

Before getting on to other things, I'd like to (somewhat differently) re-state the protection concept...because it's such an important one. When you have a protected hand, it means your opponents will have to do some heavy chasing (go way uphill) to overcome one of your directions. And, if they do overcome that direction...it's going to be very hard for them to get the other half also. [A protected hand is usually one with a Pair of Aces or even a medium Pair (such as Sevens or Eights) and a good draw on the low-side.]

STARTING HANDS GENERAL STRATEGY

There's a very important concept — common to all forms of Poker — that's super-important in High-Low. It's something you **must** be aware of whenever you're involved in a pot. It is: **how many opponents can you expect to be competing with?**

The hands you'll play (and won't play) — and **how** you'll play the hands you do play — will greatly depend on the number of players in the pot.

> **So, it'll be very important for you to consider whether you are (or will be) head-up (or not)** *not only* **on Third St. (with your starting hand) but also in the later stages of the action.**

A little later you'll be learning **specifically** what hands to play (and how to play them) depending on the circumstances. You'll also be learning the subtle distinctions you'll have to make so that you can play as close to a perfect game as possible. But, for now, I'll just give you a general idea of some of the things you must consider.

A common error is frequently made by numerous High–Low players when they have a Pair and a small card.* The error is that they don't differentiate between the Pairs when the hands are equal in value for Low.

For example, there's a big difference between a Pair of Deuces and a Six and a Pair of Sixes and a Deuce. The 6-6-2 is a far better hand. The reason is because the two hands have the same potential for Low...but the Sixes have a big edge on the high-side. The Sixes might be just the edge you need to escape with the high-end of the pot (especially in a head–up situation). But, if all you had were the Deuces, you'd find that quite frequently an opponent is going to make (by accident) a Pair of Threes, Fours or Fives and your escape-hatch will be closed. The Sixes will (often) get you out of the Trap. The Deuces, rarely.

In order to fully appreciate the enormous difference between the two hands, think about the example on the following page:

---

*A "small card" is a Seven (or lower). An Eight is borderline. A Nine (or higher) is no longer a "small card".

YOU	OPPONENT
6-6-2-A-3-4	2-2-6-A-3-4

(No Flush possible with either hand.)

As you can see, the cards broke exactly even on Fourth, Fifth and Sixth. Assuming they break even down the river (let's say, both hands catch a bad one)...here's what happens: you'll win 75% of the pot because you'll split the low-end (since you're tied) — but, you'll "scoop" the high-end.

> **The important point to remember is when you're considering playing Pairs they must be in the higher range of the lower cards...and you almost always have to have a small card to go with the Pair.** *(Specifically, a Pair of Fives is marginally playable. Sixes and Sevens are usually okay. Eights — and frequently Nines — can be played...with a small card.)*

To an experienced High-Low player, the huge difference between the Sixes and Deuces may have been fairly obvious because the two hands were **identical** for Low and the other was **much better** for High. Sometimes, however, the huge difference between two hands (that appear equal) is not obvious. When one hand has the lead for High and the other has the lead for Low, an unsophisticated player will think the hands are therefore equal. In most cases...they're **not** even close.

For example, two such hands are two Deuces and a Six vs. two Eights and a Deuce. The 2-2-6 has the lead on the low-side and the 8-8-2 has the lead on the high-side. So, in High-Low Split, the two hands are equal. Right? Wrong! It's **not** even close. The 8-8-2 would be a **very big** winner over the 2-2-6 if you just played the hands against one another *hot and cold* — that is, you simply dealt four random cards (continuously) to each hand. The reason is the Eights are a tremendous favorite to win the high-end...and only a slight underdog for the low-end. [An interesting ramification to this example highlights a point I noted earlier and which I'll discuss later in more detail. It's that certain hands (such as the 8-8-2 above) which are great in one spot can be unplayable in another. Head-up against a 2-2-6, your 8-8-2 will really take down the money. But, if a player with a Nine-up **also** came in the pot. . .then you could throw the 8-8-2 away because you'd also probably be up against two Nines (with a small card). In that case, you could be starting with the worst Low-hand **and** the worst High-hand.]

> **In High-Low Split, there's nothing worse than to be chasing in** *both* **directions.**

When you have a hand such as 8-8-2, the times you have to be worried are when you're in the pot against an Ace. You'll have two reasons for concern:

(1) The player with the Ace may already have a Pair of them (especially if no other Ace showed) *with a small card;* **or**

(2) He may catch an Ace (which he'll do about 25% of the time with four cards to come) — if the Ace isn't already paired.

So with 8-8-2 against an Ace. . .you could be in very serious trouble. If the Ace isn't already paired. . .he's going to get there one out of four times. And, if he is already paired (with a hand such as A-A-6). . .well, he's just a tremendous favorite over your hand (8-8-2). He's starting with a better High **and** a better Low.

You should **not** interpret the above to mean you'd never play a Pair of Eights against an Ace. It's just **not** playable in a head-up situation. But, if you had an 8-8-2 in a three-way pot, against, let's say, a Five and an Ace (who's in the steal position). . .then your hand is worth playing. I'll zero-in on the situation more closely by saying the player with the Five is weak and the player with the Ace is strong and really trying to steal the antes. If the Ace catches bad on Fourth, he'll probably give it up right there. You could hope for that and also hope you catch good on Fourth. You also wouldn't mind if the Five catches good...in which case you'd have a good head–up hand against the Five.

In reality, you must be very, very careful when you're up against an Ace when you have a small or medium Pair.

There's another time you have to be very careful when you have a small or medium Pair...and this instance highlights a very interesting and curious thing about High–Low. A common error made by...well, a jillion people...is they'll have a King–up and a King–Deuce in the hole and they'll play that hand. They'll even play it against an Ace! (It's incredible how badly some people play this game.) Even if the Ace isn't already paired...you've already learned it's only 3 to 1 he doesn't catch one to beat the Kings. A Pair of Kings is a hand not even worth discussing ...and I wouldn't have mentioned it if I didn't see so many Suckers play it.

It's also worth mentioning for another reason. The Suckers who play that hand (and similar high Pairs) can create problems for you. It's a problem you wouldn't have at another form of Poker...and makes the situation a strange one, to say the least.

Normally, you want to be up against (bad) players who are playing high cards. Because, when they're doing that, they're making a mistake. But, there are times when their bad play can force you out of a pot you'd ordinarily play. This may sound strange...but it can easily be explained. Here's how:

Let's say you're in the pot with 8–8–2. (By the way, this is **not** the only hand I know how to play. I've learned how to play one more hand. I'll tell you about that one later.) If you've got a Pair of Eights and you're in the pot with a Sucker who's got a bigger Pair and there's **also a player who's going for Low**...well, then, you've got to let go of your hand. His bad playing (with the high Pair) made your hand no longer playable. You'd be chasing both ways. **NEVER do that.**

For example, you start with an 8-8-2 and you're in the pot with two opponents. One has a 7-5-2 and the other has a J-J-4.

If you were in there **alone** with an 8-8-2 against a 7-5-2, you'd be all right. The two hands are about equal. You have to go way uphill to catch him on the low-end and he has a similar problem in beating you for High.

But, when the Sucker with the two Jacks gets in the pot...you no longer have anything. His (the Jacks) bad playing has forced you to throw your hand away. That might be pretty obvious because you're beat both ways.

However, there are other times that are not so obvious because a bad player in the pot with you and another expert can create a situation where you'd be forced to throw away a hand that'll probably win one-way. This unusual situation is illustrated below.

YOU	SUCKER	EXPERT
A-2-5-8-K	?-?-J-J-J	?-?-6-8-Q

On Fifth St., the expert bets. (You'll remember, the Low-hand in-sight must act first from Fourth St. on.) You know you've got a better four-card Eight than he does — and will probably win the low-end. But, in this particular situation, you can no longer play your hand. You **must** throw it away because the Sucker is surely going to raise.

The expert actually made a very good play by betting into you because he knows it's mathematically correct for you to release your hand in that situation. If you were in his spot, you should make the same play he did. He wants to get head-up with the Sucker because then he'd be almost certain to get half the pot.

The reason why you can no longer play your hand is because everytime you (and the other expert) put your money in the pot...both of you would be donating half of it to the Sucker (who'll most probably win the high-end). For you to call the expert's bet and the expected raise by the

Sucker, it would be as if you're playing in a game where the pot is being raked 50%. That's another thing you NEVER want to do. So you get rid of your hand. Many players make the mistake of calling in that spot thinking their call is correct because they have the potentially best hand for Low. They're right about having the potentially best one-way hand...but they're wrong about making the call.

Another mistake many players make is that they'll slow-play a good hand because they don't want to chase anyone out of the pot. That's a very common error. So here's another profitable principle of play you should have etched in your mind:

> **It's *almost* NEVER correct to slow-play your hand.**

Always remember, the bigger the pot is...the less you gain by (slow-playing a hand) and letting someone in cheap. (This is true in all Poker — not only High-Low Split.) Even if the player you let in the pot is a big underdog to you... you **can't** let him get in the pot cheap. If you do, then you're letting him get the best of it.

For example, let's say there's $800 in the pot. The man in front of you bets $100. You can call for $100 or raise to $200 because you've got a very good hand. Your hand is so good that the man behind you is an 8-1 dog. So you want to let him in by merely calling the $100. If you do that, the pot'll be $1000 when the action gets to the player behind you. That means he'll be getting 10 to 1 when he calls...so his call would be a good one since he's only an 8 to 1 dog. But, if you raise and make it cost him $200 to call...you'll be cutting down the odds he'll be getting to 5½ to 1. If he called in the latter case, he'd be taking the worst of it. And that's what you want. So **don't** give your opponents the best of it by slow-playing your hands.

Now that you have something of a foundation on which to build your strategy I'll discuss the specific hands you should (and should not) play and how to make your decision depending on the circumstances.

ALWAYS PLAYABLE HANDS
general considerations

Certain hands in High-Low Split are always playable...
no matter what circumstances. (There are rare exceptions.)
But, even though those hands should always be played...
there are ways you can play them so they'll be even more
profitable than they might otherwise be. You'll soon see
what I mean because I'll show you how to extract maximum
value from them.

Your primary consideration in deciding **how** you want to
play a particular hand (that you'll always play) is whether
you want to reduce the action to a head-up situation (or, at
most, two opponents) or whether you'd rather be involved in
a multi-way pot.

For example, let's say you had a 3-4-6 (offsuit). With a
hand that good you might be forced to slow-play it
depending on your position and how the action went. If
you're first to act, you should raise with it. It shouldn't be
slow-played. Play it the same way you'd play a hand that's
not quite as strong. But, if there's a raise in front of
you...you're almost forced to slow-play it (by merely calling
the raise).* If you put in a raise yourself, you'd lose most (or
all) of the players behind you. They'd have to call a
double-bet *cold* — which is not likely.

When you have a near-perfect starting hand (such as
3◊-4◊-5◊)...you want a lot of customers. So take a
"chance" with it and let 'em come on in. You could catch a
perfect card (the 2◊ or 6◊) on Fourth...and you'd be in
great shape to scoop a three-way (or four-way) pot. And
that's what High-Low's all about — scooping the pot...
especially a multi-way pot.

But there are other hands you'd always play that are
most profitable when played head-up. So, with hands in that
category...you want to maneuver yourself into a head-up

---

*Remember...I said you should *almost* never slow-play your hand.

situation. Such a hand would be a Pair of Aces and a Five. Of course, you'd always raise with that hand. What's more, if there's a raise in front of you...you **must** raise yourself. It's absolutely mandatory. In contrast to the previous situation, you **want to** restrict the field. Whenever you have a hand with good scooping possibilities (but one that's **only a** favorite to scoop in a head–up situation), you want to force the players behind you to call a double-bet. With a hand such as 7-5-A, you'd also make the same play. Don't even think about it. **Automatically re-raise** when you have a hand where you want the action head-up.

There are also hands where it wouldn't make too much difference whether you had to play them head-up or multi-way. Such a hand would be A-2-3. It's kind of a head-up type hand, but it would be debatable whether or not to re-raise with it. It would depend on the situation.

For example, if a man raised in front of you — and you think he's bluffing (on the steal) — you should re-raise. But, if you think he's really got a hand...you then have to decide whether or not you want other people in the pot. Since this is **not** an automatic re-raise situation...you'll have to (quickly) evaluate the situation. Your evaluation will be based on many factors such as who's behind you, what cards they have and the tempo of the game. Then you'll have to exercise your judgment. That's always the case in situations that aren't "cut-and-dried". Of course, your judgment will get better and better as you gain more and more experience.

Occasionally, you'll be faced with a problem after you've re-raised. You should know how to handle it.

The problem is, whenever you put extra money in the pot with a double-bet, you'll find it more difficult to fold your hand on Fourth St. when you catch a Paint and your opponent catches a little one. It would still be correct to fold your hand...but it's not a clear-cut decision. You'll simply have to make an on-the-spot evaluation. Your decision will depend on the particulars of the individual situation. It may be that your hand is not that much worse than your opponent's and you could be getting a good price (pot odds) if you call.

In general, the type of hand you have, your position and how the action went before it got to you are the factors that'll determine **how** you'll play a hand you'll always play.

> If you're in an early or middle position and you have a hand you'd prefer to play head-up with...then you put in a raise (or double-raise). With a hand that's most profitably played with many players...you may or may not raise (or re-raise) depending on your position. In an early (or middle) position, you might want to *limp-in* (just call). In a late position, there'd be less reason to slow-play your hand.

With certain hands (such as the 3♡-4♡-6♡), you're "forced" to take two cards (go to Fifth St. with the hand) — regardless of the card you catch *on the Turn* (Fourth St.). So, when you're the last man (to act)...and you have one of the dynamite hands in this game...**always double-raise.**

SPECIFIC HANDS THAT ARE ALWAYS PLAYABLE

The stronger the hand you have to start with...the more ways you'll be able to win. The more things you have going for you, the more Outs you'll have. It's simply a matter of common sense...and probabilities.

In most cases, three small cards are always playable. That's a strong hand. If they were three to a Straight, they'd be even stronger. Three to a Straight-Flush is stronger still. The latter hands are "dynamite" starting hands.

Three-Four-Five is **probably** the best possible starting hand. I say "probably" because in a head-up situation — two Aces and a Baby card comes close to it. Especially if the Baby card is a Deuce. That hand (A-A-2) would then have three of the cards that would greatly improve the 3-4-5.

As you can see, in evaluating and ranking hands (strength-wise) a lot depends on the cards that are out. But, in general, A-A-Baby is not quite as good as 3-4-5...but it's better than a hand such as 7-5-2.

If you think about all the things and specific hands I'll discuss **from a conceptual point of view** — rather than just memorize them — your feel for the game (judgment) will be far better than if you just play like a robot.

As an example of how to think conceptually, I'll discuss a hand such as 7-5-2. Most players would consider that to be a "super" starting hand. It's a good starting hand, but there's nothing super about it. Yet, I've seen players *jamming* (raising and re-raising) pots with it. When they do that...they're playing badly. You should always have a three-card Straight to jam a pot. (A little rule of thumb is that a Deuce and a Seven won't *stretch* to make a Straight.)

Sometimes that hand (7-5-2) or a similar hand isn't even playable. If you think you're going to be in a head-up situation with it...you should throw it away (especially if your opponent is a tight player and it's a low-ante game). You wouldn't want a hand like that in a head-up situation anymore than you'd like a Pair of Kings head-up. Why? It's simple! **How** are you going to win both ways?

> **So, if your starting hand is the kind that** *won't* **give you a chance to win both ways...then you should** *not* **play it when it looks like you could be head-up.**

Here's an example of the way that situation could come up: a player with an Ace-up raises in front of you. You have a 7-3-2 (all **different** suits). You should throw your hand away. He almost surely has a better hand than you do. You shouldn't care what he has — there's no chance your hand's as good as his. **I would rather have an A-8-9 than a 2-3-7.**

In fact, 2-3-7 (in three different suits) is so bad in that spot that there's no question it should be thrown away. It's a hand that's only about equal to an Ace and two **random** cards.* It's a definite dog to an Ace and two **good** cards. The reason is: it's just a one-way hand. And to play it head-up against a hand that could scoop you would be a very bad play. Very costly. Very unprofitable.

> **Never lose sight of your primary goal which is to win** *both-ends* **of the pot. And always remember that when you scoop a pot — especially a three-way or four-way pot — you could almost lose the rest of the night and still show a profit.**

That's why I suggested earlier that you slow-play a hand like 3◊-4◊-5◊. It's because you can win a real big pot with that kind of hand.**(Of course, a hand like this is an **exception** to the rule that you should **not** slow-play a starting hand. It's also why I stated you should **almost** never slow-play one.)

If the high-card (the player who's forced to bring it in) is to your immediate right...you shouldn't raise with a dynamite hand. You want to give the players behind you every opportunity to get in the pot...because you want to give yourself a chance to win a real big pot. It's true that the players behind you might know what you're doing (slow-playing a big hand)...but the fact that they can get in cheap will probably be an overriding consideration. So they'll most probably come on in. Which is exactly what you want.

However, if there's a raise behind you after you limp-in...then you must play your hand when the action

---

*You might want to see this for yourself. Start one hand with a 7-3-2 (all different suits). Deal it four more cards. Start the other hand with a single Ace. Deal it six more cards. You'll find that, on average, the two hands are about equal. That is, each hand will scoop about the same number of times.

**You'll have about a 35% chance to make a Straight or Flush with a 3-4-5 *suited*. That's why it's such a great scooping hand to start with.

gets back to you. "Slow-play time" is over. You put in a raise yourself and continue to play your dynamite hand as aggressively as you can.

Now that you have something of a conceptual framework around which you can build your starting-hand strategy...I'll put in capsule form the **always-playable** hands. Then, I'll discuss the important things you should be aware of that are pertinent to the items in the table below:

ALWAYS PLAYABLE HANDS
Action Preferred

Head-up	*Multi-Way*	*No preference*
7-Baby-A	**3-Babies***	**3-card Sixes†**
A-A-Baby	**3-card Sixes****	**3-Card Sevens††**
A-A-6		**3-Card Eights** (suited only)
A-A-7		**Trip A's, 7's, & 8's**
A-A-8		

*Three different (unpaired) cards. (2-4-5 is O.K.; 2-2-4 is not.)

These (unpaired) Sixes **must have Straight possibilities (even if it's a broken Straight possibility such as 6-4-2).

†The (unpaired) Sixes that have "no preference" are those with an ace.

††These Sevens **must** have **strong** Straight or Flush possibilities.

Hopefully, the above table will enable you to quickly determine those hands you'll **always** play...and **how** they're most profitably played. (You should read the footnotes **carefully** since they're a **precise** definition of the hands categorized in the table.)

Each hand has been put into a category according to the action you'd **prefer** to have (**not** the action you must have) with that particular hand. A hand in the "head-up" category (7-Baby-Ace or A-A-Baby) is there because it's most profitably played one-on-one. With those hands, you'd try to force the action (by strategic raises) to a head-up situation. But, if you were unable to get the action you'd prefer (head-up) on Third St. — you'd still play the hand. Then, you'd try to get head-up on Fourth St. (assuming, of course, you didn't catch a bad one).

The reason you want to play those hands head-up is because they have a greater probability of scooping the pot when you're up against only one opponent. Against more than one opponent, they're still winning hands. It's just that in a multi-way pot, you'll more likely have to settle for a split.

Similarly, the two hands in the multi-way (action preferred) category are the type of hands you'd like to play against several opponents. They're the dynamite hands that'll get you off to a great start on your way to scooping a big pot. At the very least, they'll be **very strong** one-way (enabling you to split a big pot) should they lose their scoop potential. As already discussed, your strategy with this type of hand should be to get as many customers as you can.

The hands in the "no preference" category are those that'll do equally as well in a head-up or multi-way pot. If you had to play any of those hands head-up...it's O.K. If you got involved with them in a multi-way pot...well, that's O.K. too.

It should be quite obvious why most of the hands in the table should always be played. But, rare circumstances could exist when you might not want to play some of them. The most common of the rare situations is when you felt almost positive one of your opponents had wired Trips. If your hand has possibilities for **only** the low-end of the pot and you were **not** a **big** favorite to win that half...you'd do well to refuse to play one of the always-playable hands. A better spot will come up later. (Remember...a pot like that is equivalent to one that's raked 50%.)

Also, if you felt reasonably certain you were up against Trips **and** three Babies with A-A-8 (or lower)...you'd have to pass this "always-playable" hand too. Once again, you **never** want to be in a multi-way pot taking the worst of it on both ends. It's bad enough being in a multi-way pot with the best hand one-way and the worst the other way. To have the worst hand in both directions is just a catastrophe.

Another rare case that could occur when you would **not** play an always-playable hand is when all (or almost all) of the cards you need are gone. For example, let's say you had a

6-5-3 and when the action gets to you, you're faced with calling a double-raise *cold*. Normally, you'd like that situation because you have exactly the type of hand you'd want to have in a multi-way pot. But, in this case, you notice that **all** the Fours are gone. Your hand just wouldn't be playable in that spot. You can't make a Straight...so you're left with a one-way hand. And because of the double-raise, you're obviously up against dynamite. (If you saw only two Fours out, you'd probably want to fold a 6-5-3. With only one Four out, you should definitely play the hand.)

There's an interesting point you should be aware of related to the always-playable Trips (Aces, Sevens and Eights). Not only are those hands strong enough to give you a good escape-hatch (because you're going to go all the way through with them)...but you can win the **whole pot** with them **at any point**. If you're in a head-up situation with those Trips and your opponent catches bad, he might well decide to give it up **before the end**.

A Pair of Aces and a small card is very strong against one player. It goes down in value dramatically against many players. Against two players, it would be all right — especially if you think one of them might fold at some point in the hand. Even if both players stayed all the way, your Aces might stand-up for High...and you'd still have a shot at the low-end. But, **against more than two opponents**, two Aces and a little one is a hand that loses a lot of its value.

The reason it's such a good head-up hand is because it gives you a lot of scooping possibilities. The only way one player can overcome your High is when he makes a Straight, a Flush or Two-Pair — a long uphill road to climb. And if he makes Two-Pair, he almost surely won't beat you for Low. So it's also a hand with a lot of protection against one player.

When you have that hand, (A-A-small), you should always make every effort to play it head-up. If the man to your right (in front of you) raises...double-pop it (trying to knock out everybody behind you). If no one has raised in front of you...you should definitely raise.

On Fourth St. also, you should continue to do everything you can to get into a head-up situation. As you'll later learn on page 312, you could be in an ideal position to check-raise enabling you to force a head-up situation.

Although the various ways to play the always-playable hands have by no means been exhausted, I think you now have a good general idea of how to play them. So we'll move on and discuss hands not quite as stong — the *usually-playable* hands.

USUALLY-PLAYABLE HANDS

You'll have to exercise considerably more judgment with a hand that's *usually*-playable than you would with a hand that's always-playable. The key word is, of course, **usually**. To be certain you don't misinterpret my meaning, I'm going to define it precisely. What I mean by *usually*-playable is that you'll play the hands in this category most of the time...but **not** all the time. By definition then, they're quite different than the *always*-playable hands. Generally, your only concern with the always-playable hands is **how** you'll play them — **not** whether you'll play them. With a *usually*-playable hand, you'll have two considerations to make:

(1) **Whether you should play them, and**

(2) **How you should play them.**

In some spots they're as good as the always-playable hands; in others, they may be only marginally-playable; and, in certain spots...they're non-playable. The relative value of the hands you'll usually play depends, to a great extent, on the hands you're likely to be up against.

For example, let's say you have a 7-7-3 (which is a hand you'll usually prefer to play head-up). A Queen brings it in for $25. You make it $75. No one behind you calls your raise. The Queen wants to "save" his force (as most Suckers do)...so he calls your raise. Now...your slightly weak hand has become very strong. You're a big favorite in this spot. Here's why:

It's **unlikely** the Queen is paired since he was **forced** in. But even if he is paired, you have a very big lead on the low-side. Assuming his *side-card* (kicker) is a Baby, he'd have to catch four (almost perfect) cards to your three to beat you. The far greater probability is that he has two Babies in the hole. (He must have "something" to have called you.) In this case, you're (at worst) a slight dog on the low-side. But...you have a comfortable lead on the high-side.

The major point is that his only reasonable hope is to beat you one-way. You, on the other hand, are protected against getting scooped...with a fair opportunity to scoop him.

Now, I'll give you the same hand (7-7-3) in a different situation. A King brings it in and an Ace raises. A Queen calls cold. You're next to act. What do you do? You get rid of your hand just as quickly as you can! That usually-playable hand has become **unplayable** in this spot. It would be unplayable against the Ace alone. When the Queen called cold, it's as if he showed you his hole cards. You know there's at least one more Queen there (giving him a Pair of Queens). So you'd be chasing in both directions if you called. And, in High-Low Split, there's nothing worse than that.

Of course, many of the things I discussed in the previous section (on *always-playable* hands) will be applicable here. You'll also be able to relate the things I'll now discuss to those hands. In fact, the general guidelines you'll now learn could have been discussed earlier. They're more appropriate here because the always-playable hands can almost play themselves. This is **not** true of the usually-playable hands.

Once again, the hands will be categorized (in the table below) according to the action you'd prefer to have with them: head-up, multi-way or no preference.

USUALLY **PLAYABLE HANDS**
Action Preferred

Head-up	*Multi-way*	*No preference*
A-A-9 & A-A-10	**Trip 10's**	**3-card Nines & Tens**
9-9-Baby*	**J's, Q's, K's†**	*(suited only)*
	Trip 2's, 3's,	**3-card Sevens‡**
8-8-Baby*	**4's, 5's, 6's, 9's††**	
7-7-Baby*		
6-6-Baby*		
3-card Eights**		
7-8-9-**		

With these hands, head-up action is not merely preferred...it's almost mandatory. If you're not successful in getting the action head-up on Third St., you can play for a card and try to get head-up on Fourth St.

These Eights Must have Straight possibilities (even if it's a broken Straight possibility such as 8-6-5). If no Straight is possible, the Eight must contain an Ace (e.g., 8-4-A).

****This is the only Straight Nine that's "usually-playable." As you'll see, the other Nines with Straight possibilities are "borderline" hands.***

†You definitely want multi-way action with these Trips.

††These Trips can be played head-up or multi-way, but you're probably better off playing them in a multi-way pot.

‡Any 3-card Seven not in the "Always-Playable" table. (Such a hand is a 7♡ - 5♠ - 2◇.)

The "head-up" hands are going to be discussed last because how and when you play those hands (medium Pairs) is one of the most important strategy decisions you'll have to make. Knowing exactly what to do with them will play a significant part in whether you'll be just a good High-Low player...or a very good one.

You might have noticed that the hands in the "multi-way" category above are quite different than the hands in the same category in the *always-playable* table. This is so because two very different types of hands are most profitably played against more than one player.

The first type of hand is the one that has good scooping possibilities in a multi-way pot. Such a hand is three little cards with Straight and/or Flush possibilities. Hands like a 3◇-4♠-5♡ or 3◇-4◇-6◇ are the ones you'll **always play** and would **prefer** to play against a lot of players.

The other kind of hand you'd prefer to have a lot of action with is the one that's **unlikely** to scoop a pot...but is very, very strong one-way. Such a hand is three Kings. If you're going to play a hand like that...you want as many players as possible. You can't win anything unless you get a lot of players because you're "dead" for one-end of the pot. All you're going to do is get your money back (and not always) if you get involved in a head-up pot.

Therefore, with a one-way hand, you need at least three players going all the way to the end. And that means you better have four or five players to start out with because one (or two) will most probably drop out before the end.

A hand on the low-side that's essentially a one-way hand is a 7♡-5♠-2◇. This kind of Seven (**no** probable Straight or Flush potential and **no** Ace) is in the "no preference" category in the *usually-playable* table because it's **not** an absolutely one-way hand such as three Kings. But, it **is** the kind of hand that would be more profitably played in a multi-way pot. Nevertheless, I'll leave it in the "no preference" category because it's more appropriate there.

This little discussion points out a very important general rule that should constantly guide your play. That rule is:

> **When you have a hand with little or no scooping possibilities...that hand must be very, very strong one-way.**

It's also important to note that when you have a one-way hand such as three Kings...it could become **unplayable** after you get involved with it. For example, if the pot started out four-way and then, on Fourth St., two players dropped out...you'd have to throw those three Kings away. You just **can't** play a hand like that head-up because it's going to cost you too much money to go the rest of the way with it. The best you could hope for is a split...while you might get scooped.

But, in a multi-way pot, three Kings is a hand that's going to show a profit (although you won't win every pot with it). It's usually enough to win the high-end without any improvement. More than that; you're going to make a Full House about 32% of the time or Fours (four-of-a-kind) about 8% of the time. So, approximately 40% of the time you'll be the nuts to get half the pot. And it could be a big one if somebody makes a Straight or Flush when you do improve. That'll somewhat compensate you for the times you don't improve and lose to a Straight or Flush (which will happen about 10% of the time).

The reason why the always-playable Trips (Aces, Sevens and Eights) are better hands than the high Trips is because they're something of a two-way hand. However slight, there's a chance (with three-Sevens, for example) you could end up with a low-hand that might win that end of the pot too.

Another thing is with a big card like a King showing, you won't be able to drive anyone out of the pot. But, with a small card showing (as with three Sevens)...you might be able to win the **whole** pot **before** the end.

Three Sevens is also a better hand than the low Trips (such as three Deuces). The reasoning here is the same as that discussed earlier explaining why two Sixes and a Deuce is a better hand than two Deuces and a Six.

In comparing the low Trips (Deuces and Treys) to the high Trips (Kings and Queens)...the former are somewhat better hands because they have some low potential.

An interesting thing about starting with Trips (excluding Kings and Queens) is that the average low-hand you can expect to make is a Jack-low. That's why three Jacks is almost as good a hand for Low as three Sevens.

But, with three Sevens, you can *represent* (that you're going for Low). With three Jacks, you can't. That fact alone makes the Sevens a superior hand since they give you a chance to win the **whole** pot before all the cards are out.

Everything I discussed should help you understand why Aces, Sevens and Eights are Trips that are always–playable and why all other Trips are just usually–playable.

The rule you learned earlier — that a one–way hand must be very, very strong in the direction it's headed — is, in a way, related to another rule (better — a concept) you should also understand. That concept is:

> **When you have a two–way hand...it's all right if your hand is only of medium–strength in both directions. And any two–way hand is better than a one–way hand.**

This new concept will enable you to make the subtle distinctions between hands that've been grouped together. For example, a 6–7–8 is a better hand than a 7–3–2 (offsuit). The latter hand, as I already noted, is essentially a one–way hand. The 6–7–8 is only of medium–strength (for both High and Low)...but is a legitimate two–way hand. And because it's going in both directions, it's also a better hand than 8–8–3. Yet...all three hands are in the same category — usually–playable. So, the rule you just learned should help you to differentiate between hands that are similarly ranked.

Two–way hands have (by definition) some reasonable probability of scooping and a good probability of making "something" (that will win at least one–end). Because of that, you should want to play them in almost all cases.

A 6–7–8 is a good example of just such a hand. It's a hand with potential that's often overlooked by many players. It has scoop potential beyond the obvious Straight that can be made with it. The medium cards it has could pair by "accident" — and that Pair could be just what you need to scoop the pot. At the very least, it could save half the pot for you when your opponent makes a very good low hand (with no–Pair or just a little Pair). You should really like the hand because it offers you a good degree of protection from being scooped.

The other hands in the "no–preference" category of the usually–playable hands are those that you'd want to play if you can get in the pot fairly cheap. You'd also tend to play them in a pot with a weak player.

Knowing how to play the medium-sized Pairs (Sixes through Nines) is one of the keys to being a real good High-Low Split player.

> **Medium Pairs (Sixes through Nines — with a Baby)** *must* **be played head-up. If you can't get head-up with them. . .you** *must* **be able to throw them away. Also, even when played head-up, the medium Pairs lose much of their strength when they're up against an Ace (and in a multi-way pot with a Sucker who plays high Pairs).**

The reason you want to play the medium-Pairs head-up is because they afford you a lot of protection in that situation (except against an Ace). They're **not** nearly as strong a hand in a multi-way pot (and should **not** be played) because they can be beaten very easily (by Suckers who play high Pairs). Once the high-side is taken away from you, you're in big trouble. The (high-side) protection you have head-up is then stripped. And your two-card low is **not** very good either. Once again, you'd be taking the worst of it both ways.

I learned that painful lesson early in my career. And to this day, I remember a pot I was involved in many years ago. A player led off with a Jack and a little-card raised it. I had an Eight-up with an Eight-Deuce in the hole. I re-raised it because I wanted to play head-up. But, when it got back to the Jack, he also put in a raise. The little-card called (it was a three-raise limit). . .and so did I. I made a bad call because I had the worst hand both-ways.

Normally, my play wouldn't have been bad because most players — even if they had two Jacks — would throw them away. But a bad player is going to come on with them. Consequently, you can't play a medium-Pair against a low-card that came in raising when there's a bad player in with a face-card up. Because, if that face-card's paired, he'll play it. And you'll be caught between a better High and a better Low.

Like a 6-7-8, a 7-8-9 is a hand you want to get head-up with. You're always looking to scoop and (against several players) a Nine **isn't** going to scoop very often. Nor will the medium-Pairs you might make be of much value in a multi-way pot. But, a 7-8-9 can easily scoop against one player.

Most of the playable hands have been discussed in the two major classifications. There's a minor group of hands that can sometimes be played. I'll now discuss them.

BORDERLINE HANDS

The borderline hands are those **just below** (in quality) the hands that are usually-playable. They're the kind of hands you'd play **only** against a bad player...**except** when you want to steal with them. This last point is an important one. It gives the borderline hands a new dimension. Trying to steal with them makes them very playable in the right spot.

A borderline hand (which by definition is questionably playable) takes on a new dimension when you have the opportunity to steal with it. They become definite plays when that opportunity exists. You can *represent* with them...and that gives you a chance to win the pot **before** all the cards are out. Whenever you have a borderline hand, you should always keep the following concept in mind:

(Excluding the exceptions soon to be noted), **anytime you have a hand that's almost (but not quite) worth playing, it's very bad to call with the hand...but definitely correct to raise with it** *because there's an extra chance to steal the antes or win the pot at any point in the hand.*

If no one is in the pot (except the "force") when the action gets to you...and there's only a couple of players you have to go through...you should raise (going after the antes) with a borderline hand. That's generally the way these hands should be played. You should raise with them — not call.

But, there'll be times when you might want to call with them because you think you can play them cheaply. For example, if you're in an early (slow–play) position you might want to limp–in with a Baby in–sight. That kind of play could make the people behind you freeze–up. Since you'd make a similar play with a real good hand (and your opponents know that), they might put you on such a hand and be afraid to raise. So you could play a borderline hand cheaply that way.

Another way you could get in cheap with such a hand is by merely calling when you were very confident there wouldn't be a raise behind you.

When you're **not** looking to steal (or get in cheaply) with a borderline hand...you **want** to play them **head–up** against a bad player — the kind of player who'll give you action on Fourth St. when he catches a Paint.

I'll discuss some **specific** playing strategies with the borderline hands after you've looked at the table below.

BORDERLINE HANDS
(Head-up action preferred)

2-2-Baby	5-5-Baby	3-card Eights*
3-3-Baby	9-9-Baby	3-card (Straight) Nines**
4-4-Baby	10-10-Baby	Paint-Baby-Baby *(suited only)****

(The small Pairs are borderline on the high-side.
The other hands are borderline on the low-side.)

*These Eights are the ones that are **not** "always" or "usually" playable. (That is, any 3-card Eight with a Trey and/or Deuce and **no** Ace is considered borderline.)*

These Nines **must have Straight possibilities (even it it's a broken Straight possibility such as 9-7-5; however, a 9-8-5 is **very** borderline because the "8" makes the Nine a very "**rough**" Nine-low).*

***You prefer multi-way action with this particular hand.*

Whenever you try to steal the antes with a borderline hand you're *semi-bluffing*. It's not a complete bluff because you're doing it with a hand that has *Outs*. As with any bluff, you **don't** want to get called when you make the play...but, if you do get called, you're not really in terrible shape because you do have something of a playable hand.

For example, you're in the steal-position and there's only one low-card behind you. You make a play for the antes by raising with an 8-3-2 (with the Deuce-up) or a 3-3-A (with the Ace-up). You want to win the pot right there. But the low-card in back of you calls. Now, you're in a little trouble...but it's **not** serious. You've got a few Outs. If you catch good on Fourth, and he catches a Paint...you'll then become the favorite. (Of course, if he catches good on Fourth and you catch a Paint...you automatically fold.) If you both catch good, you'll have to make an on-the-spot evaluation of the particular situation. If you can legitimately hope to escape (profitably) with the hand you have on Fourth St., you continue to play it. If not, you pass. It's that simple. Use the **ESCAPE TABLE** as a guide...but **don't** get tied-on to a hand that cannot be profitably played (for an escape).

Besides noting that a player constantly plays the very big Pairs (Jacks, Queens or Kings)...one of the easiest ways to recognize (and then label) a bad player is when he's in a pot with you and gets stubborn by continuing to play his hand after he catches a Paint. (I'm going to restate this situation because an important concept follows from it.)

Even if he had you in trouble on Third St. because he started with three small cards and you started with a borderline hand...you're in great shape once he catches a Paint. For example, you make a play for the antes with 10-10-3. A bad player behind you calls your raise with, let's say, a 7-5-2. On Fourth St., you catch a Four and he catches a King. Here's what the situation looks like now:

YOU	OPPONENT
10-10-3-4	**7-5-2-K**

On Third St., you were a dog. But, on Fourth St., you became a big favorite. Here's why: you have a big lead on the high-side and are only slightly behind on the low-side. [On four (cards), a Pair of Tens is a much bigger favorite over no-Pair than a 3-card Seven is over a 3-card Ten.]

In head-up situations, you have to evaluate your lead in one direction and relate it to how far you're (probably) behind in the other direction. When you do that, you'll be able to determine whether or not you're the **real** favorite.

It's the **relative** lead that's important. So, once again, when you have a big lead in one direction and are only slightly behind in the other direction. . .then, you're the **real** favorite.

> These situations constantly recur in head-up situations. A rule of thumb to guide you is: *the high hand is* **usually** *the favorite* **but** *not* **if the low hand has a Straight or Flush draw.**

I covered the gamut of all the starting hands that have profit potential. You now know exactly what starting hands can be played. . .and how and when to play them. You know what you **should** do. I'll now discuss what you **shouldn't** do.

UNPLAYABLE HANDS

I've mentioned or discussed every hand that's conceivably playable in High-Low Split. If a hand's not *always-playable, usually-playable or borderline*. . .you simply **don't** play it. So there's really no need for this little section.

But I'm going to discuss some of the unplayable hands anyway because there are players who "think" some of them are playable.

A simple rule you can use to immediately isolate a *completely* **unplayable** hand is this:

ANY starting hand that has two Paints in it is
UNPLAYABLE *(even if all three cards are suited).*

There are a lot of people who play the King and Queen
of Spades with another Spade. They shouldn't. It's an
unplayable hand. Also, a J-10-5 (suited) is unplayable. And,
as already discussed, some people think very high Pairs are
playable. They're not. Many people will play a 9-10-J. They
shouldn't.

The reason so many people play those unplayable hands
is because it's a carry-over from Seven-Stud. But a hand
that's considered pretty good in Seven-Stud is very often
not good enough for High-Low. A similar mistake is made
by Razz (Seven-Stud for Low) players. However, the Razz
players are more apt to make their mistakes at High-Low
after the first three cards (when they catch a Paint on
Fourth St., for example).

Excluding the exceptions already noted (in the playable-
hands tables)...you should simply remember that in
High-Low Split there's no room for Kings and Queens. A
Jack is bad enough (and a hand with a Jack and two Babies
wasn't noted even in the "borderline hands" table). But,
when you're anteing real high...you have to go with a Jack
sometimes if you strongly suspect a player's on-the-steal.
**However, with a King or Queen it doesn't make any
difference**...it doesn't matter if a player's stealing or not.
Barring the one exception I'll now discuss, there's just no
room for Kings and Queens in High-Low.

The exception is the borderline hand of Paint-Baby-
Baby *(suited only)*. Let's say you have a **K♠-A♠-2♠**. There
are situations where you might want to play that hand — in
both a multi-way pot **and** head-up. If the Ace or Deuce is
showing, it's a good hand to try to steal with. If you get
caught — you won't like it...but you'll be all right. You'll
have some Outs with the hand. If the King is showing, you
might play it with a lot of players in the pot because they'd
be less likely (than just one player) to give you credit for
two Spades in the hole if you catch a "perfect" card (the
3♠-4♠-5♠ or **6♠**) on Fourth. The only time you might want
to play the hand (with the King in-sight) in a head-up

situation is against a player you know is stupid enough to continue giving you action if you catch "perfect" on Fourth. [A real good player will be able to put you on Spades (with two Spades in-sight) and you won't get any more action from him. He'll know that he's a big dog and he'll just throw his hand away.]

If everything I've said up to this point has not impressed those of you inclined to play a hand with a Paint and two Babies (against someone with an automatic steal or not) — one last point you should remember is this:

> **Whenever you play a hand with a Paint in it...most of the time you'll be playing six cards against your opponent's seven.**

Consistently giving your opponents **that much** the best of it is simply an edge you're **not** going to be able to overcome. Conversely, when **you** have a consistent advantage like that (combined with all the things you've just learned about this game)...you'll find High-Low Split very, very profitable.

> **So play** *playable* **hands...and**
> *refuse* **to play** *unplayable* **hands.**

SUMMARY OF POSITIONAL CONSIDERATIONS

This will be a summary of some of the things you should consider — that is, the general way you should play the various playable hands — depending on whether you're in an early, middle or late position. *Early* is the first two positions after the high card; *middle* is the next three positions; *late* is the last two positions.

In an early position, the first thing you must do is dismiss any thoughts you might have about bluffing or trying to steal the antes.* If you're going to play your hand from an early position...you **must** have a legitimately playable hand (**not** a borderline hand). Your only thought should be: *"how am I going to play it — should I call or raise?"* The answer to that question is:

> **You raise with the hands you want to play head-up. With a hand that you'd like to play in a multi-way pot, you might call...or you might raise. It depends.**

You might want to just call with a "dynamite" hand such as 3-4-5 (suited) in a small or normal ante game — even if your opponents **may** know what you're doing (slow-playing). However, you **shouldn't automatically** slow-play a big hand. Exactly what you'll do will depend on the quality of players you're up against. If you're the first low card and you **just** call...and you're up against very good players — they'll **know** you've got a hand. In that case, you might just as well come in raising because you won't gain anything by slow-playing. More than that, you could actually lose some potential profits by slow-playing because then your hand is an "open book" to a good player. He'd be more inclined to gamble with you when he knows you've got an "automatic" raise. But, if he suspects you of *sandbagging*, he probably won't give you any action.

Also, in a **high-ante** game, you should come in raising with **any** hand you're going to play from an early position.

In a middle position, you should play your hand in basically the same way you would from an early position. The only difference is that, as more and more people fold, you start to consider raising with a borderline hand if you think there's a chance you can steal the antes.

If everybody has folded and you have a low card up, you're in the *steal* position if there's only one low card

---

*An exception to this is when there's only one or no low-cards behind you.

behind you. You should usually raise in that spot even if you've got a *bad one* (a Ten or higher) in the hole. With two bad ones, just give it up.

If there's **two** low cards behind you, you **must** have a playable hand. But you can take a shot at the antes with, let's say, a 9-7-5 (if the Nine's in the hole). Raise it...and try to steal the antes. If you don't get away with it, it's all right. You've got a playable hand.

If someone has raised before it gets to you, you surely must have a hand. An exception would be when you're the last low card and the raiser is the next-to-last low card. Since he may be taking advantage of his steal-position, you don't have to have quite as good a hand. In fact, you may want to try to re-steal it.

In any re-steal situation, you should be guided by your evaluation of the particular player who does the raising from the steal-position. If you know that he's an aggressive player and you have any kind of a hand...it's mandatory that you re-raise. The reason why your re-raise is mandatory is because (if he is stealing) you don't want to give him two ways to win. (The first way he could win it from you would be if he stole it; the second way would be if you just called his raise and gave him an easy opportunity to outdraw you.)

So even if you have a relatively weak hand such as 7-6-2...you must re-raise. If he does have a bad one, he'll fold...or he'll call your re-raise with a bad one which is O.K. too. What you **don't** want to do is give him the opportunity of stealing there...and then give him an extra chance to win by outdrawing you on Fourth St.

If you run into a big hand in that situation (which is going to happen once in a while), there's nothing you can do about it. But you **can't** give him that free shot to outdraw you on Fourth St. If you do that, you've allowed him to gain the full value of his semi-bluff. He'll have gained not only the chance that you'll fold now...but also the chance that you'll fold later (which you'll do if you catch a Paint on Fourth). By re-raising, you'll force him to have a hand...and you'll have taken away the **free** chance he'll have of winning by simply out-drawing you. And, if he gets stubborn and calls your re-raise with a bad one...well, that's going to hurt him even more.

When you're in the absolute last position with a small card...and everybody else has folded...you should raise no matter what you have — as long as a Paint had to force it. It's worth going after the antes and you won't be doing much gambling because you'll just have the high card to contend with.

Before going on to discuss strategy at the other stages of play, you should be reminded that how you start in High-Low Split will have a lot to do with how you'll finish. So if you get off to a winning start...you'll be much more likely to end with a winning finish.

FOURTH STREET PLAY

The general principles you've already learned still apply to your strategy from Fourth St. on. You want hands that can scoop. You want to avoid hands that can get scooped. And, you must realize that when you're in a three-way pot, every dollar you put in is going to get back only fifty cents if you can't scoop it...but it'll get back two dollars if you can scoop. That's a big difference.

Probably the most important thing to remember about Fourth St. is the **PAINT RULE**. Because, when you catch a picture card on Fourth...any chance you had of scooping the pot is practically gone. If you wind up with a high hand of Two-Pair or Trips...the best Low you can have is whatever picture card you caught. Your only real chance for a scoop (once you catch a Paint) is to make a small Straight or a Flush to go along with your Low...or to make a good Low with a Pair which may occasionally scoop.

So when you have a Paint and your opponent has two small cards...you can realistically forget about scooping it. In a head-up situation, you'll have to put in a lot of money just to get back half of what's in the pot at that time...and it's almost never worth it.

In a multi-way pot, if all the other players caught small cards and you caught a Paint. . .there's almost no question that you should fold. The only exceptions would be when you started with a 3-card Straight-Flush draw (such as 3◊-4◊-5◊) or a three-Flush and the Paint you caught was of the same suit. . .or, if there was so much money in the pot because of prior raising that you're almost forced to play since the pot would be laying you such tremendous odds. (These are legitimate exceptions to the **PAINT RULE** because you should be a slave to the rule **only** when you started with an **average** 3-card hand.)

In a head-up situation, if both you and your opponent caught picture cards. . .and you caught the lower picture, you'd be in better shape than he would **unless he has an Ace in his hand**. For example, let's say he caught a King and you caught a Jack. Well. . .your Jack would give you a little value for Low. . .but if he has an Ace-King, you'd have to overcome that (for High). But, it's really not very important how you play your hand when the two hands are very close on Fourth St.

Of course, when you don't catch a Paint on Fourth and your opponent does. . .you bet.

When you both catch good, it could mean several things and you have a few options. For example, the small card you caught could've paired you or not. So you're either going to have a four-card hand or a three-card hand with a Pair. . .and, once again, there's a lot of difference between a Pair of Deuces and a Pair of Sixes (or Eights).

If you have a four-card hand and you're first to act. . .you can do one of three things if your opponent also caught good. Your options are to bet, perhaps consider check-raising or maybe even to check and then call (if you think your two hands are about equal).

The weakest of the three options is to check with the intention of raising. You may **not** get the opportunity to raise. If your opponent calls your check. . .you'll have lost a bet. Also, if you bet, you might get raised. . .and then you'll be able to get in another bet if you think your hand's good enough to re-raise.

Checking and calling with a hand you think is about equal to your opponent's hand (or maybe even slightly better than his) is not that bad a play against an aggressive player. By doing that — rather than check-raising him — you've made him think that your hand is worse than it is and he might get tied-on to his hand.

For example, let's say you have 2-6-5-3 and you're up against an aggressive player with a 7-5 showing. By checking and calling, he may think there's something wrong with your hand (like maybe the Three paired you) and that's why you didn't bet. You may be able to get him to stay in all the way by showing a little weakness. You wouldn't want to lose him with a hand that good on Fourth.

If you're in a pot with more than one player on Fourth St....once again, you have to decide what kind of action you'd prefer to have with your hand — head-up or multi-way.

When you have a hand where you'd like a lot of action...you play it accordingly. For example, there's a 2-3 in front of you and a 7-J (a bad player) behind you. You have a 2-3-4-5. When the 2-3 bets...it would be foolish to raise because you want the 7-J to keep on coming.

If you have a head-up type hand and you're in a position to raise...that's what you do. The medium-Pairs are basically the hands you want to get head-up with because when you do...you can scoop with them. But, when you don't get head-up with them...it's unlikely that you'll scoop. So, you want to do **everything you can** to get head-up with them (or any other hand that you'd prefer to play head-up with).

If you can't get into a head-up situation and you have a hand that you're **not** likely to scoop with...then it **must** be a hand that's **very strong** one-way so that you can at least count on splitting a big pot.

Above all, you must avoid falling into the Trap and getting scooped. And always keep in mind the big money difference there is between scooping and just getting half the pot.

FIFTH STREET PLAY

Here's where you have to make the really crucial decisions. Fifth St. is the **key** to High-Low...because once you decide to go with your hand here, you'll almost always go on through to the end. It's that simple.

On Fifth St., you have to ask yourself: *"can I scoop?"* If the answer is *"NO"*...then you must have an extremely strong hand in one direction. It cannot be just routinely good. You've gotta be very, very good.

You've got to be ready to get away from some hands on Fifth St. that appear to be playable...but are not good enough because they're **not** *real strong* one-way hands. The following illustration (reproduced from page 259 is an example of two such hands.

YOU		**OPPONENT**	
Hole-Cards	*Up-Cards*	*Hole-Cards*	*Up-Cards*
7♣ - 3♣	2♡ - 6♣ - K♢	? - ?	A♠ - A♡ - 8♠
6♣ - 6♡	3♡ - 3♠ - Q♢	? - ?	8♡ - 6♡ - 5♠

As already discussed, the hands you have above would be considered playable by most players because they think they can escape with them. And, as I noted, they **can** escape with them...but **not often enough** to make it worth continuing to play them. So you have to get away from hands like that on Fifth St. If you **don't** release them... you're headed for the Trap. Remember...escaping two times out of three is **not** good enough on Fifth St. where, if your goal is to escape, you must do so at least three times out of four. And the hands you have in the situations shown above are just **not** strong enough to escape with 75% of the time.

Knowing what you know now, it'll be relatively easy for you to get off a hand on Fifth St. — especially in a head-up situation. Here's another example to prove how knowledgeable you've become. Let's say you have 2-6-7-6-Q and you're up against ?-?-8-8-8. It wouldn't take you very long to realize you're in very bad shape. Your thinking about this situation would probably be very similar to what I suggested on page 262. And you'll pass on this one too.

It's a little more complex when you're up against two players...especially when one of them has half the pot locked-up and you're in a contest for the other half with someone who's foolish enough to put in a lot of action and is unknowingly donating half of his money (and, if you continue to play, **half of your money**) to the guy who has what looks like the nuts for one-end. (You might want to re-read the discussion on page 273.)

As noted in that discussion you could be forced to release a legitimately playable hand. When the best you can expect to do is get back 50¢ for every $1 you put in the pot...you're actually in a pot that's effectively being raked 50%. It's very tough to overcome something like that. So if you feel you're an underdog (even slightly) to the man you're competing with...it's almost never worth playing your hand. And, even if you feel you're a slight favorite... it's barely worth playing. You certainly shouldn't put in any action. And you're going to find it very upsetting when the player you're contesting does put in action in that spot. All he's doing is helping the other guy (who has practically a sure win one-way). He's not only hurting you...he's also hurting himself.

So, once again, the most important thing you have to know about your play on Fifth St. is that:

> **When you have no (realistic) chance to win one-end of the pot...in order to continue playing — you must have a super-hand for the other half.**

The opposite of that guideline is:

> **When you have a hand that *may* scoop (even if the scoop-chances are slight)...you can profitably continue to play that hand despite the fact it's relatively weak in both directions.**

A look at the illustration below should clear-up any possible misinterpretation of the last guideline.

YOU	OPPONENT 1	OPPONENT 2
5-6-7-9-6	?-?-7-5-2	?-?-3-8-4

The hand you have above should definitely be played against what you see in your opponents' hands. If you catch the Eight you need for your *gut-shot* Straight...you might be able to scoop that pot. As you know, there's a big swing in the money you can win when you scoop a three-way pot (as opposed to what you win when you just split). That fact alone dramatically tips the scales from what you might think is a borderline play to a definite play.

So that's another very important concept you should be aware of on Fifth when you may be faced with a critical decision. Even though your hand is weak in **both** directions ...you just need a **reasonable** chance for half the pot as long as you **also have** a scoop-chance going for you.

Many players — especially Razz players — don't know about that concept (and others). And when they try to play High-Low the same way they play Razz...they're usually in a world of trouble. For example, when a Razz player catches a Paint, he'll just ignore it (in most cases). Paints in High-Low **cannot** simply be ignored. When you catch a Paint in High-Low it's far more damaging to your hand than it would be in Razz.

Another carry-over by Razz players when they play High-Low is shown by the following illustration:

Hand "A"	Hand "B"
A-2-7-4-Q	?-?-7-8-9

A Razz player with Hand *A* **playing Razz** would be a favorite against Hand *B*. However, with the same hand against Hand *B* in High-Low...he would have a **definitely**

inferior hand. The reason is, of course, that Hand *A* is essentially a one–way hand and Hand *B* is a two–way hand and therefore has much better scoop potential.

Those are two major differences often overlooked (or not even considered) by Razz players when they're in a High–Low game. They're similar to the mistakes made by Seven–Stud players who think they can automatically play solid Seven–Stud hands in High–Low. As you now know, it's not that simple. Certain hands that are money–makers in Seven–Stud and Razz are **losers** in High–Low.

Another concept you should know is when you have the better Board (meaning you must act first)...but you **don't** have the best hand...it's usually **not** worth betting if you **know** your opponent will call.* What's more, if your hand is much worse...you should check and if your opponent bets, you should fold. That'll save a bet. If you bet you could easily get raised by a good player who knows he's got the best hand. And that'll cost you **two** bets. So your play is to check...and hope to get a free card. If your hand is only slightly worse...you **should bet** so you don't show weakness (and also because you can stand a raise if it comes).

The two examples below illustrate the two situations just discussed.

EXAMPLE "A"		EXAMPLE "B"	
YOU	*OPPONENT*	*YOU*	*OPPONENT*
5-2-8-5-A	?-?-7-7-5	4-3-2-3-6	?-?-7-7-4
CHECK		BET	

In example "A", your hand is much worse...so you should CHECK. If your opponent bets...FOLD.

In example "B", your hand is only slightly worse...so you should BET (so you don't show weakness).

---

*This is truer in High–Low than another form of Poker (such as Seven–Stud) because calling is much more automatic in High–Low. In Seven–Stud, you might bet with the worst hand because there's a chance your opponent might throw his hand away.

The important point to remember about the illustration above is that in example "*A*" you gain nothing by betting and showing false strength. In fact, a bet is a *losing* play so that's why you should check. In a situation like that, don't worry about showing weakness. You'd be far better off saving the bet.

Because your hand is only *marginally* worse in example "*B*", a bet is the correct play since you can show strength that could enable you to win the pot right there. And, even if you get called (or even raised), you've got a lot of Outs with your hand — a Six-low, a small Straight and Two-Pair or Trips.

You should now have a very good idea of what to do on Fifth St. with various types of hands. Because the betting limit doubles here (from $100 to $200). . .the probability that you'll get something out of the pot must be high enough so that you can profitably continue to play your hand. If there's no chance for you to scoop. . .then your one-way hand must be very, very strong.

SIXTH STREET PLAY

If your hand was worth playing on Fifth St., it's unlikely that it won't be worth playing on Sixth St. when there's even more money in the pot. Folding on Sixth is not nearly as common as folding on Fifth (where some hands that look to be playable are actually not).

Because you're almost sure to go through with your hand if you've made it to Sixth St. (or you shouldn't even be there). . .there's really not much I can tell you about what to do at this stage of the action.

As you'll recall from the *ESCAPE TABLE*, when you're about even-money to escape on Sixth St. it's worth it to continue to play.

In almost all cases, you'll probably·have at least a 50–50 chance to escape. But, as always, there are exceptions. The illustration below is an example of **a very obvious** situation where it would not be worth it for you to continue with your hand.

YOU	OPPONENT
2♣-6◇-4♠-5◇-6♠-K♠	?-?-5♡-2♡-3♡-4♡

With the hand you have above against your opponent's Board on Sixth St., it's quite obvious you have less than a 50% chance to escape. Not only did you have a somewhat shaky (although legitimate) call on Fifth, but in light of the way the cards broke on Sixth...you could actually be *drawing dead* for **both** High and Low. So there's no question you have to give it up on Sixth in a situation like the one above.

Sometimes, however, the situation is not quite so obvious (as illustrated below).

YOU	OPPONENT
A-2-3-6-K-Q	?-?-A-7-5-A

Most people with the hand you have in this new example would think a call is justified on Sixth. It's not. You **won't** escape half the time on Sixth in that situation. You'll have to call $200 on Sixth and you **must** make your Six–low or it's not worth it. But what if you make an Eight? Then, you'll have to put in another $200...and you may get scooped. The price just isn't right for you to call on Sixth in that spot. So, once again, you'll have to give it up.

The two examples you've just been shown are unusual in that you'll play your hand through **in most cases** once you get to Sixth St. But, because there are exceptions...you should use the following rules to guide you:

(1) **If you decided to go on Fifth and the cards broke approximately even...then there's no question you should call on Sixth St. But,**

(2) **If you had a** *close* **decision on Fifth (because you caught a bad card) and now all of a sudden on Sixth St., you catch another bad one and your opponent catches real good...** *then you must certainly fold your hand.* **Your escape-hatch will have effectively been closed.**

PLAY ON THE END SEVENTH STREET

If you're in a multi-way pot when all the cards are out, you should be in one of the following two situations:

(1) **You have a (fair to very good) chance to scoop the pot; or**

(2) **You have a super-strong one-way hand and are virtually certain to get at least half the pot.**

The only time you should **knowingly** be in any kind of jeopardy of losing it all is in case (1) above when your scoop-chances are only fair. That's one of the few times you'll be doing any "gambling". But, you'll do it **knowingly** because you understand the big money swing that occurs whenever you scoop a pot.

Of course, there'll be other times when you'll **unknowingly** be in trouble because someone makes a real longshot draw down the river and cracks a hand you thought was "virtually certain" to get one-end. There's nothing you can really do about draw-outs...except to hope the Suckers who try to draw-out on you remain in the game. If they do, you'll get your money back...plus. You can't go *uphill* consistently in Poker (any form) and expect to be a winner. The laws of probability eventually catch up with the Suckers who try that consistently.

On Seventh St., more often than not (and especially when you're in a game where all the players are reasonably good ones)...you'll find yourself in a head-up situation.

> **In such a case, it's very important to be able to recognize when you have the nuts (or practically the nuts) for** *at least half the pot.*

Although you may have some difficulties, at first, immediately recognizing when you have the nuts (for half the pot)...after a while, you'll find it to be relatively easy.

It will make it even easier to see when you're in a nut-situation on the end if you look ahead at an earlier stage. For example, if your opponent catches a Paint on Fifth St. and continues to play against you...you should immediately begin to consider how you could have the nuts.

Let's say, he catches a Queen. I'll even say you caught a Jack. If you were playing Razz, it wouldn't mean too much. Both of you would disregard the Paints. But, in High-Low, it makes a big difference. (This is another fact overlooked by Razz players when they play High-Low.)

You're in a much better position because you caught the Jack. If you both wind up with Two-Pair (a situation that frequently occurs)...your opponent (with the Queen) is **dead** for Low. With Two-Pair and a Queen in his hand...the best he could have for Low is a Queen-low. He may have the higher Two-Pair and he'll be able to escape because of that. **But, he's NOT going to win it all.** As I noted earlier, you should always be aware that:

> **If your opponent has Two-Pair or Trips, the** *best* **Low he could have is represented by the** *highest* **card in his hand.**

You should use that rule to guide you whenever you have Two-Pair and, say, a Jack-low. You'll know that if your opponent has a King or Queen...you'll have the nuts for at least half the pot (unless he makes a Straight or Flush).

Knowing when you have the nuts is an important concept for you to understand...and use. So you should always be trying to figure out when you're in that enviable situation. When you are...you'll be able to bet with impunity. You can literally bet your house (and anything else you own) when you know the **worst** that can happen is that you'll split the pot.

It's very easy to see when you have the nuts in a game like Hold 'em. It's not quite as easy to see that in High-Low...but it's really not very difficult either. The following two examples will show you what I mean.

Let's say you're in **separate** pots with two very good (and very aggressive) players. But, as good as they are...they don't completely understand the concept of *having the nuts for at least half the pot*. I'll also say they don't know that you know the concept and they try to "run over" you. Well, you can slow 'em down...although you would probably be better off **not** smartening them up...and, more importantly, **not** making it so apparent you know exactly where you're at. In any case, here's what one of the situations might look like down the river.

YOU		OPPONENT	
Hole-Cards	*Board*	*Hole-Cards*	*Board*
9-A-6	3-3-Q-K	?-?-?	2-2-K-J
			(four different suits)

As you can see, you don't have much of a hand. But the Nine you caught on the end gave you a Queen–low to go with your Pair of Threes. And, against his Board...that's enough to give you the nuts for half the pot.

When he bets...you can raise him. He might even re-raise you — trying to make you think he could scoop. It would be a futile attempt because you'd know that was impossible. So you can put in another raise. He'll slow down and call you. Your last raise **wouldn't** really be a good move because it would smarten him up for his future play against you...and would also be a wasted effort since you know you're going to split it.

The reason you'd know you had a sure split was because he has to have either:

    (1) a Jack-low; or

    (2) Two-Pair or Trips.

If he has (1), you'd win the high-end with your Pair of Threes.

If he has (2), he'd get the high-end...but, then your Queen-low would stand-up.

His raises would show he didn't realize you had the nuts. More than that...it would show he didn't know that you knew what you had.

Here's another example of a situation where you have the nuts and should never stop raising because there's a slight chance you could win it all.

YOU		OPPONENT	
Hole-Cards	*Board*	*Hole-Cards*	*Board*
5♡ - 3♡	7♡-J♡-K♡-Q♠	A♣ - 3♠	5♠-5♢-5♣-2♡

As you can see, on Sixth St., you have a Flush made and also have a Queen made for Low. (You can improve your low hand down the river to a Jack-low if you catch any card that doesn't pair you.) So, no matter what happens, you have the nuts for at least half the pot. What's more, you have a chance to scoop the pot...a chance your opponent doesn't have.

When you bet your hand on Sixth and if your opponent raises you...well, you could continue the "raising war" until you run out of money. There's no way you could lose...and you could win it all. Your opponent will probably slow down and quit raising before you get all-in. It'll probably dawn upon him that you have a Flush made...and have a cinch for at least one-end. But, maybe not. In any case, I'll discuss why you must at least split the pot...and why there's a small chance you could scoop on the last card.

All the possible cards he could catch are shown below:

(A) 4

(B) A, 2 or 3

(C) 6, 7, 8, 9, 10 or J

(D) Q or K

In case (A), he would make a *Wheel* (Five-high Straight). That would win the Low for him, but his Straight would be wasted against your Flush.

In case (B), he would fill-up. That would beat your Flush, but then he'd have a Pair for Low...so your Queen (or Jack) would take the low-end.

In case (C)...he wins the Low, but you get the High.

If case (D) occurred...he'd **lose it all.** He'd make a Queen or King-low which would lose to your Jack or Queen...and your Flush would take care of his Trips.

He has no Outs. You do. So, as you can see, it's quite important to know when you have the nuts. There'll be times when you'll have to make some tough decisions — an example of which is below:

YOU		OPPONENT	
Hole-Cards	Board	Hole-Cards	Board
8-6-4	3-A-3-J	?-?-?	7-6-5-2

In a situation like the one above, you'll have some problems. If that Eight in your hand was a Nine, you couldn't call on the end. As it is, you have a legitimate (though shaky) call. Your Eight-Six **might** get the low-end ...and your Pair of Threes **might** get the high-end. But there's a good chance you **might** get scooped.

As you know from the **ESCAPE TABLE**. . .a call is justified only when you think you have at least a 25% chance to escape. If you don't think you have that "good" a chance to escape. . .you have to lay it down on the end. In that case, a call would be unprofitable.*

Admittedly, it'll require a certain amount of judgment to gauge the possibilities and then determine what your escape-chances are. As I noted earlier, your judgment will get better and better as you gain experience. In any case, you'll have standards to guide you. . .and that's something most of your opponents won't have. At least, you won't be making desperation calls on the end — something many unsophisticated players do all the time.

Most importantly, when you **don't** have a tough decision to make when the cards are out. . .you now know how to determine whether you have the nuts for at least half the pot. That's also something the large majority of your opponents won't know how to figure out. As you know, that could give you a big edge in the right spot.

CHECK-RAISING
and
BLUFFING

If you're in a multi-way pot with a hand you'd prefer to play head-up, you must try to maneuver yourself into that situation. And one of the best ways you can do that is to check-raise when you're in the right spot.

> You should pay close attention to the follow-ing play because there are going to be many times you want to reduce the play to head-up.

---

*Assuming a single bet on every Round, in a $100 and $200 game, you'll have to risk $200 to get $600 (which is half the pot on Sixth St.).

The situation will present itself on Fourth St. when you're in, let's say, a four-way pot. You have a hand like three Babies with a small Pair. You have the low-Board. The player in front of you (to your immediate right) also caught good on Fourth, but his Board is slightly higher than yours. The other two players on your left (behind you) caught relatively bad cards on Fourth. The situation I just described might look something like this:

(man on your right... in front of you)		(men on your left...behind you)	
OPPONENT 1	YOU	OPPONENT 2	OPPONENT 3
?-?-2-7	A-6-3-6	?-?-3-8	?-?-4-9

Your object is to get head-up with Opponent 1. So you check. Opponents 2 and 3 will most probably check along. But, Opponent 1 is almost surely going to bet. When he does...you raise. That will effectively force Opponents 2 and 3 out of the pot. Neither of them is very likely to call a double-bet. So you'll have achieved your objective. You'll be head-up with Opponent 1.

You should get to the point where you make that play **automatically**. Of course, it only works when the man you expect to bet the hand is to your right. If he's on your left...you can't work the play.

There are also other automatic check-raise situations. Sometimes it's very difficult to tell who has the best hand in High-Low. So in a game with top players, if the man with the low-Board checks...the other player in the pot will just naturally assume he has the best hand (or why would the low-Board check?) — and he automatically bets. That's almost always the case with an aggressive player. So whenever you want to get in a double-bet in that situation...you have an automatic check-raise.

It's a play that could easily be worked against you, too. If someone checks it to you and you've got any kind of a hand...you must bet it. You **can't** be giving free cards. For example, a player came in raising on Third St. You called. On Fourth St., you both caught good...but he's got the low-Board. He checks. You must bet...even though you know you may be wide-open for a check-raise.

Fortunately, it won't happen to you very often because most players don't take advantage of check-raise opportunities and they completely miss some situations that are extremely obvious. The example below is a good illustration of an opportunity that most players (even very good ones) miss almost all the time.

YOU	_OPPONENT_
6-A-2-3-5-K	?-?-8-5-3-8

You have an automatic check-raise in the situation above — an opportunity to get in a double-bet that's almost invariably missed by players with your hand.

It's an automatic check-raise since it'll automatically work. Because of the Paint you caught on Sixth, you'd be in very bad shape if you also had a little Pair. You actually have a dynamite hand. But your opponent doesn't know this. So when you check...he's almost certain to bet. Then, you let the cat out of the bag...and make it two bets.

Sometimes, you're almost forced to check-raise...because, if you came out betting it could very easily work against you (by defeating a particular purpose you're trying to achieve). Such a situation would exist when you have a hand you **don't** want to get head-up with because it's more profitably played in a multi-way pot.

Let's say you're in a four-way pot and you have a 2-3-4-5 (with the low-Board) on Fourth Street. Now, you have a hand you **don't** want to get head-up with. Your objective this time is exactly opposite of what it was in the four-way pot illustrated on page 313. You checked then (with the intention of raising). Now, you **must bet** (assuming the same situation and the aggressive player is in **front** of you).

However, if the aggressive player is **behind** you...you **can't** bet if your objective is to play your hand (2-3-4-5) in a multi-way pot. If you bet you could easily defeat the purpose you're trying to achieve. This new situation (with the aggressive player **behind** you) is illustrated below:

YOU	OPPONENT 1	OPPONENT 2	OPPONENT 3
4-5-3-2	?-?-2-7	?-?-4-8	?-?-5-9

In this situation, you're almost forced to check because you want Opponents 2 and 3 to remain in the pot. If you bet, Opponent 1 (who's aggressive) is likely to raise. And his raise will force Opponents 2 and 3 to call a double-bet. As before, they're **not** likely to do that. So if you bet, you could lose them...which you **don't** want to do. Hopefully, when you check and Opponent 1 bets...Opponents 2 and 3 will call. And when the action gets back to you...then, you make your play and raise.

An interesting thing about this example is that even if Opponent 1 suspects your hand is better than his — and even if he **knows** what you're doing (checking with the intention of raising) — he **must** bet. He can't let the third and fourth best hands (Opponents 2 and 3) get free cards. He has to try to force them out of the pot by betting — or make them pay for their next card.

You now know how effective a check-raise can be if you do it in the right spot...and use the play properly to achieve the objective you want. In Limit Poker, the opportunity for *plays* are very restricted (as compared to No-Limit Poker). So when the opportunity to *make a play* exists in Limit Poker...you should always take advantage of it. It would serve you well to re-read the examples I show you and **really study them** so you can execute them to perfection whenever you're in similar situations.

The limited opportunities for *plays* in Limit Poker includes bluffing, of course. And of all the Limit games I discuss, High-Low Split is probably the one game that has the fewest opportunities to bluff. It goes back to what I noted earlier when I said that *"throughout my experiences, I've discovered that most Poker players are continually looking for an excuse to get in the pot. And High-Low Split offers the average player more opportunities to get in the pot and play than any other form of Poker."*

Because High-Low players want to play...because they're always trying to get half the pot...they just don't fold as often as they would at another form of Poker. That fact of human nature severely restricts the opportunities you'll have to bluff at High-Low.

The only real chances you'll have to bluff are on Third St. (before the players get much money in the pot), an automatic bluffing oportunity in the middle of a hand, and a special bluffing situation on Seventh St. That's a rather sparce "menu" for someone like myself who thrives on making plays. And it's why I said High-Low is a game more suited to a mathematically-oriented player than a psychologically-oriented one.

So you'll have to restrict any bluffing you might want to do to Third St. (when you're in the steal or re-steal position) and when you've got a much better Board than your opponent on Fifth St., for example, and you bet what you know is a bad hand because your opponent will almost have to fold against what he sees.

There's also a special situation on Seventh St. when you'll have an opportunity to bluff. As you'll soon see, it's a very important bluff for you to try when the proper elements exist. But, before I discuss it, I want to be sure you understand an important general rule you should observe when all the cards are out. It is:

> **When you *know* you *can't* win the whole pot (when the cards are out) you should (*generally*) check your hand...especially when you also *know* your opponent will call if you bet.**

Such a situation would be like this:

YOU	OPPONENT
J-7-5-3-2-4-J	?-?-?-A-A-5-K

In the situation above, you're looking at a Pair of Aces. You can't beat them. So you **know you can't** win it all. But, you **can** lose it all (if he started with perfect cards in the hole and caught a miracle card on the end). You also **know** he's going to call if you bet. So you might as well check.

However, there's a very important exception to that rule. It is:

> When there's a chance your opponent *won't* call on the end...you should bet — even though you *know* you can't win it all.

That rule relates to the special opportunity you'll have to bluff on Seventh St. The proper elements for that bluff would exist in a situation like this:

YOU	OPPONENT
9-8-5-4-2-3-7	?-?-?-A-5-Q-J

Most players would check your hand in that situation because they know they can't beat the Ace-Queen high. But, a check would be a very bad play...because, if you bet, you have a chance to steal the whole pot. What if he *busts-out* (by catching an 8, 9, 10 or K on the end)? If he does that, he probably won't pay you off and he'll throw away his Ace-Queen for High and maybe his Eight, Nine or Ten for Low because it looks like you're almost sure to have him beat both ways.

You have almost nothing to lose and everything to gain when you bet in that situation. You won't cost yourself a bet because if you check and he bets...you must pay him off. So you might as well bet it yourself. When he does make a perfect hand (that'll scoop you)...it'll only cost you an extra bet when he raises.

It's probably about even-money that he'll beat your Seven-low or bust-out. In the first case, all you'll lose is one bet (his raise). But, in the second case, you'll win the whole pot. And the pot will be laying you a very big price for just an even-money shot.

Admittedly I got very technical at various times in discussing the many subtleties of this game. But, that's the kind of game High-Low Split is. More so than any other form of Poker, it lends itself very well to a clearly-reasoned analysis of a particular situation — the kind of things you can put in concrete form (as opposed to the imaginative plays you can make in No-Limit Hold 'em).

You won't have to conjure up intricate psychological maneuvers — and you really **don't** have to be a gambler — in order to do very well at High-Low. As you know, there are all those Suckers just waiting to be TRAPPED.

HIGH-LOW DECLARE

a brief overview

Another way of playing High-Low is with a declaration. In this variation people usually declare with chips or coins. After all the cards are out everybody has, for instance, two coins. They take the two coins and put their hands under the table and then come up with a clenched fist. All the players open their hands **simultaneously** and the number of coins indicates which way they are going. It is usually set up so that zero coins is Low, one coin is High and two coins is both ways.

(High-Low can also be played with a **consecutive** declaration, but this gives the last man to declare such a tremendous advantage that it **isn't** much of a game. I haven't heard of it being played recently.)

In *Declaration* the rules are as follows: When you declare High, that means you **must** have the best high hand. It makes no difference what your Low hand is. You're saying that you have the best High and if you do, you'll get at least half the pot.

If everybody declares High, then whoever has the best high hand wins the whole pot. If everybody declares Low, whoever has the best low hand wins the whole pot. (When you declare Low your high hand no longer matters.) If everybody else declares High and you declare Low, you **automatically** win half the pot no matter what you have. You could have a Full House and declare Low — which I've done. Or you could have a Six-low and declare High and if you're the **only one** to declare High you automatically have half the pot.

If you declare **both-ways** (High **and** Low), it basically means you're saying you're going to win both-ways. If you do, in fact, win both-ways. . .you'll win the whole pot. So, normally, if you declare both-ways, you're either going to lose or win the whole pot.

There's a little bit of variation in the rules if you declare both-ways and you **tie** one-way. Some players play that if you declare both-ways and you tie one-way and win the other way you get three quarters. Some players say you **can't** even tie — once you're declared both-ways and you tie. . .you're out of it. In my opinion, the ¾ way is a better way of playing.

If you declare both-ways and you do, in fact, **lose** one-way — but **not** the other way — again, they have two ways of doing it. Some players say if you are trying to *scoop* and have the best High but don't win Low. . .then a man you beat for High "backs into" half the pot. That's one way of playing, but it's **not** the good way. The much better way is that if you declare High, someone else declares both-ways, and a third player declares Low. . .then, if the player who declares both-ways can't beat you High, but beats the other guy for Low — you should get the whole pot with your high hand. So, in general, the better rule is that if the man who declares both-ways beats everybody except one player — the player who beats **him** gets the whole pot.

There's a very important reason why it's better to be able to win the whole pot in the way I just discussed. For example, if you have a draw to a Full House and you **suspect** you're up against a man who's going to go both-ways, it becomes much more worthwhile to draw to your Full. If you make it, you'll win the whole pot instead of half the pot. And, as I've already said, in a three-handed pot, that's four times as profitable.

> **Therefore, one of the interesting strategic concepts in** *Declare* **is to play hands to get a man to declare both-ways so you can** *scoop* **when all you have is a one-way hand.**

But, of course, you must first establish which set of rules is in effect in order to avoid misunderstandings.

I want to discuss the differences, in general, between *Cards Speak* and *Declare*. One of the better ways of doing it is to give an example. There was a hand in the *Cards Speak* part of this section where a man had three-of-a-kind on Board and was drawing to a Bicycle. The other man had an obvious K-J Flush made (see page 310). In *Cards Speak*, I said the K-J Flush would never stop raising because if the man with the Trips and the draw to a Bicycle makes a Full House, he'll get the Low. If he doesn't make the Full, the Flush will get the High.

In *Declare* — believe it or not — if he were playing, for instance, No-Limit *Declare* (or even Pot Limit). . .if the Flush bets, the three-of-a-kind should raise and the Flush should **fold**. The reason is: the man with the Flush **doesn't know** *what* to declare. He's looking at what he knows may be a Full House already. . .and he has to **totally guess** which way to declare. The other guy has three-of-a-kind and a draw to a Bicycle. So, he can put in an extra raise and the man with the Flush can no longer go High because he's afraid the guy might be making a play with the Full House made already. He's got to go Low. And that gives his opponent a free shot. The guy with the Trips has an automatic split if he wants it. All he has to do is declare High. If he does make his Low he wins the whole pot. He can always escape for one-end. . . with a freeroll to scoop.

In comparing *Declaration* to *Cards Speak*, another example of the same principle is the situation where in *Cards Speak* you know you have the *nuts* for one-way (or the other), but you don't know which way. That comes up all the time in *Cards Speak*. In that situation, where you'd have the *nuts* in *Cards Speak*...you're in **extreme trouble** in *Declare* **because you have to guess**.

Anytime you know you have one-way cinched, but you don't know which way...you're in a lot of trouble if your opponent has been betting and indicating strength. Either you're going to declare the right way where you get half the pot or you're going to guess wrong and lose the whole pot.

Here's a good example: if a man has a 2–3–7–J showing and you have Two-Pair of Tens and Nines with a Ten-low... you have to guess whether he has Jacks-up or a Seven-low — if he's been betting with any kind of authority.

In the above paragraph you have the *nuts* (for one-way) in *Cards Speak*, an opponent will have the better hand in a *Declare* game because he can always go Low. You **can't** go Low. He can always declare Low if, in fact, he misses his hand...even if he **doesn't** have you beat for Low.

The major difference between *Declare* and *Cards Speak* is that your Board is very important in *Declare*...much more so than in *Cards Speak*. If you have a strong Board, you can have the *nuts* in *Declare*. This is especially true if you're head-up with somebody...even if you really **don't** have very much (of the hand represented by your Board).

For instance, if on Fifth St. I have a four-card Six and a Pair of Deuces and my opponent has 6–7–8 showing...I have the better hand in *Declare*. In *Cards Speak*...he's got the better hand. In *Declare*, I've got the better hand because I have for instance a 6–3–2 showing and a Deuce-Ace in the hole. I don't care that he may have a Straight or even be drawing to a Straight because he has already committed himself to going High. He can no longer afford to declare Low. I have a 6–3–2. He's got a 6–7–8. So I'm the one that's freerolling. From this point on (Fifth St.), I know I can get half the pot by declaring Low. If I back into a Full House, I get the whole thing because he's going to declare High and I'll declare High also.

I **may** want to take a chance and declare High if I make a Straight or 3-Deuces or Aces-up, and now he may get the whole pot...if I feel like gambling.

If, for instance, he has a 6-7-8 and catches a **non-dangerous** card like any face-card, then I may go High if I make Aces-up or better. But I always have the option to go Low. Because I have the better Low Board my opponent is forced to declare High and I have a virtual freeroll. If I have three little cards showing and keep on betting, my opponent has problems. He **can't** think that he can escape by just showing down his hand (as he could in *Cards Speak*). Once you have a dangerous Low Board, even if you have junk in the hole, you're freerolling because you can always escape by declaring the way your Board indicates.

Trips are a good starting hand in *Declare*, **except** if you're up against a good player who would suspect you have Trips if you started with, for example, a King showing. Head-up, 3-Kings wired is *almost* **no better** in *Declare* than in *Cards Speak* because the other player will probably suspect you have 3-Kings and he'll be on a freeroll just as much as he would in *Card Speak*. The reason he can assume you have 3-Kings, is because playing with a King showing is *rarely* correct in *Declare*. Starting with a King-up gives your opponent too many options. In *Declare*...you **can't** have bad cards showing — not even medium-sized cards. You **must** have good low cards showing.

The principle of playing to scoop holds exactly the same in *Declare* as in *Cards Speak*. The **ESCAPE TABLE** holds true in *Declare* also. Playing only for Low is an equally bad way of playing *Declare* as it is for *Cards Speak* — although for somewhat different reasons.

When you're playing in a *Cards Speak* game (rather than playing purely for Low) you should play hands that can scoop like middle-size Pairs or middle-size Straight draws. In *Declare*, you want to play scooping hands like small Straight draws and Pairs in the hole. Those hands will entice your opponent to try to *escape*. What'll actually happen is that he'll wind-up declaring the same way as you do.

A Pair of Aces in the hole becomes a great hand in *Declare* — especially against only one (or two) opponents. If I'm up against an opponent who goes **just for** *Low*, I'm **not** too worried about him. I can escape for High against him simply by declaring High. So, once again a man who just tries to go for Low is in a lot of trouble (in *Declare* as well as in *Cards Speak*).

However, a man who plays very low cards and has a low Board is in a **more powerful** position in *Declare* than in *Cards Speak*. For example, a 6-7-8 (especially with the Eight showing) is **not** a very good hand in *Declare*. As you know, it's a very good hand in *Cards Speak*. In that respect a man who plays *Razz*-type hands would be better off in a *Declare* game. The disadvantage to that type of (Razz) play is that such a player would never get to profit from hands like big Pairs in the hole and a low card up.

An interesting thing about *Declare* is that more than any other game you can slow-play your hands. If, for instance, you have a Pair of Eights showing and you have a Full House on Fifth St., you can really profit by slow-playing if it will occasionally entice everybody to declare High. If, by not putting in a raise when you make your Full on Fifth, you can get a man to declare both ways...then making that raise and scaring him into going only Low is a terrible play. You've given up half the pot for an extra bet or two if there are other players in the pot.

So, frequently in *Declare* you're doing things to deceive your opponents as much as to win money from them. Anytime your deception wins you the whole pot (or lets you escape with half the pot) it's so profitable that you're not worried about one bet in comparison to the whole pot (or half the pot). You can also do the opposite and put in a raise with a weak hand simply to get an opponent to declare opposite from you so that you'll escape with half the pot. The deception necessary to win the whole pot as often as you can — and to escape as often as you can — makes *Declare* very much different from *Cards Speak*.

Naturally, a good strategy player will **escape more** in *Declare* than in *Cards Speak*. When I say the **ESCAPE TABLE** holds true for both games I'm talking about your percentages. But, you can play much different cards in *Declare* and still have the same percentages.

If it's Fifth Street and a man bets, you must have a 75% chance of escaping. However, there are many more hands you could play in *Declare* that will give you that 75%.

Reading **hands is obviously more important in** *Declare* **than in any other game. If you know a man's cards you've got the** *nuts* **because it's** *not* **very often that a man will have a hand where he can declare both ways.**

Anytime you can *read* a man's cards with a high degree of accuracy...you're almost freerolling because you can escape even if you **don't** make your hand. **Simply declare the opposite way you think he will.**

When you can *read* your opponents, the ways to escape increase greatly — especially in head–up situations. In these instances you will **not** fold nearly as often as in *Cards Speak* because it's much harder for your opponent to back into a scoop.

A man's **never** going to scoop you with a Pair of Three's and a Seven-Low because he's only going to declare Low. If you think you're up against a low hand...he's **not** going to make a small Pair to win the whole pot from you — even if you don't have a Pair.

The similarities between the two types of High-Low stem from the fact that in both games pots are split. Therefore, the general theory of going for the whole pot versus half the pot, and what your chances have to be, hold true for both games. If you do suspect you're going for half the pot...it's **not** very good. If you have a hand that can get the whole pot...it **is** very good. The differences are in the cards that would put you in those possible scooping positions in *Declare* as opposed to *Cards Speak*.

One-way hands can easily be scooping hands in *Declare* because if your opponent declares the same way you do...you can win the whole pot. One-way hands which are deceptive, particularly hidden high hands, can be very strong. When you have a low Board and a concealed high hand your opponent will naturally go High. In a head–up situation, a Pair of Kings in the hole and a small card up is quite a **good hand** in *Declare*. It's absolutely **unplayable** in *Cards Speak*.

That's just one example of the variance in starting hands between the two games. Of course, in either game you'll still play three good low cards. . .and the ones that can make Straights are even better. Strangely enough, a hand like 2-2-5 which really is very borderline in *Cards Speak* is quite playable in *Declare* — especially if the 2-Deuces are in the hole. The reason is that if you hit a Deuce you may win the whole pot if your opponents go High.

I said earlier (in *Cards Speak*) that 6-6-2 is a much better hand than 2-2-6. In *Declare*, they're almost equal in value because which Pair you have is **not** going to matter if you go Low. But 2-Kings and a Queen is, for example, still **unplayable** even in *Declare* because you have no deception.

I'd rather play *Declare* with weak players because you can play so many more hands and have so many more opportunities to outplay them. In *Declaration*, you can frequently play a hand like a Q-A-5 if the Ace or the Five is showing. I'll even play A-K-J against bad players if the Ace is showing. You can take a card with it against real bad players who are playing Jacks and Kings. If there are two players who obviously have Kings and Jacks, I'll just sit there and play with my Ace showing and play the whole hand with absolutely nothing and get half the pot. Playing a hand like A-K-J to win half the pot by planning to escape for Low is a play which can **only** be made in *Declare*.

There are certain hands which can be played in *Cards Speak* that **can't** be played in *Declare* and vice versa. But on average. . .more hands can be played in *Declare*.

> You can play much more mechanically in *Cards Speak* **than in** *Declare*. **Contrary to what many people think,** *Declare* **is the** *least* **mathematical of all Poker games. It's more of a people game than any other form of Poker.**

There's another variation in rules that can have somewhat of an effect on your play. It's whether there's a **bet after** the declare. Many people play that there's one further round of betting after the declare and some players play that there is no betting after the declare.

**The major effect of this rule variation is that
you can play a little bit more freely if there's**
no bet after the declare **and just take a** *shot.*

That's especially true in a three-handed pot. For
example let's say a man has a three-card Seven and there's
only one or two cards to come. If there's **no bet** *after the
declare*, you can try to make an Eight and hope it's good and
declare Low. If there's going to be even more bets after the
declare, there's that many more bets you have to worry
about — especially if there's a third player in the pot who's
going High and could put you in the middle.

There's even more skill necessary to play this variation
as the following example will show. In this variation the
man with a "lock" (one-way cinched) always bets first.

One of the very interesting advanced plays (when
there's a bet after the declare) is putting a man in the
middle. Let's assume I'm in a pot with two other players.
One of them is obviously going High...and the other is
obviously going Low. There's a bet and, of course, raises
after the declare — with $100 in the pot. The bet after the
declare is $30 — but four raises are allowed.

Let's say I know the man to my left (behind me) is
going Low. In that case, I'd go High — almost regardless of
what I had. That would put the "man in the middle" (in
front of me) in a predicament.

The Low hand would bet $30 after the declare. The
"man in the middle" knows if he calls and I don't have very
much I'll just fold. So he'd be risking $30 to win $50 (half of
what was in the pot before the betting after the declare).
But, if I do have something, I'll raise. The other man (behind
me) would re-raise and that would put the guy in front of
me in the middle. So, he has to fold...unless he has a real
strong hand because he's either going to win a little bit or
lose a lot. So, at times, if I'm not sure which way to go, but
I know the man on my left is going Low...I'd ignore my
hand and simply go High...even if I figured the man on my
right (in front of me) was going High also. Now, the man on
my right is in jeopardy.

He's in a much worse position than I am because if my hand is better than his — and we both call — I win half of those two bets. But, he's got to put his money in **without knowing** whether I'm going to call. He's in a bad spot.

That's just one play that changes when there's a bet after the declare. Of course, you can also make very sophisticated plays against good players. For example, I've gone both-ways with Aces-full when I was very sure my opponent had a Full House. By going both-ways, I make him think I have a Straight and because of that, I can get at least one extra bet out of him after the declare.

I declare both-ways with a Full House because I know he's going High. The Low part of my declare is irrelevant because head-up I **don't** have to beat him for Low.

Then there's another type of play which we named the *"Jones Option"* after a weak player I played with. (*"Jones"* is a fictious name, but the play is a real one. It's so-named because a friend of mine used it against the real *"Jones".*)

Here's the way it came about. Jones started with a Three-up. He caught a Five, Jack and Queen (in that order). My friend's Board was something like a 7-6-3-2. When all the cards were out, my friend had a 7-6-4-3-2 for Low with a Pair of Sevens and a King.

How do you declare against a man who starts with a 3-5-Q-J and is looking at a 7-6-3-2? The answer to that question is you go **only** High. You **don't** go both-ways and you **don't** go Low. You go **only** High and you take the chance that the man snagged a Queen or a Jack on the last card. Here's why: if he caught a 3, 5, 8, 9, 10, K (or if he paired)...he'll go High trying to escape your Low. He **won't** go Low with an Eight-low. He'll only go Low with a better Seven or a Six.

The point is that he **won't** declare Low unless he thinks he has you beat. But, he'll frequently declare High **without** being able to beat a Pair of Sevens. So you gain nothing by going Low or going both-ways. If you go both-ways and he goes Low...you lose. You go **only** High. That's the *"Jones Option"*...and it's just another example of an advanced play that you can make in *Declaration* when it's apparent that your opponent is frequently just trying to escape.

An interesting hand in which I made the **wrong** play is the following example. We were playing that Straights couldn't *swing* (go both-ways) — they were only Straights. I had a 2-3-4-5-6. I had no Low at all, but I did have a Straight...and I did have low cards showing. A man with an A-A-5-4 raised me on the end. He was a good player and I knew he would raise me with a Six-low. I also knew he would raise me with Aces-full. Because of the cards that were out, I thought there was a better chance he had a Full House. I declared just for Low...a hand I **didn't** have. He had a 6-4.

I happened to lose that pot, but the important point I want to make is this:

> **Once it becomes apparent that your hand has no value, you just try to go the *opposite* way from your opponent — even if that means going the *opposite* way of your own hand.**

I've frequently gone Low with Trips or a Straight.

> **The *art* of declaring is one of the most important, if *not* the most important part of the game. It's *so* important that if I'm playing against mediocre players, not real wild loose players but just mediocre players, I could probably win playing *every* single hand and *never* folding.**

I could escape many times by reading their hands and by doing various things like putting in an extra bet to help myself escape.

High-Low Split *Declare* is a complicated variation. I've given you some of the basics...and an idea of the sophisticated strategies that can be used.

SUPER/SYSTEM's TWIN COURSES IN

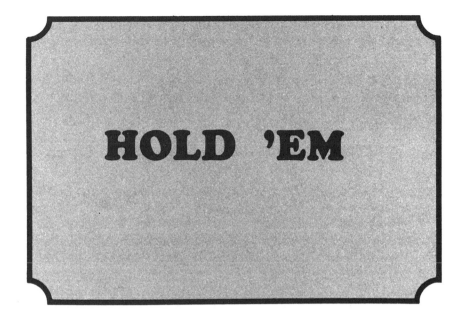

HOLD 'EM

Course #1: Super/System's Power Poker Course In Limit Hold 'em.

Course #2: Super/System's Power Poker Course In No-Limit Hold 'em.

Hold 'em...

Tomorrow's most popular form of Poker. It's already the game played to crown the *World Series of Poker* grand champion every year at the Horseshoe Club in Las Vegas.

Taught to you by...

Doyle *"Texas Dolly"* Brunson
1976 World Champion
1977 World Champion

and

Bobby Baldwin
1978 World Champion

Class Begins...

HOLD 'EM

Limit and No-Limit Similarities and Differences

If you've never played Hold 'em, you're about to learn about the most fascinating of all the various forms of Poker. If you have played it, then you know what I'm talking about.

Hold 'em has more variety to it than any other form of Poker. And more complexity. It has something for everybody...the mathematicians and psychologists...the "loose-gooses" and the "hard-rocks".

Above all, it has action...more multi-way action than any other game. Almost every pot you get involved in will be tremendously exciting. The thrills and frustrations are never-ending. Once you play Hold 'em...you may never want to play any other form of Poker again. It could become your main game. It's converted a lot of other players.

But, of course, it's Poker...so it's similar in many respects to other Poker games — especially Seven-Card Stud. However, there are enough differences — in the strategy you use and the mathematics you apply to Hold 'em — to make it a truly unique game. The mere fact that it can be played with as many as 23 players is an oddity that alone distinguishes it from any other form of Poker. (However, Hold 'em is rarely played with more than 11 players in the Limit version and No-Limit Hold 'em is most often played with nine players.)

Because Hold 'em may be unfamiliar to you, it's the only game where I'm going to discuss its simple mechanics. In both Limit and No-Limit, the game is always played with a *Blind*. The first player to receive cards is said to be *in the Blind* and must make a forced bet to start the action. It's also a *live* Blind which means the player *in the Blind* has the option of raising when the action gets back to him or he can simply "call" (without putting anymore money in the pot) if his Blind bet is not raised. In Limit Hold 'em there is usually a single Blind and each player (including the Blind) must ante. No-Limit Hold 'em is also played that way. Additionally, the No-Limit version is commonly played with multiple Blinds and no ante.

In a casino, the game is dealt by a *House* dealer and a *Button* (an object that physically resembles a small Hockey puck) is placed in front of the last player to receive cards. The player with the Button is considered to be the dealer and the first player to his left is considered to be the (first) Blind. A private game may or may not have a paid dealer. If it doesn't, each player takes turns dealing. In the casino, the Button is moved from player to player after each pot.

The game starts with each player receiving two *hole-cards* — the only ones he personally receives. Then, there is the first round of betting. Quite often in No-Limit play that bet is also the last round of betting because someone makes a huge bet (or *moves-in* with all the money he has in front of him) and no one calls him. That's not an uncommon play. I do it often when I think I can *pick-up* the antes and when I feel someone has made a weak bet.

A pot in Limit Hold 'em seldom ends so quickly. There's a second round of betting after the dealer *burns* (removes from play) the top card,* deals off three cards face-down and *Flops* them over in the center of the table. (*Turn* and *Fall* are often-used synonyms for "Flop".) Those three cards are community cards. All the players still in the pot can use them with their hole-cards to make up a hand. In both Limit and No-Limit play, the Flop is the most critical point in the hand. It's here you'll make the major decision as to whether or not you want to continue to play.

There's another round of betting after the dealer *burns one and turns one*. This is *Fourth Street* (the fourth community card). The last round of betting occurs on *Fifth Street* (after

---

*The top card is always "burned" because it might be marked. . .and any player who knew how it was marked would have a tremendous advantage.

the dealer *burns and turns* again). That's when *all the cards are out*. The pot is won by the player with the best five-card hand — made up with both (or one) of his hole-cards combined with three (or four) of the community cards. Occasionally, a pot is split by two players with identical hands (usually Straights) and in rare instances the *Board* (all five community cards) is the best hand. In the latter case, the pot is divided among all the players who have called all the bets on the end.

That's all there is to the mechanics of Hold 'em...but it's hardly all there is to acquiring a mastery of the game so you can win at it consistently. What's more...there's a vast difference in the strategies you'll use in the Limit and No-Limit versions of the game.

In Limit play, you must play solid hands because it's almost impossible to run anybody out of a pot. But, in No-Limit play, you can make your opponent(s) lay down a hand by using your position and your money.

You must also have a certain aptitude to be a strong No-Limit player. In a word, what you must have is "Heart". Not everyone has that. Of course, you must have respect for your money and know its value...but if you want to be a strong No-Limit player you can't think you're betting a Lincoln Continental everytime you bet ten or fifteen thousand dollars. If you do think that way...you'll never make it playing No-Limit.

There are also Limit players who can't rise above a certain class. I know of many such players who are super-strong players when they play $30 and $60 or $60 and $125 Limit...but, when they try to move up and play in a much higher limit game — say $200 and $400 or $400 and $800 — they just can't cut it. I've seen it over and over and over. They try to move up and play in a higher game than they're used to and they get busted out. Of course, that's not true of all players. Some make the big move...and do it successfully. But most don't. So you should always bear that in mind when you try to step up in class. Don't be in too big a hurry. And if you've got what it takes...you'll make it. A lot of what you'll need is right here on these pages.

I won't get into all the specific differences in strategy you'll use at Limit and No-Limit Hold 'em until the two versions are discussed individually in the pages that follow. For now, I'll just continue to discuss some of them and also the things that make Hold 'em the unique game that it is.

Every Poker player has heard that drawing to an inside Straight is usually a Sucker play. That's generally true at most forms of Poker. But, in Hold 'em (especially No-Limit) ...drawing to an inside Straight can be a sound and justifiable play. It all depends on the situation. If you can draw to that belly-Straight cheap — and there's the possibility you can win a real big pot by breaking your opponent if you make it...then you should gamble and take that 5 to 1 shot.* The reward makes the risk worthwhile. I make plays like that all the time (as you'll soon learn).

There are also times when you'll play hands that would be completely unplayable if the ordinary standards you applied to other forms of Poker were applied to Hold 'em. But Hold 'em is a game in a class by itself. More so than in any other game — and especially so in No-Limit — any two cards in Hold 'em can get the money.

I'm not saying you can indiscriminately play any two cards you're dealt. That's not the case at all. As in the other forms of Poker I've discussed, I'm going to give you standards to guide your play. What I am saying is in Hold 'em there are more exceptions to the rules than in a more "mechanical" game such as High-Low Split. So much in Hold 'em depends on the Flop. And on your position.

> **In No-Limit Hold 'em, position is...well, it's the name of the game. It's everything. If I had position all night, I could beat the game...***and I'd never have to look at my hole-cards.* **In Limit play position's not nearly so important.**

No-Limit play is also far more complex than Limit because you can do so many more things. You can make a

---

*Drawing to an inside Straight is about 5 to 1 against you with two cards to come. And it's about 10 to 1 with one card to come.

few cute little moves in Limit play...but, as I said earlier, for the most part you just have to play a solid game. You can't get too fancy at any form of Limit Poker. When your opponent knows the most it can cost him is another bet he won't be as hesitant to call as he would be in No-Limit when you move-in on him. In the latter case, he'll usually be in a quandry. He won't know whether you're bluffing...or whether you have the nuts.

That's another thing that distinguishes Hold 'em from other games (except for the now nearly-dead game of Five-Card Stud). It's very easy to see when you have the nuts (or very close to it). It's not so easy to know when you have the nuts at other forms of Poker. You can use that fact to great advantage in Hold 'em because you can *represent* (bluff) when you don't have the nuts and when you're quite certain your opponent doesn't have them either. I'll show you how to do that. It's something else I do all the time.

Another interesting aspect of Hold 'em is that you can turn the nuts and be the *dog* to win the pot. Here's how that could come about:

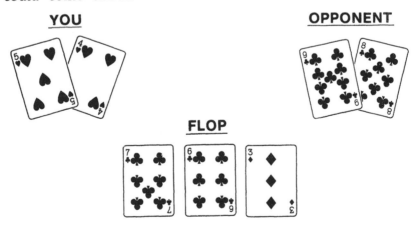

YOU   **OPPONENT**

FLOP

In the above example, you flopped a Straight — which is the nut-hand right there — but, you're **not** the favorite to win the pot. Your opponent is. He has a chance to make a bigger Straight and he also has a Flush draw. He has 14 wins — 3-Fives, 4-Tens and 7-Clubs (other than the Five and Ten of Clubs). With two cards to come, there's a 53% chance that he'll catch one of those 14 cards. That makes him a 53 to 47 (or a 6%) favorite.

There's also a case in Hold 'em where you could be in a lot worse shape than that after you flop the nuts. This interesting situation could occur as follows:

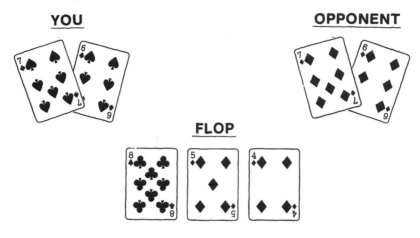

YOU   **OPPONENT**

FLOP

You flopped the nuts...but so did your opponent. More than that...he's got a cold freerolling Flush draw. You're in a near desperate situation. The best you could hope to do is split the pot. The worst is that you're going to lose more than ⅓ of the time. There are nine Diamonds he can catch to make his Flush...and with two cards to come, he's going to get there about 36% of the time. You turned the nuts...but you're up against the **pure** nuts.

Whenever you have small connecting cards that are suited, the ideal Flop would be three cards that made your Straight — two of which are in your suit to give you a Flush draw also. And if you were to run into someone else around the table who flopped the same Straight you did (and **no** Flush draw)...well, that's a No-Limit player's dream. Some of the biggest pots I've ever seen in Hold 'em came about just that way. Both players had a cinch...but one of them was freerolling for a Flush.

Situations like the two just noted could occur — but with less frequency — in Seven-Stud. For example, you could have a small Straight made and your opponent could be drawing at a bigger Straight open on both ends — with a Flush draw, too. Then he'd be the favorite. Or, both of you could have an identical Straight made and your opponent could also have a Flush draw.* But these situations are far more common in Hold 'em because of the community cards.

You'll be learning many more peculiar and interesting things about this game. For example, when you have a Pair of Aces and a single Ace flops (giving you a Set of Trips)...there'll **always** be the possibility that the next card off could make someone a Straight. (I'll discuss this in greater detail later when I tell you how I play two Aces when I flop a Set.)

In fact, Straight and Flush draws seem to be ever-present in Hold 'em. It's one of the things that makes the game so action-filled and so interesting. Most players indiscriminately pursue their Straight and Flush draws when it's clearly not justified by the pot-odds in Limit play or the potential amount of money they can win at No-Limit. I'll discuss this more thoroughly when we get into the individual sections.

You'll also discover that overcards (on the Board that are higher than a Pair you have) and kickers play a more dominant role in Hold 'em than other forms of Poker. Quite often, you'll find that your hand will become unplayable when an overcard falls or when you suspect you've got "kicker-trouble". But again, I'll get into all of this shortly.

Most players think of Hold 'em as a draw-out game because someone always seems to be making a Straight or Flush...or "spiking" a card on Fourth or Fifth that pairs their kicker. But, in reality Hold 'em is much less of a draw-out game than it appears to be. That's an important point for you to remember.

> **In Hold 'em, whenever you have a hand against a hand** *(as opposed to a hand against a*

---

*There's a difference between the "Identical Straight" situation in Hold 'em and Seven-Stud. In Hold 'em, when two players have identical Straights made, but one of them has, in addition, a Flush draw...the Flush draw is a pure freeroll due to the community cards (since both Straights improve the same way). In Seven-Stud, the Flush draw may not be a freeroll because the other player's Straight could get higher (if it's not already Ace-high).

draw)... the draw-out possibilities are severely
limited — *because of the community cards.*

For example, when you've got A-K and your opponent's
got A-Q...you've got him to the point where he can catch
only one (type of) card (a Queen) to win the pot (assuming
he doesn't have the possibility of making a Straight or Flush
after the Flop). In a game like Seven-Card Stud, you almost
never have an opponent waiting to catch just one card.
When there aren't community cards, your opponent usually
has a variety of cards he can catch to win the pot.

In No-Limit (and occasionally in Limit), the reason you
see so many big pots won on a draw-out is because it's a big
hand against a big draw. You'll rarely see a big pot played
when it's a Pair versus a Pair. Unless you have a Pair of
Aces or Kings (and sometimes Queens)...you simply must
not play your Pair too strongly. If you do — and you're up
against a bigger Pair — you're going to be a big underdog.
What's more, when you have a Pair and your opponent has
two overcards, you're a slight favorite.*

In light of this (see footnote), you should never re-raise
with two Queens or two Jacks (all the way down to a Pair of
Deuces) before the Turn expecting to get all your money in
the pot in No-Limit. You don't want to...because if you get
played with — you're either a big dog or a small favorite.

Unsophisticated players tend to play Pairs (especially
Queens) much more strongly than they should. Another
time they give far too much value to a hand is when they
flop the bottom Two-Pair. An example is when they play
small connecting cards such as a 8-7**and the Flop comes
K-8-7. Well, if they're up against an A-K...they're in a very
dangerous situation. I know.

---

*For example, a Pair of Kings against a Pair of Aces is more than a 4½
to 1 dog. And a Pair of Queens versus Ace-King is only about a 6 to
5 favorite.

**To be consistent throughout the discussion on Hold 'em, all two-card
hands will be stated with the higher card first.

I've gotten broke more times playing the *bottom* **Two-Pair than with any other hand playing Hold 'em.**

In that situation, the man with the A-K can win with another King or with an Ace...and he can cripple your hand with a *running* Pair on Fourth and Fifth. If the Board doubles-off with even a Deuce-Deuce on the last two cards...you're gone. He's made Kings and Deuces...and your hand was not helped at all. So you must **proceed with caution** when you flop the **bottom** Two-Pair.

You should also **go slow** when you turn the **top and bottom** Pair. It's only when you turn the top Two-Pair that your opponent's chances are considerably reduced of drawing out and breaking you. But, the danger in this (and other such situations) is far greater in No-Limit than Limit because your entire table-stake could be in jeopardy. In Limit, your only danger is a few extra bets.

Another reason you'll have to be extremely careful with the small connecting cards is because, if you follow my advice, you'll be playing them often. They're my favorite playing hands at No-Limit Hold 'em.

An interesting point about those particular hands such as a 6-5, 8-7, 9-8, 10-9 — which I play about the same way — is that the J-10 is the **best** of the connecting cards. It's better than the others because it's the only two cards in the deck that'll make four Straights and they'll **all** be the nuts. It can make a nut Straight with a 9-8-7, Q-9-8, K-Q-9 and A-K-Q. A Jack-Ten **can't** make a bad Straight — they're **all** the best hand.

All the connecting cards from a 10-9 down to 5-4 will make four Straights...but **only three** of them will be the nuts — one of the Straights will be the little-end. If an 8-7-6 falls, a 5-4 can be beaten by a 9-5 or a 10-9...and, if a K-Q-J falls, a 10-9 can be beaten by an A-10.

Also, when the cards are one-card apart as with a 7-5...you can only make three Straights — and **only two of** those will be the nuts.* (You can have the nuts with a 6-4-3 or an 8-6-4...but you **won't** have the nuts with a 9-8-6.) Similarly, when you've got a hand that's two cards apart...you can only make two Straights with **just one** being the nuts.** (With an 8-5, you can make a Straight with a 7-6-4 and a 9-7-6...but **only the former** will give you the nuts.) As you can see, when the cards in your hand are separated, it not only reduces the number of Straights you can make...but it also means that you'll be able to make fewer nut hands with them. This consideration is the reason why a 7-2 offsuit is the worst Hold 'em hand there is. It's the one hand that has the smallest probability of success.

Another very interesting point is that even though a J-10 can make four nut Straights...it's **not** a hand you'd prefer over, let's say, a 9-8. The latter hand is prefered because you can make **more money** with it. Here's why:

If the Board comes A-8-8, you'll have a pretty good hand (with a 9-8)...and you can feel reasonably confident (especially in a raised pot) somebody else **didn't** turn three Eights. If they did, they probably have an 8-7, a 9-8 (like you have) or possibly a 10-8. I mean they're **not** likely to be in there with a Q-8 or K-8. (There are people who play those hands, but if you're in there with a good player he's **not** likely to have such a hand.)

Now, if you have a J-10 in a raised pot, and the Board comes J-J-4...well, you could very well have "kicker trouble". There's a lot of players that'll play an A-J, K-J or Q-J in a raised pot. Or, if the Board comes 10-10-4...you could have a similar problem since you could be up against an A-10, K-10 or Q-10.

There's other interesting points to be noted about the small connecting cards that might go unnoticed. Let's say you play the 7♣-6♣ and the Flop is 6♠-6♦-2♥. If an off-card falls on Fourth St. and you continue to play your hand pretty strong (in No-Limit) and someone's still in there with you...it's likely you're in there with another Six. Now, you have to decide what your kicker's worth. It's bad — only

---

*An exception here is Q-10 which will make three nut Straights.

**An exception here is K-10 which will make two nut Straights.

Seven-high. So you might think you've got "kicker trouble". But, do you? If he's a good player, what's his kicker likely to be? If it was a raised pot coming in...you could put him on one of three probable hands — a 7-6 (like you have), a 6-5 or an A-6. It's **not** likely to be anything else. Because of the raise before the Flop, he probably **didn't** play a 10-6, J-6, Q-6 or any of those trash hands — **even if they were suited**. So your Seven-kicker is **not** so bad after all. Most people would think that if you're in there against another Six, there's just no chance your Seven could be a good kicker. But it could. It's a lot closer than it looks.

There are times you can even know more than the fact that your kicker's probably **not** as bad as another player might think it is. Quite often, when you know you're up against a good, sound player in the situation described above...you can do more than merely put him on the other Six. **You can name both his cards because you can know what suit he's got**. He's either got the A♡-6♡, 7♡-6♡ or the 6♡-5♡. So if there's a *back-door* Flush possibility (a Flush made with two *running* Hearts on Fourth and Fifth), then you could get a read on him there, too.

You can't always analyze the possible hands your opponent might have and read the situation that well. If you know a player's style and the hands he's likely to play...you can usually come pretty close. But, if you're up against a weak player or somebody who's just *speeding around* (playing real loose and with no definable pattern)...then you can't say such a player couldn't have, let's say, a Q♠-6♠. He could have. As I've so often said...a big part of winning play is knowing your player. You've just got to know people...and watch (carefully) how they play.

A good example of knowing your player can be illustrated by a pot I played with Gary *Bones* Berland (the man who came in second to me in the World Championship Hold 'em event in the 1977 *World Series of Poker®*). Bones said that that pot was the turning point in the whole tournament for him. It probably was. I know it was a key pot for me because it gave me a lot of chips to operate with. Here's what happened:

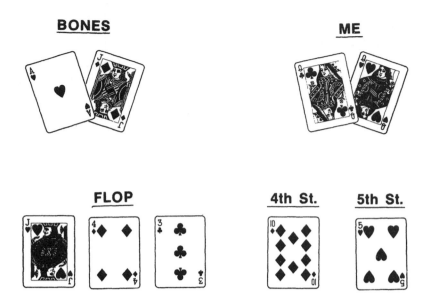

BONES

ME

FLOP　　　　　　**4th St.**　　**5th St.**

Before the Flop, Bones and I got about $6,000 each in the pot. On the Flop, he was first to act and bet $7,000. I just called. The reason I **didn't** raise was because I thought he had just exactly what he did have. I **didn't** want to take him out of the lead since I knew he was going to make a big bet on the next card.

The big tip-off (as to what his hand might be) was his raise **before the Flop**. He was in the first seat (after the Blind) and made it $6,000 to go. **He never raised** in the first seat with two Aces or two Kings in the whole Tournament ...or any other time I saw him play. If he'd have had two Kings or two Aces...he'd have called it and *sent it around* hoping somebody would raise behind him so he could make a big move before the Flop. Of course, he could've had three Jacks in that spot, but I didn't think he did. I put him on Ace–Jack or King–Jack.

When he bet $18,500 on the *Turn* (Fourth St.) — that big a bet — I was close to certain about his hand. As I said, when he made his first bet, I thought there was a small possibility he might have three Jacks. But all my doubts about his hand were removed when he bet the eighteen-five. Then I knew what he had...and knew he was trying to shut me out of the pot right there. So I called the $18,500 and moved-in with the rest of the money I had ($13,800). He called my raise even though he was pretty sure I had him beat at that point. It was a pretty big pot — almost $78,000 before Bones called the last bet. I could've been bluffing. I've been known to do that on occasion. Bones' call swelled the pot to over $90,000...which put me in a commanding position for the rest of the Tournament.

That pot illustrates another thing about my play that's misunderstood by a lot of people. I've heard that I was "lucky" in that pot because Bones had the hand he did. But, as I've explained, it wasn't luck at all. I knew his play. As you'll later learn, I've got something of a reputation for being a "lucky" player. Of course, it's unfounded. It's rather difficult to win millions of dollars playing Poker and be on a "winning streak" for nearly 25 consecutive years. To do that...you need a lot more than luck.

As you can see from the discussion of the pot I played with Bones, there's both art and science to putting a player on a particular hand. It's not always easy to do. It requires experience, close observation of your opponents, and a keen analysis of their style of play. I hope I'll be able to teach you how to do it with a reasonable degree of accuracy.

But there's another aspect to Hold 'em that doesn't require any special qualities...and yet it gives a lot of players a lot of trouble. It's the simple matter of reading the Board and being able to relate it to your hand. Correctly.

You'll remember that the winning Hold 'em hand (when all the cards are out) is the best five-card hand made up with both (or just one) of your hole-cards and three (or four) of the community cards on the Board. So it's really a very simple matter to figure out what your best hand is. But, occasionally, it gets a little confusing and even very experienced players will make some horrible mistakes. I'll tell you about one such mistake shortly. But, for now, let's see if you can figure out who'll win the pot in this situation:

Player _A_　　　　**Player _B_**

BOARD

Think about it. Who wins? To an experienced player it looks like a simple question. But most beginners will answer it incorrectly. In any case, you'll find the correct answer in a footnote on page 348.

The problem posed here may seem very simple — and it is — but I've seen players overlook their hands completely. . . and for a lot of money. I saw a very big pot played where the Board was K-K-4-4-7 and one guy bet eighteen thousand on the end. The other guy called with two Deuces in the *pocket* (hole). He called that $18,000 bet with absolutely the worst possible hand. He couldn't even beat the Board! (Remember: you play the best five out of seven cards — the best combination of the two cards in your hand and the five cards on the Board.)

That was an oversight of enormous proportions. It's unforgivable. But, Hold 'em is a remarkable game. As I noted earlier, you can turn the nuts in Hold 'em and have the worst hand. There are so many interesting things that can happen in Hold 'em. . .some that border on the miraculous.

The situations in Hold 'em that appear to be miracles are when a player has to *catch perfect* in order to win. . .and he does. A *perfect catch* is the biggest draw-out in the game. It's when a player is "dead" to only two cards in the deck — no other cards will win it for him — and he catches both of them to pull-off the "miracle". I've seen such "miracles" on several occasions. They're hard to believe when you see them. Especially when you're on the losing end of them. I know. It happened to me in what was probably the biggest Poker game the world has ever seen.

The game was at the **Aladdin** (in Las Vegas) a few years ago and it went round–the–clock for about three consecutive months. There was over a million dollars on the table at all times. It was quite a game. And this particular pot I remember very well. I lost over twenty thousand in it.

I had two Kings in the pocket and the guy in the pot with me had two Sevens. The turn came K–2–2. He moved in on me. I called him. I flopped a Full...but I didn't win it. He caught 7–7 on Fourth and Fifth. That was the only way in the world that he could win...and that's what he did.*

I saw a similar situation in that same game. (In three months of 24–hour play a lot of things can happen...and they usually do.) Here's what happened in this one:

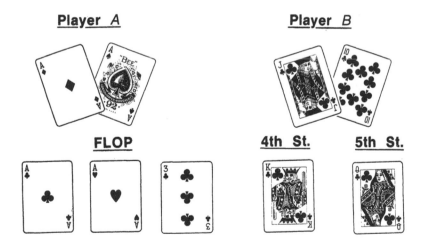

| Player *A* | Player *B* |

| FLOP | 4th St. | 5th St. |

Player *A* flopped the nuts...and what looks like an unbeatable hand. But, Player *B* beat it by catching perfect on the last two cards.

Other very "strange" things can happen in Hold 'em. One time, about eight years ago in Reno, I won a $27,000

---

*It's almost 1000 to 1 against catching two perfect cards (989 to 1 to be exact).

pot with a Six-high. Here's how that happened:

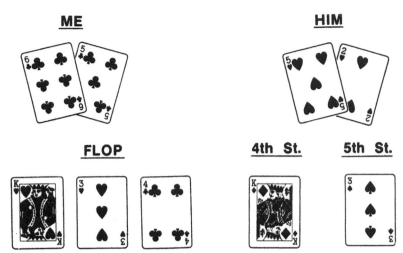

I bet on the Flop and he raised me. I moved-in on him — which, as you'll discover, is usually my style of play at No-Limit once I take a position (bet) in a pot. Well, he called me. After the last two cards were dealt, he had Kings and Treys with a Five-high. I had the same hand **Six-high.**

If you play Hold 'em often enough, you're sure to see about everything that can happen in the game. I'm sure I have seen everything. One night at the **Dunes** (in Las Vegas) I was involved in an unusual pot. I flopped a Set (of Trips) and had to settle for a split (pot). Here's how it happened:

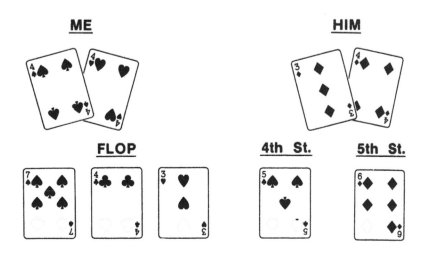

Here's a last illustration of the very strange things that sometimes occur in Hold 'em. This interesting situation happened at the **Horseshoe** in one of the side-games (of which there are several) during Tournament time. I didn't see it, but I'm sure I've got it right because it was talked about for days after it happened.

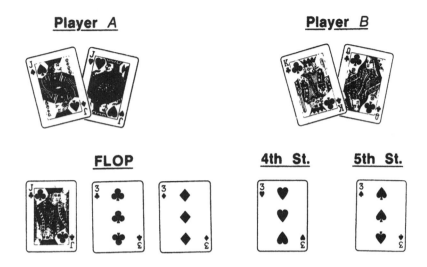

Before the Flop, *A* brought it in and *B* raised it. *A* called. On the Flop, *A* checked and *B* bet. *A* called again. The action was the same on Fourth. On the end, *A* checked again and *B* moved-in on him. At that point, *A* couldn't beat the Board... but, in frustration, he called. *B* won the pot, of course, with four-Treys, King-high. *Bad Beat*.

The brief discussion of the similarities and differences between Limit and No-Limit Hold 'em that you've just read was for some quick information only. Because Hold 'em is not as widely played as Seven-Card Stud, for example, this little introduction was written for those of you who know nothing at all about the game. Hopefully, even experienced players were able to learn something from it.

Actually the differences between play at No-Limit and Limit Hold 'em are far greater than the similarities. They're really worlds apart. Proof of this is that I've known very few players who can really play both forms *jam-up*.

It stands to reason that's true. Limit Hold 'em — in fact, any form of Limit Poker — is very much a mechanical game. There's only so much you can do when there are restrictions on the amount of money you can bet. That's **not** to say you **can't** *put a play on* a man in Limit. You can. You just can't get **too** "fancy"...because there'll be someone there to *look you up* most of the time.

However, in No-Limit, it's quite a different story. There's so many things you can do when you've got almost as much freedom as you could want. The many options available to you in No-Limit play is what makes the game so much more complex than Limit. This will become quite apparent now that I'm going to discuss the two versions separately.

The answer to the little problem posed on page 344 is that the pot gets split. The Eight kicker doesn't do Player *A* any good because he has a Pair of Kings with an Ace, Queen, Jack...and so does Player *B*.

SUPER/SYSTEM's
POWER POKER COURSE
IN

LIMIT
HOLD 'EM

LIMIT HOLD 'EM

Table of Contents

Bobby Baldwin

BOBBY "The Owl" BALDWIN

My Expert Collaborator
on
LIMIT HOLD 'EM

"Bobby won all the money again"...that's what my friend *"Iron Man"* told me a couple of years ago during one of his frequent visits to Vegas. After having played twenty years in Texas I was naturally curious about what was happening. Everytime I talked I got the same answer.

Some young kid I didn't even know had taken over where I had left off. I couldn't believe it possible that some unknown like Bobby Baldwin would come along and dominate the group of good Poker players I knew inhabited the southern States. Quite frankly, I was getting pretty irritated hearing about this "Bobby". I thought to myself: *wait until I get this kid across the table from me...I'll destroy him.*

Well, I finally got him across that table. The first thing I knew I was forty thousand loser trying to run over him. I finally settled down and got even in that game but *Bobby won all the money again.* I knew how Pat Garrett must have felt about Billy the Kid about a hundred years ago.

After I finally got to know Bobby, it wasn't very hard to understand how he mastered Hold 'em in such a short period of time. He approaches **all** Poker games with such professional diligence and intensity he absorbs the "fine points" much easier than most.

The longer I play with *"The Owl"*, the more I watch in amazement at the subtle, intricate maneuvers and strategy he uses that took me years to perfect.

Even though Bobby is my expert on Limit Hold 'em, it's obvious he's an all-around Poker player. This fact was borne out in the 1977 *World Series of Poker* when he won both the Seven-Card Stud championship ($45,000) and the Deuce-to-Seven Lowball championship ($90,000). He also made it to the last table in the No-Limit Hold 'em championship. He's quite a Poker player...no matter what the game is.

Bobby is one of the handful of Poker Professionals who doesn't care who's playing, what they're playing or how high the stakes are. He simply walks up to the table and says *"deal me in"*. He has so much raw talent that he can at least hold his own in **any** Poker game. And he's so super-aggressive that I sometimes wonder if he doesn't get a sore arm from shoving all his checks to the center of the pot so often. However, his aggressiveness belies the fact that he's one of the most pleasant and gracious persons I've ever known...a true Southern gentleman.

Bobby lives in Tulsa, Oklahoma and has no immediate plans to move to Las Vegas where gambling is legal. He prefers the life of a traveling Poker player, going where the action is at that particular time. And that includes the very big games in Vegas. Since he's only a phone call away, he "mysteriously" shows up **whenever** there's a No-Limit game or when they're playing $1000 Limit Hold 'em.

Being on the road constantly is a tough life — I can tell you from experience. Chasing that white line down the middle of the highway is an exciting and rewarding way of life...if you're good at what you do. And Bobby is **good** — one of the best in the world. There's a lot of self-satisfaction running down the toughest Poker games...and beating them.

And the one thing I know that's abundantly clear is this: Bob Baldwin is a young man who won't be satisfied until he reaches the top. And, I rather expect I'll be meeting him again and again across that green felt battlefield.

Note: In May of 1978, just *after* **Super/System's** First Edition was published, Bobby Baldwin won the World Championship.

LIMIT HOLD 'EM
Undergraduate School

INTRODUCTION

As I've already mentioned, there are many differences between Limit and No-Limit Hold 'em. In fact, the games are so different that there are **not** many players who rank with the best in both types of Hold 'em. Many No-Limit players have difficulty *gearing down* for Limit, while Limit players often lack the courage and "feel" necessary to excel at No-Limit. As "heart" and intuition diminish in importance in Limit, other qualities increase in value. In the following pages, I'll discuss these qualities and supply you with other information you need to play top-notch Limit Hold 'em.

Many of the high-powered strategies that are available to the aggressive No-Limit player **can't** be used to great advantage in Limit. Specifically, bluffing and *picking-up* small pots are much more difficult when the game limits you to a maximum bet. Despite this, there's an important similarity between good Limit and No-Limit play. This similarity is an aggressive style. The nature of Limit Hold 'em makes it necessary to keep a tighter rein on your aggressive play...but when you play a pot, you play it strongly — much as in No-Limit. That's Power Poker.

One of the most significant differences between Limit and No-Limit is the number of players per pot. Since the amounts of money you can bet in Limit are fixed, you have **much** *less* leverage and therefore less chance of significantly narrowing down the field. Big No-Limit pots usually involve two players, occasionally three. Large limit pots are often played among five to seven players, sometimes even more. Small and medium-sized pots in Limit may also involve multiple hands more readily than No-Limit. The problems, which are presented by having a number of opponents in most pots, make the ability to "read" your opponents' hands one of the most important strategic tools for a Limit player.

In addition to being able to accurately assess the strength of the hands out against you, it's usually necessary to start out with an above-average hand yourself. This means, very simply, *playing* **big** *cards* **most** *of the time.* The straight-forward, somewhat mechanical nature of Limit Hold 'em means that most of the time you have to show down a hand, and you'll make the best hand more often with big cards than little ones. In Limit, you **can't** take a 7–6 suited and *double-through** a man with two Aces, because he **doesn't** have to jeopardize very many chips. Consequently, the small, suited connectors (which are my favorite No–Limit hands), are **not** as valuable when I **can't** *move all–in* on a man. I still play them, but the situation has to be right.

There are also a couple of "intangibles" which can be the difference between success and failure in Limit Hold 'em play. These qualities (which are also useful in other forms of Poker) are almost indispensable in playing Limit. The intangibles I'm referring to are patience and self-discipline while playing, attention to what the other players are doing — whether you're in the hand or not — the good judgment to know which games are best to play in and, once you're in the game how to decide whether to continue playing or to quit.

> Lack of patience and self-discipline are the downfall of many players who otherwise are technically sound enough to be winners. I know many players who are extremely tough when they are winning, but who *fly open* if they get off to a bad start during a session. Similarly, I have seen many players who go *on tilt* when they get a *bad beat,* and their play gets ragged and sometimes deteriorates to the point where they have almost no chance to win.

---

*Double your entire stack.

Hold 'em can be a very frustrating game when you are going badly, and it's important to play each hand and each session without letting past events affect your play or hamper your judgment. I've seen players who were *running bad* believe that they were going to lose and play so defensively that they usually did lose. Nobody likes to lose a big pot on the last card (and in Hold 'em it can be particularly annoying when your opponent has only two or three cards he can catch to beat you), but you must play the next hand the same way as if you'd won. That's self-discipline.

Patience pays its dividends during the periods when you're losing and cannot pick up a playable hand. You have to keep throwing them away until you get one you like. You need to resist the temptation to play hands that you **wouldn't** even consider if you were winning. These guidelines seem simple to follow when you are reading them (like you are now), but it's another matter entirely when you get caught up in the emotions that go with winning and losing your money.

Paying attention to as many things as possible while you're playing helps you to get to know your opponents. While this aspect of the game is more crucial in No–Limit, it counts in Limit, too. It's particularly important when a new player sits down that you observe him carefully for a while to get a *line* on his play.

There are two main things to watch for in your opponents: *Tells*. . .and your opponents' general approach to the game. *Tells* are physical mannerisms which may betray information about the content of a man's hand. You're more likely to profit from this type of information if you're playing with relatively inexperienced players. (Most Professionals will be aware enough to reduce this type of indication to a minimum.) A *Tell* is nice if you discover it, but even **more valuable** is the ability to evaluate an opponent's style from careful observation. If you follow my suggestions in this section, you'll have ample opportunity to observe your opponents, because much of the time you'll be on the sidelines waiting for a good hand. Cool, objective observation is easier when you're **not** in the pot and have nothing else to do but watch the action. (This is also a good time to practice the important art of "reading" hands.) The time you spend watching the other players will be very useful when you do play a pot with them and are able to recall how they reacted in a similar situation.

> **The important questions you want an immediate answer to are:**

(1) **How many hands does he play?**

(2) **Does he bet a lot or is he a** *Calling Station?*

(3) **Does he bluff?**

(4) **Can he be bluffed?**

(5) **Does he have a good knowledge of the game or is he a weak player?**

(6) **Is his play thrown off by a** *bad beat?*

(7) **Does he always play the same hand the same way or does he mix-up his play (by** *changing gears*)?

The answers to questions like these are important in adopting a proper strategy towards each new opponent. It can also be helpful to watch players and learn from the way they play hands or read opponents hands.

The question of when to play and when to quit is an important one for the Professional player who has the chance to play every day. Players looking for an excuse after a losing play often will say, *"I should have quit when I got those Aces beat,"* or *"I should have quit when I was $300 ahead."* Whether you're winning or losing, what happened on a particular hand should have nothing to do with your decision to quit or not to quit. You should continue playing as long as you feel you're in a good game, where you are the favorite to take down the money. If your mental or physical condition starts to deteriorate...you have a sign to either take a break or get ready to give it up.

> Play only as long as the game is good and you
> feel good. If your resources of patience and
> concentration are dwindling, and you hit a
> bad streak, it may be time to quit. *Not*
> because you are running "unlucky", but
> rather because this set of circumstances tends
> to destroy discipline — and ultimately leads
> to inferior play towards the end of a session.
> If you *aren't* up to your best effort, *usually*,
> you should go home. The exception to this is
> if it's an unusually good game and you think
> you can win — even at less than 100%
> efficiency.

Try and think of all your plays as one long session (I
know it's hard), during which you are going to try to win as
much money as possible. In order to do this, you have to try
to play longer when the game is good and quit sooner when
it may be too tough. Try to recognize the days when
personal problems are going to interfere with your play, and
avoid playing then. *Don't* **take your troubles out on your
bankroll**.

Also, it is important to learn how to go home loser,
particularly if the game is not very good and shows no signs
of improving. If, when behind, you ask yourself the
question: *"Would I continue playing in this game if I were
ahead?"*, and give yourself a *"No"* for an answer, then it's
time to quit. Remember, it's all one long session. Nobody
wins every day.

I have been talking about the general topic of money
management. *Money management* is a phrase which is
sometimes misunderstood. It **doesn't** mean setting yourself a
limit of how much you feel you want to win or lose in one
play. It means how you handle your money when you're
gambling. If you sit down at a table and there are a couple
of players you know are pretty easy, maybe you figure you
can win a couple of hundred in the game. Let's say after
three or four hours you are a couple of hundred ahead. Do
you quit? If you look around and see that the easy spots
have gone broke and a few tough players have replaced
them, then you probably should quit. But, if the weak

players are still there and have lots of chips, and a couple of really *solid* players are stuck and are now gambling, then the game is better than when you sat down — and you should keep at it.

> Playing Limit Hold 'em is like a job — the more hours you work, the more money you'll make. Money management and the self-discipline from which it comes are almost the most important factors in Limit, second only to learning how to become a good player. If you can't manage your money, you won't have any.

One last word on the size of your playing bankroll: relative to the game you're in I believe about 200 times the upper limit — $4,000 for $10 and $20 — should be sufficient to allow you to absorb a few substantial losses. With this amount you can take an occasional shot in a bigger game without putting yourself (your bankroll) in serious jeopardy. If you run into a sustained losing streak (or have to withdraw some of your capital for other reasons) it is **NEVER a bad idea** to play in a smaller (and hopefully easier) game — to build your cash back up to a comfortable level. (It is **never** a good idea to gamble with money that you can't really afford to lose. This situation will tend to limit the aggressiveness of your game and affect the accuracy of your decisions.)

You should also train yourself to treat **with utmost seriousness** the money you are playing with. I've heard it said of one Las Vegas player that he plays the same whether he's betting $1 checks or $100 checks. That's a good way to be. Not many players can do it. **If the game you're in is worth your time, the money you're playing for is worth your best effort.**

ANTE and BETTING

STRUCTURE

I'm now going to describe the structures of the $10 and $20 and $15 and $30 Limit Hold 'em games as played at the **Golden Nugget** in **Las Vegas**. The games at the **Nugget** are among the toughest anywhere, and anyone who beats them regularly deserves to be called a top player.

The $10 and $20 is the standard game, and is played almost every day of the year. It's eleven-handed with a 50¢ ante, and the player to the left of the *Button* ("Dealer") has a $5 Blind. Each subsequent player may call the $5 or make it $10. If someone makes it $10, that's considered to have completed the initial bet (rather than being considered as a raise). Any player may now call the $10 or raise it to $20. There is a four-raise maximum which allows a *jammed* pot to go to $50 before the Flop. I'd estimate that between one-half and two-thirds of the pots are unraised. Usually, you can get to see the Turn for $5. [If the pot is **not** raised by the time it gets back to the *Blind*, he has the last chance to make it play for $10 — or he can merely "call" (by not putting any additional money in the pot).] All bets and raises on the Flop are in increments of $10 (again, to the $50 limit), while the last two cards are $20 "Streets", and the maximum that can be put in is $100. (However, in a two-handed pot, there's **NO** limit on raises.)

The $15 and $30 is set up differently and encourages **faster** play. There are ten or eleven players, with the *Button* having a $5 Blind and the first player a $10 Blind. Each player can either call the $10 or raise it to a total of $25. Again, there are three more ($15) raises, to a maximum of $70. Bets of $15 must be made on the Flop and the betting limit doubles on the last two cards to $30 bets.

The fact that you can raise it to $25 before the Turn, but only bet $15 on the Flop gives the ($15 and $30) game a considerably **looser** format on the Turn since the pots are often quite large, and many players take a $15 card. (If you put in $25 before the Flop, it's proportionately more of the total a hand is likely to cost you than the $10 equivalent in the $10 and $20 game.)

Not counting raises (after the Flop), a hand in the $10 and $20 game will cost you $10, $10, $20 and $20, a total of $60 — while in the $15 and $30 game it'll cost you $25, $15, $30 and $30, a total of $100. Thus, you put in ⅙ before the Flop in the $10 and $20, but ¼ in the $15 and $30. Also, if you put in $10 in the $15 and $30 game you are subject to be raised 2½ times, while in the $10 and $20 game the raise is only double. The consequences of this is that you need a stronger hand to come in with in the $15 and $30 game — **especially** *in the early positions.* (If the game had an ante, in addition to the Blinds, it would be less conducive to *tight* play, but as it is, it only costs $15 a Round.)·

INTRODUCTION TO THE PLAY OF THE HANDS

There are 1,326 possible two-card hands in Hold 'em. But if you consider just the *numerical* values of 8-7, K-10, A-5, etc., there are only 91. If you distinguish between suited and unsuited cards you must add 78 more. (Of the basic 91 hands, 13 are Pairs and cannot be suited.)

The preceding might not sound like the raw material for an interesting Poker game, but if you deal two cards to ten or eleven players, then give them five common cards, the resulting situations can be complex, exciting, and as fascinating (or even more so than) any other form of Poker. Recognizing which of the two-card hands to play (and when to play them). . .and learning how to evaluate the various situations that can arise are the two most important technical requirements for a Limit player. There are a couple of fancy things you can do, and I'll tell you about those too, but you **can't** "dance around" too much in Limit play. **Solid** *play* and **solid** *hands* get the money in the long run.

There are four betting rounds, and thus four decisions you may have to make in a Hold 'em hand. The first one, whether to play or pass, affects the nature of the others. When you play an A-K you're going to be up against a different set of problems as compared to when you have a 6-5.

> **The decisions you make on the Flop are by far the most important — once you have decided to play your hand. Fourth St. presents fewer intricacies, although there are still a number of difficulties which consistently appear at that point. The final decision (on Fifth St.), which you'll make when all the cards are out, is almost always simple and relatively mechanical.**

I'm going to give you the information you'll need to know in order to understand, recognize and solve the problems that you'll continually face in Limit play. Of course, there's no substitute for experience, and only by playing, with your money at stake, will you develop the confidence in your judgment and the self-control and discipline which will eventually enable you to be an expert player.

PLAY BEFORE THE FLOP

There are very few things I'm going to tell you about Limit Hold 'em that will **not** have an occasional exception. It's a good tactical move (especially against experts) to mix-up your play by treating the same situation in different ways. (The one disadvantage a solid player has is that his alert opponents can often figure out the "texture" of his hand. I'm going to give you a solid approach...but I'll also tell you to refrain from being too predictable.) As I just implied, you must create some doubts in your opponents' minds or you'll be too easy to "read". An occasional departure from your basic style will effect two ultimate objectives: it will **not** only keep your opponents off balance, but it will also make your play **less** mechanical. But first I want to give some general guidelines...then, I'll deal with how to vary your play as we go along.

Position is **always** a big consideration in Hold 'em. It's more important in No-Limit than Limit — but it's still vital to this discussion. The first information that you have about a Hold 'em hand (even before you get your cards) is the nature of your position.

Roughly speaking, the table can be divided as follows: Player 1 — the Blind; Players 2-4 — early position; Players 5-7 — middle position; Players 8-10 — late position; Player 11 — the *Button*. Since position is fixed throughout a hand, (unlike Stud), you have to give it **strong consideration** in your decision whether to call the first bet or not. You **can't** *consistently* take marginal hands in **bad** positions. I try not to play too many hands "up front", especially if the game allows a sizeable raise like the $15 and $30 game I described. I play Limit with what I call a "big card theory". I prefer the big cards, and this is particularly true when I'm in early position where the exposure to a raise is great. A certain percentage of pots is always going to be raised before the Turn, and each game has its own character as far as this is concerned. Sometimes this character changes from one hour to the next. A game which has seen very few raises can suddenly turn into a shoot-out, with almost every pot raised — and many pots will be double-raised.

How *loose* the game is, is also a factor in what hands you play "up front". For example, if in most raised pots a couple of players are calling the raise *cold*, you're going to get more play on your hands and you can come in with slightly weaker hands, as compared to a game where a raise tends to drastically narrow down the field.

PLAYABLE HANDS
before the Flop
in an
EARLY POSITION

In the three spots to the left of the Blind I like to have a hand I can raise with, or one that's strong enough to stand a raise. I'm talking about a Pair of Aces, Kings or Queens, A-K (suited or not), and A-Q or K-Q (suited **only**). I'd also play the medium Pairs — Eights to Jacks. I'd probably play the smaller Pairs, — Deuces to Sevens in a game set up like the $10 and $20 I described, but they would be *very* **marginal** *hands* in the $15 and $30. Also, I'll play A-J, K-J, Q-J and J-10 when they're **suited**. I **don't** put a lot of value on hands like Q-J and J-10 suited when I'm in very early position. I **don't** think that you lose anything by passing them. An A-Q or K-Q **offsuit** are marginally playable, but I'd feel better with them if the pot doesn't get raised behind me. I sometimes raise coming in with these hands, but just as often I'll simply call.

If I have one of the three highest Pairs I almost always *bring it in* with a raise. Once in a while (especially if a lot of pots are being raised), if no one has called the Blind, or I'm in the number two position, I'll *limp-in* with two Aces or two Kings and hope I get a chance to re-raise. [Although it's **best** to raise coming in with big Pairs, slow playing them (**not** raising) about 10% of the time can have some benefits. This is because nobody will be able to put you on a big Pair, and other players will have it in the back of their minds in other pots, that you may be in with an overpair, when your actual hand is **not** that strong.] Two Queens is a hand I *almost* **always** raise with — because it only figures to stand up if you can thin out the field. Ace-King **offsuit*** is a hand I generally raise with in middle or late position. Up front I sometimes just call, but most of the time I'll raise it there too. Here again, some of the value you lose from **not** raising

---

*From this point on, if I don't specifically state that a hand is *suited*, you should assume I'm talking about an *offsuit* hand.

can be made up because your hand is disguised. If you catch a good player in with A-Q and an Ace flops, he'll probably think his kicker is good if he figures you'd have raised it coming in with A-K. I raise **less** *often* with A-K **suited** because I want to let players who may make a smaller Flush come in. If it gets raised behind me, my hand is strong enough to *play back* now that the pot is fairly large.

There are two sound reasons for raising with big Pairs and A-K:

(1) **You get more money in with a good hand.**

(2) **You tend to narrow down the number of opponents (and this is the more important reason).**

Big Pairs **decrease in strength** according to the number of hands out against them, and a raise is really your only means of protection. If you have two Aces and someone wants to try and *run you down* with two Fours or a Q-10, then you want to put them in the most disadvantageous position possible. Anytime you do **not** raise you're concealing the nature of your hand, and this can work against you as well as in your favor. If you *limp-in*, you're taking the chance of losing the pot to a player who **wouldn't** have gotten involved had a raise given him a clue as to the strength of your hand. Naturally, if you **don't** raise and six or seven people call, **you must proceed** *very* **carefully** *on the Flop.*

An A-K, while a very strong hand, is still a *drawing* proposition. One large benefit in raising with this hand (especially in late position) is that many times you can see a *free card* on Fourth St. if you **don't** turn a hand. This is a great advantage to you, because you **always** have two overcards, and sometimes if big cards flop, a possible inside Straight draw. If the pot is played short-handed, you can often win with A-K simply by virtue of having raised, because usually you'll either have the best hand (even when you **don't** turn a Pair), or your opponents will fold marginal hands (like a small Pair in the hole or bottom Pair on the Flop) if you bet.

The other hands that I mentioned earlier in this section are almost always *calling* (rather than raising) *hands* in early position. Hands like K-Q **suited** or K-J **suited** tend to do well in *volume pots** — where no one has indicated strength before the Turn. If you raise with these cards you're (unfortunately) going to tend to eliminate the types of hands you want in...and you'll get called or re-raised by hands that are probably better than yours.

I'd like to mention one more type of hand before I discuss play from the middle positions. A-X** **suited** is, I believe, *one of the* **most** *overrated* Hold 'em hands. It's a hand that you want to **play for as little as possible** before the Flop, since most of its value comes from gambling with it when you turn a Flush draw. You only flop a Flush draw about one out of nine times, and you only make a Flush about 5% of the times you do hold the hand. If you flop an Ace and get any kind of play, you're probably up against a better kicker. Most players play this hand religiously — regardless of position — but I do **not** consider it to be a good enough hand to merit a call in early position. This is because it's **not** that much stronger than A-X **offsuit**, which is definitely a hand you want to pass in most positions. I do prefer A-2, A-3, A-4 and A-5 to A-6, A-7, A-8 and A-9 since the former hands give you the additional Straight potential.

PLAYABLE HANDS
before the Flop
from
MIDDLE or LATE
POSITIONS

In the 5th through 7th positions, I can loosen up my standards a little. The chances of getting raised are lessened considerably, and not as many players will have the

---

*Large number of players.
**"X" is any card.

advantage of acting behind me as the hands develop. In the 5th, 6th and 7th seats there'll usually be (in addition to the Blind) between one and three players in the pot, when the action comes around. Once again I'm going to raise (or re-raise) with the top hands — Aces, Kings and A-K. (Some very tight players, who only raise with big Pairs if they're in an early position, are **not** the kind of players you want to re-raise when you have A-K. In fact, if I'm fairly sure they have a big Pair, I might even pass A-K.)

Two Queens is a difficult hand to play behind a raise. I generally re-raise to *define* my hand, narrow the field, and find out where I'm at — assuming the original raiser is the type of player who **often raises** *without* a hand better than two Queens. If I get re-raised by the original raiser (or by somebody behind me), I have to put them on Aces or Kings — because they know that I have to have a good hand to re-raise in my position. I'll take the Flop and if I **don't** improve I'm probably going to be done with it.

When you hold two Queens or two Kings, against a higher Pair, it's very difficult to avoid losing some checks — (unless you're up against an unusually tight player). By re-raising with these hands, I protect them if they're the best hand and I'm still able to get away from them if I'm convinced I'm beat. If I just call against an opponent who may have raised with Jacks, Tens, Nines, A-Q or A-K, I'm just asking to get my hand beat by somebody behind me — who has a hand that he'll call one raise with...but **not** two raises.

> **My play in the middle and late positions illustrates a saying which applies to every Poker game I know:** *"Play solid in front and loose in the back."* **I** *don't* **have any hard rules for what hands to play in what positions, but that's one thing I'm always thinking about when I have a hand that's NOT a** *premium hand* **(the ones I play in early positions).**

Hold 'em is a game in which you can get good odds on your money with certain hands in certain situations. The small Pairs and small connectors are hands you want to play against a lot of players. When I get these hands, I have to decide how it looks like the pot is going to be played.

Let's say I have 7-6 **suited** in 7th position. (Now I'm assuming it's a tough game and when people come in early they're mostly playing the *premium* hands like I am.) There are three types of pots that can come up.

(1) The first type is where one person in an early position calls and everybody passes to me. I pass, too, because there's no reason for me to play a short-handed pot **without** a *premium* hand, with perhaps one more player who may come in behind me. Worse yet, I may get raised from someone behind me. Then I have to put in more money before the Flop in a pot where I **don't** expect to win much — even if I do make the best hand. If I'm going to play a *light* (weak) hand in Limit, I want to have the chance to win a big pot with it.

(2) The second type of pot is the one where three (or more) players have called in front of me. Now...I'm getting the kind of *price* I like with my hand. I'm going to call and let the rest of the field *trail in* if they have anything.

(3) The third type is when the pot's already been raised. Now I need to know that I'm going to get four-to-six-way action. If a couple of players called early, number five raised it, and number six called the raise, I know that if I call, there's a good chance we'll pick up somebody in the back who's attracted by the size of the pot. Now my position is good (next to last), and I have a hand I can *easily* **pass** if I **don't** get a good Flop. (There's one more small possibility, and that's a *double-raised* pot. When I play a *double-raised* pot, I like to be one of the raisers. When two players in the first half of the table raise, I'm probably **not** going to get the number of people in the pot that I want...so I'm usually going to pass.)

When I'm in a middle to late position, and the pot looks like it's going to be played four-to-six handed (or even more), I'm going to take quite a few Flops in **both** raised and unraised pots. I'm going to call with the small connectors and the small Pairs — whether the pot is raised or not.

But the play of some of the other hands depends on whether or not it has been raised. This is especially true of the "trouble" hands (see page 505). I'm going to pass with these hands in Limit, the same as I would in No-Limit, if the raiser is in an early position. I know that up-front they're raising with the same type hands that I am. I **don't** want to be calling raises with hands if I **don't** know what I want to catch with them. If I call a raise with K–Q, I **can't** feel comfortable with my hand if I turn a King or a Queen. The raiser is "telling" me he's probably got a big Pair or A–K suited or A–Q suited. By the same reasoning, I **don't** like to call raises with A–X suited. If I turn an Ace I'm in "kicker trouble", and if I beat two Kings or two Queens I'll only win a **small** pot.

I **don't** want to call a raise and be forced to turn a Flush draw, which **I'm going to miss** 65% of the time, or two big Pair, in order to be able to play the hands through.

I'm usually going to call a raise in middle position with suited hands like K–10, A–10, J–10 and 10–9 — but I'll proceed cautiously (unless I get a big Turn) as in No-Limit.

In **unraised** pots the "trouble" hands go up in value. They're even better if the first three players pass, indicating that none of the dangerous *premium* hands are out up-front. Now...other players are going to start playing all kinds of hands, and I have a good hand and good position. Hands like Q–J and K–J, which in other spots are passes or marginal calls, become raising hands. A–J, A–Q and K–Q are very strong hands — especially against one or two players who have just called. These hands are sometimes strong enough to re-raise. If everyone has passed to the sixth or seventh player, he's likely to raise with any kind of a reasonable hand in order to pick up the Blind. You should re-raise, for a number of reasons:

(1) First, you probably have an equal or better hand;

(2) Second, because you have position; and

(3) Third, in order to take the lead.

> [*Many times (in two or three-handed pots) the player who raises or gets in the last raise before the Flop has the chance to win the pot by betting on the Flop, when nobody turns a hand or a draw.*]

I want to get back to the small connectors for a moment. If I've got a lot of people in, I'm going to take a turn with these hands most of the time — although I like to have the additional value of being suited in a raised pot. The more people in the pot and the closer to the Button I am, the more likely I am to call. It's also better to have a hand like 8-7 than one like 8-6, 9-7 or 10-7 since you'll flop more Straight draws and because your kicker will rarely be a factor.

The "trouble" hands in late position become closely related (in value) to the small connectors (assuming the pot was not raised up-front and a couple of people have come in). If the pot was raised in a middle position, especially by a *fast* (action) player, I'm going to take a *turn* because this type of raise is not as threatening as a raise *under the gun*. Sometimes, I'll even play-back — so I don't let him (the action player) make a caller out of me all the time.

If I'm *on the Button* and it **hasn't** been raised, I'm going to take a lot of *turns* if I have any kind of hand. I'll play hands like 7-5, 9-6 and 10-7 (offsuit), which I'd ordinarily throw away. If a lot of the players in a pot are in the last half of the deal, I know that a lot of them are in with the type of cards I have. This is an indication that I have to be careful **not** to get very involved on the turn, if *Rags* fall, unless I **flop** a fairly strong hand. You **don't** want to risk a lot of money with a weak hand — unless you get a big Flop.

That brings me to a play I like to make when I have a suited hand like 8-7 or 7-6 *on the Button*. Let's say, a man in an early position raised and a couple of others have called the raise up-front. Now I know that they probably all have big cards and I'm going to re–raise and gamble with them. Now I've got to believe that the callers will probably have good enough hands to stand a double–raise in case the first raiser *hits it* (raises) again. I know the type of hands they have...but they know nothing about mine. In addition, I have the Button and I can always throw my hand away if I **don't** get a *turn*. One big side benefit I'm going to get from this play is that once my opponents have seen it, they're going to give me a lot more action when I pick up two Aces or two Kings near the Button. This type of play and some of the other things I've mentioned are going to work best in *solid* games, where you can get a good idea of the *texture* of your opponent's hands from their position and actions.

> **If you're in a *loose* game, where the first man is as likely to have 7–6 as A–K, and where almost every pot is being raised, you can normally *forget about* putting people on hands before the Flop. You can also *forget about* doing anything "fancy". You're going to have to show down the best hand to win. That's all there is to it.**

I like to raise once in a while in a middle or late position with any hand which I was going to call with. Small or medium Pairs, or **suited** connectors like 8–7, 9–7, 9–8, 10–8 or 10–9 are worth an **occasional** raise to keep your opponents off balance. If you only raise with big Pairs and Ace–King, you'll be giving too much information to strong opponents. Once they know that you might raise with 10–9 suited, they'll be forced to put less pressure on you if you've raised and the Flop comes 8–7–6.

A good player who turns a Pair and a Straight draw will make it very tough on someone he's sure has an overpair. I **don't** like to overdo the *play* of raising with these hands since a good player only has to see something once for him to remember it a long time.

There are quite a few hands which some people play which haven't been mentioned. I won't play a King or Queen suited or offsuit with a card less than a Ten. I'll also play Q-9, J-9 or J-8 suited. I don't want to get involved with hands like K-9, Q-8, J-7 or 10-6 where you can only flop one Straight and it's not the "nuts", and where, if the hand is suited, you will be trying to make an intermediate Flush. If you follow my advice almost all the Flushes you make will be the nuts or fairly small ones, because with the exceptions of the "trouble hands", you won't be drawing to King, Queen or Jack Flushes.

Of course, all hands with one big and one little card are passes except perhaps when you're in very late position trying to pick up the Blind, and playing your Ace or King for the best hand. Any hand with two cards below a Seven, except 6-5 and 5-4 are almost always a pass, although 4-3, 5-3 and 6-4 suited may be good enough for a "Button call".

PLAY ON THE FLOP
preliminary considerations

The most important thing in Hold 'em, once you have mastered the rules and have an idea of what hands to play, is an **aggressive** approach to the game. **I've** *never* **seen a top player who was a "caller"**. If you play sound hands and use good judgment about when to be aggressive, you'll be well on your way towards winning at Limit Hold 'em.

In addition, as always, it is important to know your players in order to evaluate which techniques to use in specific instances against individual opponents.

There are a few things that you need to be aware of in every pot you're in.

(1) **You should know how many players are in;**

(2) **who, if anyone, raised;**

(3) **how many players are behind you, and**

(4) **how much money is in the pot.**

(A fairly accurate estimate of the money will be good enough for all but extremely close decisions.)

THE BEST HAND
on the Flop

There are two general types of situations I want to talk about for Limit Hold 'em. The first is when you turn a **good** *hand* and the second is when you turn a **good** *draw*. (Occasionally, you'll get a Flop with **both** these advantages.) Because of the common-card aspect of Hold 'em, there are often several different draws out in the same deal. It becomes necessary to recognize which cards are likely to make someone a complete (Pat) hand, and this makes the ability to "read" hands extremely important.

I'm going to discuss the play for a variety of Flops when you're likely to have the best hand and your opponents are trying to outdraw you. Of course, the play of the individual hands will vary with your position, the number of players, the action before the Flop and the size of the pot.

The most common, and most difficult, situation is when you *turn* "top Pair" on a Flop where there is **no** Pair on the Board. There are a number of types of Flops that you'll see when you have the top Pair. (In the examples, that follow (FLOP 1 through FLOP 5), I'm going to make the following assumptions:

(1) You have the **A♢-K♡** and an Ace or King will flop.

(2) The discussions will assume a fairly tough (solid) game. That is, your opponents will not be chasing everytime they turn a Pair or an inside Straight draw. (In a very loose game, it's much more difficult to put your opponents on a hand. In that kind of game — where there's several players taking a turn with just about anything — you've got to find a hand you like and go as far as reasonable with it. I can't give you any hard-and-fast rules in such a situation because so much depends on the texture of the particular game you're in.)

(3) The third assumption is that another player with the top Pair will also be involved in the pot with you.

FLOP 1

FLOP 1 is a very "safe" Flop to your hand. There's **no** Flush draw, and **no** probable Straight draw. The hand that's most likely to give you a *play* is an Ace with a poorer kicker. If you get more than one or two callers with a Flop like this and one of them raises, you'll probably end up looking at three Eights or three Deuces.

The number of people calling after the Flop gives important information about the proper way to continue on the fourth card. With *FLOP 1,* I would probably always bet on Fourth St. with the one exception that I might be tempted to check if another Eight fell and more than one player had called on the Flop.

When more people call than you would expect from the "texture" of the Flop, you have to give them credit for something. If A–K is the best hand, it is not too dangerous to give a *free card* in a spot like this (when an Eight falls), but of course you've lost a bet against a player who was going to call with, for instance, A–J.

FLOP 2

This is still a fairly safe Flop, but one on which you are likely to get more action. Although there's no Flush draw, you're likely to get a *play* from a variety of Straight draws. The two most probable drawing hands are J–10 and 7–6.

For *FLOP 2*, the number of callers becomes more important to the subsequent play. If I got called in three places on the Turn I'd probably bet if it was checked to me on the fourth card. The most dangerous card for my hand would probably be a Queen, which would make a Queen-high Straight or (less probably) Aces and Queens. Other cards which would set off the "warning bell" in my head would be a Ten or Seven. Any card which makes a three-Straight (7-8-9 or 8-9-10) is a potential danger. My bet on Fourth St., if one of the cards that I'm concerned about falls, is an example of betting to "find out where I'm at". If I get raised, or check-raised, I'm probably going to have to fold. With four players in the pot it is **unlikely** that I'm being bluffed, because the number of callers prevents anyone from getting too fancy — since they'd have to be afraid of running into the "nuts".

I **don't** want to check on the fourth card for a couple of reasons. I want to be the aggressor and make my opponents guess whether I have a "big hand" or not. Once I check and show weakness, my opponents are going to bet, and now I'm on the defensive and have no way of knowing what they may be betting. When you bet and get raised, you can be pretty sure that you're up against a big hand. There are also many hands that I might be giving a free draw (if nobody bets) and I also check on the fourth card. There are many cards which may beat me on Fourth St. but unless I'm reasonably sure I'm beaten, I'm going to continue to bet my hand, hoping for the best, until somebody's play changes my mind.

FLOP 3

This is a Flop that calls for **caution**. . .even though you have top Pair and an inside Straight draw. There's a good chance someone has turned Two-Pair (or even a Straight). The only hands you're likely to be up against where you'd be the favorite, are K-Q and Q-J. Of course, you probably do **not** want to hit your kicker after this Flop since it will probably make someone a Straight. If you do flop the best hand (or even if you're up against Jacks and Tens), the **best** continuation for your hand (outside of .catching a Queen) would be a· small *running* Pair. The worst cards for you would be an Ace or Nine.

With *FLOP 3*, I'd want to try to "find out where I'm at" as quickly as possible. With this type of Flop no one is going to *slow play* a hand unless perhaps they have A–Q. I want to play my hand on the Flop and see whether any of my opponents have enough of a hand to play back at me. If there's a lot of action on the Flop and the fourth card **doesn't** help my hand, I'm going to have to decide whether I want to call on the "expensive street". If I do, I'm probably committing myself to also calling on the end, even if a *blank* falls. This type of Turn (K–J–10) is going to *hit* a lot of people and so if nothing comes on the fourth card it's important to see if the action slows down at all. If a *blank* hits, it may slow down the *come hands* and give me some further indication as to whether or not I have the best hand. In a game with aggressive players it isn't possible to avoid mistakes on this type of hand. A "fast" player may play K–Q or K–J the same way after a Turn like this, and you simply **cannot** avoid (sometimes) throwing away the best hand or calling with the worst hand. (However, your opponents have the same problems, and what determines the winners is an overall consistency of judgment — which keeps errors to a relative minimum.)

If you feel you're beat, **DON'T hesitate** to pass. All good players throw away the best hand occasionally. You shouldn't be embarrassed or ashamed if you're out-maneuvered once in a while — it's inevitable in a tough game. The major mistake many players make is to let one marginal, incorrect judgment put them "off balance". Then, they proceed to compound the error with a series of mistakes which they would not normally make.

FLOP 4

A Flush draw is the **most** *likely* hand for you to be against with *FLOP 4*. If someone plays this hand *fast* against you, they have, in all probability, K♣-Q♣, A♣-"X"♣ or, the most dangerous possibility, A-J.

FLOP 4 presents an interesting example of how the number of callers on the Flop determines what you do on the next card. Naturally, the thing you're concerned with here is a Flush card on Fourth St. It's the most likey draw and certainly is the only *beat* you can get away from. (If someone makes a Straight or hits their kicker when, for instance, the 10♥ falls, it is much more difficult to pass.) If there are one or two callers and the Flush card (a Club) comes, I'm going to lead at it and make them guess if I've completed my hand or if, perhaps, I have A-K with the A♣ and am now drawing at the nut Flush (with the top Pair). I can't check, because that would give an opponent a free draw if he has any Club in his hand. If someone has a Pair and a small Club, it'll be very difficult for him to call because there's a strong chance that he's *drawing dead*. Once again (remember this pot is short-handed), I want to put my opponents to a guess. Most of the time when you check and call your money is bleeding away. That's the position you want to put your opponents in.

The situation changes greatly, as the number of callers goes up. Three callers makes a Flush draw probable, four makes it almost a certainty. There isn't too much else they can have with a Turn like *FLOP 4* — there are only two more Aces in the deck (although a Set of Jacks or Sixes is always possible). Now a check is called for because to bet again would be foolhardy. (**Don't** consider trying to *represent* a large Flush. In Limit, if you're up against a complete hand, you're going to get called.)

FLOP 5

A Flop like this, with two cards of the same suit and two connected cards which help a Straight draw, is the type

Example **377**

most likely to involve a lot of players and yet your one Pair will probably be the best hand.

With *FLOP 5*, you might get anywhere from one to ·perhaps as many as six callers, and still have the best hand. It is **not** difficult to imagine the following hands:

Caller 6

FLOP

Caller 1

Caller 5

Caller 2

Caller 4

Caller 3

YOU

As an exercise, figure out how many cards will beat your hand on Fourth Street. (There are 27: 7-Spades, 3-Jacks, 2-Sixes, 3-Fours, 2-Nines, 2-Sevens, 2-Fives, 2-Queens, 2-Eights and 2-Tens.) Every card **above** a Three which does **not** help your hand makes somebody at least Two-Pair. There would be no possible way to know that such an unusual situation actually existed, but obviously **the point is — when you get five or six callers...proceed carefully**.

When you are playing one Pair for the best hand, there's one tactic you usually want to use if you get any kind of action on the Flop. You want to play your hand **as fast as possible** to thin out the field and to find out where the other strong hands are. The bets on the Flop are **only** *half* the size of those on the next two Rounds, so you should use the "cheap street" to find out where you're at and possibly save (if you feel you're beat), or gain, extra bets later.

> **Be straightforward...** *not* **fancy...in your betting tactics. Some hands you get will virtually play themselves. Your ability to make the most, or lose the least, with one Pair will probably be the difference between winning and losing.**

When you have top Pair with a Pair on Board, the number of draws that you'll face is greatly reduced. The most important aspect of these hands is the denomination of the Pair. If you have A–K — a Flop like A-3-3 is much **less** *dangerous* (because the Pair is **small**) than a Flop like A-J-J. Naturally, more people play the big cards, and when a Pair of Face-cards flops you must be wary. When a **small** Pair flops, I'd play my hand aggressively (when there's a Flop like A-3-3) — much as if the Flop did **not** contain a Pair. Here, again, you must be aware of the number of players who have taken the Flop, whether or not the pot was raised, and, of course, how many people call on the Turn. Naturally, if six people took the Flop, you're more likely to run into a Three than if only three people were in against you. **Whether or not the pot was raised is** *very* important. You're much **less** *likely* to find somebody in a raised pot with very small cards than when they can call (limp–in) for the minimum.

Your opponents' actions on the Flop is the most important factor of all in the hand. If your bet gets called by two players (and no draw seems probable), you have to resort to an either/or decision. Either both the other Aces are out, or one of the players has a Three. Many times in Hold 'em (especially in loose games which have a number of weak players) you'll be involved in hands where it just doesn't seem reasonable that your opponent can have a particular hand — in this case a Three in the hole. But if you stop to think, you'll realize that the chances of him *representing* a Three and not having it are pretty minimal. Therefore, he's probably got one.

If someone *plays-back*, you'll have to decide whether they have an Ace and a big card or 3-Treys. **Where** they raise is often important. Most players who turn Three-of-a-kind on the Flop like A-3-3 will slow-play the hand and wait until the fourth card to raise. Consequently, if you get raised on the Flop, it **may** be a sign of weakness from a player who has something like A-J and is trying to find out if his kicker is any good.

If a medium Pair flops (for this discussion, let's say it's a Pair of Sevens thru Tens), you must proceed, from Fourth St. on, almost as carefully as for the high Pairs. If you're betting (and I do **not** recommend checking these hands on the Flop whether you have Two-Pair or Three-of-a-kind) your opponents will **not** know the strength of your hand. If they play their hand strongly on the Fourth card, it means they're **not** too worried about your hand and you'll usually be looking at Trips.

When you're fortunate enough to have 7-6 against A-K or two Aces, and get a Flop like K-7-7 play it "full steam ahead". Very few players can get away from an A-K in Limit Hold 'em with a Flop like that...especially if they raised coming in. You'll win more money if you play this hand as *fast* as possible.

For Flops like A-J-J most of the previous comments apply. Once again, if you have a Jack, play at *full speed* most of the time. As the Pair on Board gets higher, it becomes more likely that two players will turn Three-of-a-kind. This occurrence is especially common when two Aces flop, since many players will play **any hand** with an Ace in it...and that's all the more reason to *lead off* with your hand. If nobody has anything on a Flop like this, you **won't** gain too much by checking. Only the weakest players will be deceived by an attempt to "trap" them by means of a "free card" with a Flop like A-J-J (or any other big Pair).

Another reason to bet is that if you are up against an inside Straight draw you may lose a big pot if you let a card fall off without betting. *Slow-playing* is only good when it appears unlikely that you'll get called on the Flop, but that you may get called by a weaker hand if you let the field *catch-up*.

This type of hand illustrates another advantage of being an aggressive player. If you make a lot of bets without having a really big hand, your opponents are going to start *checking you out*. A lot of times what they'll be checking out is the *nuts*. If you're known as a tight player, it's hard to get much action when you bet three Jacks on a Flop like A-J-J because your opponents will assume that that's what you have. But, if you make many sensible *value* bets in pots like this, your opponents will gamble more with you when you do have a big hand.

There are two more points I want to make about Flops with Pairs on the Board. The first is that if you're playing a hand like A♡-5♡ and the Flop comes A-10-10, you're in a position where if you bet and get called you're *almost* certainly beat. If someone else bets, you should definitely **not** call.

The second point is the possibility of Flush draws. Although it's generally **not** advisable to get involved with Flush draws when the Board is paired (especially if it comes with a large Pair), many players ignore this important strategical concept. When there's a two-Flush and a Pair (on Board), some players will draw to Flushes and, even worse, Straights. A Flop like **10♣-9♣-9♡** may find A-10 as the best hand — even when several people are in. You may find opponents who'll stand a lot of pressure to go to the' last card (after Flops like that) with draws as weak as 8-7 or two small Clubs. If this is the case, you must adjust your values. Try to sell some marginal hands with which you would usually be reluctant to go very far.

The presence of two **suited** cards on the Flop is a definite indication to play "full steam ahead" when you flop a Set (of Trips) because you're more likely to get a *play* and you can easily be hurt by giving a free card. In addition, some players will *put you on* a Flush draw, or perhaps a "weak Ace", (one with a bad kicker with a Flop like A-J-J) and *play-back* at you right away — thereby giving you a chance to build a big pot.

I'm **not** suggesting you always play Three-of-a-kind as "fast" as you can, but it's important to be able to distinguish between the times when you're likely to get a play on a big hand from the times when it's more appropriate to *slow-play*. It's important to **avoid** any patterns through which your opponents can "read" your hands. Play the same hand differently (and the better the hand, the more variety you can safely introduce) and play different hands as though they were the same. Bet your big hands, your draws and your occasional bluffs in a similar way.

For instance, gamble with a big draw on the Flop as strongly as if you had turned the *nuts*. Even if you **don't** make your draw, you'll be rewarded in extra action, when you do turn a big hand. There's a saying: *"You must give action to get action."* Giving a little bit should go a long way in Hold 'em. Most players hate to be bluffed or *run over*. They don't like to lay down the best hand. Showing them occasional glimpses of your *fast gear* will pay for itself in the inevitable dozens of "loose calls" that you wouldn't get otherwise. Maybe you'll even get lucky while you're playing *fast* and have the cards *run over you*. That's how you get on a *rush*. It's one of the best feelings in the game.

I mentioned earlier that some hands play themselves. But, you have to expect that in a game with eleven players, there'll almost always be someone drawing to beat you. Getting **extra** bets with your good hands is an important part of Limit play. You can often get these additional bets on Flops where you have Two-Pair or a Set and it's quite clear that you have the best hand.

The hands that are so big that they play themselves are often **not** very profitable because no one else has enough of a hand you for to get a good play.

The ways of saving bets will be discussed when I get to the situations where you're drawing and want to try and minimize the money you'll have to pay before making your hand, and also in the section where I discuss "payoffs".

How to get
EXTRA BETS

I'm going to give examples of getting extra bets when you have at least Two-Pair. This does **not** mean that you cannot use the same techniques in other situations when your hand is not as strong. Any time you think you can get an extra bet **without** jeopardizing the pot you should do so. (I'm using "big hands" as illustrations to eliminate the possibility that a strong opponent will *play you off* the best hand when you try to get him for an extra bet.)

One of the commonest methods for getting an extra bet is the check-raise. As you know, it's **not** a strategy I use very much. . .even in Limit play. If you lead off with a hand you're certain to get one bet in and there's a chance that they'll *play-back* at you, allowing you to get in three bets. If you check it, you're liable to win nothing or, if they bet, you can win two. It's simple arithmetic. *Leading* with your hand gets you one bet or three bets, while check-raising gives you zero or two.

Nevertheless, there are certain times when I think a check-raise is a good play. When I'm up against an aggressive player who bets me every time I check, I want to show him that my check does **not** *always* mean I don't have anything. Many *fast* players will try to *run over* you (especially in short-handed pots) whenever they think you're weak. . .and particularly when they have position on you. I want them to know they can't just keep betting me and not expect to get played with. Of course, a lot of the time I'm going to lead off with my hand, if I think they'll call or perhaps raise.

I resort to check-raising when I feel it's **not** likely that they're going to call if I bet. When I have a big hand or when I believe my opponent is weak, the only way I'll be able to win something is to check, knowing that there's a good chance that he'll try to *pick-up* the pot. (This strategy will **not** work well against a player who you know to be a "caller" and generally **un**aggressive.)

Another good use of the check-and-raise is when you expect a bet from a player who is one or two seats to your left (behind you). If, for instance, the man right behind you raises before the Flop, and you turn a Set, you do **not** want to lead right into him. Let **him** *take the lead* and you'll get the rest of the players in the middle. If you led off in this pot, he might raise and cut off the other callers. **This** example illustrates another *important point* about the check-raise — which is that *you must feel quite sure* that somebody else is going to bet before you use it.

A third occasion for check-raising is when you're in a pot with a lot of players who've taken the Flop and you're trying to get into a head-up situation. The bottom Two-Pair is the best example of this type of hand.

Let's assume that you're in the Blind with an 8-7 and a player in a late position raises. You call and there are four other calls. The Flop is K-8-7 (of three different suits). You're reasonably sure that you have the best hand, but it's **not** strong enough so that you want to play it against many opponents. Usually, everyone will check to the raiser. He'll now bet many hands with which he would have raised. Naturally he'll bet with any hand with a King or a Pair of Aces, Queens, Jacks, Tens or Nines. There's also a good chance that he may bet with a hand like A-Q and hope that he won't get called if a King is not out in another hand. Now...you check-raise. You've made it very difficult for anyone else to call if they have a Straight draw with a 10-9 (for example) because **not** only do they have to call a double-bet, but they are in jeopardy of being raised by the original bettor.

Almost all Limit Hold 'em games are set up so that the bet on the fourth card is twice as large as the bet on the Flop. This structure provides several ways to get extra bets or to maximize the amount of money your extra bets are worth. Here are a few examples:

FLOP

Player D

Player C

Player B

Player A

Player *A* has raised the pot before the Flop in an early position. Player *D* knows that he probably has A–K or two Aces and that furthermore Player *A* is a strong, aggressive player who will figure that he has the best hand and will play accordingly. After *B* and *C* calls, *D* immediately raises, knowing that *A* will probably *put him on* a draw for which he is trying to get a *free card*. *A* does exactly that and re-raises. *B* and *C* get trapped for two raises and now *D* just calls in order to convince *A* that he's drawing. The **5♠** falls on the fourth card and *A* leads again. *D* raises and gets extra bets on both cards.

If you're against a player who you feel will not *play-back* on the Flop, there's another way to get an extra bet. You *smooth call* on the Flop and wait until the fourth card to put in a raise. Here's another example of that play:

FLOP

Player C

Player B

Player A

On the Flop, Player *A* leads, *B* just calls, and *C* also calls. The fourth card is the **7♣** and *A*, believing from the play on the Flop that he has the best hand, bets again. Now *B* raises. This puts a lot of pressure on *C*, who must decide whether to call two **full** bets with only one card to come.

Waiting to raise until the fourth card has the advantage of winning more money from *A* (than if *B* raised on the Flop), and it also puts *C* in a position where he has to put in two (**expensive**) bets to draw to his Straight. (It **wouldn't** make sense to play this hand like the previous example and hope that *A* would think *B* was drawing. *B's* position, in the middle of the table, would make raising the initial bettor with a draw on the Flop a **poor** play.) Also, notice that if C does call on the fourth card, that A is *drawing dead*.

There's one more situation where, although you do **not** need a big hand, raising on the fourth card may gain you an extra bet. The Flop is:

FLOP

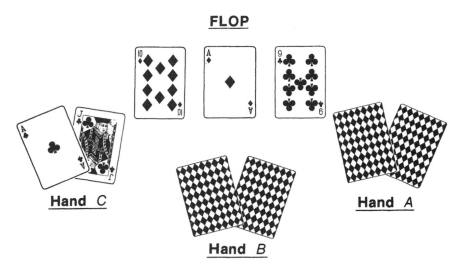

Hand C

Hand B

Hand A

You have hand C. On the Flop, A bets, B calls, and you call. You feel like one of them is probably drawing and one probably has an Ace. (If A is drawing, then B may have a *Rag* kicker — and be afraid to raise with it. If A has the Ace, probably with at least a Jack kicker, then B has a draw and does **not** want to raise and narrow down the field.) You have a hand which **may** be the best on the Flop, but you cannot think so with any certainty. However, you have the additional value of being able to pick up a big draw on Fourth St. if a Club, an Eight, or a Queen falls.

You've decided that the situation is close enough that you may want to call twice anyway, so if you pick up a draw, you raise. If you make the hand on the end, you'll win an extra bet; if both your opponents are weak, you may win the pot on the fourth card; if you miss the draw, you can still show the hand down on the end for the same two bets that it would've cost you had you called twice. Of course, if the fourth card does **not** give you a draw, you have to decide there whether to *pay it off* or fold.

Limit Hold 'em presents many more hands (compared to No-Limit Hold 'em) where it's a good idea to slow-play. If you check a hand in No-Limit, you're endangering all your chips when an opponent makes a gut-Straight or catches one of his paired hole cards. This can happen in Limit, too, but the results are *not* nearly as devastating. It's often worth taking this chance, if by doing so, you also allow someone to *catch-up* by making a second-best hand which they'll think is good.

For example, if you have Q-J, and the Flop is Q-Q-3 — you're **not** likely to get called if you bet, unless the other Queen is out. But if you check, and an Ace or King falls (on Fourth), you'll probably get a play. If there are inexperienced players in the game, they'll often call when you bet on the fourth card, if it pairs them, because they think your bet means you've made Two-Pair also. You can't depend on that kind of "loose" action — but it does happen. Usually, if somebody else also turns Trips your check on the Flop **won't** hurt you. You'll get plenty of action from them on the fourth and fifth cards. Sometimes, they'll slow-play a bigger hand than you did and you'll be the one trying to *catch-up*.

On the rare occasions when you turn a big Full or Four-of-a-kind, you can't expect anybody else to have much, and so you check, hoping that someone will bluff at it or that they'll make a hand on the next card. If the Flop comes with a big Pair and a little card (with no Flush draw), then it's also usually wise to check. If a two-Flush (A♣, A♠, 6♣) is present, you may get some play from player(s) who have a Flush draw, a medium Pair, or the idea that you're *stealing*. If you check this type of Flop sometimes, and lead at it sometimes, and bluff at it sometimes, your opponents will not be able to *read* you.

When you turn the **nut** *Flush* with three little cards on the Flop, you may want to *slow-play* it, because nobody may have a hand they can call with. If someone else flops a Flush, you'll get plenty of chances to play with them — whether you check or not.

Straights on the Flop should be played **strongly**, because usually you'll be able to get calls or raises from other players who are drawing.

I've discussed Flops like 6-6-K, when you have a Six, and the same general comments applies to the *underfull*, when, for instance, you have two Threes and the Flop comes K-K-3. However, if the Turn is 4-4-3 you have a situation where it's more likely nobody will be able to call.

HOW TO PLAY OVERPAIRS

The next thing I'm going to discuss is how to play when you have an *overpair* and you think it's the best hand. This will be a continuation of the discussion of the play of big Pairs that I began earlier in the sub-section: INTRODUC-TION TO THE PLAY OF THE HANDS. I'm going to assume that you raised the pot coming in, and that the other players will play accordingly.

There are many similarities between having an *overpair* and having *top Pair* and *top Kicker*, as in the examples with A-K. The main difference is that an overpair gets a lot of play from the person who has the top Pair and top kicker. When you have two Kings against an A-Q, and the Flop is Q-6-3, you'll have an overpair and there are very few players who will lay down the A-Q. The Flop I just gave you is the type that you want when you hold Aces or Kings. You want to get a Flop where you catch one person, or better yet two, with top Pair — and a very small chance to draw out.

Many times, of course, the Flop will come with two to a Flush or a probable Straight draw, like Q-J-3. Many of the Straights you look at when you have two Aces or Kings are big ones — because more players will call in raised pots with hands like J-10, Q-J, K-J and K-Q than with two small connectors. Even though you're going to look at some Straights, this is the kind of action you want to get when you have a big Pair.

Generally speaking, you play an overpair *fast* on the Flop. (This is even more true when you hold the medium Pairs, because the danger of overcards on the fourth and fifth cards makes it necessary to narrow the field down as much as possible.) You play them for the best hand on the Turn, and you try to figure out what type hands are out — whether there are draws or smaller Pairs, or both. If you get any play, the **worst** card for an overpair is when the top card on the Board pairs on one of the last two cards. Other than that, you have to be concerned with the same *beats* that you'll look at when you have top Pair.

Aces and Kings, in particular, present some problems to many Limit players who do **not** understand what they should expect from these hands. They're **stronger** hands in Limit than No–Limit...because when you get them beat, you **don't** have to jeopardize as many chips.

The secret with the big Pairs is to **expect to get them beat** *about half the time.* Any hand that you take up against an average of three to five opponents is going to lose in many pots. If you win 50% of the hands, and get an average of four-way action, you're going to come out a big winner. Many players cuss out two Aces when they get them beat, and say that they would be happier if they never got them again. I'll be glad to take their share and take my chances with them in Limit Hold 'em.

One of the reasons that Kings and, even more so, Aces, are disliked is that people "fall in love" with them and lose much more money than they should. There are a number of types of Flops which reduce an overpair from a big hand to a very marginal one. It's important to learn to recognize these Flops and thus enable yourself to *get away from* overpairs **with a minimum loss.** (These comments apply equally to Aces or Kings with the obvious exception that it's fairly easy to *get away from* Kings if an Ace flops.)

If you hold  the following types of Flops are **very** *dangerous:*

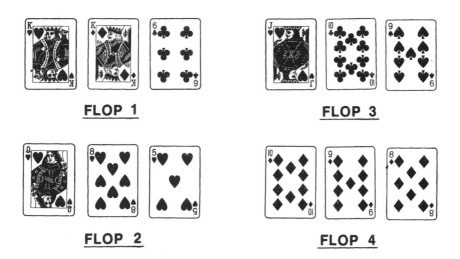

FLOP 1   FLOP 3

FLOP 2   FLOP 4

The first Flop obviously presents the danger of three Kings and you can't stand very much action and expect to have the best hand.

The second Turn is a more difficult one. The play on the Flop will give you indications as to whether you're against a Flush, Set, or just the nut Flush draw.

The third example is a problem because even if you have the best hand...you're only a little better than even-money against a player who has a Pair **and** a Straight draw. This type of Flop tends to make you a small favorite or a huge underdog. Therefore, it should **not** be too difficult to *get away from* when you have two Aces.

The last Flop combines all the bad aspects of the second and third and is therefore worse than either. If there's any action, most players will be hesitant to get involved with a hand that can't beat two Aces.

If you hold two Aces and get a good Flop, there are still several dangers that you should be aware of. Any Flop which contains two cards from a King down to a Ten presents the possibility of Two-Pair or Straight draws. When a third *Paint* falls on the fourth or fifth card in these situations, you're often going to have the **worst** hand because of the prevalence of people playing the "trouble hands" in raised pots.

Another problem that you can face with big Pairs, especially Jacks and Queens, is when overcards flop. This is **not** an ideal Flop, but it does **not** mean that you're beaten. Usually I play it like this: If more than one overcard flops, I am **not** going to bet. If one falls, and it's checked to me, I bet — if I get called I have to use my judgment as to whether the Flop makes it look like he's drawing or whether he has checked the top Pair. When someone bets into me, I have the same decision to make: Is he pushing a draw or am I beaten?

There's no easy answer, as different hands have different factors to take into account.

A Flop of one overcard to the medium Pairs (for example, 10-7-4 when you have two Nines) usually calls for a bet, if it's checked to you. You want to try to win this pot here...before another big card falls and cripples your hand altogether.

When you have two Aces and someone else has two Kings or two Queens, you're in an ideal situation. You're going to get a lot of action and you're a big favorite over his hand. When **two** big Pairs are out, you often get *jammed* pots — where several players put in the limit of raises **before** the Flop. It's especially important in these pots to protect your hand as much as possible at every opportunity, because players will want to try to make many hands (even *back-door* draws) that they would normally **not** consider if the *pot odds* were not so great. (If you get *head-up* with a man that has Kings or Queens, you can usually use your "trick plays" to good advantage, if you want. You can let him make you stop raising before the Flop in order to make sure he pays you off later. Also, you can wait until the fourth card to reveal the strength of your hand. Whether you're first or last, and what type of player your opponent is, will determine the best way to get extra bets.

How to Play
WHEN YOU FLOP
A SET

Sets are the most difficult hands to read and, as a result, can be played fast because your opponents will almost always *put you on* the wrong hand. If you turn Second or Bottom Set, you'll very often get a good play from someone with Top Pair...especially if the top card on the Flop is fairly high. When you flop a Set of Queens or Jacks, it's **always** good to have an Ace or King come on the Turn.

The only time that I **sometimes** slow-play a Set is when I'm in a fairly small pot where, for instance, I had raised with two Aces and the Flop was A-9-3 of different suits, or I had two Nines and the Flop came 9-4-2 with no Flush draw. In the first case, I would hope that someone might think I was checking Kings or Queens and try and take the pot away from me, or that they might make a second-best hand on Fourth St. In the second case, I would want an overcard or a draw to get someone involved on the next card.

I've covered all the common types of situations where you feel you have the best hand on the Flop. Now I'm going on to a part of Hold 'em that helps make it the unique Poker game that it is.

How to play
DRAWS
in general

I heard a Hold 'em player at an adjoining table complaining about how they kept *drawing out* on him. Finally, an old man next to him, tired of the grumbling, turned and said, *"What do you mean draw outs? It's a seven-card game."* Probably the most misunderstood parts of "Hold 'em" are the drawing situations.

Because of the five common cards, there's no other game where you can have either as much of an edge or as much of a disadvantage when you have a draw, as you can in Hold 'em. Draws are often more valuable in Limit than No-Limit because you're getting action from more players. The other side of the coin is that you're also *drawing dead* more often.

In one respect, Hold 'em is **much** *less* a draw-out game than Seven-Stud. When you hold a Pair over a Pair or A-K against A-Q, you're a much bigger favorite than you would be in a game where the players do not have five community cards out of seven. When you have a poorer kicker there are a maximum of only three cards you can catch to help your hand. If **you have** A-9 against A-K, and the Flop comes A-10-10, you can hope to split with the *case* Ace or a Ten. But your **only** *win* is two *running* Nines. The hands I recommended earlier in this section tend to reduce "kicker trouble" and keep you out of unpleasant situations like the one above.

The two most common draws are, of course, Straights and Flushes. In some instances, the value of either of these hands can be strengthened by the presence of a Pair. Flush draws are of two varieties. The more common one occurs when a player has two suited cards in his hand and two of the same suit flop. The other possibility is when you have one in your hand and there's three on the Board. In both instances, the Flush can be made (with nine remaining cards) about 35% of the time (with two cards to come). Straights can be made with eight cards and will be completed 31.5% of the time (with two cards to come). In general, you want to get two calls on the Flop and on Fourth St. — and one call on the end in order for the *pot-odds* to justify your draw. The large majority of pots in Limit that are not head-up will call for you to draw. Some of the three-handed pots will be marginal, but almost all the others will be worthwhile.

DRAWS
that are the Favorite

How you play draws varies a great deal with the cards on the Flop, the number of callers, and the relative strength of what you're drawing to. Sometimes you want to *jam* the pot on the Flop. Other times you want to get in for as little as possible. The strength of some draws is so great that it's **not** uncommon in Hold 'em for the player with the best (made) hand to be an underdog with two cards to come. **Some examples are:**

EXAMPLE 1

"Best" Hand   FLOP   Favorite

EXAMPLE 2

"Best" Hand   FLOP   Favorite

EXAMPLE 3

"Best" Hand   FLOP   Favorite

These big draws can have even more value when there are other callers in the pot besides the person with the best hand. (A Pair and an open-end Straight–Flush draw — the second example — is the biggest draw you can have with the "worst" hand.)

DRAWS
that should be played
AGGRESSIVELY

There are two different types of situations where you may want to lead off and bet a draw. The first is when you feel there's a chance that your bet may win the pot right away. It's consistent with the aggressive approach I've been suggesting to lead with many hands that you're going to call with anyway. The "texture" of the Flop determines your chances of winning the pot without a call. Let's say you have:

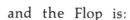

and the Flop is:

you are much more likely to win the pot with a bet than if the Turn comes:

If you do get called on the first Flop, your hand is strong enough to be the favorite over the top Pair and to have the best Flush draw most of the time.

Whether to lead at the second Flop is a matter of judgment, based on your position and the actions of the other players in the hand. Many times it will be profitable to lead at this Turn. If there are many people in the pot, your draw is big enough to gamble with, even if someone raises it. If there are only a couple of players, then you may not get called unless there is an Ace or another big draw out. The type of situation that it pays to avoid is leading with a draw, when you suspect you may be raised immediately to your left, thus cutting off potential callers — and reducing the *price* you're going to get on your hand. It becomes more correct to lead, the more people that have checked and the closer you are to the Button, since your chances of getting called are substantially reduced. The exception to this, is, for instance, a raised pot, where you feel someone wants to check-raise you on the Flop. In this case, it's better to check and hope to make the Flush free.

Since it's usually **not** possible to tell who's going to give you action, I often lead with big Flush draws and take my chances on how the hand is going to develop.

The second type of draw you want to lead with is one where your hand is big enough that you're hoping to get raised — so that you can get in several bets on the Flop. **Here are some good examples:**

EXAMPLE 1

YOU   **FLOP**

In Example 1, you have the top Pair (and top kicker)...with the nut Flush draw.

Turning second, or third, Pair and a Flush draw (Example 2) gives you less chance of having the best hand, but a greater chance to draw out against A–K.

YOU   **EXAMPLE 2**   **FLOP**

The strength of this hand (Example 2) varies greatly according to whether you have the best hand on the Flop.

YOU   **EXAMPLE 3**   **FLOP**

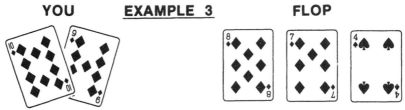

This draw is so big (Example 3) that it's even a favorite over a player with a 6-5 who has turned the *nuts.*

YOU   **EXAMPLE 4**   **FLOP**

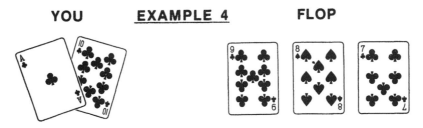

An open–end Straight and the *nut* Flush draw (Example 4) is a powerful *come* hand whose value is increased by the fact that you're likely to get a lot of play with a Flop like this.

YOU   **EXAMPLE 5**   **FLOP**

This is an excellent Flop (Example 5). You have a good chance to have **both** the best hand and the best draw.

YOU   **EXAMPLE 6**   **FLOP**

An open-end Straight and small Flush draw (Example 6) illustrates another unusual feature of Hold 'em. Many times it's better to make a lesser hand (Straight instead of Flush in this case), as it's the only way to have the *nuts*. A lot of action after a Turn like this probably means that there's a bigger Flush draw out and the 6♡-5♡ can only win with a Deuce or a Seven.

If you turn a big draw, and somebody else bets into you, whether to raise right away, or not, will be determined by your position and the number of additional players that you may get in the pot if you just call. There are some situations where *smooth calling*, with a hand that's worth a raise, is the best way to play the pot. Just as you lead more with draws (the closer to the Button you are) you also raise more with big draws as your position improves and as the number of callers between you and the initial bettor increases.

There are occasions when leading **twice** with a Flush or Straight draw will win the pot — even if you do **not** complete the hand. If your bet on the Flop is **not** raised, and you are **not** called in too many spots, it often means that your opponents have marginal hands that they want to try and improve at a minimum cost. Leading on Fourth St., when you were going to call anyway, will sometimes result in winning the pot at that point. An aggressive player, who is always betting, will win a certain number of pots without a hand, simply because his opponents **don't** have enough to call. A player who's always checking and calling can **never** win money in this way.

There are also occasions when you improve on the fourth card — **without** making a Flush or Straight. Many times, pairing an overcard will give you a good chance of having the best hand on Fourth St. The presence of overcards, to the Flops in your hand, give important added value to your draw. **Here are two examples:**

Hand 1   **FLOP**   **Hand 2**

Either an Ace or Jack will probably give Hand 1 the best hand on the fourth card. Hand 2 (which is **not** up against Hand 1 — it's merely a different situation) will probably have to make the Flush to win.

Hand 1   **Hand 2**

FLOP

Hand 1 may be able to make the best hand by pairing on the fourth card. However, his hand will be weaker than the previous example — because either of his cards (the Jack or the Eight) may make another player a Straight. It's interesting to note that when you are **not** drawing to the *big end* of the Straight (Hand 2), it's always better to catch the lower card (a Six makes him the *nuts*), rather than the higher one (a Jack, which makes the third nuts).

DRAWS
that should be played
CAUTIOUSLY

There are many draws which require less aggressive play. Small Flush draws and some Straight draws fall into this category. When I play the small suited connectors I'm hoping to make a Straight, Trips or Two-Pair rather than a

Flush. If I turn a Flush draw to these hands, I want to proceed more slowly than if I flop a Flush draw to A–K suited. If I had:

and the Turn came:

I would probably try and make my hand as cheaply as possible. In a late position — where I would be most likely to play this hand — I would have most of the betting in front of me and be able to judge my chances. If I felt, from the action on the Flop, that I might be *drawing dead*, I would try and *get away from* the hand before I got involved.

This **difficult** decision of *getting away from* the hand has to be made quickly, because the more money you put in, the harder it is to pass in a pot like this. You can't ever know for sure when you're *drawing dead*. You have to consider what the pot's laying you against your chance of making the hand, and the further possibility that you **might** lose even if you do make it.

The medium-sized pots are the ones you're most likely to win with a small Flush, because as the number of callers on the Flop increases, the chances of a bigger Flush draw goes up greatly. Incidentally, this is the type of hand that you may want to raise on the Flop against timid opposition. If you think you can "slow down" your opponent (by raising on the Flop and then checking if you don't make it) and see all the cards for $20, rather than $30 (by calling $10 and then $20), you should use this chance to save half a bet.

How to play
STRAIGHT DRAWS

Straight draws are both more difficult to play and more difficult to read than Flush draws. (All Flops that **don't** have a Pair, except K–7–2, K–8–2, K–8–3 and Q–7–2 can make a Straight on the fourth card.) It's important, when drawing to a Straight, to be reasonably certain that your hand is going to be good if you make it. There are two factors which can greatly decrease the value of a Straight draw:

(1) Possible Flush draws and

(2) higher Straight draws.

If you're trying to make a Straight when a Flush draw is out, you are *drawing dead* to two of your eight "wins".

YOU   FLOP   OPPONENT

The 7♡ or Q♡ make your J–10 a second-best hand. If you make your hand **without** a Heart on the fourth card, your opponent (the Flush possibility) will re-draw more than 20% of the time. The chances of you making the best hand are greatly reduced, and the amount that you will lose as a second-best hand is greatly increased when there's a Flush draw, also. Of course, a Flush draw is **not** always out when two suited cards turn, but one is **often** present, especially in pots that get jammed on the Flop.

Another disadvantage is that if the Flush card comes off on Fourth St., and there's a bet, the Straight draw is usually forced to pass and is thus cut off from making a hand on the end, which will sometimes be good. (This is yet another reason for leading with a Pair or two-Pair when a Flush card comes on the fourth card — if there was a reasonable doubt whether somebody was drawing at a Flush.)

> **The first rule of Straight draws should be:** *"DON'T draw at the low end."* **Many players have discovered (at considerable expense) that it does** *not* **pay to draw at the** *dead* **or** *ignorant* **end. If the Flop comes 10-9-8, and you have a Seven, it** *doesn't* **pay to call a bet to make your hand.**

The presence of Pairs on the Board also diminishes the value of Straight or Flush draws. It's usually correct to pass these draws in pots where a Pair comes on the Flop and there's a fair amount of action. (Any time the Board is paired you **may** be *drawing dead*.)

The difficult decisions with a Straight or Flush draw usually come when the Board pairs on the fourth card. The most dangerous card to pair is the top card since that usually makes someone at least Three-of-a-kind. When the middle or bottom card pairs, it's less dangerous, but you may still be *drawing dead* if someone has turned Two-Pair (or better). The chances of *drawing dead* are quite a bit less when the Board shows something like 9-6-6-3 or J-8-8-4 than if it has Q-J-J-5 or, even worse, K-K-J-5. (The tendency of most players to play big cards always makes high-card Flops more likely to produce a Full.)

Straight draws also present the problem of drawing to split pots. Flops like 8-6-5, 10-8-7, Q-J-9 or K-Q-J are likely to find several players with the one card which makes an open-end Straight. The chances of winning the whole pot after Flops like these are much less than when two cards are necessary as part of a Straight Draw. [You should **not** play any draw too aggressively, when it appears that you're probably drawing for a split. Three-way (and even four-way) splits are **not** unusual in Limit Hold 'em.]

When you make a Straight with 9-8, after a Flop like K-7-6, you have a very well-disguised hand. If you expect action behind you, this is a perfect spot to check–raise — whether you led on the Flop or not. However, if you got a Turn like 8–7–6 to the same hand, it pays to lead if a Five or Ten hits, because the four-card Straight on the Board will slow down anyone who doesn't have a Straight — and if you check expecting to raise...you probably **won't** get the opportunity. So, you should· bet in this case.

When there are three suited cards on the Flop, there are a few things that are important to keep in mind. The Ace-high (Flush) draw is really the **only** one that can be played with any confidence on Flops like this. Drawing to the King-high (Flush) is likely to make you a second-best hand, and any lower draw should **not** even be considered. If you flop a small Flush, it's best to play it *fast*. You want to find out quickly if a bigger hand is out against you, and if you have several people drawing you want to charge them as much as possible.

Remember, if you get a lot of action with a small Flush in a tough game, it usually means the other players are **not** going to be playing weak hands with a three-Flush showing, and there's a good chance that a bigger Flush is out.

The value of a Straight–Flush draw if the Flop comes 10◊–9◊–8◊ is **much** *less* than it appears. If you have the J◊, and one of your opponents has the A◊, you are in reality, drawing to only two Diamonds (the 7◊ and the Q◊).

Inside Straight draws are sometimes worth going for if you can take the card off cheaply in a good-sized pot. (This possibility is another reason to raise on the Flop when ·you think **you** have the best hand...so you can shut-out an opponent who might be drawing to a belly-buster Straight. It is a lot more difficult, and less profitable, to put in $20, rather than $10, to draw to a belly-buster.) If you're going to take a long-shot draw, you want to be drawing at the *nuts*. If the Flop comes, for example, 10–9–3, you would only try to make a gut-shot with K–J or K–Q. It's also better if there are **not** two suited cards on the Flop, as that may reduce your "wins" from four to three. An inside Straight draw is 10¾ to 1. You must be certain that the pot is going to lay you the **correct** *price* before you try to make this or any other draw. (This does not necessarily mean that there is 10.75 times the money in the pot already, but rather that your average overall win expectation, including the times you lose, is at least 10.75 times the $10 you are calling.)

QUESTIONABLE DRAWS

Draws to hands **other than** Straights and Flushes are **seldom** *good choices* in Hold 'em, because of its common-card nature. When you think you do **not** have the best hand, and you are **not** drawing to a Straight or Flush, you have only two to five cards which will help your hand. (There are only two cards that'll help you if you have a Pair in your hand. Five cards will help you if you flopped a Pair — two more to your Pair and three to your kicker.) What's more. . .you can **never** be assured that the cards that improve your hand will **not** *also* help someone else even more.

Chasing, when you have few Outs (and no certainty that you'll make the best hand) is a losing proposition. This does **not** mean that you always have to have top Pair or better to play. There are many pots when nobody turns any kind of hand. Knowing when a marginal hand, like second or third Pair, is likely to be the best, and worth a "value" bet, is something that only comes with a lot of experience.

There are a few hands when it pays to try to make Trips when you have second Pair or go to the fourth card to try to pick up a draw. But, they are exceptional cases. You must have the opportunity of winning a very large pot. . .or it's **not** worth the gamble. Extreme discretion should be used in choosing when to *go uphill*. It can get to be a bad habit — the habit of a loser.

Another situation that you want to avoid is being in a position on the Flop of having to play the hand out — with the idea of getting a split. This usually happens when you turn top Pair with a weak kicker. It's better to give the hand up, rather than put in a lot of money trying to get half the pot. There are some occasions when the fourth card makes a split probable (for instance, when the Board is A–K–2–2) and you're only going to have to call one more bet. In such a case, it may pay to call, even though you think you can't win.

How to
READ HANDS

A lot of what I've already discussed has been related to *reading* hands. Anytime you bet *to find out where you're at*, make a *value* bet, *put someone on* a draw, or pass because you think you're *drawing dead*, you're partially involved in *reading* hands. In this section I want to analyze several hands in detail, but first I want to give some general hints.

Reading hands, like much of Poker, is a combination of art and science, with art — in this instance — playing the major role. I say that because there isn't any exact method for *reading* hands. You have to come to your decisions based on information that's put together so fast there's no time to analyze it methodically. I usually go with my first impression. I try to stay with it while refining it as I get more information. Now, I'm speaking about a pot that I'm playing head–up, or a situation where there's one player who concerns me more than the rest.

To begin with, you *give a man* (put him on) one of several hands from his actions on the Flop. What he does on Fourth St. often helps you to narrow his hand down further.

For instance, if he has a draw and doesn't make it, he may play differently than when he has turned a Set. This is where knowing your players comes in. Experience and recall tell you what this man has done in this situation before, and this is a big factor in *reading* him. By the fourth card, your judgment should be pretty well set. **Don't** change it on the end because a "funny" card comes up and now you could be beaten in some way you didn't expect. If he made that hand, he's going to have to show it down. Many times...when something feels wrong to me about a hand...I pay it off.

If somebody deviates from their pattern or bets when a seemingly unrelated card falls, I become suspicious. Sometimes they've made a gut-shot or caught Trips on the end. This is especially true of weak players who only bet out when they have a big hand. Other times I catch others *out of line* and more than make up for the hands I pay off.

The main methods I use in figuring out what a man made on the last card is reconstructing the hand from the Flop. If I can't figure out what a man could have called with on the Flop — in order to make the hand he seems to be *representing* on the last card — I'm going to *look him up*. Suppose I have:

and the Flop is:

It's checked to me, I bet, and a player to my right in a middle position calls.

The next card off is:

He checks again, I bet, he calls.

On the end comes:

Now he leads into me and I have to stop and think. Naturally it looks like he's got a Nine. But how? If he had 10-9 or two Nines, he probably would have led on the Flop — considering his position. If he had 9-8, he made his hand on the fourth card, so why didn't he play it there? I don't think he would go to the last card with J-9 or 9-6, and since I have two Sevens, 9-7 is an unlikely possibility. I **can't** *get away from* my hand **unless** it's a player whom I have never seen bet anything but the *nuts* on the end. In that case, I know he must have slow-played his Straight on the fourth card, and had his planned check-raise ruined when the Eight fell. With this amount of doubt, I'm going to pay it off.

Another example of a reconstruction is the following deal on which I made a big hand on the end. I have:

And here's the way the Board came:

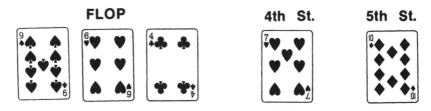

I bet the hand all the way and get raised on the end. I know it is probably a split, but I want to play-back as long as I'm pretty sure he **doesn't** have the *nuts* (which is J-8). I don't see how he would call on the Flop with that hand, so I don't hesitate to re-raise. If there had been two suited cards on the Flop, and there was a chance he might have been drawing to a J-8 Flush, then I would just call the raise.

When there are a number of players who are gambling on the Flop, it isn't going to be possible to put each one of them on their hand. In these situations you should try to satisfy yourself that you have the best hand (or the best draw) and if possible, try to distinguish who's drawing from who already has a hand. (Some mistakes in these pots are inevitable. So, don't be shocked, if somebody you thought was trying to make a Flush has a Full instead.) By the fourth card, the action usually slows down and you can get a more precise idea of where you stand.

One important thing to **avoid** when you're *reading* hands is seeing a threat in every card that falls. You don't want to get so "clever" that you paralyze yourself with indecision because somebody might have made something. Aside from Flushes and obvious Straights, there are **not** too many draw-outs that you can **get away from** for nothing. And...**don't** slow down with what you think is the best hand...until you get raised.

One of the **most common mistakes** that players make is to check when they've turned the top Pair and an overcard comes on the fourth card. If you have Q-J and the Flop comes J-8-2 and you bet and get called it's **not** likely that a King or an Ace is a dangerous card. If you were against K-J or A-J, you'd probably have been raised on the Flop and you were beat anyway.

In this instance a Queen **may be** the most dangerous overcard. Although it makes you Two-Pair, it also may complete the only probable draw, which is 10-9.

In a similar situation, when there are two suited cards, an overcard becomes somewhat more dangerous because of the possibility that it might pair a player with a Flush draw. Despite this danger, you must lead again, even if an Ace falls, unless you're reasonably sure the *nut* Flush draw is out because of the action on the Flop.

How to
SAVE BETS

When you get raised, you have to decide what your opponent has, whether or not you're beaten, and if you are, whether you should try to re-draw. The subject of getting raised brings up a point I want to mention. If you bet on the end and get raised or check-raised, by someone other than a very poor player, you'll often be wise to fold if you can't *play-back*. Each pot will have its own unique features which will influence your decision, but my overwhelming experience is that your opponent's raise (on the end) indicates that he has the *nuts* or very close to it.

On almost every occasion that I've paid off a hand on the end — just because of the size of the pot — I've been throwing away the final bet. (Of course, if the pot is very large, you must be very sure, because any mistake will cost you a great number of bets.) Don't let it be known when this situation comes up — that you're saving the last bet, because your opponents may start to play-back at you if they see that you may not call. When you're up against good players, it's impossible to avoid making some pay-offs. But. . .you have to let them know they **can't** *run over* you. Within this context, try to cut down on unnecessary, reflex payoffs when it's clear that somebody has made a hand. If you use discretion and good judgment, you'll be amazed at the number of bets you can save at the end of a week's play. Limit Hold 'em is a game of what you save — as well as what you win.

Every time I hear someone say *"I have to pay it off"* or *"You got me"*. . .I smile to myself. **I know** they're going to be right and what's more — **they know it too.** When you have that urge to call, stop for a moment and think about all the *"you got me's"* before you act on your hand.

How to play
against
WEAK OPPONENTS

The importance of reading hands goes down as the caliber of your opposition goes down. You can't read a man if he doesn't know what he has himself. The best strategy to use against weak players is straight-forward play. All you have to do is show them the best hand. Keep in mind that they'll often bet weaker hands than a tough player would. So you can give them some *looser* calls.

Now I want to go over a few hands. On the first one I had A–K in an early position and raised the pot. I got two *cold* calls.

The Flop was:

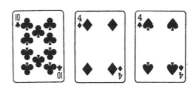

I led off and bet. The first player passed, and the second one called. Now I knew the player and I knew he had to have some kind of hand to enter a raised-up pot before the Flop. When he called, I thought he probably had a hand like mine, a medium Pair, or possibly a Ten. The next card was 8◇.

I bet again and he called. Now it was certain that he **didn't** have a Four. The last card was 2♠.

Now, I checked because I knew that if I bet and he called. . .I couldn't have the best hand. I also knew that if he had gone this far with a Pair he was going to call the last bet. Somewhat to my surprise, he bet.

I was fairly sure that (on the end) this player would not bet a Ten (or a Pair in his hand) in this way. I knew he didn't have a Four and there wasn't any kind of draw he could've made. I thought there was a reasonable chance I had the best hand — so I called. He had the K◇-J◇. He picked up a Flush draw (on Fourth St.) and was "forced" to bluff on the end. If he had raised on the fourth card, it would have put me to a hard call.

The next hand is a case where your opponent has either a big hand or nothing. In this particular pot, I was up against a very "fast" player — which influenced my play.

I had raised before the Flop and several people called. Here's what the Board looked like:

FLOP   **4th St.**   **5th St.**

I had the A♢-K♠ and led at the pot. All the other players passed — except the last man, who raised. I re-raised and he called. I thought he probably had a Flush draw or an Ace and a good kicker. When the Jack fell I bet again and he raised again. I still felt he might have a Flush draw, and I was hoping that this card made him a Straight draw rather than Two-Pair. When the last card came, I couldn't beat anything except a Flush draw **without** the Queen or Seven. He bet again and I called. I knew he could tell from the play of the hand that I probably had A-K. Therefore, he also knew that each card made my hand weaker. I stuck to my first impression and fortunately I was right. He had the K♣-9♣. He flopped a Pair, and the *nut* Flush draw — and decided to gamble — even though he knew I had him beat.

I **don't** want you to think that I always come out on the best end. I remember one pot, in particular, that I was almost starting to count before it was over. I had K♢-J♠ and the Board came as below:

FLOP · **4th St.** · **5th St.**

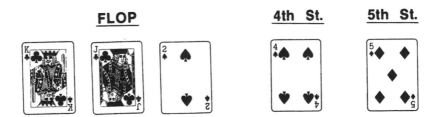

Four people put in the maximum number of bets on the Flop. I felt pretty certain I had the best hand, unless someone had turned three Deuces. When I led and nobody raised on Fourth St., I was sure that I had the best hand. I thought I was up against A-K (probably), Q-10 and a Flush draw. I felt good about the last card...so I bet again. Surprisingly, the man right behind me raised. I could see what had happened. He was drawing at one hand and *back-doored* a different one. This was one of those hands where I knew he couldn't be bluffing. He had to be there. I thought there might be a slight chance he had the same hand I did so I called. He didn't. He showed me what I was afraid of — the A♣-3♣.

Here's an example of a big draw that **wasn't** what it appeared to be. You run into some hands like this when you get a lot of players taking the Turn. The hands and Flop were as follows:

FLOP   **4th St.**   **5th St.**

Player *E*   Player *A*

Player *D*   Player *B*

Player *C*

Player *C* turned a Straight-Flush draw, and got trapped for three bets on the Flop. Since the **10♣** was in *E's* hand and two of the other Tens were out, *C* had only one win — the **10♠**. To make things worse, *B* made the *nuts* the next card, when the J◊ fell. *C* was now completely dead. **The moral of this hand is** — *don't* **fall in love with your draws**. When **five** *people* called **three** *bets* on the Flop, it should have been clear to *C* that his Jack-high Flush was **not** going to win. When the Jack fell and *B* check-raised *D's* bet, *C* should have had enough. On the end he caught another Jack and paid off *A*, who won the pot.

Afterwards, C said the pot was laying him a long price. It actually wasn't laying him anything, since he had **no win** after the J◇ fell.

BLUFFING, PICKING-UP POTS and SHORT-HANDED PLAY

The things I'm going to discuss here will probably be the most difficult. Situations will be discussed where you have to play largely by "the seat of your pants". The only way to really master this material is to get out and play a lot of Hold 'em. Only after you get accustomed to the type of play that characterizes short-handed games, will you be comfortable playing in them. Some of the techniques and *plays* I am going to describe have applications in *Ring* games too, but I'm talking about them because they are particularly relevant when the table is half-empty. Even if you never play short-handed games, there are many short-handed pots in full games to which these comments will apply.

The most important thing to remember about short-handed situations is that you're **not** always up against a hand. Many times nobody will Flop anything that they can play very confidently. That's why, when it comes down to a short-handed pot, I always try to be the aggressor. If I raise before the Flop and everybody misses their hand, I've got a good chance to *steal* the pot.

I **don't** like to call in a short-handed deal — I like to be the one that's doing the raising. If I can't *play-back*, I'm going to pass and wait for the next hand. Many people think that because the Blind comes around faster, which results in the ante per hand being higher, that you have to play *looser* in a short-handed game.

The answer is *not* to play more hands, but rather to be more aggressive on the hands you do play. Remember — as the number of players decreases, the value of many of the intermediate hands goes up. Good examples of this are medium Pairs and the "trouble hands". The "trouble hands" are no longer going to be as dangerous to play, because people will *not* be waiting for "premium hands" to raise.

Short-handed pots give you some of your best opportunities to use bluffs profitably. Let's say you're in a full game and call in 4th position with A-J **suited**. Only one other person calls. . .so you're playing three-handed with the Blind. There's $20 in the pot. If the Blind checks after the Flop, many times it will pay to bet — even when you **don't** Turn a Pair. You're risking $10 to win $20. If you are successful one-third of the time, you'll break even.

In actual play, you'll win more often than that. You'll only get called when the third player has flopped something and on the rare occasions when the Blind has checked a hand. If you check, there's a good chance that the last player will bet at it and you won't be able to call.

Picking-up small pots like this isn't very spectacular, but it adds up. In the example I used it wasn't clear, before the Flop, that there were only going to be three players. When you see this short-handed situation, it should be a signal for you to *change gears* after the Flop, and play the hand as though you had raised it coming in.

Betting in next-to-last position camouflages the fact that you're bluffing. Sophisticated players expect the last man to try and *pick-up* the pot when it's checked to him. . .and they'll sometimes check-raise him without a hand. By taking the chance of betting on the Flop, with a man behind you, you make it more difficult for your opponents to *put a play on* you. Most of the pots that you'll try to *pick-up* will be so small that some opponents will pass when they have a draw rather than try to make their draw in a head-up situation (with poor pot-odds). The "pick-up" should be used with discretion, rather than as an automatic play. It's a lot better to bluff when the Turn comes 10-6-2, than if it comes 9-8-7. You want to bluff at Flops that make it appear unlikely that somebody will have turned a hand **or** a draw.

If you get called on your first bet, most of the time you'll have to check next time...unless you help your hand. This is especially true against the type of player who checks and calls a lot. In addition to the texture of the Flop, you should take into account the styles of the other players who are in the pot before you try a "pick-up" or any other bluff. Bluff more against the good players than the weak ones. Don't jeopardize your money bluffing against a player who'll call you every time you have the best hand. When you are up against a player who **won't** bet his hand you can use his style against him. If he consistently checks the best hand, he's giving you free cards to beat him. Take as many as he'll give you.

Proportioning your bluffs according to the game you're in will further increase their effectiveness. If you see that you're in a game where everybody has it *screwed down* and won't bet unless they turn a big hand, you can bluff a little more. Another factor which will help your bluffs is having an *Out*. If, for instance, you turn a belly-Straight draw, or have two overcards, you'll have something to draw to if you're called. It will also be true that **sometimes** you'll be "bluffing" with the best hand. In short-handed deals, an Ace or bottom Pair will often be the best hand. These hands call for "value" bets which would be unprofitable if there were more callers.

If the game gets down to five players or less, the play of (and against) the Blind(s) becomes quite important. Much of the play in the game now focuses on *picking-up* the Blind's *dead money*. All hands that are worth playing are **now worth raising with**. Your raise can now have a new dimension of getting the pot down to a two-handed contest with a man who usually has a weak hand. If **you're** in the Blind you have little choice but to let such a strategy succeed.

You'll be better off calling raises with **only** good hands in the Blind, rather than trying to "protect" your investment with any two cards.you happen ·to pick up. You'll lose more calling with a bad hand in bad position than if you simply pass. When you do have a playable Blind-hand — *play-back* before the Turn. Your opponents will be raising you with a lot of mediocre hands — trying to force you to pass. Put them on the defensive instead. The player who has the initiative on the Flop is often as well off (strategically) as the player who has the best hand.

Similarly, **don't** raise the Blind (trying to steal the antes) unless you have a hand that you'd play anyway. **Don't** try to take control with the "trash hands", because everybody might start playing *fast* and you **don't** want to call a raise before the Flop with a nearly hopeless hand.

Small cards go down in value in short-handed games because you're seldom getting the number of callers you want with them. Suited cards are of minimal importance because Flush draws and Flushes will not be significant. Small Pairs become stronger because they're quite valuable in head-up pots. Any hand with an Ace in it also increases in value. An Ace and a small card will **not** get you in trouble nearly as often as it would in a Ring game because kickers will not be a deciding factor as often.

As you'll discover (after you read the section on No-Limit Hold 'em)...my playing philosophy is completely different when there's a limit on what you can bet. A "big card theory" is the winning way to play Limit Hold 'em because of the mechanical nature of the game. Follow the advice I gave you in this section — discipline yourself to wait for the big cards and good position — and you should be able to beat **any** Limit Hold 'em game.

SUPER/SYSTEM's
POWER POKER COURSE
IN

NO-LIMIT
HOLD 'EM

NO LIMIT HOLD 'EM

Table of Contents

Editor's note: At the time of this book's original publication, the first three community cards were known as the "turn," the fourth community card was known as "fourth street," and the fifth and final community card was known as "fifth street." Although these terms have changed over the years to "flop," "turn," and "river" respectively, readers should be aware that in the following chapter, the older (and original) terminology is maintained.

NO-LIMIT HOLD 'EM
The Cadillac of Poker Games

INTRODUCTION

There's a story I've been hearing all my life around Poker games. It's related to a colorful player down in south Texas named Broomcorn. Whenever there's someone in the game who's playing real tight, the opposing players will needle him by saying: *"Well, you're gonna go like Broomcorn's uncle."* He'd perk up and respond sharply: *"What do you mean I'm gonna go like him?"* And they'd say: *"Well, he anted himself to death."*

That's a little story you should always keep in mind. Because whenever you find yourself playing a very tight and defensive style of Poker...you'll be in danger of anteing yourself to "death". As I've said throughout these pages... the ante determines how fast you play in any Poker game. Since you'll generally play in a normal (or medium) ante game... if you play an aggressive style of Poker, you'll have way the best of it.

That's the way I play...and it works. This is especially true of No-Limit Hold 'em which, in my opinion is the Cadillac of Poker games. That opinion is **not** because No-Limit Hold 'em is my best game. It's an opinion shared by many of the world's best Poker players...some of whom are only beginning to appreciate the great variety of skills you need to be a top-level Hold 'em player. As I've said, although Hold 'em is similar in some respects to a game such as Seven-Stud...there are enough differences to put it in a class by itself. And it's truly a game that requires very special talents in order to play it at a world-class level.

Above all else, No-Limit Hold 'em is a game where you have to be aggressive...and you have to gamble. One of the great things about Hold 'em is that there are so many different combinations of hands and different things you can do in different situations. As opposed to other forms of Poker, you can represent a lot of different hands in Hold 'em. You can also put your opponent on any one of several hands. It's a very complex game. You're forced to do a lot of guessing. So is your opponent.

It comes to a point where you have to take a chance. If you want to be a winner — a big winner — at No-Limit Hold 'em...you *can't* play a solid, safe game. You *must* get in there and gamble.

My philosophy of play at No-Limit Hold 'em is a simple one: I try to win big pots...and the small ones I *pick-up* (win without a contest). It's a philosophy that necessitates a gambling style of play. My style. And it's this style that's fostered a lot of comment from countless players about how "lucky" I am. I've been hearing that for a lot of years. The simple fact is it's **not** true. Everyone gets lucky once in a while. But no one is **consistently** lucky. So it has to be something other than luck to account for the fact I've been a consistently big winner through the years. It is something else. You'll soon discover what that "something else" is.

I've appeared to be a "lucky" player because every time a big pot came up, I've usually had the **worst** hand. There are good reasons for that. I'm a very aggressive player. I'm reaching out and picking up small pots all the time. I'm always betting at those pots...hammering at them. And I **don't** want anybody to stop me from doing that. I **don't** want anyone to **defeat** my style of play.

Consequently, if I've got any kind of a hand, any kind of a draw...I bet. And if I get raised...I **don't** quit. I go ahead and get all my money in the pot knowing I've probably got the worst hand — that I'm the underdog to win the pot.

Sometimes, I'll even call a *Post-Oak bluff* (a very small bet in a big pot) **just to get a chance at a draw**. Of course, if

I'm going to gamble like that...the player I'm in there with must have a lot of chips on the table. For example, I'll have a 10-9 and the Flop comes 8-3-2. And, let's say, there was $10,000 in the pot before the Flop. Now, with a raggedy Flop like that, a tight player might try to pick-up the pot with a Post-Oak bluff of $1200. Well, that's a **gutless** bet* and I'll call it trying to catch a Jack or a Seven just so I could get an open-end Straight draw on Fourth St. I'm in a good position to pick-up the pot on Fourth **whether or not I get the draw I want**. The tight player who made that weak bet on the Flop is asking me to take his money. And, in most cases, that's exactly what I'm going to do when the next card falls — regardless of what it is. I'm going to move-in on that tight player because I feel confident he's going to throw his hand away and **not** put his whole stack in jeopardy.

Since I play that way, I've got a reputation of being an extremely aggressive player. And I don't ever want to lose that reputation. It's what enables me to pick-up more than what would normally be considered my share of pots.

In most cases, my opponents are afraid to play-back at me because they know I'm subject to set them all-in. So, when they **don't** have a real big hand, they let go of the pot...and I pick it up (in a way similar to what I'd do when somebody makes a Post-Oak bluff at me). The accumulation of all those small pots is a big part of my winning-formula. It's the bonus I get for playing the way I do...and it's the "secret" as to why I win.

If I win ten pots where nobody has a big hand — ten pots with let's say $3,000 in them...then I can afford to take 2 to 1 the worst of it and play a $30,000 pot. I've already got that pot paid for with all the small pots I picked up. And when I play that big pot...it's a freeroll.

As I said a little while ago, when a big pot's played... I've usually got the worst hand. I'd say over 50% of the time...when all the money goes in, I've got the worst hand. Obviously, I couldn't overcome that unless I had something

*I **NEVER** make a Post-Oak bluff.

to compensate for it. And my compensation is all those small pots I've picked-up.

Of course, I'm *almost* never completely out on a limb in a big pot. Whenever I make a substantial bet or raise...I've *almost* always got an *Out*. Betting with an Out. That's what I call it. And it's the Out I have that makes me appear "lucky" when I'm a *dog* in a big pot and wind up winning it.

You'll have additional compensations for playing the aggressive way I recommend. You'll be able to break a lot of players because you're in there gambling all the time...and, because of that, you'll get a lot of your real good hands paid-off. Tight players don't get their real good hands paid-off because they make a *move* so rarely that their hands are an "open book" whenever they do. And they almost never *change gears* (start playing loose). But you'll be out there betting, betting, betting — all the time. Your opponents will see you're an aggressive player. They'll know you're out there trying to pick-up all those pots...so they'll sometimes give you a little loose action. And, since you'll hold a few hands (you **won't** always be out there with the worst hand)...you'll break one or two of them. After that, they'll be scared to get involved with you.

So your style of play will be very deceiving — it'll get **all** the other players befuddled. They **won't** know whether you've really got a hand or not. They **won't** know whether you're going to set them all-in or not. Because they might have to put all their money in the pot **not** knowing if they have the best hand...they **won't** know what to do. And anytime you get your opponents in that confused situation ...you'll have an advantage over them.

Of course, you **don't** play every hand aggressively. Occasionally you slow down...and sometimes you completely stop and throw your hand away.

> **You should never start out bluffing at a pot and keep bluffing at it *without* an Out.**

For example, whenever I raise the pot **before** the Flop...I'm going to bet **after** the Flop about 90% of the time.

So if the Flop comes completely ragged (one that doesn't look like anyone can have much of it)...I'm going to bet at the pot and try to· pick it up even if I **don't** have a piece of the Flop. But, if I get called...I'm usually going to give it up — unless I have some kind of an Out [even as little as *Third Button* (a Pair made with the lowest card on the Flop) or an inside Straight draw]. Sometimes, you can keep hammering on certain players and drive them off even when you **don't** have an Out. But, you're usually better off when you have some kind of escape-hatch.

The reason I go ahead and put all my money in on occasion when I know I've probably got the worst hand deserves repeating since it's so important for you to understand. I do it because I **don't** want somebody playing-back at me and trying to stop me from being the aggressor. If I allow that to happen...it'll cramp my style. I'll no longer be able to pick-up all those pots when nobody has a hand. And nobody's got anything a big percentage of the time. Somebody's got to get the money that's left out there. I want it to be me.

An example will best show you what I'm talking about. Let's say I raised before the Flop with a type of hand that's one of my favorites: small connecting cards that are suited. I'm in the pot with one player who called behind me. At this point, I put him on a couple of big cards or a medium Pair. That's all right. It's what I want him to have. Now, here's what'll happen if the following Turn comes up.

ME   **HIM**

FLOP

With that Flop, I'm going to lead right off and bet. If he plays-back at me, I'm now going to be quite sure he's got two Aces (or better). So, I'm about a 9 to 5 dog. The pot (odds) will compensate a little bit for that price...but it **won't** be laying me enough to put the rest of my money in. Yet, I'll go ahead and get it all-in there because I **don't** want that same guy, who might be a pretty good player, taking a Jack-Ten and making that same play when I **don't** have anything. To let his play succeed, I have to throw my hand away and give him the pot. Because **I** want the pot...I can't let him succeed. I want him to fear me. I want him to have the opinion I'm going to defend the money I put out there. I don't want him to have any doubts. So I go ahead and put the rest of my money in.

In making that play on the Flop, there's a good chance I can win the pot right there. Because I'm known to play any reasonable hand (and some "unreasonable" hands in a short-handed high-ante game)...I've really made it tough on him. I could've flopped a Set (of Trips), Two-Pair or even the Straight. I've put him on the defensive...and he's got a lot of guessing to do.

If he decides to call me...it's **not** all that bad because I've got an Out. If I make my Straight, I'm going to break him. And if I draw out on him...it appears like I got lucky again. Well, I did...and I didn't. When I moved-in on him, I was gambling to pick-up the pot. When I **didn't** succeed because of his call...you might say I got unlucky. What's more...I **am** supposed to make my draws once in a while. In fact, in that specific situation I'll draw out more than one third of the time (by making my Straight or back-dooring Two-Pair or Trips).

A very interesting thing about that particular hand of 7-6 is that I'd rather have it than a 9-8. The reason is that when you turn a Straight with a 9-8...you'll frequently find that somebody is on top of you. A good example is when the Flop comes Q-J-10. An A-K will have you nutted and even a Sucker who plays a K-9 will have you beat. I've turned many a Straight with a 9-8...but when a Q-J-10 falls, I'm always **real cautious** with the hand. Because people play the higher cards more frequently than the lower ones, you're less likely to be in trouble when you turn a Straight with a 7-6 than you would be with a 9-8.

I'll discuss the general category of small connecting cards in great detail a little later. As I previously noted, they're one of my favorite hands. Another of my favorites is a hand where you can turn a **double** belly-buster (two-way inside) Straight. It's one of the most deceiving hands there is...and I especially like it in No-Limit. Because it's so deceptive, I almost invariably raise with it when I can win a big pot. It has all the advantages of an open-end Straight... but it's **not** as easy to read.

An example of turning a double belly-buster is when you have a Q-10 and the Turn comes A-J-8. As you can see, it's very deceptive because you can make a Straight with a Nine or a King. What's more, if you catch a King and there's someone in the pot with you with A-K...you can see all the trouble he's in.

Since double belly-busters are such good gambling hands (because of their deceptive qualities), you might find the following quick rule of thumb useful for now.

> It's possible to turn a double belly-buster with any two cards that are part of a Straight such as a 7-6, 8-6, 9-6 and a 10-6. Also, two cards with five gaps between them such as a Q-6 can also turn a double belly-buster draw. (In the *Supplement* at the end of this section you'll find a complete rundown on all the hands that have double belly-buster potential.)

When you turn a double belly-buster draw, you should very carefully note which of your possible Straights will be the nuts. For example, if you have a J-9 and the Fall is K-10-7...both an Eight and a Queen will make you a Straight. However, only the Eight will give you the nuts. If a Queen falls on Fourth, someone with an A-J can beat your Straight. So you must be careful — especially in No-Limit play — and you must know how to read the Board **perfectly** (to see what hand is the absolute nuts). Practice at home, until you **don't** make a single mistake. You're sure to learn after you get broke a few times with what you thought was the nuts, but was actually the second best hand.

A good case in point is the example noted in the above paragraph. A player could easily think he had the best Straight when the Queen fell...until someone showed him an A-J for all his money.

> **An easy way to determine whether your Straight is the nuts is by using one of the following observations. You'll have the nut Straight if:**
>
> **(1) the high-end of the Straight is made up with the** *highest card in your hand;* **or**
>
> **(2) the high-end of the** *highest possible* **Straight is already on the Board.**

Drawing to a double belly-buster is one of few exceptions in No-Limit where you might be drawing to an inside Straight that **won't** make the best hand. As I noted earlier, inside Straight draws can be real good plays in No-Limit Hold 'em because for a few chips you have the opportunity to win a very big pot. But, you *almost* **never** draw to a **(single)** belly-buster Straight that will **not** be the best hand if you make it. They're longshot plays...so when you do make them, you want to be **sure** they're the nuts.

For example, let's say you held a Q-J and the Fall was 9-8-4. Now, you **might** want to draw at that belly-buster trying to catch a Ten — even in Limit, but mostly in No-Limit. You know if you catch that Ten, you'll have a cinch hand. But if you held a 6-5...you'd **never** draw to it (with the same Fall) because there'd be two different Straights that could beat you if you catch a Seven. (You'd lose to a 6-7-8-9-10 and a 7-8-9-10-J.) If a man makes a Straight with you, he's either got you tied or he's got you beat. So, you **never draw** to the *dead-end* of a (single) belly-buster.

Before you decide to draw to a belly-buster, you **also** want to feel reasonably certain that your opponent is going to gamble with you if you do make it. I mean, they're good plays...but **only** if you can win a big pot if you make your longshot. So you want your opponent to have the best hand possible on the Board. If it came a 9-8-4 (as above)...ideally, you want your opponent to have 3-Nines. You **don't** want him to have a Pair of Kings or A-9. You want him to have at least Eights and Nines, or better, 3-Nines. You want him to have a **very big** hand. Your Q-J would be a very good hand against 3-Nines. It **wouldn't** be as good against a Pair of Nines because it **won't** make enough money. Your opponent will release a Pair far more readily than he'll release a Set.

So if you can get in real cheap and have the potential to win a big pot...belly-buster Straights are good gambles. But, you also have to be **very selective** about the belly-busters you do draw to. You **don't** want it to be apparent to your opponent that you could've made a Straight. In the illustration just used, you might **not** get the action you want if a Ten falls off on Fourth Street. A Queen-Jack is actually a **weak** hand when the Flop is 9-8-4. Your opponent might put you on a 7-6 and, when the Ten came, he might be very leery about calling a big .bet you made. The Straight possibility might even scare him off completely.

But, if a possible Straight *wasn't* **so apparent** when the Ten came off...then, you could probably win a lot of money. Let's say, you had the Q♡-9♡ and the Flop was J-8-2. You might want to pick the Ten off there...because that would be a very deceptive belly-buster draw. And that's the kind of inside Straight you want to draw for to win a big pot — the ones that *aren't* **so obvious**.

If you graduate from Limit Hold 'em to No-Limit, you'll find that you'll be doing many things (besides drawing to inside Straights) that simply **won't** work when all it can cost your opponent is another bet.

A good example of a bluff that has a lot of power to it in No-Limit, but will **rarely** work at Limit play is when the Board's one card off a Straight on Fourth. Let's say there's an A-K-Q-J out there and your opponent bets. You've got a Ten in the hole so you've got the nuts. (There's no Flush possible.) Your opponent bets, you raise and he plays–back. Now...there's no question he's got a Straight also.

An unsophisticated player would move–in on him right there because he knows he can't lose. But, what good is that? He's only going to get a split.

However, add some drama and a little acting to your play and there's a chance you could win it all. You know you're going to call his re-raise...but you **don't** have to do it instantaneously. Take your time. Just stall around. Study the Board real hard and shake your head several times making it appear as though you overlooked the possible Straight. You could even pick up your cards slightly and make him think you're going to throw them away. Then...put them back down and say *"O.K., I'll call it."*

With all your agonizing, he's got to give you credit for a Set. You've made him think you're gambling the Board will pair so you'll make a Full. If the Board **does** pair on the end...you bet him all your money. There's almost no risk to that play. You represent a Full and many a time your opponent will throw his hand away. It works a lot of times. (Of course, it's harder to do in Limit because all the guy has to do is call one bet.)

As you can see from the play just described, bluffing often involves a lot of "art". But, there's "science" to it also. There's even science to **calling** a bluff. The following pot I was involved in will clearly illustrate what I mean.

It was a small (ante) No–Limit game early in my career. I was on the Button so I limped–in with a J–10 in the hole. (There were two players in the pot in front of me.) Here's what the Flop looked like:

FLOP

As you see, I had two to a (belly) Straight. Since there

was **no** raise before the Flop, I was reasonably sure **neither** of my two opponents had very strong hands.

On the Flop, the guy in the first seat made a *reasonable (size) bet** and the player in front of me called it. Both players had a lot of money in front of them...so I also called.

The. fourth card was the 2♠. They both checked on Fourth St. — and so did I. The last card was the 3♦. The Board now looked like this:

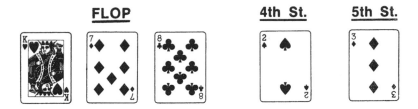

When all the cards were out, the guy in the first seat checked again. I felt when he bet (on the Flop) and then checked twice (on Fourth and Fifth)...he had the top Pair with a small kicker. I felt the guy in front of me was drawing at some kind of Straight (and, obviously, missed his hand). Much to my surprise, he made a real out-of-line bet on the end — far bigger than the size of the pot.

When he did that, it looked to me like he was clearly trying to steal the pot. I was also sure I had him high-carded. (As I said, I felt sure he was drawing at a smaller Straight than I was.)

If I was correct in thinking I had been drawing at the highest possible Straight...I "knew" I'd win the pot if I **just called**. (I also "knew" the other player **couldn't** *overcall* because his hand wasn't strong enough.)

So I called that out-of-line bet...and my analysis proved correct. The player with the Pair threw his hand away and the guy who over-bet the pot **was** drawing to a little Straight. So I won the pot with a Jack-high.

---

*Throughout these discussions, a *reasonable (size) bet* **means about the size of the pot.**

I didn't tell you that Poker story because I won the pot with a Jack-high. And you shouldn't remember it for that reason. It has a more significant message.

I stated that I "felt" neither guy had much of anything. I then went on to explain why I had that *feeling*. Obviously, it was **more** than just a nebulous feel that I had. I had played with both those guys often...so my feel was a certain amount of reasoning and a process of elimination was involved. And a lot of it was based on recall.

Whenever I use the word "feel"...you should understand it's **not** some extra-sensory power that I have (although, as I noted in the section on *GENERAL POKER STRATEGY*, I **do** believe there **is** something to the theories relating to ESP). I recall what happened...even though I might **not** *consciously* do it...I recall that this same play came up (or something close to it) and this is what he did or what somebody else did. So I get a feeling that he's bluffing or that I can make a play here and get the pot. But, actually my subconscious mind is reasoning it all out.

You build up a history of every player you ever played with...I mean everyone that you've ever done any serious gambling with. You've got some kind of information on them. It's there...buried in your mind. And you **don't** have to concentrate to get it out. When the time comes to use it, it'll come naturally — you **won't** have to force it.

All **good** Poker players have tremendous recall. They reach back into the depths of their mind and remember what a certain guy did in a similar situation. A good player might not realize what he's doing...and he might not know exactly what it is...but he feels he can make a real big play or make a super call when he feels a guy's bluffing. The vibrations are definitely there. He just **knows** it.

And what it actually is, is a sense of recall. The same (or similar) situation existed some time ago...and he knows **exactly** what to do in this one. It's usually a stress situation — when a (relatively) big amount of money's involved — that these things are always true.

There's another kind of "feel" you can have in a game

that **doesn't** depend on recall. This type of feel depends on close observation of what's going on during a particular session. You acquire this feel when you notice that a certain player is really off his game and playing far below the quality of play he's normally capable of. You see this happen all the time. A lot of players lose control and go *on tilt* after they get one (or more) big hands *cracked* (beaten). They become *unglued* (lose their composure). To recoup their losses, they start playing weak hands...and they play those hands badly. Very badly. It's easy to capitalize on those situations. Here's how:

Let's say you're in a game with a high–ante structure (a subject I'll soon discuss) and naturally everybody's playing real fast. You played a 9-6 and the Flop came A-9-8. Normally, if you got played with, you'd be very concerned about that Ace (and also your kicker). But, in this case, you're in the pot with a player who's losing and, from what you've been able to observe, he's playing very badly. You check on the Flop...and so does he.

Now, all of a sudden, you get a "feel" that all he's got is the *Third Button* (a Pair of Eights). The reason why you feel he got "something" (a small piece of the Flop) is because he checked. He **didn't** bet because he wants to get the hand shown-down. If he had nothing at all...he would've bet to try to steal the pot. And, you "know" he doesn't have an Ace. You know the worst that can happen is that he could also have a Nine and *run you down* (chase you). Well, what you want is for him to run you down with an Eight — which is what you really think he has. You know if you're really off-base...he might have a Nine.

But, you feel confident you're **not** wrong and if a Rag falls off on Fourth...you bet. You know he's going to call you...almost out of desperation because he's losing. So you make some money on Fourth and also on the end. You know he's **not** going to show you a hand unless he gets lucky and pairs his kicker.

The very surprising thing about the previous discussion is that the player I was referring to who's *on tilt* is actually a very good player. He could even be *world-class*. Of course, the super-stars of the Poker world — those who I play against on a regular basis — are able to exercise far more control than the average player. Yet, even a real good player has moments when he's playing considerably off his usual game. So, you have to be observant and take advantage of such opportunities when they present themselves. You'll have far more opportunities to do that against the average player simply because they lose control far more often.

There's something else that's extremely important that you'll have to be constantly aware of. It's this:

> **You'll have to be able to categorize your opponents** *as to the quality of their play.* . . **and you'll have to play** *very differently* **against strong players than you do against weaker ones. This is of crucial importance in No-Limit play.**

Shortly, I'm going to go into considerable detail on this very important subject because I've seen very good players fail to adjust their strategy when they're in a pot with a certain type of player. In fact, as recently as the 1977 *World Series of Poker*® (in the World Championship Hold 'em event), some of the best players I know made such amateurish mistakes that I wouldn't have believed it possible if I hadn't seen it with my own two eyes. But, before I get into the specific details, I want to give you two **general** rules to guide you in this matter.

> **(1) Against a low-grade player** . . . **you simply make the obvious play. That is, you** *don't* **try to get fancy when you're in a pot with a weak player. You** *don't* **try to make subtle moves that'll be far beyond his capacity to understand or appreciate. You play** *fundamentally* **better (rather than strategically better) than a weak player. In a word, you** *outplay* **him.**
>
> **(2) Against a higher-grade player** . . . **(someone who could be thinking along the same lines as you)** . . . **you** *must* **mix-up your play.** *Sometimes* **you make an obvious play against a**

> strong player (as you *always* would against a
> weak player). . .and *sometimes* you go at it
> another way and make a play that's *not* so
> obvious. Most of the time. . .you have to *put a*
> *play on* (outmaneuver) a strong player.

In a nutshell, that's all there is to it. And it seems
simple and logical enough. There's even very good players
who **know** that that's what they're supposed to do. But
knowing something. . .and being able to execute it — are **not**
the same thing. As I said, I saw some *world-class* Poker
players make mistakes in the 1977 World Championship
Tournament that only an idiot would make.

There was a particular player who entered the Tournament for the first time. . .and, almost immediately, it was
easy to see that he was a weak player. He was the supreme
example of a *calling station* — a player who's next-to-
impossible to bluff.

Even though I had never played against him before, it
didn't take me very long to recognize the type of player he
was. I've played with thousands just like him throughout my
career. So I knew what to do when I was involved with him
in a pot. More precisely. . .I knew what **not** to do. I was **not**
going to try to bluff him. **Not even once.**

I quickly decided that if I was in the pot with him, I was
going to show him a hand. And, if he got lucky enough to
beat me. . .well, he was going to beat a hand. My mind was
made up about that.

But there were other very good players in the Tournament who tried to *run over* him — tried to force him out of
a pot. They would bluff at him constantly. . .and they were
rarely successful. If he had anything at all. . .he *looked 'em up.*
As I said, he was the ultimate *calling station.* He looked
enough of them up often enough to finish far higher than
he was legitimately supposed to. He was probably about a
1000 to 1 dog to finish as high as he did. The reason he did
was simply because so many players — and some very
experienced ones — just handed him their money. They
almost literally gave it away to him.

What they should **not** have done is try to bluff him. It takes an idiot, in my book, to bluff at a man who you **know** is going to call you.

You simply **can't** bluff a **bad** player...because a bad player will play when he's got some kind of a hand and will pass when he doesn't have a hand. I mean...it's clear-cut. You **don't** have to be an expert psychologist to figure out what he's doing. All you have to know is if he's in the pot...he's got something. And you're **not** going to get him out of the pot by trying to bluff him.

Above all...**you** *don't* **want to gamble with a** *weak* **player**. Forget about that...show him a hand. You do very fundamental things against a bad player. Obvious things. That is...no tricks...no strategic plays...nothing fancy. Play straight-forward Poker against a weak player.

For example, if a weak player raised the pot coming in (before the Flop) and then checked it on the Flop and checked again on Fourth St. — well, I would automatically bet (regardless of what I've got) because I'd know he didn't have anything at all. It's simple to outplay him because his actions tell me whether he's got something or not. There's no mystery about it.

I could also outplay him by adjusting my style to his. For example, I noted that I'm always stabbing around trying to pick-up pots. I could still do that with a weak player in the pot...but I'd **adjust my play** because he's in there. Like I might raise him without looking at my hand. Now, here comes the Turn and he checks. Well, I'm going to bet at that pot in the *dark*...because I know he doesn't have any-thing — and I also know he's probably going to pass. He checked, didn't he? If he had something, he would've bet.

Of course, I might have to make a further adjustment. If he checked (on the Flop) and then called me...I'd give him credit for something. If there's no Straight or Flush draw out there...he's probably got a **small** piece of the Board. (If he had a **big** piece...he would've bet.) If he checks again on Fourth and calls me again...then I'd know I'm going to have to show him a hand on the end — unless I thought he was drawing and missed his hand. Only then would I think I had a chance to steal it on the end.

Another way I'd adjust my style when I was in the pot with a weak player is when I turned a real big hand — say, a Set of Trips. As you'll learn, I **don't** *slow-play* that hand. I always lead with it. But, against a **weak** player...I would check it because I'd know that if he had anything, he would bet. And I'd get to break him anyway. If he didn't have anything, I wouldn't mind giving him a free card. I want him to improve his hand. I want him to make something so I could break him there.

It's more difficult to outplay a strong player. You can't do simple things against better players — you've got to *put a play on* somebody who knows what's obvious. And if **he** does something that's obvious — like I think he's trying to pick-up the pot...well, I'll *put a play on* him and raise him with nothing because he might throw his hand away. But if a weak player bets at me, I'm **not** going to raise him... unless I've got something.

Since a good player will understand the obvious, I must try to deceive him. I'll even put a play on **more than one** good player. For example, if someone *brought it in* (raised it) in an early position and three players just called it...I might try to pick-up that pot. I might move-in with nothing.

Against a good player, you'll have a lot more tools to work with...many different strategies to use. You're effectively restricted to a "pickax and shovel" — basic, fundamental things — against a weak player. Never forget that. **Don't** try to devise elaborate strategies to use against a bad player. They **won't** work against him. Use sophisticated plays against a good player. They'll work against him.

Another point you should note about weak players is that they come in several varieties. They're not all like the one I just described. Some are completely opposite. There are some who check their good hands and bet their bad hands. They like to bluff...and they do it almost all the time. So, with a player like that, you keep on checking it to him...and let him bluff his money off to you.

Note that I **didn't** say you check-raise him. You **don't** want to take the play away from that type of player. In fact, check-raising is a strategy I rarely use. I think it's a weak play. I'll do it occasionally. . .but **not** often.

However, I suppose I encounter more check-raising than the average player because I play so aggressively. If a player makes a hand, he'll check it to me thinking that I'm going to bet. . .and he's usually right. Most of the time, I will bet. So he checks it to me. . .and after I bet — he raises.

As I said, I don't do too much check-raising myself. I'll usually do it when someone seems to be trying to take the play away from me. Perhaps, I might check it. . .and move–in on him or something like that. But, I don't do it often. Check-raising is **not** really a part of my philosophy of Poker. I do it on occasion — you have to keep people in line — but I **don't** look for opportunities to check-raise somebody.

Surprisingly, if you employ my style of play at No–Limit Hold 'em. . .you **won't** be in constant fear of getting check-raised. By playing aggressively, you might think that *"well, they're probably going to get me this time"* every time you bet. But, even though you'll probably encounter more check-raising than most players, you'll be amazed at how many times your opponents keep throwing their hands away whenever you bet.

It all reverts back to my basic style of play. My opponents know that if I've got any kind of a hand — any kind of a draw — and they do check-raise me. . .then all of my money (and theirs) is going to the middle. And. . .because they know that. . .it keeps them off me — it stops them from playing–back at me.

There are other things that my aggressive style of play does for me. Not only does it give me an "umbrella of protection" from getting played–back at (in most cases) and not only does it make my opponents constantly fear me and therefore make it easy for me to pick–up numerous pots without a contest. . .but it has other advantages as well. I've already told you I also get a lot of loose action. This may seem contradictory. . .because how can I pick–up pots easily on the one hand and get a lot of loose action on the other? But, it's easy to understand when you realize that the pots I pick–up are when nobody's got a hand. And, as I said, that's a big percentage of the time. When I get so-called "loose action"...it's when somebody **does** have a hand. At those times, all the money is subject to go to the center. And when it does — as you now know — I've usually got the worst hand.

But I can also find a hand when I look down. And, once in a while, it's the **best** hand. When I'm up against another hand at those times...the pot gets to be a mountain. It wouldn't be nearly as big if I wasn't the aggressive player I am. I'd never get the action I do when I've got a hand if I was known to slow-play hands...or do a lot of check-raising. That's why I rarely do those things.

An example of why being known as an aggressive player — and constantly playing that way — is the most profitable way to play Poker is clearly illustrated by the following situation.

Let's say I turned a big hand on the Flop — a Set of Trips or even Two-Pair. I'm first to act and I'm in the pot with someone who raised before the Flop. He's supposed to have a strong hand. He's probably got a big Pair in the hole — bigger than anything that showed on the Flop.

> **In this situation, there's a principle I always apply in Hold 'em.** *I always make it a habit to lead into the raiser whenever I turn a big hand.*

Most players will slow-play their hand in that spot...or hope to get in a check-raise. When they do that, they're playing it **wrong**...as you'll now see.

By betting right into the raiser, you make him think you're either trying to take the pot away from him or you've got some kind of draw or a mediocre hand. Consequently, he'll almost invariably raise you. At that point...you can get all your chips in. And it's tough for him to get away from his hand because he has so much money already in the pot.

The raiser expects you to check to him on the Flop. I mean, he knows **you know** he's supposedly got a strong hand. He raised coming in, didn't he?

When most players turn a Set with a small Pair (or turn Two-Pair with small connecting cards)...they do the obvious. They check...waiting for the raiser to bet. And then they put in a raise.

That's the **wrong** way to play it. That way **they give the raiser an opportunity to get away from his hand at a minimum** loss. But, if you lead into him...and he raises — there's no savings. He's almost committed to get the rest of his money in the pot.

Even if it's a raggedy Flop — **without** a Straight or Flush draw — you should still make the same play. Perhaps even more so...because with three Rags out there a bet would indicate weakness rather than strength to most players. Since it does look like you're weak (and like you're trying to take the pot away from him)...the average player will respond to your bet by raising.

The only risk you take when you play the hand that way is that the raiser might **not** raise you on the Flop because he might **not** have a hand...but he might bluff at it if you check and you'd win the amount he bluffed.

However, it's far more probable he **does** have a hand. He's supposed to have a hand! He's represented a hand. He was the raiser. On that very reasonable assumption, I go ahead and lead into his hand. When compared to check-raising in that situation, it's the bigger money-making play, by far. **I think it's one of the strongest plays in Hold 'em.**

If you turned a Set in an **unraised** pot (and it was a raggedy Flop)...you'd have to play the hand quite different-ly. Depending on what Set you flopped, you might not even play it at all. You'll see what I mean in a minute. But, the concept you should understand is this:

In No-Limit play, you must be very careful you *don't* lose all your chips in an *unraised* pot.

Here's what I mean: let's say you and six other players got in for the absolute minimum — that is, you all limped-in for a $50 *force* (the Blind bet). Everybody just called. Nobody raised...so the field wasn't weeded out at all. Now, a J–4–2 flops. You turn 3-Deuces. In the previous situation — with this same Flop — you should lead right into the raiser with your Set. He's probably got an overpair and will raise as expected. But, in the present situation, you must play it carefully. Very carefully. You turned a hand that's easy to get broke with. There's nothing in the pot...and you **don't** want to get broke in a "nothing" pot.

The six people in the pot with you tried to turn the nuts for free. And one of them might have the nuts. Or close to it. So when one of the players commits all his money when there's only a few hundred dollars in the pot...you better watch out. Your 3-Deuces probably **aren't** any good.

You could be up against 3-Jacks, but that's **not** as likely as 3-Fours since there was **no** *raise* **before** the Flop. That's the hand you should be afraid of — 3-Fours.

I'm **not** saying you shouldn't play the hand. That's not the case at all. I'm just saying that you have to play it carefully because nobody showed any early strength. Therefore, you're **not** likely to be up against a big Pair. However, you could be facing another Set. Nevertheless, if it's checked to you, **you've got to bet it**. But you **don't** want to get broke with the hand because it was a nothing pot to begin with. If you get raised, your own judgment in the particular situation will have to prevail. With the Third Set (Deuces), you might want to go on with the hand...and then you might not. With the Second Set (Fours)...you just could **not** get away from it. Someone's going to have to show you 3-Jacks. That's all there is to it.

An important point for you to remember is that in a judgment situation *you're always better off* **sticking to your** *first* **impression. Once you decide what a man's most likely to have — especially in No-Limit play — you should** *never* **change your mind. You'll probably be right the first time...so** *don't* **try to second-guess yourself.**

With constant observation of your opponents' play...
you'll learn how to put them on a (probable) hand. Once you
do...**don't** change your mind. Stick to your **first** impression.
Have the courage of your convictions!

Having courage is one of the most important qualities
you must have to be a good No-Limit player. If you don't
have it...you'll have to restrict your play to Limit Poker.
You need courage in Limit too...but not nearly to the
degree you must have it at No-Limit.

A lot of Limit players — and now I'm talking about the
very best Limit players — just **can't play** No-Limit. They
don't have the "heart" for it. What's more...they **can't
adjust** to the complexity of No-Limit play — and they find it
very hard to go from what's essentially a mechanical game
(Limit) to one that takes in everything (No-Limit). Only
very special players can make that transition successfully.

You also have to have a different "feel" for No-Limit
play. I mean, you have to be right just about all the time —
especially when your entire stack's at stake.

In Limit play, you're **not** going to get knocked out of a
game by one or two mistakes. You can make several
mistakes in a Limit game and still win the money...because
your opponents are making more mistakes than you are.
Playing No-Limit, you can make just one crucial mistake at
any time and you can lose all your chips.

It not only takes a lot of "heart" to play No-Limit...it
also takes a lot of "muscle". You need "muscle" in Limit
too...but you need much more of it at No-Limit.

A strong No-Limit player can keep "slapping you
around" — just "lean on" you and keep "leaning on" you
until you melt. Of course, that could happen in Limit
too...but, again, **not** to the same degree.

The very best players I know are extremely aggressive
players...and that's what makes them the great players they
are. The more aggressive they are...the better they are. It's
that simple. And I firmly believe that's what accounts for
the difference between a very good player and a truly top
player. It's the dividing line. That's for sure.

There's not a man alive that can keep beating on me. I refuse to let somebody keep taking my money...and all the other truly top players are the same way. An aggressive player might do it for a while...keep leaning on me. But, at the first opportunity I get, I'm going to take a stand and put all my money in the pot.

It's like that little boy who keeps sticking his head up and keeps getting slapped all the time. Well, sooner or later he's **not** going to stick his head up any more. So if a guy keeps going on and on and keeps pounding on me...then me and him are fixing to play a pot.

Like me, all the top players know you have to be extremely aggressive to be a consistent winner. You have to bet, bet, bet...all the time. If I find somebody I can keep betting at and he keeps saying *"take it Doyle"*, *"take it Doyle"*...well, I'm going to keep pounding on him. I'm **not** going to let-up. And that poor guy **never** will win a pot from me. He's going to have to have the nuts to call me.

That's what most players do...they keep throwing their hand away. They're weak. They sit down and try to make the nuts on you. That's hard to do. So you keep whamming on 'em and whamming on 'em and you just wear 'em down. And, sooner or later, you'll win all their money.

Perhaps now, you can see more clearly what I explained to you earlier. When a big pot comes up...I've usually got the worst hand. That weak player finally picked up the nuts...and that's what I usually look at in a big pot. But, I've already paid for that big pot with all the other pots I've won. So I'm freerolling with all that weak player's money (and the money of all the other weak players in the game).

You **can't** do that against a truly top-player in No-Limit ...because he's fixing to make a stand and play-back at you. And that's the big difference between a merely good player and a great one.

Another important difference is that a real top-player can win money with a marginal hand. A weaker player can't do that. They don't know how...or they're afraid to put any money in the pot in a borderline situation. They want the nuts (or close to it) before they'll jeopardize any of their chips. They don't want to do too much gambling. . .so they check a lot of hands that I'd bet for value.

Betting for value is what it's all about. For example, if it came down to a tough situation on the end and a tight player had Two–Pair, but there's a *possible* **Straight** out there. . .well, that tight player would probably check it trying to show the hands down.

In that same situation, as long as I felt reasonably sure my opponent didn't have that Straight — I'd be more aggressive. I want to make some money on the end. I want to get value for my Two–Pair. So I'd bet. . .and try to *sell* my hand for the most money I thought I could get.

I **don't** have to have the nuts to bet my hand on the end. If I feel like I've got the best hand. . .I'm going to bet it — and get value for it. A more conservative player would check it on the end and he'll get his check "called". So he'll lose that last bet.

I never was a tight player. . .even when I first started to play. Experience has taught me a lot. Early in my career, I didn't know how to start at a pot and quit. . .like I can now.

A very big part of winning consistently — and winning big — at No-Limit is to get the other guy in a position where if he makes a bet he's actually jeopardizing all his chips as opposed to you jeopardizing all of yours.

> **That has always been the *key* to No–Limit play as far as I'm concerned. I want to put my opponent to a decision *for all his chips*.**

For example, if a guy's got twenty thousand dollars in chips and you lead–off for six or seven thousand. . .you're really betting him twenty thousand. This is because he knows if he calls that six or seven thousand. . .well, then, he's got to go for the rest of it.

You're betting seven thousand. . .he's betting twenty.

However, if he bets me seven. . .it's just the reverse. So, I always try to make the bet that puts him in jeopardy. . .not me. If he's right. . .and I'm bluffing. . .he's going to move–in with his twenty thousand — and I'm **not** going to call him. So he'll win seven thousand. But, if he's wrong. . .and I've got a hand. . .he's still going to move–in. But now he's going to get called — and he's going to lose twenty thousand.

So he's laying me about 3 to 1 — his twenty thousand to my seven. I put the commitment on him. I make him commit himself. I'm **not** committed. Whether he thinks I am or not. . .I'm not. That's the beauty of it. He's thinking about my bet. . .and wondering how much more he's going to have to put in there.

It's an either/or situation. Either I'm bluffing. . .or I've got the nuts. And against me, he knows it **could** cost him twenty thousand — his whole stack — unless he throws his hand away.

And, boy, you'd be surprised how many times they say *"take it Doyle"*, *"take it Doyle"*. They just throw their hand away and throw their hand away. . .over and over and over again. I mean. . .even **I'm** surprised. I think to myself *"well, he CAN'T throw this one away"*. . .but I bet anyway. And there goes his hand. . .chunk! It finally gets to be mechanical with them. And I've won another pot.

I've stolen so many pots I couldn't begin to count them. And most of the time, I've actually had to force myself to bet. I'd be playing and I hadn't held a hand all night. Yet. . .I won every pot because I hadn't bet into the nuts yet.

It goes on and on like that. I pick up a hand and I've got nothing. The Flop comes out there and I've still got nothing. So I kind of have to hit myself to bet at it because there's a guy I've been pounding on and pounding on. And, all the time, I'm thinking *"how can he throw his hand away this time"*? But I bet. . .and away it goes. Chunk!. . .one more time.

If he takes a stand and raises me. . .it gets back to my basic philosophy. If I've got a hand. . .I'll go with it — even though I know it's sometimes the worst hand.

By now, you should have a very good idea of how I play No–Limit Hold 'em. I hope this somewhat lengthy introduction gave you a sufficient "feel" for my style of play. . .and I also hope it will help you to understand how I play specific hands in various situations. I'll discuss those shortly.

However, when you read those discussions you should realize it's quite difficult to state **exactly** what I'd do with a specific hand in a particular situation. So many things are involved. No-Limit Hold 'em is a very complex game.

Most of the things I'll say will be an accurate reflection of what I'd **generally** do. But, I might do something else — or even something completely opposite — depending on who's in the pot with me and whether or not I have position on him.

> **Always remember...No-Limit Hold 'em is a game of position — and people.**

There'll be a lot of times when only your good judgment will dictate the proper play. Situations will come up all the time when a hard-and-fast rule will prove inadequate. Poker — especially No-Limit Hold 'em — is **not** a game you can learn to play well in "ten easy lessons". A thousand **hard** lessons might not be enough. There are simply too many variables involved. Even the most sophisticated computer in the world would be unequal to the task.

Nevertheless, the "lessons" you'll soon be learning will go a long way in helping you to master No-Limit Hold 'em. The **general** principles and concepts that I'll discuss about the play of specific hands will give you a far greater command of the game than almost all the players you could expect to be competing with. I wish I knew all the general guidelines you'll soon be reading when I first started to play. It would've made things a lot easier for me. That's for sure.

But before I get into how you should (generally) play specific hands...there should be a discussion of the ante, betting structure, bankroll requirements and other considerations you'll have to make before you sit-in on a No-Limit Hold 'em game. So that's what I'll do now.

THE ANTE
and
other considerations

If I had to choose a particular size game that would be close to "perfect" for No-Limit Hold 'em...it would be nine-handed. Of course, I'm talking about a *Ring* (full) game.

Actually I prefer to play in a short-handed game with about four or five players. The reason is that in a short-handed game — with a high ante — you're forced to get in there and play. You can't just sit there and wait for the big Pairs or Ace-King or even small connecting cards. If you do..."*you'll go like Broomcorn's uncle*". So, a game like that suits my style just fine. It gives me plenty of room to muscle the game.

A "full" game with nine players is all right, too. That's just about the right amount of players for a Ring game where there'll be good action. I mean, there'll be people coming in the pots because they'll know they won't have to be looking at the nuts every hand.

However, when that nine-handed game all of a sudden turns into an eleven-handed game...well, the complexion of the game changes completely. What was once a relatively fast and loose game becomes a thing of the past. The players no longer get in there and play as often. The game begins to screw down real tight.

There's a lot **more combinations** out every hand with eleven players than with nine players. So everyone **stops** playing borderline hands and they start waiting for the really good ones. In short, they **don't** do as much gambling...so the action really dries-up.

Many Poker games are like that — and they stay like that unless "something" happens to change the character of the game. More than anything else, the "something" that'll change that tight game back to the loose game it once was is for one of the players to start giving a lot of action. As I've said...that's what I do. I'm known as an action–player. It's an image I've always had. Because I give action...I get it.

I mean, I'll get into a Poker game and almost from the very first hand I'll start gambling. I'll be taking chances... betting...raising...re–raising...moving–in. That'll stir–up a game real fast. One player can do it. That's all it takes. And that player's usually me.

I don't merely talk loose...I prove I'm loose by my actions. You kow the old cliche: *"a first impression is a lasting impression"*. Well, that first impression I create lasts throughout the session...even though I might *change gears* (go from loose to tight to loose) several times during the course of a game.

Being able to adjust your playing *speed* is a very important part of being a top player. There are a lot of reasons for this.

(1) You **never** want to get yourself stuck in an identifiable pattern. You **must** mix–up your play. If you do...you'll always keep your opponents guessing.

(2) As I said, you also want to create an image... the image of a loose, gambling–type of player who gives a lot of action. But, it has to be the image of a **good** loose player — **not** the image of a fool who's *throwing a party* (giving his money away).

(3) Since you'll most likely get off loser if you play as I recommend and start *plunging around* (playing very loose) almost as soon as you begin to play...you'll have to *gear down* (start playing tight) after you've laid your (image-creating) groundwork. Then you'll start play-ing loose again...and you'll continue to vary your *speed* throughout the session.

(4) You'll also want to adjust your speed to the varying speeds of particular players. If there's a guy in the game who's *speeding around*...then

you do exactly the opposite by gearing down — and remember to play **only solid hands** against him. On the other hand, if you notice that a certain player is playing real tight... then you can start bluffing at him.

(5) The game itself might dictate the speed at which you'll have to play. If everyone is playing real loose and all the pots are being jammed...then you start playing real tight. Conversely, when the game's so tight you can hear it squeaking...you should play loose and pick-up all the pots you can.

(6) When players start dropping out of the game (and their seats **remain** vacant)...you have to move into "high gear". As I said, you **can't** sit back and wait in a short-handed game. If you do, the ante will get you because the good hands **don't** come often enough. So you **must** *play*...or you might as well quit the game.

(7) And, of course, there's the ante. That's the main thing that determines how fast you play. Actually, the absolute size of the ante is **not** what's important. It's the relationship of the ante to the amount of money you have. A $10 ante in a No-Limit game would be quite high if all you had was $500. But, if you had $5000...that $10 ante would be very low. In the first (high-ante) game...you'd have to play pretty fast. You could slow down considerably in the latter (low-ante) game.

The ante is such an important determining factor as to how fast you play that the *trouble* and *trash* hands I later discuss would become big hands if you were anteing high enough. In fact, that's the case in the World Championship Hold 'em Tournament because of the way it's structured. It starts with each player anteing $10 and there's a $50 Blind. According to a predetermined time schedule — and, as players are eliminated — the ante and Blind get higher and higher as the tournament progresses...until it's down to the final two players. At that point, each player antes $1000 and blinds it for $2000. If you sit around and wait putting in that kind of money every pot...you'll go faster than Broomcorn's uncle.

You've got to play **almost every hand** when you're anteing that high. At the very least, you've got to see the Flop. So, it's really **not** all that surprising I won the 1976 and 1977 World Championships with "trash" hands. The only thing that is surprising is that in both years the hands were almost identical.

In 1976, when I won $220,000, the last pot had $176,000 in it. I won that pot with the **10♠-2♠**. All it had on the Flop was a Pair of Deuces...but I caught two *running* Tens on Fourth and Fifth. Jesse Alto (a very experienced **non-professional** who owns an automobile dealership in Houston, Texas) was the man who came in second.

As you know, in 1977, Bones was the young man who came in second to me. (He's a Pro who's now living in Las Vegas, but is originally from Los Angeles, California.) In the last pot with Bones I had a **10♦-2♥** and flopped a Pair of Tens. This time, I caught a Deuce on Fourth St. — but I filled up with a Ten on the end. That last pot was worth $130,000 and I won $340,000 in the 1977 Tournament.

Of course, in a normal-ante Ring game, it would be a rare case when I'd play those hands. There's little reason to when the ante doesn't "force" you to play. A major exception would be when I play a pot for the sole reason of trying to steal it. Then, it doesn't make any difference what I have. I mean, I could be playing the hand **without even looking at my hole cards**. At such a time, I'd be playing my money, my position and a particular player. My hand wouldn't matter. If I was forced to look at it (because I got played with), I might find two Aces, Ace-King...or trash.

You'll almost surely have to get some No-Limit experience under your belt before you'll be able to play a pot completely blind. So, in the beginning, I suggest that you restrict the way you'll play specific hands to the recommen-dations I'll soon be making. However, it's important for you to understand that those recommendations as to the hands you should play and the way you should play them are what I would do in a normal or medium-ante Ring (nine-handed full) game. In a game different from that...you'll have to adjust your play as previously discussed.

In order to help you determine what constitutes a normal (medium-ante) game, you should use the following table as a guide.

NINE-HANDED GAME — NO LIMIT HOLD 'EM

Type of ANTE-GAME general description	ANTE with each player	single BLIND 1st Seat only	multiple BLINDS			BUY-IN* absolute minimum
			Button	1st Seat	2nd Seat	
Very Low	$ 1	$ 2	$ 1	$ 2	$ 5	$ 200
Low	2	5	2	5	10	400
Medium	5	10	5	10	25	1000
High	10	25	10	25	50	2000
Very High	25	100	25	50	100	5000

*Twice the *minimum* buy-ins listed here would be much better. More than twice would be better still.

In the above table, the *very low* ante game where each player antes $1 (with or without the Blind) would be approximately equivalent to the game with the multiple Blinds of $1, $2 and $5. Assuming there are nine players, it would cost you $9 a Round in the first case. (It would be an additional $2 if each player had to take the Blind once a Round.) In the game with the three Blinds, it would only be $8 a Round. As you can see, it doesn't make much difference whether everyone antes or the multiple Blind structure is used.

Sometimes, the game is structured where the "dealer" (*Button*) and the first Blind have to blind it for an identical amount. This would be the case when the Blinds in the *low* ante game were $5, $5 and $10 instead of the $2, $5 and $10 seen in the table. Also, there are some games that have **four** Blinds. The effect of that would be to move a game as classified in the table to a higher classification. For example, a game with four Blinds of $5, $10, $25 and $50 would be a *high* ante game...**not** a *medium* ante game.

Of course, all the terms in the table from *very low* to *very high* are applied to the ante on an **absolute** basis. That is, because of the antes, they would be called very small and very big No-Limit games, respectively. But, when you consider the various games listed **relative** to the **minimum buy-ins** in the table...there's actually very little difference between them. (To get around the table in each of the games shown, it'll cost you about 4% of your buy-in if you sit down with an absolute minimum buy.)

You wouldn't want to sit down with less than the minimum buys shown. As the footnote states, you should definitely consider buying-in for more.

When I play in a game with three Blinds of $25, $50 and $100...I never sit down with less than $20,000. What's more...I like to have as much as (or more money than) any other player at the table. If my stacks are not approximately equal to the guy with the most money then I couldn't break him, could I?

And...I practice what I preach. I start playing fast right away. I've always played like that. Even when I was just starting out. Back then I'd buy-in for a thousand (in a small No-Limit game) and I'd usually get *stuck* (lose) that first thousand. Then, I'd *pull-up* and start playing tighter and I almost always got even...or won.

About three out of four plays, I'd lose that first thousand...but, on that fourth play, I'd get on a *rush* (winning streak) and I'd more than make up for those first three losses. I mean, I'd be playing so fast and winning so many hands when I was rushing that I'd literally break every player in the game. It's because whenever I hold a bunch of hands, I usually get action on them.

I've never won a bunch of pots *on the bank* (watching the other guys play). If I'm *striking* (making a bunch of hands)...I'm in there — I'm **not** on the side. **If you're going to have a rush...you've got to let yourself have one.** You've got to sustain that rush. And to do that, you've got to get in there and play.

After I've won a pot in No-Limit...I'm in the next pot — *regardless of what two cards I pick*

up. **And if I win that one. . .I'm always in the
next one. I keep playing every pot until I lose
one. And, in all those pots, I gamble more
than I normally would.**

If you don't play that way. . .you'll **never** have much of a
rush. I know that scientists **don't** believe in rushes. . .but
they make about fifteen hundred a month. I've played Poker
for almost 25 years now. . .and I've made millions at it. A big
part of my winnings came from playing my rushes.

There's only one world–class Poker player that I know
of who **doesn't** believe in rushes. Well, he's wrong. . .and so
are the "scientists". Besides, how many of them can play
Poker anyway?

If you want to take the money off. . .I mean, make a big
score. . .then, you've got to play your rushes. It's that simple.

At this point, you should have a very good feel for my
style of play. It should help you to understand and
appreciate the things I'm going to say about the way I play
specific hands. . .from before the Flop on through each stage
of play until all the cards are out.

In all the situations that I'll shortly discuss, an
important assumption has been made. That is:

> *Unless otherwise noted,* **the way I'd play a
> specific hand at No–Limit Hold 'em is how I'd
> play it in a pot against other** *top* **Poker
> players. . .and** *not* **the way I'd play it against a
> weak player.**

The reason that assumption has been made is because,
as you already know, against a weak player (or a drunk) you
have to play quite differently. All you try to do against a
weak player is make the best hand and then extract from
him the largest amount of money you can. Just outplay him.

HOW TO PLAY SPECIFIC HANDS

An important qualification you must be aware of before reading what follows is that the recommendations I make are how you should **generally** play the hands discussed. That's the way I **generally** play them. But, you should **never** fall into a pattern playing Poker. I don't. I always vary my play...I try to mix it up as much as I can. I **never** consistently repeat my action on any, hand. I **don't** play like a computer that's programmed to do the same routine over and over again. The high-quality of players I play against on a regular basis would easily detect a pattern to my play if there was any. So I **never** do the same thing with the same hand from the same position against the same player. I'm always changing speeds during the course of a game.

However, for your purposes, my playing recommendations for a particular hand are a good way for you to play them...until your opponents learn your style. When they do...you start *shifting gears* — up and down continuously — until there is **no** noticeable pattern.

I'm going to break the game down into four major — and very broad — categories as follows:

- I. **PAIRS**
- II. **SMALL CONNECTING CARDS**
- III. **BORDERLINE HANDS**
- IV. **TRASH HANDS**

How to play your hand when you have a Pair in the pocket is going to be discussd first. That category will be sub-divided and discussed as follows:

- a. **Big Pairs — A-A, K-K and A-K**
- b. **Q-Q**
- c. **J-J down to 2-2**

I've grouped an Ace-King with a Pair of Aces and a Pair of Kings because it's a very strong hand. As you'll learn, I would rather have A-K than A-A or K-K.

I'll discuss each of the hands as I'd play them in a nine-handed game from an **early** position (first three seats), **middle** position (next three seats) and **late** position (last three seats). A medium-ante game is assumed (unless otherwise noted).

A-A and K-K
how to play
before the Flop

With a Pair of Aces or Kings in an early position before the Flop...I would probably limp-in with them (*just* **call** the Blind) hoping that somebody would raise it behind me so I could re-raise.

In a middle position — if nobody in the early seats came in — I would play them the same way. But, if somebody in the early seats did come in...I'd put in a raise with them (of about the size of the pot).

In a late position, I'd obviously raise with them and hope that somebody *trailed their hand around* to me — that is, slow-played their hand so they could re-raise me. If they did, I'd play-back, of course, and might move-in depending on the circumstances. If I did play-back and got about half my money in the pot before the Flop with two Aces or two Kings...there'd be no question that I'd get the rest of it in on the Flop — regardless of what came on the Turn. Nothing could stop me. If my opponent didn't set me in on the Flop...I'd move it all-in myself. The reason I'd do that is because there are too many ways I could outguess myself... and I'm **not** going to try. If I get either of those big Pairs cracked...well, I'm just going to have to lose my money.

Conversely, a rare situation could exist where you'd consider throwing away two Kings before the Flop when you got raised. It's a hard hand to get away from. . .but if a real tight player moved-in on you — a player you know to be so tight that he **wouldn't** make that kind of play unless he had two Aces — then, you might want to throw them away. Of course, you'd have to be almost certain about your man before you'd do that. One way I make this rare decision is to put myself in my opponent's position. I ask myself if I'd re-raise (if I were him) with two Queens (or less). If the answer is NO. . .I'd throw the two Kings away.

I'm going to discuss how to play a big Pair **on the Flop** in a moment. But, this is a good point to note that when you have two Kings and there's a *single* Ace on the Flop. . .it's complete judgment as to whether or not you should go on with your hand. If you put your opponent on an Ace* . . .that's the end of the pot right there. If not. . .you play your two Kings as if you had the best hand.

A-A and K-K
how to play
on the Flop

Regardless of the hand you have, the Flop is where you'll make your most crucial decisions. It's **THE** *key point* in the hand. It's where you put people on hands. . .decide what they've probably got. Usually, everything after the Flop is more or less cut-and-dried.

---

*There's a lot of very interesting facts on Hold 'em probabilities in the *Appendix*. **Particularly relevant here are the following two facts:**

(1) In a nine-handed game, when you have two Kings, the probability that no other player has an Ace is about 20%. . .or, a player *will* have an *Ace* about 80% of the time. (See *"Hold 'em — Absence of Aces before the Flop . . .by numbers of players."*)

(2) Also, an Ace (with two unpaired cards less than Kings) will flop about 18% of the time. (See *"Hold 'em — Flops for selected hands: Selection B."*)

Of course, you put people on hands before the Flop, too...but, on the Flop, you're in a much better position to determine what a man probably has by the way he calls — whether he's drawing to a Straight or Flush and so forth.

I play a Pair of Aces or Kings very cautiously from an early position when there's three cards that'll make a Straight or a Flush on the Flop. This is especially true if there are two or more people in the pot with me. The guys that called behind me are liable to have anything. In that position, they've either got a hand that could break me...or I'll win a very small pot if I bet. So, in an early position, a bell rings (reminding me **not** to bet) when I see three to a Straight or Flush on the Flop when I've got Aces or King in the pocket. Consequently, I immediately start playing that hand slow...and usually I just check in a front position.

Now, if I'm in a late seat...and somebody had *trailed-in* in the early seats...I might go ahead and bet once. If I got called...I would immediately become defensive again with that hand. **Anytime** there's three cards to a Straight or Flush, I play the hand with extreme caution.

The quality of the possible Straight that's out there also has a big influence on the way I'd play that big Pair. If it came 9-8-7, 10-9-8 or J-10-9 and I've got two people in the pot with me...**I immediately give it up.** Almost any two cards that those two people have will fit into those Flops somehow. They're either going to have a hand that's already got me beat or they're going to have a hand to draw at that would make my hand no better than even-money shot.

If it comes 10-9-8 and one of them's got a Q-J...then, he's got the Straight made. If he's got a J-10...then, he's got a Pair with an open-end Straight draw. He could catch a Seven, a Ten, a Jack or a Queen. Anyone of those cards will beat me. There are 13 of them* in the deck and he's got two shots at them. That makes his hand as good as mine at that point — he's almost exactly even-money to beat me — so I don't want to put myself in jeopardy and get myself in a position where I could get broke.

---

*4-Sevens, 4-Queens, 3-Jacks and 2-Tens.

I **don't** always give up the pot in that situation. I just play extremely cautiously. That is, I **don't** charge. . .and try to win the pot right there.

If just a J-10 falls — say the Flop is a J-10-2 — well, there I'd really play my two Aces because any combination of big cards would give, my opponent some kind of hand. A King-Queen will give him an open-end Straight draw. . .an A-K will give him two overcards and a belly-Straight draw. . .an A-J, K-J, Q-J, A-10, Q-10, or K-10 will give him a Pair — so I'd go ahead and play my two Aces in that situation. If he's got Jacks and Tens (or better). . .well, more power to him because he's got a hand with which he can win a big pot from me.

> **If you know your player. . .you'll be able to figure out what hand he's likely to have. You have to use common logic in putting your opponent on a hand.**

I'm **not** as leery of a three-card Flush on the Flop as I am a three-card Straight. There's not as many possible hands that could beat you. . .although a guy could have a Pair and a Flush draw if he's in there with you.

The first thing I'd do would be to see if either one of my two Aces (or Kings) matched the cards out there. If three Hearts fell. . .and I had two red Aces. . .I would immediately play that hand. It's a big hand. But if I had the two black Aces or **didn't** have the A♡. . .I might be a little more hesitant to play it.

As I said, if I had the A♡. . .I'd play the hand fast on the Flop. If I get called. . .I'm in a position to win it anyway. I know where the nuts are.

> **That's one of the most important things about No-Limit Hold 'em. If you can avoid it. . .you never want to get your money in dead.**

You **don't** want to be drawing for a Flush wh n there's a Pair on the Board. A man could have a Full House. And, you **don't** want to be drawing to a Straight when another man could have a Flush. If the Board comes three Hearts and you've got an open-end Straight draw — you **don't** draw at that Straight. You throw your hand away. All the top players try to keep from ever getting their money in completely dead.

If there's a Pair and a Rag on the Flop. . .and I had a Pair of Aces or Kings in the pocket. . .I'd bet at that pot from an early position. If I got called. . .then, I'd proceed cautiously. I mean, when the next card was turned. . .I'd check it to him. If he bet. . .maybe I'd call it or maybe I wouldn't. It would depend on what I felt that he had. I mean, I'd know he's got something that he likes.

For example, if the Turn is 6-6-2 and I bet and he calls. . .he's telling me he's got some kind of hand. He's probably got a Pair in the pocket (anywhere from Sevens to Tens) or else he's got a Six or 3-Deuces. So, I'd use my judgment at that point. . .and I'd be cautious again.

If there were a couple of players in the pot in front of me — and one of them turned a Set (of Sixes) — he'd probably check it to me. That's what most players do in that situation. They check a Set into the raiser. But, as you know, that's the **wrong** way to play it. A *player* would **know** the right thing to do is to lead into you.

If it was checked to me — and there **wasn't** a Straight draw on the Board (say the Flop was 7-7-2) — I might check it also. . .and give a free card. I'd do that for two reasons:

(1) **If he didn't have a hand, I'd want him to help his hand enough to continue playing. For example, if a Jack or Queen fell off on Fourth St., it might pair him.**

(2) **Another reason I'd check would be to eliminate the possibility that I'd get broke if he does have a Seven.**

But, if the Flop was 6-6-2. . .I would bet. . .because I wouldn't want a Three, Four or Five falling off and making somebody a Straight.

> In brief...you *don't* give *free* cards where that *free* card could break you. If there's a possible Straight or Flush *draw* on Board...you *don't* give a *free* card.

A Flop that's 6-6-5 is a lot different (because there's a Straight draw) than one that's 6-6-K. If I had two Aces with the latter Flop and it was checked to me...I'd probably check it back. If he's got a King...he's going to play it on the Turn (Fourth St.) because you've made him think he's got the best hand when you check — plus, if he does have a Six, as before, you might be able to hold your losses to a minimum.

> **What it all boils down to is that with a Pair of Aces or Kings...you're waiting until you get kind of a cinch hand before you really play a big pot. You're *not* looking to play a big pot where you might have only a small percentage the best of it or one where you're a big underdog.**

In general, with those big Pairs on the Flop...you play them a little more aggressively from a late position than from an early position. Also, you **shouldn't** be concerned that someone might be checking the nuts to you (such as 3-Sixes in the examples used). You **never** worry about that. I've heard people say: "*Well, I was afraid to bet because I was afraid he'd raise me.*" **Never** worry about getting raised. You have to go ahead and play and if it happens, it happens... and then you worry about it. **Don't** cross that bridge **until** you come to it.

> **You *can't* play winning Poker by playing safe all the time. You must take chances...gamble. And you have to *feel* aggressive to *play* aggressively. That's my style of Poker. And it's a winning style.**

I've re-stated my general philosophy of play at this point because I'm discussing the play of a Pair of Aces or

Kings in the hole. In most cases, I play them slowly (not slow-play them). That is, I play them cautiously. This is **contrary** (to my **general** style of play and) to the way most people play them. Most players feel that they're so hard to come by that when they do get them they want to win a big pot with them. So they play them real fast. That's usually wrong. (But, there are exceptions I'll soon discuss.)

The fact is, with a Pair of Aces or Kings...one of two things will usually happen. Either:

(1) You'll win a small pot

or

(2) You'll lose a big pot

The reason the above is so is because a player is not going to get a lot of money in the pot unless he can beat your big Pair or when he has a Straight or Flush draw. In the latter case, as you'll soon see, I'm going to make him pay to draw to his hand.

Another time I play two Aces or Kings **slowly** is in the rare instance a Set of Trips flops — say, 3-Sevens or 3-Jacks. But, this time I do it for somewhat different reasons. Now...I want someone in the pot with me to *catch-up* (improve his hand). So I check it...but, *just* **one time**. I want to give them a free card — so they can catch a Pair...or give them a chance to bluff at it.

It's tough to win anything in that spot by leading off...unless you catch somebody with a Pair in the pocket.

Of course, there's a small chance you could run into a Set of Fours. But, anyone who made that hand will "let you know" they made it by the way they put all their money in the pot. It takes experience to recognize something like that...but it's just like any other situation where somebody's betting the pure nuts at you. You have to use judgment to evaluate it. After a while, you recognize it. As always...it boils back down to people.

The one situation where I stand to lose a very big pot with a Pair of Aces (or Kings) is when there's two to a

Straight or Flush on the Flop. For example, there's a J–10–2 out there. If somebody bet at me...I'd move–in a lot of chips. I could win the pot right there. If not...they're really going to pay to draw to their hand. If I was first to act, I'd check...hoping I'd get to raise it. (It's one of the few times I check–raise.)

If I get called, I'll probably put my opponent on a Straight (or Flush) draw. And, of course, on Fourth St. — I'll go ahead and bet again if a *Blank* (meaningless card) fell.

Again, a lot of judgment's involved...because my opponent might have been fortunate enough to make some kind of hand that would beat my two Aces (such as Jacks and Tens). In that case, I'd go ahead and pay him off... because, as I said earlier, I'm **not** going to try to out–guess myself.

If the Board fell completely ragged, say a 10–6–5, I would bet from any position. As in all the hands I discussed, there's always the chance that someone could've turned a Set. But, again, I'm going to cross that bridge if and when I come to it.

In this situation, I'd know if my big Pair was beat... especially if I had raised with my hand from an early position before the Flop. All good Hold 'em players would interpret that as a sign of strength. I mean, the first thing you usually give a man (credit for) when he raises (especially the weaker players) is a big Pair.

So if it comes a 10–6–5 (and I had raised from an early position)...the other players will think that I have a strong hand — possibly a big Pair, which I've actually got. Then...when I bet on the Flop and get raised by somebody in a late position...it gets back to people again. You've just got to know your players. He's representing to you that he can beat a big Pair. If he's a good, solid–type player...what else can he have besides a Set of Trips or, possibly, Two–Pair? So, you make up your mind right there whether or not to go ahead with your two Aces (or two Kings).

Of course, it's possible that he could have a Pair of Queens or Jacks in a back position and didn't raise you before the Flop...and, now, on the Flop (because he's got an overpair) he's decided to test you. Then, you might want to call his raise one time...if it's **not** too big a bet. The next time, you check it to him and see what he does. If he bets again...he's usually there.

Up to now, I've discussed how I'd play a Pair of Aces or Kings on the Flop *assuming* I *didn't* **turn anything that helped my hand**. Now, I'll discuss the situations where I get some help.

If I turn a Set...I **never** *slow-play* it (with the exception of a situation I'll soon discuss). I almost always come right out and bet...and I **don't** make just a nominal bet. I make an extra-large bet because the only way you'll win a big pot is when somebody else turns something with you...or puts you on a bluff...or tries to run you down. So...I really come out smokin' right there.

You might remember the point I made earlier (on page 337) that *"when you have a Pair of Aces and a single Ace flops (giving you a Set of Trips)...there'll always be the possibility that the next card off could make someone a Straight."* The reason why that's so can be seen in the examples below.

FLOP *A*

With a **single** Ace on the Flop **and** any card Five-or-under...there's always a draw to a Five-high Straight. As in **FLOP** *A*...if a Deuce, Trey or Five fell on Fourth St. — it **could** make someone a small Straight.

The same thing applies whenever there's a **single** Ace on the Flop **with** any card Ten-or-above.

FLOP *B*

With **FLOP** *B*...a King, Queen or Ten on Fourth would mean someone **might** have made an Ace–high Straight.

If there's **no** draw to a Straight that **includes** an Ace, then there'll be a draw to a medium-Straight because there'd have to be a two–card combination of the other four cards...namely, a Six, Seven, Eight or Nine (an example of which is below).

FLOP *C*

The Straight possibility is more obvious with something like **FLOP** *C* because there are seven different Straights that can be made. (If anyone has a J–10, J–8, 10–8, 10–6, 8–6, 8–5 or a 6–5...they could make a Straight with the next card off.)

You should always keep this interesting discovery in mind whenever you see what appears to be a raggedy Flop with an Ace in it. The threat that someone could make a Straight will **always** be present.

So when you flop a Set of Aces, you **immediately** go to betting — and you bet a **large** amount to prevent somebody from drawing at an inside Straight cheaply. A **good** player will know it's worth it to take a cheap draw at a belly-Straight...and, if he makes it, he can break you.

However, if you flop a Set with two Kings...you could possibly give a free card when it comes ragged where there's **no** Straight or Flush draw. For example, say a K-8-2 falls. Now, you can give a card with that Flop because you'd have the nuts if any card other than an Ace, Eight or Deuce fell. An Ace might give someone 3-Aces and an Eight or Deuce could possibly make someone Four-of-a-kind. Since you **don't** realistically worry about a Set of Fours...you really want an Eight or Deuce to hit the Board on Fourth St.

In the rare instance when you turn a Set of Fours (say, four Aces) you're happy to have them...but you really **don't** have a very profitable hand. You've got the deck crippled. There's nothing left that your opponents can have. (The situation illustrated on page 345 is so rare that you might not see four Aces get beaten like that in a lifetime of playing Hold 'em.)

So, when you turn a hand that big, you just have to check along and maybe try to win a small bet on the end. Or — if you're extremely fortunate — you might get somebody to try to bluff at it. They just might try to pick-up the pot by representing **your** hand. You **could** get lucky that way. But, most of the time, you just play it very slow and take what you can get...meaning that you always bet on the end from any position.

Another time I would almost always check it is when I flopped the *big Full* (the highest possible Full House). And, that's what you would have with two Aces if the Flop was A-3-3 or with two Kings if it came K-7-7.* You'd have some leverage then so you could give them a free card. (There's an exception to giving a free card which I'll discuss shortly.) After you check it once...you then bet on Fourth...hoping that somebody hit something there.

Whenever you've got a hand that's so big you've got the deck crippled or one that's very **unlikely** to get beaten...you should play it very slow on the Flop for two reasons:

---

*With an Ace (or Aces) on the Board, you might *not* have the big Full with a Pair of Kings.

(1) First, you want to give your opponents a chance to bluff; and

(2) You want to give them a chance to catch something if they *don't* bluff.

With a Pair of Aces or Kings, there's a chance you could flop a Straight or Flush draw. It would almost always be a gutshot Straight draw (with the exception of a Q-J-10 when you had Kings). In any case, if I flopped a Straight draw, I'd be cautious with my hand. You're probably beat at that point because any Flop that would give you a Straight draw could easily make your opponent Two-Pair. I wouldn't fool with that hand.

But, if I've got the two red Aces and three Diamonds flop...well, as I noted earlier, that's a very big hand. I'd *play that hand from the hip*...and I'd be willing to put all my money in with it.

> **You should always remember that the Flop is practically the whole game in Hold 'em. That's where your major decisions will be made. The play on Fourth St. and Fifth St. is pretty basic.**

For example, on the Flop, you put your opponent(s) on a particular hand. And, all your thinking follows from that. If you think he's drawing at a Club Flush...you bet. You must make your opponents pay to make their draws. If the Club doesn't come on Fourth St. — you bet again. Obviously, if the Club comes...you check it — if you think your opponent made his hand.

> **If you think you're beat, naturally, you check it...and if you think your opponent's drawing ...you bet. That's the whole thing.**

On the end (Fifth St.), if it looks like your opponent has missed his hand...there's usually no reason to bet any further. So you just show your hand over. . .or you check it and give him a chance to bluff.

That's No-Limit Hold 'em in a nutshell. . ..but, as you know, it's a far more complex game than that.

A-A and K-K
how to play
on Fourth and Fifth

So far I've given you **general** guidelines on how to play a Pair of Aces or Kings before and on the Flop. I'll continue to discuss the play of those big Pairs in the latter stages of action (Fourth and Fifth Sts.). Later, I'll also discuss how I'd play various other hands at the different betting points.

> **But, when you read the discussions you should always be aware that my advice is of a** *general* **nature. I keep re-emphasizing this because it's so important that you understand it. There's** *not* **a single play I make that's of an absolute nature. I mean. . .***there's no play that I'll make with a particular hand.* **Every hand I play is subject to be played differently depending on the circumstances at the time. The standards I have — the ones you've read (and will read) —** *generally* **guide me (as they should you). But, sometimes, even I** *don't* **know exactly what I'm going to do until the situation comes up. Whatever my** *first feeling* **(impression) is at the time — I'd go with that.**

For example, I said I'd check my Pair of Aces (one time) if there was an open Set of Trips on the Flop. On Fourth St., if a man made a big bet or if I bet and he moved-in on me. . .I'd probably go ahead and pay him off. If a man's lucky enough to flop a Set of Fours when I've got two Aces. . .he'd have to show me the fourth one — unless I've got a lot of money in front of me and there's **not** too much money in the pot.

I'll put some numbers on what I'm talking about so it'll be more clearly defined. However, even what I say now I might **not** do (or do just the opposite) at a particular time. It would depend. On a lot of things. Especially the guy in the pot with me. What do I know about him? So it's back to people again. Nevertheless, here's what I **might** do.

Let's say there's $20,000 in the pot. I've got $70,000 on the table. My opponent's got $20,000. . .and he moves-in on me. In that case, I'd probably pay him off. . .if I knew him to be a *Player* (as opposed to a *Rock*).

However, if my opponent also had $70,000 and overbet the pot by moving-in his entire stack. . .well, then I'm **not** sure what I'd do. As I said, I'd go with my *feelings*. I'd look at him. . .and then I'd decide.

To start with. . .if he made a move like that. . .I'd turn my hand face-up on the Board. And I'd watch him real close. I'd want to see what his reaction was when I turned the two Aces up. It would take a strong man **not** to show some kind of emotion. And from the emotion I saw, I'd judge whether he had a Set of Fours or not. Then I'd react according to whichever way I felt.

As I noted, you continue to bet your big Pair on Fourth St. when it rags-off and it **doesn't** look like it completed the Straight or Flush draw that showed on the Flop. If your opponent(s) want to draw again. . .you make them pay for it.

In the situation where **you** flopped a Set, you should also continue to bet on Fourth even if it **does** look like someone could've completed a Straight. You can't worry about it because you **don't** know which Straight it is (and if it was made at all). Just disregard any Straight card. . .and go ahead and bet.

But, if a *third* **Flush** card fell on Fourth. . .then I'd probably check it. If someone bet. . .I'd call it. I'd be thinking that I was probably beat. . .but I'd be trying to make a Full. I mean, I wouldn't know for sure that I was beat. . .but I'd call knowing there was a strong possibility I was. And I'd call a pretty big bet.

If the man moved all-in on me in that spot, I'd probably give him credit for the Flush. Then it would be simple mathematics whether or not a call was justified. There'd be ten cards out of the 45 left that would help my hand.* That means it's 35 to 10 (or 3½ to 1) that I **don't** improve my hand. If the pot's laying me more than 3½ to 1. . .I'd call. If not. . .I'd throw my hand away.

Of course, the above math **only applies** when you feel very strongly that your opponent has the Flush made. If you thought you could have the hand wrong — where the man **might** have the second (highest) Set of Trips (or some other hand) — then, you might call if the pot was laying you only 3 to 1. You could accept a smaller price because you have some doubts.

So much depends on your judgment in situations like that. This is especially true on the end (Fifth St.). If I didn't make my Full there. . .it would be complete judgment if I was forced to call another bet.

When I discussed how I'd play my big Pair when I flopped a Full (on page 463), I said I'd *"almost always"* check it. The exception would be when two of the cards on the Flop were **suited** (or maybe even two to a Straight). In that case, I would **not** check on the Flop. I would bet. I'd be trying to get a man in there drawing to a Flush and hoping that he'd make it so I could break him. And, if a Flush card did come on Fourth St. — I'd make a big bet. . .expecting to be raised. . .hoping to be raised.

I'd play the hand similarly if I had flopped a Set and the Board paired on the end making my Full and at the **same time** making a possible Flush for somebody. Whenever you've got a Full and a three-Flush comes, it's **exactly** the situation you're looking for. You go ahead and bet — even an extraordinarily big bet — and you can break your opponent. (You should **not**, by the way, bet as much with a

---

*The case (last) Ace is *assumed* **to be still in the deck and so are three each of the other three cards on the Board that could pair and make my Full.**

three-card Straight out there because your opponent **may** *not* **have** the nut Straight. He may even be drawing. So, in either case, if you've got him *dead*...you'd want him to play his Straight if he made it **or** you want him to draw at it...and a very big bet might scare him off.)

In the case where you flopped a Set and the Board pairs on Fourth or Fifth...but there's **no** possible Straight or Flush out there (say the Board is A♠, 6♡, J♣, J◇)...you should lead with your Full. **Don't** slow-play it. In fact, you should make a **big** bet (bigger than the size of the pot).

There's a good possibility that your opponent was calling you on the Flop with the Second Button (or possibly the Third Button). So, when the Board paired, it might've made him a strong hand...and you'd be in a position to break him. He'd probably play-back if he made Trips when the Board paired. Also, knowing your aggressive style of play, he might think you're trying to represent **his** hand...and you might get a good play because of that.

But, if a Flush draw was out there on the Flop and the Pair on Fourth **didn't** complete the Flush...well, then I'd make a **small** bet (smaller than the size of the pot). I want him to call so he'd have an opportunity to make the Flush on the last card.

The situations I've been discussing are those where you've made a *very* **big** hand with your two Aces or Kings...and the way you should play it in order to extract the most you can from your opponent(s). It's more likely that you **won't** make a big hand and will have to play a Pair of Aces or Kings **very carefully** in certain instances on Fourth and Fifth Sts.

For example, if there were three Rags on the Flop and then the Board paired on Fourth or Fifth...I'd *definitely* **slow down**. This is **not** the same situation as when a Pair came on the Flop. When the Pair shows **after** the Flop, the possibility is **much stronger** that it helped your opponent there. He's already called you on the Flop...indicating that his cards fit into the community cards. His call clearly meant that he had something — a Pair or some kind of draw. So, I'd be cautious again in that situation.

It's a *somewhat* **different situation** when there are four Rags out there and the Board pairs on Fifth St. Exactly what I'd do would depend on whether I bet the two previous times (on the Flop and on Fourth). . .and on which card was paired. If the top card (and possibly the second card) paired. . .I'd suspect I might be beat. They'd be the two most dangerous Pairs. If the Third, or Fourth Button paired. . .I wouldn't be concerned if I had bet on the Flop and on Fourth St.

Another time you should **not** be at all concerned is when the Flop is, say, 8-8-5 and then the third Eight falls on Fourth (or on the end). You just don't worry about a Set of Fours. . .so actually your hand got stronger on Fourth St. Before the third Eight showed, there was the nagging possibility your opponent had Trips. That's far less likely now. . .and he's probably in there with an overpair.

A very tough situation could exist on Fifth when there's four to a Flush (or Straight). . .and you **don't** have any of it. With a big Pair in that spot, it's back to judgment again. You have to evaluate what you think your opponent was drawing at. . .and whether or not he's got one of the cards that would complete the Straight or Flush.

You should **never** bet in that situation. If he's first and he checks. . .you just show it down. If you were first, you'd check it. If he bet. . .well, you're back to people. You'd just have to evaluate your player.

That situation brings to mind a play I often make. I've played a lot of pots against tight players when I've made a very weak call on Fourth St. hoping the last card will make a four-card Straight or Flush on the Board so I could represent the Straight or Flush by making a big bet. For example, my (tight) opponent has raised before the Flop and I feel he has a big Pair in the pocket. The situation might look like this:

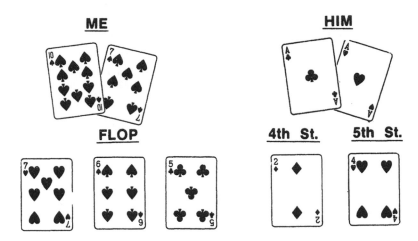

My opponent bets on the Flop and I call. The next card is the 2◊ and if my opponent bets again, I'll call *not* because I think I have the best hand...but because of the tremendous bluffing opportunity I'll have if the last card is a 3, 4, 8 or 9. Either one of those four cards will mean the Board is one card off of a Straight. I'll almost certainly win the pot if I make a substantial bet on the end (representing the Straight) if, as in the example, a Four fell on Fifth. I might also catch a Ten or Seven on the end. I'd win a nice pot in that case, too...so I'm justified in calling on Fourth St. I do a lot of gambling like that on Fourth and on the end. And they're good gambles because I know a tight player wouldn't jeopardize all his money when one card would beat him.

It's not only tough for a tight player to make a call for all his money in a situation like that...it's tough for anyone to do it. But, if you know your player...it does make it easier. If the Straight or Flush is a *back-door* job (made on Fourth and Fifth Sts.), then you may want to reconstruct the play of the entire hand and try to determine whether it's logical that that particular player would go as far as he did to make the hand. Of course, a lot of times a player will literally back into a hand like that. For example, he may have started with a small Pair on the Flop and he might have picked–up a Straight or Flush draw on Fourth. And he got there on the end without really trying.

With two Aces or Kings, you're going to have to use a lot of judgment when all the cards are out and your hand never got better. You'd have to go back to what you originally felt your opponent was drawing at on the Flop and on Fourth St. If you thought he made what he was drawing at on the last card...well, obviously, you'd check it — whether you were first or last to act. If you thought he was drawing at a hand and completely missed it...and you were first — you'd still check. But, this time, you'd be doing it to give him an opportunity to bluff at it. If you were last and it looked like he missed his hand and he checked it to you...you'd just turn your hand over to avoid being wrong in your judgment. He's **not** going to call you if he missed his draw. But, if you put him on the wrong hand to begin with...you could get raised.

A-K — *how to play*
before the Flop

I've already mentioned that I'd rather have Ace-King than either a Pair of Aces or a Pair of Kings. A lot of players will probably find that surprising. But it's not. You'll soon see why.

Of course, I know that an A-K would **never** outrun A-A or K-K if you played them against one another *hot and cold*. An A-K **couldn't** even beat a Pair of Deuces. I know. On a proposition bet, I once took the Deuces and two other guys took the A-K. The proposition was to play the two hands against one another *hot and cold*. We simply dealt out five cards to see which hand would win more times. It was an even–money proposition...and we bet $500 a hand. I won several thousand dollars before they quit.

They weren't convinced the first time because we did it two or three different times. They'd lose some money...and then they'd quit. They'd go away...come back (after doing some "homework") and then we'd do it again. And I'd beat them again.

But, I'm **not** talking about playing *hot and cold* here. Now...I'm talking about playing Poker.

An A–K is a "better" hand than two Aces or two Kings for two very important reasons:

(1) You'll *win more* money when you make a hand with it; and

(2) You'll *lose less* money when you miss a hand with it.

And I can't think of two better reasons than those to prefer an A–K over the very big Pairs.

The reason why you can make more money with an A–K than with two Aces (or Kings) is because it's a drawing–type of hand as opposed to a made hand. I mean, you **don't** have anything with an A–K unless you flop something. So you can get away from it real easy. You're **not** tied–on to it like you might be with a Pair of Aces (or Kings). And that's why you'll lose less money with it.

Another reason why you can make more and lose less with A–K than with the very big Pairs is because when you have A–K and you pair the Ace or King on the Flop...it's **much harder** for your opponent to make his hand if he's playing something like two connecting cards. For example, if someone's playing a 7–6 and the Board comes A–9–8, he hasn't made anything yet...because when you pair one of your hole cards — there can be only **two** cards that'll help him.* But, if you had two Aces *in the pocket*...the Board could come 9–8–5 — or any **three** cards that could help his hand (such as a Pair and a draw). That one **extra** card considerably improves his chances of cracking your Aces.

---

*The exception to this would be when the Flop is three to a big Straight with maybe two to a Flush, like: A♠–J♡–10♠ or K◇–J◇–10♣...and the Ace or King helps both you and your opponent.

Ace-King is also a *more flexible* hand (in the way you can play it) as you'll soon see.

There's also a big difference between A-K *suited* and A-K *offsuit*. (Any time the cards are suited it's a somewhat stronger hand than when they're offsuit. This is especially true with A-K because you can make the nut Flush.) The big difference between the two hands is that it only takes three cards to make a Flush with A-K suited. True, you can make one of two Flushes with A-K offsuit. . .but it takes four cards to make either one. That's a lot harder to do. And, with one of them (the Flush you might make with the King), you may not have the nuts.

In the discussion to follow, the difference between the two hands is sometimes ignored. That is, I'm going to suggest playing them the same way. But, you should always remember that A-K *suited* has more value than A-K *offsuit*. . .and it can always be played a little stronger.

The reason why A-K is **more flexible** than A-A or K-K is because you can play an A-K in the lead or you can play it slow to raise with it. Also, I'd play A-K **from any position** for a reasonable size bet. And, on occasion, I'd get all my money in **before** the Flop (as I'll very shortly discuss).

Specifically, in an early position, I'd *bring-it-in* (raise the Blind) for whatever the normal bring-in was for that particular game. If I was raised, I'd probably call. . .although I **don't** like to call a raise with A-K (as most players do). I like to raise with it.

If I was in a middle position and someone else had brought-it-in. . .I'd just call with it. I **wouldn't** raise because I'd probably be raising just one man. I'd want at least another player to come in.

In a late position, I'd probably raise with it — especially if I was on the Button.

There are times I might even move all-in with an A-K. Let's say I brought-it-in in an early position and a couple of people behind me just called. When it gets to the guy on the Button...he raises. Well...if he did that, I'd think he was trying to pick-up the pot since he'd probably think the only person he had to *come through* (worry about) was me since the two people behind me showed weakness. So I **might** move-in in that situation.

Or, if I was on the Button, and three or four people were already in the pot...I **might** move all-in. At that point, I'd be trying to pick the pot up...even though I'd know if I got called I'd probably be an underdog.

A-K - *how to play* on the Flop

As long as I **don't** help my A-K on the Flop, I'm going to play the hand the same way...regardless of whether or not the Flop might've helped someone else. For example, if three Rags flopped...or a Pair...or three to a Straight or Flush...or anything that did **not** help my hand — the way I play A-K is quite simple. Barring the exception I'll soon note, here's what I'd do.

> If I was the bettor to start with...or if I was the raiser — I'd bet *from any position.* If I called with A-K — I'd check...or if there was a bet in front of me — I'd pass.

As I've already said, I play (almost) all my hands that way because if I was the bettor or raiser before the Flop then I've represented a hand. So, I'll bet on the Flop regardless of what comes. I'll do it nine times out of ten.

You might have noticed that this is **quite different** from the way I'd play two Aces or two Kings. With either of those Pairs in an early position, I'd check it if there were three to a Straight or Flush on the Turn. Remember. . .I "hear" a bell ringing in that situation that reminds me **not** to bet. So, if I've got a hand (a Pair in the pocket). . .I play it slow. But, if I'm bluffing. . .I go ahead and play it fast. I mean. . .I'll take one shot at it.

The reason I do that is because I know for sure I'm **not** going to go **any further** with an A-K if somebody plays-back at me. With two Aces or two Kings — if somebody plays-back it puts me to a decision. But, when I have nothing, I can bet A-K with confidence because I'm gone if I get raised. I just throw my hand away because there's **nothing** for me to think about. Now you can see why you're less likely to lose a big pot with A-K than with two Aces or two Kings.

When I do go ahead and play the hand (when there's nothing on the Flop that'll help me), I'll make a reasonable bet — somewhere in the neighborhood of the size of the pot. But, as always, there are exceptions. In an unusual situation, I'd revert back to the same philosophy I use with Aces and Kings. For example, if the Fall was a J♡-10♡-9♡. . .I'd **never** bluff. I wouldn't even fool with the pot if **only two** of those cards were **suited**. You know somebody's going to have something. Here again, you have to use your judgment. It's an extreme situation.

That also explains why I'll bet on the Flop 90% of the time (and **not** all the time) if I played my hand strong **before** the Flop. There are times when you know somebody must have flopped something. And bluffing at a pot in that situation will rarely succeed. So you just give it up.

If I get some help on the Flop (by catching an Ace or a King), I'd make a reasonable bet at the pot from any position. The only time I might check-raise in this situation is when I had called in a middle position before the Flop and the original raiser (before the Flop) was behind me.

When someone plays-back at me in the above situation . . .I'll either move-in or release my hand. It would depend on what flopped. In order for me to move-in. . .I'd have to put my opponent on a hand where I thought he was drawing. For example, if the Turn came A♣-10♡-9♡. . .I'd put him on a Flush draw (or maybe a Straight draw) — and I'd move-in. On the other hand, if it came off ragged like a K♡-8♠-2♢...I **might** release my A-K. My thinking would be that he possibly turned a Set — and I **might** give up.

By the way, in the first situation (when the Flop was A♣-10♡-9♡) a man could've turned 3-Nines and he'd be in an ideal position to win a lot of money. It would look to me like he was drawing at a Straight or a Flush (or both) — and if he was lucky enough to have turned a Set...well, there's nothing magical I could do. I'd just have to go ahead and pay him off.

If a Pair of Aces or a Pair of Kings flopped (giving me Trips) — and the other card is **not** one that'll give someone a Straight or Flush draw — I **might** check-raise with my hand, but I *probably* **wouldn't** because I like to lead with it. It's a very strong hand and as long as a Pat hand (a Straight or Flush) **can't** be dealt off on the next card...you **might** want to· give a free card in that situation so your oppo-nent(s) would have a chance to make something on Fourth St. But, you'd only give a free card if you were last to act. If you were first to act...you wouldn't. You should lead with that hand.

If you turned Two-Pair (Aces and Kings)...you'd play them almost identically to Trips. It's almost the same hand.

> **The important thing to remember is that anytime there's a possible draw on the Flop...you should** *almost never* **check — you should** *almost always* **bet.**

In the extremely rare case when you turn a Set of Fours...you **don't** have any alternative. There's nothing else left...so you have to check it. If you bet you **could** catch a man with a Pair of Queens or Jacks and he **might** accidentally pay you off. But, realistically, you check it and hope that a Ten, Jack or Queen will fall on Fourth St. and pair someone...and then you bet hoping someone will call you with a Full.

If a Q-J-10 flopped (giving me the nut Straight)...I'd lead again if I was the raiser. Only this time it would **not** be a reasonable bet. It would be an abnormal size bet.

I'd overbet the pot when that Turn came because somebody figures to have made something. They could've made a smaller Straight...possibly Trips...or Two-Pair...or a Pair and a Straight draw. That's the type of hand most players move-in with. So, you'd probably get him to bet all his money...and he'd be almost dead.

If I was a caller (**before** the Flop)...I'd also raise it with A-K. I **wouldn't** slow-play it. I'd raise because the original raiser figures to have a hand that would fit that Flop (Q-J-10). He could have two Aces or two Kings...or he might have 3-Queens or 3-Jacks...or a Pair of Queens with an Ace or King kicker. He'd be subject to go all the way (to Fifth St.) if he had any one of those hands...and he'd get all his chips in the middle.

When the Flop came like a J-10-2 where I'd have a belly-Straight draw and two overcards with an A-K...I'd call a reasonable bet. I'd really be trying to catch a Queen...because if I caught an Ace or King, I'd have to be careful with it. It might've made someone else a stronger hand than my own — say a Straight or Two-Pair.

But, if you flop two of your Flush cards when you have A-K **suited**...you'll have a very powerful hand. At that point, you'll be a favorite over any other overpair — with the exception of a Pair of Aces or Kings.

I'll lead with that hand, of course, and I'd also lead off and bet if I actually turned a Flush with A-K **suited**. You should **not** check-raise with your Flush because your opponent **doesn't** figure to have made much on the Flop. But, he might call you with one Pair...or he might accidentally have a small Flush. It's also possible he'd think you were drawing to a Flush — especially if you're an aggressive player — and he might call you all the way through with just one Pair.

A-K — how to play on Fourth and Fifth

The way you'd play A-K on Fourth and Fifth Sts. (if you made a Pair on the Flop) is almost the same way you'd play a Pair of Aces or Kings *in the pocket*. If you think your opponent made the hand he was drawing at...you check. If you **don't** think he made it...you bet.

The only exception would be when you thought you had a man out-kicked. That is, you might keep betting with A-K if you put your opponent on a hand that's a little bit worse than yours. For example, you think he might've paired Aces (or Kings) with you...but, he's got a smaller kicker. In this case, you'd try to *sell your hand* (bet the maximum amount you think he'll call). You wouldn't try as hard to sell a Pair of Aces (or Kings) *in the pocket* because he might've been drawing to beat them. With A-K, however, there's a good chance he's got the top card (an Ace or King) paired with you...but your *sidecard* (kicker) is higher.

The important point to remember when you have A-K is that it's a drawing-type hand where A-A (or K-K) isn't. It's therefore a much easier hand to get away from than the very big Pairs.

How to Play a Pair of Queens

I've put a Pair of Queens in a separate category for the simple reason that it's a particular hand that deserves special treatment. You'll soon see why.

When I get two Queens *in the pocket*...I play them very carefully. I try **not** to play them too strongly from any position. Unless a good situation arises...I **don't** want to move-in before the Turn with two Queens. By a good situation, I mean that I'm in a very late position (possibly *on the Button*) and four people have called a raise in front of me. Here, I might try to shut them out by moving–in. I'd be using the combined strength of my pair of Queens and my position.

If you're up against two Aces or two Kings with a Pair of Queens...you're about a 4½ to 1 underdog. And, if you're up against A–K...you're only a little better than a 6 to 5 favorite. When people go all–in before the Flop...they usually have one of those three or four hands.

So, your money's in a lot of jeopardy when you get it all–in **before** *the Turn* with two Queens. If you get called, you'll usually be up against A–A, K–K or A–K...in which case you'll be a big dog or just a small favorite. You can pick a better spot than that to get all your money in.

That's **not** to say two Queens don't have a certain amount of value. They do. They're a considerably better–than–average hand. But, for the reason I just mentioned, I **seldom** *raise–back* with a Pair of Queens from any position...unless it's an unusual situation.

But, I **will** raise (the Blind) a reasonable amount with two Queens from any position **if** nobody else raised in front of me.

In a middle position, if somebody raised in front of me...I'd just call — as I would with any Pair. I'd just call with them in a late position, too. I **wouldn't** re–raise (except as I mentioned).

I also play two Queens **very slow** *on the Flop*. Whenever I play them...I'm really trying to catch a third Queen.

If either an Ace or a King came on the Flop...I'd play the hand as slowly as possible. If anybody bet with any degree of authority...I'd probably give them the pot.

As long as an Ace or King **didn't** fall...I'd play two Queens almost **exactly** the way I'd play two Aces or two Kings — and that includes the play on Fourth and Fifth Sts., too. So, you might want to re–read the way I'd play those two hands.

Excluding the times when there's an Ace or King on the Flop, the only time I'd play Queens differently from two Aces or Kings is when there's a Flush draw on the Flop. In that case, I **wouldn't** be eager to get all my money in. A man with a Flush draw could also have an overcard (an Ace or King). If he did...it would make his hand practically as strong as mine. Whereas, if I had two Aces or two Kings against only a Flush draw I'd be about a 9 to 5 favorite.

Keeping these differences in mind, you can play two Queens on the Flop, Fourth and Fifth as if they were Aces or Kings. In fact, I play all Pairs *in the pocket* in very much the same way...as you'll now see.

How to Play
Any Pair
other than
Aces, Kings or Queens

I'm going to call all the Pairs from Jacks down to Deuces a *small* Pair (except when I name a particular Pair). However, it's obvious that the bigger the Pair is...the more valuable it is. And that principle extends all the way down to the very small Pairs. That is, a Pair of Fours is better than a Pair of Treys for the simple reason that when the Flop is 4-3-2, if someone turned 3-Fours he'd be a huge favorite (about 22 to 1) over someone who turned 3-Treys.

I also have a breaking-point that I use in my play with a Pair of Jacks, Tens and Nines. I mentally segregate them from the other *small* Pairs and I play them a little stronger than the others. I do it simply because they're bigger Pairs and it's pretty easy for three Rags to fall. When that happens...you'll have an overpair. But, if you've got two Fives or two Sixes, it's hard for a Turn to come without there being at least one overcard. And, with an overcard out there, your hand is kind of dead so you don't want to get too much money involved.

Progressively, then, each Pair is a little bit better than the others...but I play them all as if they were a *small* Pair.

Before the Flop, with any of the *small* Pairs (**except** Jacks, Tens and Nines)...I'd limp-in (call the Blind). If somebody raised it from an early or middle position...I'd call it. I **wouldn't** re-raise.

I'd almost always take a Turn with any *small* Pair. I'd be trying to turn a Set so I could break somebody.

With a Pair of Jacks, Tens or Nines...if somebody raised from an early position, I'd probably just call. But, if it was raised from a middle or late position...I might re-raise with two Jacks, Tens or Nines if I felt the raiser was weak.

The reason I might do that is because (as I noted) the probability is good I'll have an overpair on the Flop. In that case, I'd play the Jacks just like I'd play two Queens. The same strategy would apply.

However, I want to note a *very unusual* **exception** I make in a special situation.

One of the reasons I like to play the *small* Pairs from any position is because they give me an opportunity to slow-down and not appear to be overbearingly aggressive when it might work against me. They also give me a chance to show a little respect for a particular opponent.

As you know, if I raise a pot before the Turn...I'm going to bet on the Flop (**whatever it is**) about 90% of the time. So, if I raised the pot with two Nines...I'd bet on the Flop nine times out of ten.

But, let's say I'm in the pot with a guy I've been pounding on and pounding on all night long. And that guy's a *real* **good** player who I know is getting very tired of me pounding on him. I also know I've probably got him beat. But, rather than bet him out of the pot, I'm going to

purposely slow-down against him. An example will best show you what I mean and I'll explain why I do it.

Let's say I raised him with two Nines **before** the Flop. He calls. The Turn comes 10-2-3 and he checks it. I check along. Another Rag falls off on Fourth St. He checks again. Now, I'm reasonably sure my two Nines are the **best** hand. But, I'm **not** going to bet it. I'll check along with him to show him some respect. The Board's awful looking and I'm pretty sure he doesn't have any of it. I'm also quite sure that if I bet I'm **not** going to get called. So I **don't** bet.

It has nothing to do with feeling sorry for the man...because if I thought there was a good chance he'd call me, I'd surely bet. But, instead of pushing him out of the pot once more and getting him hotter (angrier) than he is...I check along with him to cool him off a little.

Remember...he's a real good player. And, although I'm quite sure he **won't call** me...I'm **not** so sure he won't play-back and put pressure on me when I've got a hand that can't stand much pressure.

What's more, if he doesn't put some kind of play on me in this pot...he could do it at any time. If I keep pushing him out of every pot, sooner or later he's going to **stop** "sticking his head up". And, I won't be able to "slap" him anymore. Then, he's going to make me guess. I don't want that. I don't want him to start getting aggressive. That's the hardest player in the world to beat — a guy who you bet at and who's always playing-back at you. That's **exactly** the kind of opponent(s) I **don't** want to play against. I want all my opponents to be docile.

So it kind of cools him out when I just show down a hand. He knows that I know my two Nines are the best hand. But, by **not** betting them, I show him some respect. And because I showed the hand down...I've got him back to thinking that when I bet I'm either bluffing or I've got a hand I'm going to go with. He's back to guessing again. And that's exactly where I want him. I **don't** want to antagonize him to the point where he starts making **me** do the **guessing**. It serves a lot of purposes to slow down in a situation like that.

A short time later, I might pick-up another Pair of Nines (or Tens or Jacks) in a very late position (or on the Button) and I might raise with it again. Now...he might play-back at me. If he did...he'd get the pot. I'd give the pot to anyone who re-raised me **before** the Flop.

> I'd *never* **stand a re-raise when I have a small Pair** *before the Turn*. **I won't take any pressure with them. If someone puts a play on me...I throw them away.**

But, if I **don't** get re-raised...I'm back to my basic style of play. If I was the raiser...I'd go ahead and bet on the Flop. Just about any Flop. If I raised with two Tens and a 7-3-2 turned...I'd bet for sure since I've got an overpair. However, the only time my Pair is of any **real value** is when I flop a Set.

Nevertheless, I'd still bet (if I was the raiser) **even if** *three* **overcards flopped**. Even if I was sure a guy had a piece of that Flop (a bigger Pair) — and even if I was almost sure I'd get called...I'd still bet. I'd be giving him the courtesy of a bet...because there's an outside chance I could pick that pot up. And it **wouldn't** be a *small* bet. It would be a *reasonable* bet.

He'd be looking for me to bet...and I **don't** want to disappoint him. It would hurt my table-image.

I'll do that 90% of the time. In this case, I'll take one stab at the pot and if I **don't** get it there...I'll try to check it out from there on. An **exception** would be when I put a guy on a draw. In that case, he's going to have to pay to make his hand.

If I got raised...I surely wouldn't go any further with the hand.

I play *small* Pairs cautiously and try to win a small pot with them. I **won't** put a lot of chips in the pot unless I turn Trips. And when I **don't** make Trips with a *small* Pair, whenever I bet...I'm bluffing from there on.

If I had called a raise **before the Turn**...and the raiser bet **on the Turn**...unless I turned a Set, I'd probably surrender the pot. That's especially true if an overcard flopped. So, right there, you can see the strength of being the raiser. He made me lay down my hand. That's why I like to be the raiser.

When you **don't** help your *small* Pair on the Flop...the important points to remember are these:

(1) **You're through with them, if you just called before the Flop...and you *don't* put any more money in the pot from there on; and**

(2) **If you raised with them, you should generally bet on the Flop trying to win a small pot, but, if you get called...you *don't* want to bet again (on Fourth and Fifth) and you try to play showdown from that point on — *unless* you think your opponent is on a draw, in which case you continue betting; and**

(3) **If you get re-raised...you throw away your hand.**

It's a different situation entirely when you turn a Set. That's what you played for. And you should play them fast. That's what I do...in almost all cases. I **don't** always raise with them...but I **never** check them.

Needless to say, if I was the raiser and I turned a Set...I immediately bet right out.* As you know, I wouldn't need a Set to do that.

If I had called before the Flop...and someone checks it to me...and there's people behind me...I'll always bet with a Set of Trips.

As you know [see pages 437 and 438], one of my favorite plays in Hold 'em is to lead right into the raiser

---

*The only exception to this would be when I was in the pot with a very weak player — and he was the *only* opponent I had. I'd check in this case — as discussed on Page 435 .

with Trips (or even Two Pair) — especially when I think he's got a big Pair in the hole. I overbet the pot right there...and, if the raiser has what he represented (a big Pair) — he'll almost invariably go ahead and move-in on me.

You'd make that play when you've got a *small* Pair (say Threes) and the Flop is 10-7-3. You lead into the raiser because you think he's got an overpair in the pocket. But, a better Flop would be one with a Face-Card — say a Q-10-3. Now...the raiser's got to have some kind of combination with a Turn like that. If he's got two Aces or two Kings...he's got to raise you (if he's any kind of a player). If he's got A-Q...he'll probably raise you with that, too. If he's got K-Q...he'll probably call you. If he's got a Straight draw...he'll call — and it's possible that he'll raise you. So, you lead right off into him. If he's fortunate enough to have your hand beat...well, again, there's nothing magical you can do about it — you have to pay him off.

If someone had called in front of me and bets on the Flop when it comes like A-8-3 and I put him on a Pair of Aces...I'd probably play my 3-Threes slowly. I **wouldn't** want to take him out of the lead.

Another time you start overbetting the pot on the Turn is when you turn the *under* Full. This would be when it came 9-9-4...and you've got 2-Fours in the pocket. Well, you start making big (**not** reasonable) bets right there because the only way you're going to win any money with your hand is when you catch somebody with a Nine...or when you catch somebody with a big Pair and they call you or even raise you. You want to be sure there's enough money involved so you can win a big pot. And, to be sure of that, you've got to lead with your hand.

Note that you play the *under* Full different from the way you'd play the *big* Full. If you remember, the way you play the latter hand (as discussed on pages 463 and 464) is to check on the Flop because you'd have the deck crippled. You want to give a free card then so your opponent(s) can catch-up.

Are there times when you might release a Set on the Flop? There are. But, they're rare. It's a very hard hand to turn loose.* However, here's a situation where you **might possibly** save some money:

You bet on the Flop. There's a man in a late position who **didn't** raise it before the Turn (so he's **unlikely** to have a big Pair in the pocket). Now...he makes a very strong play after the Turn. I mean, he moves all-in and puts your entire stack in jeopardy. At that point, you might be able to determine he's got a Set...and if you have the small Set — you might be able to get away from your hand. But, it's very difficult. In a high-stakes game...I almost never do it.

> **If you turn a Set in a** *raised* **pot...it's practically impossible to get away from it. I defy anybody,** *anybody,* **to turn a Set and get away from it** *if the pot was raised originally.*

I'll repeat that: if the pot **wasn't** raised...conceivably... you could put a man on a bigger Set than you've got. But, if the pot was raised originally, (before the Flop), it's just impossible to release a Set.

> **If I raised it** *before the Flop* **and I turn a Set...and a guy beats them...well, he's going to win a real big pot from me. If we don't get it all-in on the Flop...we'll surely be** *down to the Green* **(no chips or money left) when all the cards are out.**

---

*In addition to what I say here, you might also want to re-read the discussion on this subject on Pages 438 and 439 .

How to Play
Small Connecting Cards
Before the Flop

This is the hand I'm looking for when I play No-Limit Hold 'em. Small connecting cards **(suited)** — the 7♣-6♣, 8♡-7♡, 5◊-4◊. That's the kind of hand I want. It's my favorite. And when I get it...I want my opponent to have two Aces or two Kings and to believe (as I **don't**) that he should play them slow. If he holds that opinion he'll give me the opportunity to get a Turn. And if I do...I can break him.

Exactly such a situation occured in the 1977 *World Series of Poker®*. It was definitely THE pot of the Tournament... bigger and more important than the pot I played with "Bones" (described on page 342). Not only did I win it...but I eliminated two very tough opponents. Here's what happened:

"Junior" Whited had the big Blind for $600.* Player "X"** limped-in for the six hundred. "Sailor" Roberts passed. Bones was next and he made it $3500 to go. I called...and so did Milo Jacobson. When it got back to Junior...he went all-in for $11,300. "X" was now looking at two raises — Bones' $2900 and Junior's $8400. He called. So did Bones. And so did I. Milo passed. It was a big pot already...and destined to get bigger. The dealer got ready to turn some cards. Here's what they were:

FLOP	4th St.	5th St.

---

*At this stage of the Tournament, the ante was $200 and there were Blinds of $300 and $600.

**I'm going to keep "X" *anonymous* to avoid any personal embarrassment that might stem from this description because he's one of the world's very best No-Limit Hold 'em players.

Junior was already all-in so "X" was first to act on the Flop. He moved all-in with a huge bet. Bones passed. It was up to me. "X" could've made his move and shut me out before the Turn. He would've picked-up $26,500 had he done so. Now...it was too late. I had him. There was no doubt in my mind about that. So I asked the dealer to count-down his bet. It was $45,400. I shoved in four and a half (20 chip) stacks of grays ($500 each) and four black ($100) chips. I was the only one who had any chips left so we all turned our hands over.

As you can see...when all the cards were out, the pot was mine. It was the **only time** in the Tournament where two players were eliminated in the same pot — two very tough ones.

In order to win that $142,500 pot...I had to gamble almost $12,000 with those small connecting cards before the Flop. I'd do it again. I always do it when there's an opportunity for me to win a real big pot.

"X"...and Junior, too...had almost exactly the hands I thought they had. And when "X" made his move on the Turn, I was certain he had one of two hands...the one he did have — or two Aces. He couldn't have had anything else.

If "X" had played his hand the way I recommend...he would've won a "small" pot. As it was, he lost a big one. That's about true to form for two Aces or two Kings.

If you recall, I stated on (page 453) that *"with a Pair of Aces or Kings in an early position before the Flop...I would probably limp-in (just call the Blind) hoping that somebody would raise it behind me so I could re-raise."* "X" got the first part of that advice right. If he got the second part right and raised Junior...I **never** would've got to play my hand.

That's the whole thing about the small connecting cards. I'll come in with them in an early or middle position. I might come in for the first bet (or, as you now know, even the second if I think I can win a real big pot). I probably **won't** raise with this kind of hand because **I don't want to get shut out of the pot.** If I raise...and somebody else re-raises — I probably won't be able to play it. Or, if I have to call a double-raise *cold*...I probably won't be able to play it there either. There are exceptions, as always...but, in general, I play the hand so I can get a Turn with it.

> **Small connecting cards are a hand that's *not* designed to put a whole lot of money in with before the Flop. It *is* a hand that's designed to take a lot of Flops with. You want to get a Turn with them to try to make a little Straight, a little Set of Threes, a little Two-Pair...or something.**

With any two cards to a Straight-Flush (connected or not — except for the top and bottom cards of a Straight-Flush such as the 8♣-4♣, J♡-7♡, etc.)...I'd come in in any position. In a late position...I'd raise with them.

I'm really looking to get raised when I come in with this hand in an early or middle position. In fact, I hope someone has a big Pair in the hole and raises behind me. Then, I can put a relatively small amount of additional money in the pot...and, if I get a Turn — I can break him.

> **The beautiful part about having the small connecting cards is that if you *don't* get any help...you throw them away. If the Turn comes 9-9-2, for example, you *don't* get involved with a 7-6. You're through.**

Normally, I wouldn't want to get more than 5% (maybe, 10%) of my money involved (before the Flop) with this type of hand. If I get as much as 20% of my money in with that hand...I'd have to be *rushing*. I **wouldn't** do it unless I was on a streak.

Also, there are times when I **might raise** with something like a 7-6, if I was in an early or middle position. I
noted that I generally just call. And, as a rule...that's true.
But, if the tempo of the game was just right...I'd raise in an
early or middle position.

For example, if I was winning a lot of pots...I'd do it. I
said that I always play the next pot after I win a pot...
regardless of what position I'm in. And when I play that pot,
I usually raise it. Also, if the game had tightened down
where everybody was *dealing* (playing) the nuts...I'd *shoot it
up* with a couple of small connecting cards.

Of course, you always try to keep from getting
re-raised with that hand. So, the ideal situation is when you
think your "muscle" will keep anyone from playing-back...
and will make your opponents think you've probably got big
cards or a big Pair.

The reasons I raise with the hand in a late position are
because I don't think I'll get re-raised and since nobody's
raised in front of me, I'll be able to give my hand some
deception. And, the reasons I *usually* **don't** raise in an early
position are because I'd have to go through six or seven
players **without** getting re-raised. With a lot of top players
in the game...that's **not** likely. Also, I like to be in the
lead — and, if I make something with it, I can take charge.
So, with players behind me...I usually call with it.

Another thing is that I **don't** have to maintain my
table-image (of betting on the Flop when I'm the raiser). If I
just called (before the Flop) and somebody else raised...I
very seldom try to pick the pot up or bluff into the raiser.
The raiser commands respect. So, when I miss that hand
completely when somebody else raised it...well, it's their
pot. That's why I like to be the raiser.

The only reason I **don't** like to raise with small
connecting cards is because when somebody has the hand I
want them to have (a big Pair)...they're going to raise me
back. That's one more reason I usually limp-in with them.

When you limp-in with this hand in an early position...
you're actually playing it like you would two Aces or two
Kings. So, there's also a bit of deception there. And, if

somebody raises in a middle or late position...you can pretty well put them on a hand — that is, big cards like A-K, K-Q or a big Pair. That's what you're also looking to do — you want to be able to put somebody on a hand so you know what you're trying to beat.

If you play in the style I recommend — that is, very aggressively — you'll have to adjust your play in a **small game**. You'll probably discover you'll get re-raised **more** when **you** raise in a **small** game than you will in a **big** game. That's been my experience. Here's why:

If I'm in a game where there's **not** much money on the table — say, everybody's got only $500 or $600 — and I raise it $100...well, a guy with big cards is going to move-in on me. They do it all the time in a small game. And when I've got a 7-6 or a 9-8 and someone bets the rest of his money at me...I **can't** call it.

> **I'm** *not* **going to take two small connecting cards and try to beat two Kings, A-K and so forth when I** *can't* **win anything if I get a Turn. So, in a case like that, I throw my hand away.**

And, because of that...I have trouble winning in a game where there's **not** much money on the table.

But, it's a totally different story in a big game. If I raise it $300 or $400...and me and the other guy have a lot of chips on the table — well, he's a little more hesitant about raising me now because he knows there's a very good chance I'll play-back. The guys I play with know when I put my "children" out there...I don't like to let them drown.

But, even if I do get re-raised in this situation...it's all right. In fact, it's what I want. If he raises me $700 or $800...and I've got small connecting cards — I'll call, now. If we've both got $25,000 in front of us...then all I'll be putting in is about 5% of my money. And it's worth it. Because now I've got a chance to win something if I get a Turn. I might be able to break him.

I'll now discuss how I'd play this hand depending on what I flop.

How to Play
Small Connecting Cards
on the Flop...
when you miss your hand
completely

If I **called** in an early position with small connecting cards and **I miss my hand completely**...I give the pot up.

> I *don't* **go ahead with that type of hand in that situation. I just surrender.** *The first loss is the best loss in a situation like that.*

But, once again, if I was the raiser...I would, of course, go ahead and bet at the pot. As long as there wasn't something "frightening" out there like the **Q♠-J♠-10♠**... I'm going to bet. And, something "frightening" **won't** be out there 90% of the time.

If I had a **7◊-6◊** in an early position and had decided to raise it before the Turn (when I was rushing, for example) ...and the **A♡-A♣-K♠** flopped...I'd bet right out. A Flop like that **wouldn't** "frighten" me. Why? It's simple. My opponents **don't** know I **don't** have A-K or A-Q or K-K...or any hand where that would be a good Flop for me. They **don't** know what I've got. In fact, if I raised in an early position they might think I did have a hand with big cards.

If I had raised it from a middle position before the Flop...I'd also bet — unless someone bet in front of me. In that case...the pot's theirs. I'd know they had something... and when I've got nothing with this kind of hand, I'm usually **not** going to try to make any great play (although occasionally I will bluff at it).

If I was a caller before the Flop in a middle or late position and it was checked to me on the Flop...I'd check along. As long as I **didn't** make anything...it would probably have to be checked to me twice (on the Flop and Fourth St.) before I'd bet (which would be a bluff).

Of course, if I had raised it before the Turn from a late position...I'd almost always bet — particularly if it was checked around to me. I'd bet even if the Flop was as noted before (A♡-A♣-K♠) and it was probable that someone had an Ace. The reason I'd do it is just like I discussed on page 483. I don't want my opponents to get out of the habit of checking to me. Since they expect me to bet (because I was the raiser)...I want to fulfill their expectations. So I go ahead and make a courtesy bet for them. When I make that bet, I'm trying to do two things:

(1) **I'm trying to win the pot right there. And I will many a time because they get into the habit of throwing their hands away.**

(2) **I'm also able to maintain my aggressive image. As long as I do, they'll continue to check it to me.**

That's the way I pick-up all the pots I do. Of course, if I get check-raised...I'm out immediately. That's the risk I take. But, a guy really has to have a hand before he'll put a play on me like that. So, when he does...I let him have the pot. But, they miss their hands more often than they make them. Because of that, I pick-up more pots than I give-up.

How to Play
Small Connecting Cards
on Fourth and Fifth...
when you miss your hand
completely

I wouldn't be in there on Fourth St. with this hand if I had nothing...unless I was the bettor — or, if it was checked to me and I checked it with them.

If someone had called my bet after having checked it to me on the Flop. . .I would immediately put him on some kind of hand. If I thought he was on a drawing hand. . .and it looked like he missed it on Fourth — I'd bet again. If I thought he had a made hand — regardless of how weak it was (even the Third Button) — I **wouldn't** try to make him throw away his hand on Fourth when he called me on the Flop and had, therefore, already committed himself to the pot. For example, if the Flop was a K–8–2 and I tried to pick it up; but I got called. . .well, then I'd try to check it out all the way through. At that point, I'd be giving up the pot at a minimum loss.

And, once again, if I thought my opponent was on a drawing hand (like two cards to a Straight-Flush) and I make another stab at the pot on Fourth. . .and I get check-raised — I'm almost always going to give it up in that situation, too.

> I'm *never* going to *call* a bet when I miss my hand completely. But, I *might* play-back at a guy who I think's putting a play on me.

As a general rule, I **wouldn't** make a play in that situation. However, in an extreme situation I would. If I was **completely** convinced a guy was trying to take the pot away from me. . .I'd re-play at him. But, I'd have to feel strongly about it before I'd jeopardize a bunch of chips in that spot.

My play on Fifth St. would be just like my play on Fourth. If I'm still betting at the pot. . .I'd have to continue because there'd be almost no way I could win in a showdown. I mean. . .all I'd have would be Seven-high (assuming I didn't pair on the end). Since I put my opponent on a draw on Fourth (and that's why I bet there). . .I'd have to feel he didn't make it when all the cards were out. I'd also have to feel very strongly he **wouldn't** call my last bet. Naturally, if I felt like he completed his hand. . .I'd check.

You'd be in a tough spot on the end. . .but you just couldn't leave all your money out there without one **last** stab at the pot. The key to what you'd do on Fifth is **very** much based on your opinion of why your opponent called you on Fourth. You'd have to feel pretty sure he was drawing...or you could get yourself in a lot of trouble.

You might find it difficult to continue betting your hand when you know you don't have anything. You may think it takes a lot of courage to do that. And it does. But, all it really is, is good Poker.

You'll discover, if you use my system of play, that your opponents will be scared to give you (free) cards whenever they've got a hand. The reason they'll be afraid to do that is because they know you could be drawing at an inside Straight and betting with it. They know an aggressive player is liable to show them anything. Consequently... when they get a hand...they want to shut you out right then. They bet because they don't want you in the pot drawing at them. So there are really two good points about playing in the aggressive way I recommend:

(1) **If your opponents** *do* **have a hand...they'll show you right away. They** *don't* **want to keep giving you free cards; and**

(2) **Your continuous betting makes them throw away** *borderline* **hands so you** *can* **pick-up the pot when they** *don't* **have anything.**

Quite simply...an aggressive player has way the best of it.

How to Play
Small Connecting Cards
when you make something

I'm now going to discuss how I'd play small connecting cards when I turn something with them. The hand I'm going to use as an example throughout the discussion that follows is a 7◊–6◊. You'll learn how I'd play this hand in three different situations — when I get:

(1) a *poor* **Flop** *(slight help)*

(2) a *fair* **Flop** *(medium help)*

(3) a *good* **Flop** *(a lot of help)*

When I've got a 7◇-6◇ and a Q♠-6♡-2♣ falls...I'd consider that a *poor* Flop to my hand. And, the way I'd play it would be very similar to what I'd do when I got **no** help.

However, there's a big difference in the way I'd play in this situation. It would depend on who I was involved with...and, more importantly, how much money he had on the table. I'll gamble with the Second Button (a Pair of Sixes, in this case) — or even the Third Button — if the guy I was up against was sitting on a lot of checks. I'd do it even if I knew he had a Pair of Queens. I'd call a reasonable bet and might even put as much as 10% of my money in the pot if I thought I could break him if I got lucky and caught another Six or a Seven. I'd surely do it if I thought I could win a gigantic pot.

I might even raise. There's always a time I might raise — whether I've got a small piece of the Flop (in this case) or when I've completely missed my hand. But, those times have nothing to do with the value of my hand. I'd do it because I detected a weakness in somebody...or because of my position. Right now, I'm discussing what I'd do based on how much value I thought my little Pair of Sixes had.

Another difference in the way I'd play this hand when I got a little help on the Flop (and no help on Fourth or Fifth) is that I'd continue to bet on Fourth if I was the original raiser. You'll recall that even if I missed this hand completely, I'd bet it on the Flop as long as I was the raiser. But, if my bet on the Flop was called...I'd try to check it out from then on (unless I thought my opponent was drawing).

Now, however, I'd bet again on Fourth despite the fact that my bet on the Flop was called. I **don't** like to keep betting when I'm on a complete bluff...but I **do** like to keep betting when I've got an Out. And, I'd feel like I've got an Out because if I catch that other Six (or a Seven)...I'd feel like I'd have a stronger hand than my opponent.

So I wouldn't show any weakness with my hand on Fourth St. I'd go ahead and make a reasonable bet.

If I still didn't get any help on Fifth St., I'd more than likely stop betting. If my opponent was drawing and he didn't make his hand...my Pair of Sixes are probably good — so I'd check. And, if they aren't good, there's no sense in losing any more money with them.

In the case where I got some additional help on Fourth — say I caught a Seven — well, then I'd make an oversized bet (more than what's in the pot). I'm always out to win a big pot...and now I'd have a hand to do it with. I **wouldn't** try to *sell* my hand for a small amount of money. I'd make a very big bet on Fourth...and a very big bet on Fifth.

If I **didn't** catch that Seven until the end...then I might try to *sell* it on Fifth St. for whatever I thought I could get.

The above way I'd play this hand when I caught a Seven on Fourth (or Fifth) assumed that I was the original raiser coming in and I stayed in the lead. That is, I continued to bet on every turn of the cards.

If I was a caller coming in and had checked and called on the Flop...I'd play the hand differently if I caught a Seven on Fourth St. In this case, it would be another one of the few times I'd check-raise if there was a lot of money in the pot. I wouldn't want to take my opponent (the original raiser) out of the lead when I know he'd bet again on Fourth because the pot's so big...especially since he'd have almost no idea the Seven helped me. He'd surely try to shut me out...and when he bet — I'd raise him. I'd want to win the pot right there because the Board might pair on the end (with a Queen or Deuce) and kill my Two-Pair.

The situation where I caught a Six on Fourth St. would be different still. My hand wouldn't be nearly as concealed (as it would be when I caught a Seven). The two Sixes on the Board would look very threatening. So, even if I had been a caller up to this point...there's a good chance I'd take the lead and bet when the Six hit. And, even though the raiser could readily see that I might have 3-Sixes...he might also think I was representing them. **That, by the way, would** be a very good situation to bluff at the pot if you *didn't* have a Six in the hole.

Now, I'll discuss how I'd play that 7◊-6◊ when I got what I'd call a *fair* Flop. Any three cards that gave me the top Pair, an open-end Straight (or a Flush) draw would be a *fair* Flop. But, I'd play fast **only** with the Straight draw.

I play Flush draws extremely slowly because they're so obvious. When there are two of the same suit on the Flop, I see so many players move-in on a guy after he bets when they're drawing to a Flush. Occasionally, I do it too... because my philosophy of play is to protect my money and bet whenever I can. But, it's usually a very obvious play. Most players will put you on a Flush draw in that situation. And for that reason I like a Straight draw better.

If I get that Straight draw...well, I'm ready now. I mean really ready. The battle's on. If I was the original raiser...of course, I'd bet on the Turn. If I get raised...I'd play-back and move all my chips in. If somebody bets in front of me...I'd raise 'em.

If I **wasn't** the original raiser...this would be another time when I'd check-raise. If the guy who raised it before the Flop bet after I checked...I'd raise with most or all of my chips. I'd be the aggressor at that point...and nobody could take me out of the lead from then on.

> As I said earlier, *most* decisions are made on the Flop. I mean, that's where you steal pots. So I'd play this hand that way because I'd be in a very typical situation where I steal a lot of pots. I'd be bluffing with an Out. I could win the pot right there. If I got called, I'd have a good draw (an open-end Straight which I'd make about 33% of the time) and a small chance to back-door Two-Pair or Trips.

In the case where I just turned the top Pair (when the Board was a 6-4-2 or a 7-4-2)...I'd play it cautiously. I'm not going to fall in love with that hand...but, I'll gamble a little with it.

In other words, I'd check to the raiser...and then I'd probably call. If I was in a late position (and **hadn't** raised originally)...I'd also call if somebody bet. But, it would be a weak call — meaning that I probably **wouldn't** go any further with the hand if I **don't** get any help on Fourth and somebody bets at me again.

One of the reasons I'd call on the Flop is because my Pair **might** be the best hand. Just because the other guy raised it originally **doesn't** mean he has to have a big Pair in the pocket. So, there's a possibility I've got the best hand right now. I'd know more depending on what he did on Fourth St. If he bet again (and I **didn't** help my hand)...I'd get rid of it pretty fast. I **wouldn't** invest a lot of money with that hand without any help.

But, the **main reason** I'd call on the Flop is because of the possibility I could win a big pot if I improve my hand and beat a hand (two Aces or two Kings). And the reason I check rather than bet is because I might have the best hand and I could get myself shut-out if I bet and get raised. Then, I'd have to throw my hand away. By checking, I could call a reasonable bet and try to catch a card.

If I did improve on Fourth, I'd play it from then on just like I would in the situation where I got a *poor* Flop, but got some help on Fourth.

A *good* (or even a great Flop) to a 7◊-6◊ would be a Pair **with** a Straight (or Flush) **draw**, Two-Pair, Trips, a Straight or a Flush (even though it's a small one).

> **With any *good* Flop to small connecting cards...I'd play the hand as if it was *complete* — whether it was or not. I'd lead with the hand in an early position...and I'd raise in a late position.**
>
> **I'd play the hand to get all my money in the center to start with — even if I turned a Pair with a draw. In the latter case, I'd play it that way because I'd have *two* chances to win it...when I bet or raise (and my opponent throws his hand away) — or when I improve (if my bet or raise is called).**

Naturally, you'll be in some jeopardy — even when you get a very good Flop. But, you're almost always in some jeopardy. So you *can't* worry about somebody having the nuts all the time. If you did...you never would get to play a pot.

For example, if you turned a Flush with somebody else...yours will probably be the little one — and you'd be *dead*.* If it happened...you'd just have to lose your money because you'd (almost always) have to go ahead and pay your opponent off. It's one of the hazards of the game.

You could also flop the *ignorant* (low) end of the Straight. That would be another hazard if somebody turns a bigger Straight. And again, if your opponent bet anything within reason, you'd have to go ahead and pay him. For example, if the Flop was a 10-9-8 and somebody moved all-in on you, you'd be down to judgment. You'd have to know your player...and a lot would depend on how much is in the pot and the amount he sets you in for. If you've got $1000 in the pot and he bets you $50,000 more...well, perhaps, you **wouldn't** go for it and you'd throw your hand away. But, if you've got $1000 in the pot and he bets you $2000 more — all your money, or all his money — then you'd surely pay it off. If you're beat...you're beat.

That happens a lot, by the way. And, it's why (as you'll later learn) a K-9, J-7 and hands like that are *trash* and shouldn't be played (in a normal ante, Ring game).

With all the *good* Flops, I'd already be committed to the pot...so, on Fourth St., I'd bet — if I was first **or** if it was checked to me. But, as always, there are exceptions.

For example, if you flopped a Diamond Flush and another Diamond came on Fourth St. — your hand would be almost ruined. All you'd have is a Seven-high Flush. At that point, you **must** check your hand and hope to show it down. If you **can't** show it down...you've **got to** throw it away. Or, if you flopped a Straight and the Board pairs on

---

*There's no way you can draw out when it's a Flush against a Flush in Hold 'em...except for a Straight-Flush.

Fourth St. — you **could** also be in trouble. Usually, that **shouldn't** stop you because if a man turned a Set or Two-Pair, he would've raised you on the Flop. So, if he made a Full (when the Board paired)...you'd have to pay him off. Another hazard.

> As you continue to use my system of play, you'll discover the many advantages it has. The situation above is a good case in point. If the Flop was, say a 5-4-3 (giving me a Straight)...my opponent would've let me know *on the Flop* whether or not he had a hand (Two-Pair or Trips). That is, if he's a *good* player he would.
>
> The reason why is because he *wouldn't* want another card to fall that would be one card off of a Straight. He knows if an Ace, Deuce, Six, or Seven comes on Fourth...he's going to have to give the pot up. He knows I'll bet in that case *whether or not I have the one card that'll make the Straight.*
>
> For that reason, all *good* Hold 'em players do most of their gambling on the Flop...*not* on Fourth and Fifth Sts. Occasionally, you'll see a big pot played *after* the Flop...but, in the majority of cases, all the money usually goes in on the Flop. That's the reason the Flop is the most crucial point in the game.

You'll recall that earlier I stated it's quite inconceivable to me that anybody could get away from their hand if they flopped a Set of Trips in a **raised** pot. At that point, I was talking about a **hidden** Set (a Pair in the pocket and one on the Board). It's a different case entirely when the Pair is on the Board and I have one of the matching cards in the hole. I've turned down a lot of Sets in a situation like that when, for example, I have a 7-6 and the Flop is 7-7-2...and I bet and get called. There's really **not** very many hands someone can call me with.

So it's easy to release a Set in this case because when you get a lot of money involved you know the guy who's in there with you has probably got a Seven also. (It's especially true if he's the aggressor.) So you have to evaluate your kicker. I mean...what's it worth? The conclusion I reach is that it's usually **not** worth very much. If I really think he's got a Seven then I know the best I could hope for is that I've got him tied. Of course, I'm talking about a good player...and it's much more likely he's got me beat.

He's probably in there with a Seven and a higher card that he could've flopped a Straight with (such as an 8-7, 9-7 or 10-7). Another possibility is that he's got a high card (such as an Ace or King) that's suited. He might have a 7-6 (like I do) or a 7-5 (the only likely hand I could beat). But it's almost inconceivable he's in there with a 7-4, 7-3 or a 7-2 (although the latter hand would give him a Full).

So when I got down into the hand and I gave him credit for the other Seven because he was showing a whole lot of speed...I **couldn't** continue playing my Seven with a small connecting card. And I release **that** Set quite readily. I'd do it real quick.

When I have a Set like that with a **different** kicker, I make another evaluation. If my kicker was slightly bigger... say a Nine or Ten — I'd probably play it. If I had a **suited** Ace or King then I'd definitely go ahead and play it.

Of course, the situation could be quite different when I turn a Set with that 7-6...where I might **not** release it. This would be the case where I raised with the hand before the Flop. Now, on the Flop, everybody checks it to me...and I bet. Somebody plays-back (check-raises me). In this situation, I might go ahead with my hand figuring that the guy was trying to shut me out. He might be playing-back with an overpair or a lot of different hands he might **not** have played too strong (raised me with) before the Flop.

It would also be a different situation if I had called a small raise before the Flop in a late position with a 7-6. Now, I would **not** give the raiser credit for a Seven if a 7-7-2 fell. And I'd probably play my hand real fast trying to win a big pot.

Whenever there's a raise **before** the Turn...there's a chance you can win a big pot. But, in an **unraised** pot...it's hard to win a big one. On page 439 I noted that you **don't** want to get broke in a "nothing" pot. I'm reminding you of that now because you might try to win a big pot when you turn a Set with small connecting cards in an **unraised** pot. You· shouldn't. I **never** jeopardize very much money without a **real** good hand when I don't have anything in the pot to protect. I **don't** go out of my way to win "nothing" pots.

Another important part of my playing philosophy I want to remind you about is this:

> **You should constantly be trying to get as much value for your hand as you can. And the way you do that is to bet.**

That should be clear by now. You become a big winner at Poker by betting...raising...and re-raising — by playing aggressively. Of course, there are times you have to play defensively — when an aggressive strategy would be wrong because it could defeat your purpose by getting you shut-out of a pot. But, in general, you want to be aggressive.

That means you **can't** let every card that hits the Board constantly threaten you. As I said, if you're always worrying about somebody having the nuts...you **never** will get to play a hand. This applies to all the hands I've discussed, but it's especially meaningful here because I'm discussing how to play small connecting cards when you get a *good* Flop. That's what you're playing them for in the first place...so, when you make something with them — you want to get value for them. So you should always apply this principle:

> **If you're going to call...**
> **you might as well bet.**

You should do that at all the stages of play...but it's particularly important on the end.

If you do...you'll get paid off with hands that aren't what you thought they were. I mean, there'll be many times you'll put your opponent on a hand completely different from what he's got. I'm **not** Houdini...and neither are you. You might think a man is drawing to a Flush...but maybe he's got a Pair — just one Pair. He might have been *running you down* with a lot less than you thought he had. So, when a Flush card hits the Board on Fifth St. — it may **not** have helped him at all. I mean, you'll know he's got something when that Flush card comes...either the Flush you thought he was drawing at — or some other piece of the Flop. Or maybe he's got Two-Pair when you've got a Straight. You really don't know what he's got...but since you're going to pay it off anyway since you've got a good hand with your small connecting cards — you might as well bet.

The only exception I make is when the Board pairs on the end. Then, I'll check it...and may or may not call depending on how I feel about the situation. But barring that, if I've made a real good hand with my small connecting cards...I'd go ahead and bet.

The opposite of the case where I might be a little concerned when I **don't** have the nuts is, of course, when I **do** have the nuts. Naturally, in that case, I'll do whatever I think will get the most money in the pot.

If I thought my opponent had a strong hand...I'd make a big bet. If I thought he had a weak hand...I'd try to *sell* my hand by making a smaller bet. There'd be a lot of judgment there...judgment about what I think he's got.

My decision on how much to bet depends on whether I made my hand early (on the Flop) or late (on the end).

> **If I made my hand early...I'm *not* going to try to *sell* him anything — I'm going to try to break him.**
>
> **If I made my hand late and I *haven't* been charged a lot of money to make it** (like it was checked on the Flop and there was a small bet on Fourth and I make the nuts on the end)...**well, then I'm *not* going to try to break him —**

because he probably *won't* call a big bet. Then, I'd try to *sell* my hand for whatever I thought I could get for it.

Those of you who are new to No-Limit Hold 'em may **not** have been able to appreciate how strongly I feel about the small connecting cards. And of those of you who are experienced players were probably quite surprised. But, that's where it's all at in my opinion. You have to use a lot of judgment when you play the small connecting cards...and when you play them right — they're big money-makers. And that's what No-Limit Hold 'em is all about.

BORDERLINE
or
TROUBLE HANDS

You should commit to memory the following list of *trouble* hands. I call them that because that's exactly what they are...and I only play them in borderline situations.* They're hands you can lose a lot of money with...so you should play them **very** cautiously. You **don't** want to jeopardize much money with them.

TROUBLE HANDS
(only when offsuit)

Ace-Queen	King-Queen	Queen Jack	Jack-Ten
Ace-Jack	King-Jack	Queen-Ten	Nine-Eight
Ace-Ten	King-Ten		

---

*Two important qualifications are that I *don't* consider the *trouble* hands borderline when:
  (1) they're suited; and
  (2) I get them in a short-handed game. As you'll learn, I define a short-handed game as one with four players or less and in such a game the *trouble* hands are actually big hands.

The reason I consider those hands borderline is because I'd question calling a raise with them. If they're *suited*, I'll call a raise with them and go ahead and take a turn. When they're **not** *suited*, I **won't** call a raise if I'm *out of position*.

By *out of position* I mean that I'm in a middle position and a man in an early position came in raising. I'll pass these hands in that spot.

If I'm in a late position and the pot's been raised and another man calls...well, then I'll usually call with them — but, I'll hear another bell ringing when I do. This time, that bell will be reminding me to play my hand with **extreme caution**...unless I get an excellent turn to it.

The reason why you have to be so careful with those hands is because **with every one of them** you might be up against a hand where you'd be almost dead. Most players consider A-A, K-K or A-K to be the best raising hands...so there's a good possibility the raiser has one of those three hands. True, you can't always assume that...but it's always in the back of your mind. So, if you've got A-Q, A-J or A-10...and you're up against A-A, K-K or A-K...you've got a terrible hand.

> **It's extremely hard to win a big pot with those hands** (offsuited) **when you've called a raise. They're definitely** *trouble* **hands.** *You're much more likely to* **lose** *a big pot with them than you are to win a big pot with them.* **Even when I make a Pair with them on the Flop...I play them extremely cautiously — or about the same way I'd play when I had a Pair of Aces or Kings in the pocket.**

For example, if I played a K-Q (offsuit) and the Board came K-4-2...I'd be in a lot of trouble if the raiser's got one of the three hands I've assumed he might have. He'd have two Aces, three Kings or a Pair of Kings (like I've got) — but he'd have an Ace kicker.

Or, if I played a 9-8 and the Flop was Q-J-10...I still **wouldn't** be too excited about my hand — even though I turned a Straight. It would **not** only be the *ignorant* end of the Straight...but it would have an additional weakness because the high-end of the Straight would be made up by a very strong hand that everybody plays — namely, A-K.

Something else you have to think about with the *trouble* hands is that it's **not** as easy to pick-up pots with them when you turn a Straight draw. You'll remember that when I turn a Straight draw with small connecting cards, I play my hand *real fast* **because I have two shots to win the pot.** I can win the pot right on the Flop because with small cards out there it's less likely anyone else turned a hand. And, if I do get called, I've still got a second shot to win it if I make my Straight.

But, if I turn a Straight draw with a K-Q (say, the Flop is J-10-5...it's highly likely somebody's got a piece of that Flop — and I'm less likely to pick the pot up when I bet. So, I don't have two shots to win it anymore.

The same kind of reasoning applies to the times when you might turn the top Pair **and** a Straight draw with a K-Q when the Flop is Q-J-10. **It's** *not* **even a good hand then** because you might be *dead* (as you would be with a 9-8) when somebody has an A-K. The best you **could** be drawing for would be a split.

Even when you turn a very good hand like Two-Pair or Trips...you could be in jeopardy. If the Flop was K-K-2... you could once again be in big trouble with K-Q when someone's got A-K. The difference here is that you probably **won't** be able to get away from your hand and you'll have to go ahead and lose a lot of money.

> **The important point to remember about the** *trouble* **hands is when you do get a Flop to them you** *don't* **want to get heavily involved. You should just try to play the pot as** *cheaply* **as possible.**

A minor exception to the above consideration is when you turn a Straight (meaning that you must use **both** your hole cards as when you have, say a Q-10 and the Flop is K-J-9 or J-9-8). However, even in this case (when you have the nuts)...there's a chance you **could** lose the pot. If a Queen fell on Fourth, with the K-J-9 Flop, you **could** lose to an A-10...and with the J-9-8 Flop, you **could** lose to a K-10. So, you're **not** completely safe with some of these hands even when you turn the nuts.

When you have one of the *trouble* hands **suited**...it's a much stronger hand.* For example, if you had the **K◇-Q◇** and the Flop was **10♠-7◇-2◇**...you'd have a real big hand. Not only would you have a Flush draw, but you'd also have two overcards. Or, if you had the **9◇-8◇** with that Flop, you'd have a Straight **and** a Flush draw. That situation (with either the **K◇-Q◇** or the **9◇-8◇**) would be a good opportunity to check-raise somebody if you were in an early position. If you were in a late position and sombody leads into you...you could raise them. Now, you'd be back to the principle where you'd have two shots to pick-up the pot. You might win it right there...or, if you get called, you'd have a good hand to fall back on.

TRASH HANDS

With the exception of an Ace or a King **with any** *suited* card...I consider any hand I haven't already discussed to be a *trash* hand. An **A♣-8♣** or a **K♡-4♡** are hands that I put in the same category as the small connecting cards and I play them approximately the same way. For example, if the Flop was **9♡-6♣-2♣**, and I had the **A♣-8♣**...I'd have a Flush draw and an overcard. If I was in the pot against two Queens...I'd be about even-money to win it. So I'd play my hand in that situation like I would with two small connecting cards that were **suited** (say the **9♣-8♣**). That is, I'd play it fast...and try to win the pot on the Flop — because, once again, I'd have two shots to win it.

---

*However, the *trouble* hands suited or offsuit should be played the same way — slowly — *unless* you Flop a Flush or a Flush draw. Then, you can show some *Speed.*

But that's where I draw the line — with an Ace or a King and another **suited** card. After it passed the Ace and King...if the two cards **don't** connect — **even if they're** *suited* — I consider them *trash* hands. Hands like a Q♡-4♡ or J♠-6♠ are *trash*.

Naturally, hands with non-connecting and offsuit cards such as J♡-5♣, 10♠-3◊, 9♣-4♡ are obviously garbage. But, so are the **offsuit** hands such as K-9, Q-8, J-7, 10-6, 9-5, 8-4, 7-3 and 6-2 that a lot of people play because you can turn a Straight with them. I **don't** play those hands because if I got the best Flop I could to them (outside of a Full House)...I could get broke with them by running into a bigger Straight. Consequently, I **never** play a hand when I have the **top** *and* **bottom** cards of a Straight — except when I'm *in position*.

I always make exceptions when I'm *in position* — even with the *trash* hands. For example, I might call a raise before the Flop if I was on the Button with a hand like A-8 (offsuit) — or **any** of the garbage hands — if enough (say, five) people were in the pot in front of me...and I didn't think there'd be any more raises. I might call a small raise and take a turn with a *trash* hand because it's a good percentage play. I'd be trying to turn a Full, Trips or Two Pair. But, if I **don't** get a real good Flop to the hand...I'll throw it away. I **won't** get involved and burn up a bunch of money with one of those *trash* hands. I'm **not** going to **call** any bets on the Flop. I'll be raising...or I'll be gone.

I'd even raise with a *trash* hand if I was *in position*. More than that...I'd play it fast after the Flop, too. If the guys in the early positions threw their hands away and someone in a middle position limped-in...well, if I'm on the Button, I'd be *in position* and I'd raise it **regardless of what two cards I have**. And, if it was checked to me on the Flop...I'd bet **regardless of what flopped**.

Obviously, I **wouldn't** be playing my hand because of its value. *Trash* hands have no value. I might as well be playing with two blank cards in this situation because all I'd be doing is playing my position and my opponent. I'd feel like he's got a weak hand to begin with (because he limped-in) and if he misses it...I'll be able to pick the pot up.

Other than the exceptional situations I discussed, *trash* hands are just *not* playable.

SHORT-HANDED PLAY

A lot of times you'll be in a full (Ring) game and before the night's over you'll be playing short-handed. As I already mentioned, you have to be able to *change gears* in such a situation. You should play in the same basic style — aggressively — but you should realize that all the hands increase in value. This is particularly true of the big cards.

And, in a short-handed game, the *trouble* hands all become playable from almost any position. Also, position is probably the most important thing in a short-handed game.

The reason that's so is because you get to look at more cards and have to play more hands than you would in a Ring game. You also play your position more than your cards in a short-handed game.

When your game's down to four-handed, you need a better hand in the first two positions than you need in the last two. When you raise on the Button, the other man has to act first (on the Flop) and that puts him at a big disadvantage. It's a great equalizer when the other man has to act on his hand first.

So, in a short-handed game, you'd play your position along the same theories I discussed in a full game — except the values of the hands go up a few notches. The *trouble* hands become better hands because you **don't** figure to be up against A-A, K-K or A-K nearly as often as you might in a Ring game.

You simply play more in line with a big-card theory in a short-handed game. I mean, the bigger your cards are. . .the better hand you'll have. For instance, two Aces or two Kings is just a mountain in a short-handed game...and you could play them real fast. But, in a Ring game, you might play either hand a lot slower because there could be a lot of people taking a Turn to beat those big Pairs. That **wouldn't** be the case in a short-handed game. Consequently, they're much more valuable hands than they are in a Ring game. What you're trying to catch in a short-handed game is big cards *in position*.

INSURANCE

Many times when you're playing No-Limit Hold 'em a player will have all his money in the pot before or on the Flop (or even on Fourth St.). Since there are cards to come and since no more betting can take place (if it's a head-up situation), both players will generally turn their hands over so that *Insurance* can be considered.*

Insurance is a side-bet that's usually made between the two players involved in the pot or between one of the players involved and an *Insurance Man* who may or may not be an active player. The player with the hand having the best **potential** to win the pot is offered (or asks for) some Insurance. *Taking Insurance* is a way to protect your investment in the pot. But, it's always a **bad** bet (unless a mistake is made). As it is in life away from the Poker table, the *Insurance Man* won't be giving away anything. When he lays you a price on your hand...he'll be getting the best of it. The price you'll be getting will always be considerably less than the true price your hand is worth. (See the *Appendix* and below.) The difference between the true price and the actual price the *Insurance Man* is willing to lay is his *Vigorish* (edge or *Commission*).

I used the phrase *"best* **potential** *to win the pot"* because it's **not** always the best hand on the Flop that has the best winning potential. For example, if the Flop was 7♣-5◇-4◇ and you had the 7◇-6◇...you'd be the favorite (about 2⅓ to

---

*There's no rule that says you must turn your hand over, but such a request is rarely (if ever) refused.

1) over an opponent with a Pair of Kings (say, the K♠-K♡). You'd have 20 cards in the deck that could win for you with two shots to catch any one of them.*

I try **not** to take *Insurance* myself. I try to **lay it** because the best (potential) hand always has to take the worst of it. For example, if you're a 3 to 2 favorite. . .well, the best you can usually get is 13 to 10 (or maybe 7 to 5). So why take it? That's the edge you're looking for to start with. If you take *Insurance*. . .you're giving up your edge.

Through the years, I've heard a lot of discussion about whether you should or shouldn't take *Insurance*.

My advice is to lay the *Insurance*. . .**but** *don't* **take it.**

You can't argue with mathematical facts when you have the best of something. If you can lay 7 to 5 on a 3 to 2 shot. . .you should do it. But you **shouldn't** take 7 to 5 when you're a 3 to 2 favorite. It's that simple.

However, I can understand that if a man was on a short bankroll. . .well, perhaps then he should take *Insurance*. I guess it would be O.K. to take the worst of it so you could stay in action. But, if your bankroll warrants it. . .**don't** take *Insurance* — lay it.

I used to talk about a related subject with a very big (and very successful) gambler I've known for many years. He said *"if a man came in and offered to lay me 10 to 1 on the flip of a coin for all the money I had in the world. . .I WOULDN'T take it."* He said he just **couldn't** liquidate everything he's got — all of his property and his cash. He wouldn't risk losing it all. It would be over a million dollars. He wouldn't do it even if he thought he could get hold of another million.

But, I'd do it. I surely would. I'd just have to. I couldn't pass up the opportunity to take 10 to 1 on an even–money

---

*Your Straight-Flush draw gives you 15 wins and you have five more wins with the 3-Sixes and 2-Sevens that are still in the deck. Of course, the assumption here is that your opponent's hand *doesn't* improve.

shot. I'd do it because I have enough confidence in myself that I'd be able to come up with another million if I lost.

A FINAL WORD

Of course, I'm sure you understand that all the numerous possibilities have by no means been exhausted. No–Limit Hold 'em is a highly complex game. It's hardly possible (and certainly **not** practical) to attempt to discuss the enormous variety of situations that could occur. And, as you now know, there are certain questions I couldn't answer definitively because even I **don't** know exactly what I'd do until I was faced with the problem. As I've said, at such times, I go with my "feeling" which is really a rapid analysis of conscious and sub–conscious facts.

Nevertheless, I've given you a lot of *white meat* (sophisticated techniques and strategies) that have only been known by a few world–class Poker players — and, in some cases, not even then.

The average player has **never** had access to the kind of information you've just read. First of all, nothing as comprehensive as this has ever been written about No–Limit Hold 'em. Even if it was, unless it was written by someone who has played at a world–class level for many years — and who was a consistent winner — it would **not** be of much value. In fact, it could even be harmful. Having no information at all is better than having bad information.

So...you should do quite well at No–Limit Hold 'em now that you know almost as much about the game as I do. The rest is up to you.

HOLD 'EM SUPPLEMENT

The following tables are a contribution from

Richard Englesteen

DOUBLE BELLY BUSTER STRAIGHTS (DBB's)

There is a fourteen card straight continuum since Aces may be used in a big or little Straight.

A 2 3 4 5 6 7 8 9 10 J Q K A

You may turn a double belly buster draw with any two adjacent cards from 3-4 to J-Q. In the cases where two Flops yield a draw, the top example is of the form:

X _ Y _ _ _ Z (4-6-10)	The underscore lines
and the bottom one is:	represent "spaces"
X _ _ _ Y _ Z (6-10-Q)	between the cards.

YOU HOLD	FLOP*	YOU HOLD	FLOP*
3-4	A-5-7	8-9	5-7-J
			6-10-Q
4-5	A-3-7	9-10	6-8-Q
	2-6-8		7-J-K
5-6	2-4-8	10-J	7-9-K
	3-7-9		8-Q-A
6-7	3-5-9	J-Q	8-10-A
	4-8-10		
7-8	4-6-10		
	5-9-J		

*There are 16 DBB's of this type.

You may flop a DBB with any two cards which have 1 space between them. All flops have one of three forms:

	X_YZ (2-4-5)	XY_Z (8-9-J)	X__Y__Z (5-8-J)

YOU HOLD	FLOP**	YOU HOLD	FLOP**
A-3	4-5-7	7-9	3-5-6 5-8-J 10-J-K
2-4	5-6-8	8-10	4-6-7 6-9-Q J-Q-A
3-5	6-7-9 A-4-7	9-J	5-7-8 7-10-K
4-6	7-8-10 2-5-8	10-Q	6-8-9 7-10-K
5-7	A-3-4 3-6-9 8-9-J	J-K	7-9-10
6-8	2-4-5 4-7-10 9-10-Q	Q-A	8-10-J

**There are 24 DBB's of this type.*

You may flop with a DBB with any two cards with 2 spaces between them. The flop is always of the form: X_Y_Z

YOU HOLD	FLOP*	YOU HOLD	FLOP*
A-4	3-5-7	7-10	9-J-K 4-6-8
2-5	4-6-8	8-J	10-Q-A 5-7-9
3-6	5-7-9	9-Q	6-8-10
4-7	6-8-10 A-3-5	10-K	7-9-J
5-8	7-9-J 2-4-6	J-A	8-10-Q
6-9	8-10-Q 3-5-7		

There are 16 DBB's of this type.

You may flop a DDB with any two cards with 3 spaces between them. The bottom flop is always of the form: **X__YZ** while the top one is: **XY__Z**

YOU HOLD	FLOP*	YOU HOLD	FLOP*
A-5	3-4-7	6-10	8-9-Q
			4-7-8
2-6	4-5-8	7-J	9-10-K
			5-8-9
3-7	5-6-9	8-Q	10-J-A
	A-4-5		6-9-10
4-8	6-7-10	9-K	7-10-J
	2-5-6		
5-9	7-8-J	10-A	8-J-Q
	3-6-7		

*There are 16 DBB's of this type.

With four spaces, e.g., A-6 or J-6 you can only turn an open-end straight draw.

You may flop a DBB with any two cards with 5 spaces between them. The flop is always of the form: **XYZ**

YOU HOLD	FLOP*	YOU HOLD	FLOP*
A-7	3-4-5	5-J	7-8-9
2-8	4-5-6	6-Q	8-9-10
3-9	5-6-7	7-K	9-10-J
4-10	6-7-8	8-A	10-J-Q

*There are 8 DBB's of this type.

There are eight 5-card groups which with permutations yield ten possible DBB's. These groups all have the form: V-WXYZ. All Double Belly Busters come up on 7 card segments of the 14 card continuum. The spaces, of course, appear in different sequences.

GROUP		GROUP	
I	A-3-4-5-7	V	5-7-8-9-J
II	2-4-5-6-8	VI	6-8-9-10-Q

| III | . . . . 3-5-6-7-9 | VII | . . . . 7-9-10-J-K |
| IV | . . . . 4-6-7-8-10 | VIII | . . . . 8-10-J-Q-A |

Using **GROUP III** as an example of the permutations:

YOU HOLD	FLOP	YOU HOLD	FLOP
(a) 3-5 6-7-9		(f) 5-7 3-6-9	
(b) 3-6 5-7-9		(g) 5-9 3-6-7	
(c) 3-7 5-6-9		(h) 6-7 3-5-9	
(d) 3-9 5-6-7		(i) 6-9 3-5-7	
(e) 5-6 3-7-9		(j) 7-9 3-5-6	

Thus there are 80 possible DBB's (eight 5-card groups times 10 permutations). This is the same total yielded when you add the totals at the bottoms of each of the tables (16 + 24 + 16 + 16 + 8 = 80).

COLORFUL NAMES OF

A-A	American Airlines
A-K	Big Slick
A-Q	Doyle Brunson*
A-J	Ajax
A-10	Johnny Moss
A-8	Dead Man's Hand
3-A	Baskin-Robbins
K-Q	Marriage
K-J	Kojak
K-9	Canine
K-8	Kokomo
K-7	Columbia River
K-3	King Crab
Q-J	Maverick
Q♠-J◇	Pinochle
Q-10	Goolsby
Q-9	Quinine
Q-7	Computer Hand
J-6	Railroad Hand
J-5	Motown
5-10	Woolworth
10-4	Broderick Crawford
10-3	Weinberg

VARIOUS HOLD 'EM HANDS

10-2 ....Doyle Brunson*

9-8...Oldsmobile

6-9.......................................Joe Bernstein

3-9...Jack Benny

2-9...Twiggy

8-8..................Little Oldsmobile

8-5.......................................Finky Dink

3-8........................... Raquel Welch

7-6....................Union Oil

5-7....................Pickle Man

7-2................... Beer Hand

6-3..................... Blocky

6-2.....................Ainsworth

4-5................... Jesse James

3-5....................... Bully Johnson

2-4..........................Lumberman's Hand

3-3... Crabs

6-6-6.. Kotch

4-4-4.................................. Grand Jury

---

*The reason there are two hands named after me is because of what happened in the 1976 and 1977 *"World Series of Poker"*. In **both** years, I won with a 10–2. The A–Q has long been called *"Doyle Brunson"* in Texas because I **never** play this hand.

SUPER/SYSTEM

A Course In Power Poker

Class Dismissed...

(The Poker Statistics Section Begins on Page 555.)

GLOSSARY

GLOSSARY

Poker terminology
when the game is played

"the DOYLE BRUNSON way"

ABC
A term used to describe the first three cards in Razz and High-Low Split, when they are an Ace, Deuce and a Trey.

ACE-to-FIVE LOWBALL
See *California Lowball*.

ACTIVE PLAYER
A player still involved in the pot.

ADVERTISE
To bluff with the intention of having the bluff seen by the other players in order to get them to call a future bet that's **not** a bluff.

AGENT
Confederate (in a cheating scheme). Also see *Mechanic*.

ALL-IN (or "GO ALL IN")
To bet all the money you have on the table.

ANYTHING OPENS
A Draw Poker game where specific Openers are **not** required. Therefore, a player can open the pot with any hand he wants. Such a game is almost always *Pass Out*.

AUTOMATIC BLUFF
A bluff, usually in Lowball, that's made without really thinking about it because of a particular situation. Depending on the circumstances this kind of bluff will almost always be made regardless of a player's hand value.

BABY
A term used (especially in *Razz* and High-Low Split) to describe a small card, that is, one that has a value of Five or less.

BACK DOOR
When a player makes a hand he **wasn't** originally drawing at.

BACK-TO-BACK
See *Wired.*

BACKER
Generally a rich amateur who supplies a professional Gambler with a playing bankroll. However, another professional can also (and often does) *Back* a professional who is temporarily "Down on his Luck" — that is, out of money.

BACKRAISE
See *Play-Back.*

BAD BEAT
When you get a big hand cracked (beaten) by someone who was a big *dog* against you and made his longshot draw...you're said to have had a *bad beat.*

BR
Bankroll.

BEAT THE BOARD
Having a hand that can beat any other hand that's in sight.

BELLY-BUSTER STRAIGHT
Used interchangeably with "inside" Straight.

BET INTO
To take the initiative in the betting action with the knowledge that your opponent has a potentially strong hand.

BETTING THE POT
To bet the total amount of money in the pot in a Pot Limit (or No-Limit) game.

BICYCLE
The lowest possible hand in Lowball. In Ace-to-Five, A-2-3-4-5 is called a *Bicycle.* In Deuce-to-Seven, 2-3-4-5-7 is called a *Bicycle.*

BIG BLIND
The second (or possibly third) and largest Blind bet in a game that has multiple Blinds.

BIG DOG
A big underdog to win the pot. Also see *Dog.*

BIG FULL
The highest possible Full House in Hold 'em.

BIG HAND
1. A hand with a relatively high value such as a Full House.
2. A hand with a big draw, meaning that it has excellent possibilities of winning the pot. For example, flopping a Straight Flush draw in Hold 'em.

BIG ONE
$1,000.

BIKE
See *Bicycle*.

BLACK CHIP
A Casino chip with a value of $100.

BLANK
A term often used in Hold 'em to describe a card that came on Fourth Street or Fifth Street and is **not** of any value to a player's hand.

BLIND
The bet that opens the pot that a player puts in before he receives his cards.

BOARD
The cards that are face-up in a Poker game. For example, the up-cards in Seven-Stud are referred to as a players *Board*, and the community cards in Hold 'em are also called the *Board*.

BOBTAIL
See *Open-End Straight*.

BOTTOM DEALER
A card manipulator (Cheat) who can deal cards off the bottom of the deck. Also see *Second Dealer*.

BREAK
To draw a card instead of playing Pat. This term is often used in Lowball when, for example, a player who intended to play a "Nine" pat, throws away the Nine to draw one card to try to improve his hand. What he did was *break* the Nine.

BRING-IT-IN-FOR
The first **optional** bet in any Poker game.

BROKEN FALL
A *Flop* where a Straight cannot be made on the next card. For example, Q-7-2.

BULL
Another name for an Ace.

BULL THE GAME
A very aggressive player is one that would be *bulling* the game, that is, creating a lot of action by his continuous betting and raising.

BULLET
An Ace.

BUMP
A very amateurish term used instead of the word "raise".

BURN AND TURN
1. To burn (or bury) the top card and give the active players their card(s).
2. Usually said by the last player to act on his hand, indicating he also checks.

BUST OUT
1. Miss your hand completely.
2. Lose all your money.

BUTTON
1. When there is a house dealer, a *Button* is put in front of a player to show that he is the theoretical dealer. The *Button* is passed to each player in clockwise order.
2. Second or Third Pair.

BUY-IN
The minimum amount of money necessary to secure a seat in a particular game.

BY ME
A common, though amateurish, expression that means the player checks or passes or drops out of the pot.

CALIFORNIA (ACE-to-FIVE) LOWBALL
A form of Lowball in which the best possible hand is an A-2-3-4-5. In this form of Lowball, which is often played with the Joker (which can be used as any value), the Ace is considered a low card and Straights and Flushes do **not** count against you.

CALL
> To put money in the pot that's exactly equal to the previous bet or raise.

CALLING STATION
> A *Sucker* who's next-to-impossible to bluff and who'll call almost any bet that you make is said to be a *calling station*.

CARDS SPEAK
> A form of High-Low Poker in which there are no declarations as to whether the player wants to play his hand for High or Low. That is, the cards *speak for themselves*.

CASE CARD
> The last card of a particular rank. For example, if you catch an Ace after the other three Aces are in the discards, then you have caught the *Case* Ace.

CATCH PERFECT
> A situation in Hold 'em (or another form of Poker) where there's only one (or two) card(s) in the deck that'll win the pot. Since no other card(s) will help you, you must *Catch Perfect*.

CATCH-UP
> When you must improve your hand so that it'll be approximately equal to your opponent's.

CHANGE GEARS
> Adjusting your style of play from loose to tight or vice versa.

CHASE
> Trying to beat a hand you know is better than yours.

CHECK BLIND (or CHECK DARK)
> To check your hand without looking at it. (Many players claim to *Check Blind* when, in fact, they have looked at their hand.)

CHECK-RAISE
> To check and then raise when the action gets back to you. (To do this, of course, a bet must be made after you check.)

CHIP (or "CHECK")
> A plastic token having various denominations used in place of cash money.

CINCH HAND
> See *Nuts*.

CLOSED POKER
Poker as played when all the cards are concealed, as in Draw Poker.

COFFEE-HOUSING
An attempt, by words or actions, to confuse, mislead or misdirect another player or players in the pot with you.

COLD CALL (or "CALL COLD")
When a player who has no money invested in the pot besides the ante calls a raise **and** a re-raise.

"COLD" DECK
A term often used to describe the deck by players who feel they're not getting enough playable or enough winning hands.

"COLD DECK"
A deck that has been previously set up (that is, the cards have been previously arranged) by an individual with the intention of cheating.

COME THROUGH A PLAYER
In a three (or more) handed pot when the first player to act bets, he is *coming through* the player(s) in the next seat(s).

COMMISSION
See *Vigorish.*

COMPLETE BLUFF
A bluff made with a completely worthless hand, as opposed to a semi-bluff that's made with a hand that has slight potential.

COMPLETE HAND
A hand such as a Straight, a Flush or a Full House. Also see *Pat Hand.*

CONCEALED PAIR
A Pair where both cards are face-down.

CONFEDERATE
See *Agent.*

COUNTRY STRAIGHT
An open-end Straight to draw to. For example, 9-10-J-Q would be a *Country Straight.*

COURTESY BET
A bet (usually a bluff) when you're fairly sure your opponent is going to call or raise.

COWBOY (K-BOY)

A word sometimes used to describe a King.

CRACK THE NUT

When a Professional Gambler meets his minimum living expenses he is said to have *Cracked the Nut*. See *Nut*.

CRIPPLED THE DECK

A deck that has almost nothing left in it that can help your opponent's (or your) hand. For example, if you had a Pair of Aces in Hold 'em and the other two Aces flopped...you would have *Crippled the Deck*.

CRYING CALL

To complain while making a call.

CUT

1. To separate the deck into portions (usually in half) after it has been shuffled.
2. See *Rake* as in "to cut the pot".

CUTTING OUT

When two people have formed a partnership and one player is going to do the playing while the other player is on the sidelines, and at some point one of these two people involved decides to terminate the partnership, that person is said to be *cutting out*.

DEAD CARD

The opposite of *Live Card*.

DEAD HAND

A hand that's not playable — for example, one that has too many or too few cards.

DEAD IN THE POT

When there is no way for you to win, you're said to be *dead in the pot*.

DEALER'S CHOICE

Poker as usually played in a Home game where the deal passes from player to player and the player who has the deal makes the decision as to what form of Poker will be played.

DEFENSIVE BET

A bet that's sometimes made to limit your potential loss in a particular pot. For example, a player wants to see his opponent's hand, but he feels that if he checks, his opponent would bet too large an amount for him to call and he **won't** be able to see his opponent's hand which he **may** be able to beat. Therefore, rather than having to call a large bet, he makes a *defensive* small bet.

DEUCE
Two. A two-spot.

DEUCE-to-SEVEN LOWBALL
A form of Lowball played primarily in the South and Southwestern part of the United States in which the best hand is a 2-3-4-5-7. That hand would be the *nuts*. In this form of Lowball, the Ace can only be considered a high card and Straights and Flushes **do** count against you. Also called *"Kansas City" Lowball*.

DOG
Abbreviation for (and more commonly used among Gamblers than) *Underdog*. The opposite of *Favorite*.

DOG-IT
To **not** merely lay-down your hand, but to lay-down (get bluffed) when you have the best hand.

DOLLAR (or $1)
The .name *High Rollers* have given to $100.

DOOR-CARD
1. The card (almost always a *Baby*) that a player will sometimes intentionally expose (or simply flash) in a Draw (closed) Poker game such as Lowball. Also see *Window Card*.
2. The first up-card in a Stud game.

DOUBLE BELLY BUSTER
A two-way inside *Straight*.

DOUBLE-POP
When you immediately raise a raiser you've *double-popped* it. That is, re-raising so the next player to act must call **two** bets.

DOUBLE-THROUGH
To double the amount of chips you have on the table by winning a pot from another player. Similarly, *"Triple-Through"* would be to triple your chips in winning a pot from two other players. (This is a term that is used more commonly in No-Limit play.)

DOWN-CARD(S)
The card(s) dealt face-down in a Stud Poker game.

DOWN THE RIVER
1. The last card received face-down in Seven-Card Stud or *Razz*.
2. Another name for Seven-Card Stud.

DOWN TO THE GREEN
Means that you've got all your chips and money in the pot and you're *Down to the Green* felt table-top.

DRAWING DEAD
Drawing to a hand that it would be impossible to win with, regardless of the card or cards drawn. Also known as *dead in the pot*.

DRAW-OUT
To improve your hand and beat an opponent who had a better hand prior to the *draw-out*.

DRIVER'S SEAT
The advantage a particular player has because it appears as though he has the best hand at the time. That player is said to be in the *Driver's Seat*.

DROP
See *Lay-Down*.

DROP-IN
A stranger in a game played among a regular group of players is called a *drop-in*.

DUCK
See *Lay-Down*.

DUPLICATES
In Lowball games two cards of the same rank. For example, 8-7-4-4-2, the 2-Fours are *Duplicates*.

EARLY, MIDDLE AND LATE POSITION
The *early positions* in an eight-handed game are the first three players to act on their hand, the *middle positions* are the next three and the *late positions* are the last two.

EXPOSED PAIR
An open Pair that is in-sight.

FALL
See *Flop*.

FALSE CUT
A *Cut* that appears to be real, but actually leaves the deck in it's original arrangement.

FALSE OPENERS
A hand that does not have the proper opening requirements.

FALSE SHUFFLE
A shuffle that appears to be a real one but, in fact, does **not** really get the cards shuffled at all when it's done by a skillful card manipulator.

FAMILY POT
A pot in which most of the players at the table are involved in.

FAST GAME
See *Pace.*

FAVORITE
The player with the highest probability of winning the hand (or winning, period). The opposite of *Dog.*

FIFTH STREET
1. In Stud Poker, the fifth card dealt to each player.
2. In Hold 'em, the last community card that is dealt.

FILL
To draw a card that will make a *complete hand.* For example, to *Fill* a Straight or a Flush or to improve Two-Pair to a *Full House.*

FLAT CALL
Calling a previous bet without raising.

FLAT LIMIT
A limit that remains constant on each round of betting. (This is opposed to a limit that is increased during the latter rounds of betting.)

FLOORMAN
A Supervisor in a Casino or in a Poker Room.

FLOP
A Hold 'em term describing the first three community cards that are turned.

FLOPPING A SET
In Hold 'em, when out of three community cards (or *Flop*) and your two hole cards, three of the cards are of the same rank.

FLUSH
Five cards of the same suit in no special order, such as an A-7-3-10-2 — All Clubs. This would be an Ace-High Flush which would be higher than any other Flush in any other suit

whose highest card is lower than an Ace, except for a Straight-Flush. If, the highest card in the Flushes of two opponents is the same, the hand is then counted down to the next highest card to see which Flush is higher. This continues in case there is still a tie until it's counted down to the final card of the hand to determine the higher Flush.

FOLD
See *Lay-Down.*

FORCE (or "THE FORCE")
See *Blind.*

FOUL HAND
See *Dead Hand.*

FOUR-FLUSH
To have four cards of a suit with cards yet to come.

FOUR-OF-A-KIND
Four cards of the same rank with a side card, such as four Jacks and a Seven.

FOURTH STREET
1. In Stud Poker, the fourth card dealt to each player.
2. In Hold 'em, the fourth community card dealt. The card after the Flop.

FREE-CARD
A card that's received by each active player without any money having been put into the pot because all the active players check on that round of play.

FREE-RIDE
See *Free-Card.*

FREEROLL
1. In High-Low Split where one player has one half of the pot cinched and is competing for the other half.
2. In Hold 'em where two players have the same hand except one of the two has suited cards with one (or two) of his suit on the *Board.* The suited hand would have a *freeroll.*

FREEZE-OUT
A game such as the "World Series of Poker" that's played down to one winner. An additional requirement of a *Freeze-Out* game is that no player can add more money to his original *Buy-In.* So, when a player loses all his money, he's out of the game and cannot get back in. Such a game requires a

different playing strategy than the one you'd use in a normal game where you can buy-in as often as you want.

FRONT SEAT
The first player to act on his hand.

FULL BOAT
See *Full House.*

FULL HOUSE
Three cards of the same rank (*Trips*) and one Pair, such as 3-Fives and 2-Sevens.

GAMBLER
An unusual way this word is often used is to describe the class (that is, the quality) of a Poker player. When the word is used this way it describes the highest class of player — which actually means that the player is **not** really a Gambler at all, but a highly skilled player. Also see *Rounder, Hustler* and *Minnow.*

GAR HOLE
An unusual term to describe the situation where chips in the game are "locked up", that is, they're in the stack of a tight, tough player and will be difficult to get back into the game.

GARDENA MIRACLE
1. A very lucky draw.
2. Something that defies the laws of probability.

GARDENA RAZZ
A form of Draw Lowball played in the Gardena, California Poker Clubs in which a *Button* (placed in front of a particular player) is used to identify the winner of the previous pot. That player is the last person to act before the draw in the current pot (even though he may not be the last player to receive cards).

GEESE
See *Sucker.*

GETTING A HAND CRACKED
The situation that occurs when you have a *Big Hand* beaten when an opponent makes a big *draw-out.*

GETTING AN EXTRA BET
In Limit Poker **only**, the art of extracting more money from your opponent by check-raising him.

GIVE A CARD
To let your opponent get another card without betting him.

GO TO THE CENTER
See *Move-In.*

GO UPHILL
See *Chase.*

GUT-SHOT
See *Belly-Buster.*

HEAD-UP (or "HEAD-TO-HEAD")
A Poker game involving only two players.

HELP
To improve one's hand.

HIGH ROLLER
A Gambler who plays for big sums of money.

HIT
As in "the Ace of Spade *hit*" (came on the *Board*) on Fourth Street.

HIT IT
To raise.

HIT THE DECK
Draw a card or cards.

HOLD-OUT
To conceal card or cards for the purpose of bringing them into the game for future use. This is a somewhat common form of cheating.

HOOK
A word sometimes used to describe a Jack.

HOT AND COLD
In any form of Poker, playing one hand against the other (with no intermediate betting) until all the cards are out. It's simply *showdown* and is often done among gamblers when they disagree as to which of the two hands is the favorite...and by how much. The dispute is resolved by betting — even or with odds. The two hands are then played *Hot and Cold* for a pre-determined number of times — or until one of the gamblers quits because he's lost as much as he cares to lose. At that point, he's at least temporarily convinced he had the wrong side of the proposition.

HUSTLER
See *Rounder.*

IGNORANT END OF A STRAIGHT
The lowest possible Straight. For example, when you have a 7-6 in the pocket in Hold 'em and the Flop comes 8-9-10, you flopped the *ignorant (low-end) of the Straight.*

IN THE LEAD
A player who's aggressive and one who does the first betting on each round is the player said to be *in the lead.*

IN THE MIDDLE
A player in a position between the original bettor on his right and a potential raiser on his left. This is the **worst** possible position that a player can be in during the play of a hand.

IN THE POCKET
Hole cards.

INSURANCE
A side bet (fairly common in No-Limit Hold 'em) that's usually made between the two players involved in the pot or between one of the players involved and an "Insurance Man" who may (or may not be) an active player. In fact, the Insurance Man is often a spectator (Professional gambler) who "Books" the bet. Also see *Taking Insurance.*

JACKS-AND-BACK
A form of Jacks-or-better Draw Poker that will revert to Lowball if no player can open the pot for High.

JAM
A *jam* pot is one in which several players are raising and re-raising.

JUICE
1. Referring to favorable pot odds.
2. A bookmaker or Insurance Man's *vigorish.*

JUMP THE FENCE
See *Call Cold.*

KANSAS CITY LOWBALL
See *Deuce-to-Seven Lowball.*

KIBITZER
Spectator. Also see *Railbird.*

KICKER
Side card.

KICKER TROUBLE
When you and your opponent have the same pair, the player with the smallest side card is said to have *kicker trouble.*

KILLING IT
When someone doubles the usual Blind bet before receiving his cards.

KNUCKLE IT
1. Pass.
2. *Rapping Pat.*

LADY
Sometimes used to describe a Queen.

LAY-DOWN
1. To show your hand at the conclusion of a pot.
2. To discard one's hand after having decided **against** calling a big bet. (A more useful meaning of the term.)

LAYING INSURANCE
See *Taking Insurance.*

LEAD OFF
See *Bring-It-In-For.*

LEAK
Something wrong with someones playing technique or strategy.

LEATHER ASS
Patience.

LEGGING A HAND
See *Slow-Play.*

LIGHT
See *Shy.*

LIMP IN
To call a bet.

LINEUP
The players in a particular game.

LITTLE BLIND
The first and smallest *Blind* bet in a game that has multiple Blinds.

LIVE BLIND
A *Blind* that has the option to raise when the action gets back to him. See *Blind*.

LIVE CARD
A card that has **not** been dealt (or seen), that is, a card that's still in play.

LIVE ONE
A rich *Sucker*.

LOCAL
A permanent Las Vegas resident.

LOCK
See *Nuts*.

LOCKSMITH
A *tight player* who "peddles the nuts".

LOOKING DOWN HIS THROAT
Knowing that it's impossible for your opponent to beat the hand that you have, that is, you have him *nutted*.

LOOKING OUT THE WINDOW
An expression used to describe a player who is **not** paying attention to the action.

LOOSE PLAYER
A player who tends to play most hands, weak or strong, and gets involved in many pots.

LOWBALL or LOW POKER
A form of Draw Poker (or any form of Poker) in which the lowest hand wins the pot.

MAIN POT
A pot in which the money has been contributed by three or more players and at least one player is out of money so that there has to be a "side pot" between the two players who still have money. The player out of money has a stake in the main pot only.

MAKE A PLAY
See *Put A Play On*.

MATCHING CARD
A card that will be integrally related to a card in your hand such as one with the same value or in the same suit.

Specifically, a card in your hand in Hold 'em that will "match" one (or more) of the community cards out on the *Board*.

MECHANIC
A card cheat who is able to manipulate the cards to his advantage or to the advantage of a *confederate* (friend).

MINNOW
A player who over-extends his bankroll in order to play in a big Limit (or No-Limit) game.

MISS THE FLOP
Where your two *hole cards* in Hold 'em have no correlation to the first three community cards.

MONEY MANAGEMENT
A term used by a Professional Poker Player to describe one of the following:

1. The handling (control) of the money (his bankroll) necessary to conduct a (Professional) Poker business.
2. The handling (control) of the money necessary to engage in a particular playing session.

MORTAL NUTS
See *Nuts*.

MOVE-IN
In a No-Limit game, making a bet with all the chips you have on the table. Also see *Set Him All-In*.

NAIL
To catch a card that enables you to win the pot; especially, to catch a card on Fifth Street in Hold 'em or *Down the River* in Seven-Card Stud.

NICKEL CHIP
A Casino Chip with a value of $5.

NO PAIR
A hand with five totally unrelated cards.

NUMBER TWO MAN (Second Dealer)
A Card Cheat capable of dealing Seconds. See *Seconds*.

NUT
The minimum amount of money a professional Gambler must make to continue his current life style, that is, his overhead.

NUT PLAYER
> A player who tends to play only *Nut* hands. This descriptive term is used primarily in Hold 'em, but can be applied to a player at any form of Poker.

NUTS
> 1. The best possible hand at that point in the pot.
> 2. An absolute cinch hand.

OFF-SUIT
> A term often used to describe the first two cards in Hold 'em when they are **not** of the same suit.

OMAHA
> A name used interchangeably with *Tight Hold 'em* — a game which differs from regular Hold 'em in that **both** of a player's *hole cards* **must** be used to make a complete hand. (In regular Hold 'em, a player **may** use both hole cards but **can** only use one of them and four of the *Board* cards.)

ON THE COME
> To bet on a hand with potential as opposed to betting on a hand that is complete. For example, a player might bet *on the come* if he was drawing one card to a Straight-Flush.

ON THE BANK
> If you're **not** involved in the pot, you're said to be *On The Bank*.

ON TILT
> When a player starts playing real bad (loses his composure) — usually after he's lost one (or more) big pots. . .he's said to be *On Tilt*.

ONE PAIR
> Two Cards of the same rank with three Side Cards such as two Tens, an Ace, a Nine and a Four.

ONE TOOTH
> A Lowball term meaning the second best hand possible.

ONE WAY ACTION
> When you and only one player are involved.

OPEN-END STRAIGHT
> A four-card hand where a Straight is possible on either end such as a 4-5-6-7.

OPEN POKER
> Poker as played when some of the cards are exposed.

OUTDRAW
See *Draw-Out*.

OUTPRICE
Gigantic favorite, or gigantic *underdog*.

OUTS
When you're in a pot with the worst hand, but can still win it because there are cards in the deck that'll help your hand, you have *Outs*. Also see *Drawing Dead*.

OVERBET
A term used to describe a bet that's out of proportion (much bigger than) the size of a pot in a No-Limit game.

OVERCALL
To call a bet (usually a big one) after another player or players have already called.

OVERCARD (Sometimes Called "OVERCOAT")
A card that's higher than any card showing. For example, you have an Ace in your hand in Hold 'em and the highest card on *Board* is a King; the Ace is an *Overcard*.

OVERHEAD
See *Nut*.

OVERPAIR
A Pair *In the Pocket* in Hold 'em that's higher than any card on the *Board*.

PACE
The speed at which the action (betting) is occurring. The pace of a game would be *slow* when there's **not** much betting and raising. Conversely, a *fast* game would be one in which most or all of the players are doing a lot of *playing*, that is, betting and raising.

PAINT
A Face-Card — a Jack, Queen or King.

PAIR POKER
Someone who disdains drawing at Straights and Flushes is said to be playing *Pair Poker*.

PAPER
Marked Cards.

PARTNERS
1. Two or more players teaming up in a particular game to beat

the other players by cheating with pre-arranged signals.

2. Two or more players, playing (honestly) out of the same bankroll.

PASS AND BACK IN
1. To be able to check in the first round in a Draw game. If anyone opens, you are allowed to call.
2. Opposite of *Pass Out*.

PASS OUT
A Draw game where you **must** open the pot or throw your hand away.

PAT HAND
A hand that's *complete* or one that a player does **not** draw to.

PEDDLE THE NUTS TO HIM
Selling (or trying to sell) a cinch hand to a *Calling Station*.

PEEK
The cheating maneuver of a *Second* Dealer when he looks (peeks) at the top card to see if it will be of any value to him. If it is, he'll save it and deal *Seconds* to the other players. Also see *Mechanic*.

PICKED OFF
To get called when you are bluffing.

PICK-UP
Win a (relatively) small pot without a contest.

PIECE OF CHEESE
1. Something very easy.
2. A very bad hand.

PLAY
1. To sit in on a Poker game.
2. To get involved in a particular pot.
3. To do something dramatic or creative during a particular hand: *To make a play.*

PLAY-BACK
Re-raise (or *backraise*).

PLAY BEHIND
In some games, a player can declare (before the beginning of the hand) that he's actually playing for more money than he has on the table and in such a case that player is said to be *Playing Behind*.

PLAY FROM THE HIP
A player who plays *fast* at the beginning of a game, before he is winner or loser.

PLAYER
Someone who understands the sophisticated techniques and strategies of the form of Poker being played and who is also willing to gamble.

PLAYING OVER
A player may leave his seat temporarily and go to eat, for example, and another player may occupy that temporarily vacant seat. The new player is said to be *Playing Over* the player who has left for dinner.

PLAYS JAM-UP
Plays very well.

PLUNGING AROUND
Playing very *loose*.

POSITION
Not your seat in the game, but where you are relative to the other active players in a particular pot.

POST OAK BLUFF
A very small bet in a large pot...in the hopes the other man doesn't have anything and will give you the pot. Originated from a tight player trying to *bluff* at a pot when he didn't have enough guts to make a big bet and *really* trying to win it.

POT
1. The total amount of money bet.
2. An imaginary area somewhere near the center of the table that's generally **without** physical boundaries and where the bets of the players are placed.

POT ODDS
The price (odds) that the pot is giving you on your investment (call). See *Right Price*.

PREMIUM HANDS
The top hands in a particular game.

PRIVATE GAME
A Poker game restricted to certain members of a club or fraternal organization or one that's played among friends only (as opposed to a Public Game).

PROTECTION

Having a hand in High-Low Split that protects you from being *scooped*.

PUBLIC GAME

A Poker game that's open to anyone and one that's generally played in a specific area of a casino called "the Poker Room" or in a public facility such as the legal Poker Clubs in California.

PUMPED UP

1. An elated feeling, usually after winning a big pot.
2. To have money.

PUT A PLAY ON

When you *Put A Play On* a player, what you're trying to do is out-maneuver him by strategically timing your bet. You should **only** attempt a strategy play **against** a **strong** player.

PUT THE CLOCK ON HIM

Any player can make the request to *Put The Clock On Him* if he feels another player is taking too much time to Call his bet. In No-Limit games, there's (almost) always a stop-watch at the table. After the dealer (or Card Room Manager) starts the watch, the deliberating player has one minute to make the Call. If his money isn't in the pot at the end of that time, he's considered to have passed.

QUARTER CHIP

A Casino Chip with a value of $25.

RABBIT-HUNTING

1. Asking to see what the next card coming off the deck is after you've folded your hand.
2. Looking through the discards to see what cards have been dealt. This is something that's **never** done in a Professional game while the hand is still in play, but in a Home game, it's a somewhat common practice.

RAG

This term is often used in Hold 'em to describe the cards on the Flop that look "raggedy". For example, if the Flop was a 2♠-5♣-10◇, then a player who plays Hold 'em regularly would probably describe that particular Flop as "three *Rags*". Also see *Blank*.

RAIL

A physical barrier that can be made of wood or simply a velvet rope that separates on-lookers from players in the game.

RAILBIRD

An On-Looker. See *Rail*.

RAISE

To make a bet with more (total dollar amount of) chips than a previous bet.

RAKE

The percentage extracted from the pot by a House dealer. Also see *Time*.

RAPPING PAT

This term is used in Draw Poker. A player who decides to play the original five cards he was· dealt and **not** draw any cards is *Rapping Pat*.

RAT-HOLE

To put chips (or money) in your pocket during a game.

RAZZ

Seven-Card Stud for Low. Also a form of Draw Lowball in Gardena.

READ

Making an educated guess as to what an opposing player's hand is. Also, *putting a player on* a particular hand.

READERS

See *Paper*.

RELEASING A SET

To throw away *Trips* when you think they are best.

REPRESENT

To make it appear that you have a hand you really don't.

RIGHT PRICE

When you're getting (exactly) the right pot odds on the money you have put in the pot (or exactly the proper odds on any bet you make).

RING GAME

A Poker game that has a player in every seat, that is, a full game (as opposed to a *Short-Handed* game).

RIVER CARD

The last (or 7th) card dealt face down to a player in *Razz* or Seven-Stud.

ROCK (or HARD ROCK)
A very good player. Usually a very *tight player* also.

ROLLED UP
An expression in Seven-Card Stud when the first three cards are of the same rank. For example, three *Rolled Up* Jacks.

ROUGH
A term often used to describe a Lowball hand. For example, an 8-7-6-5-3 would be a *rough* Eight. An 8-4-3-2-1 would be a *smooth* Eight. Another example: an 8-7-3-2-1 is an Eight that's *rough* because the Seven is in the hand, but it gets *smooth* after the Seven.

ROUNDER
A very good Professional Poker Player who makes the "Rounds" of various games. However, a *Rounder* is a lower class of player than a *Gambler*.

ROYAL FLUSH
The highest ranking *Straight-Flush* (and in a game with no Wild cards, the highest-ranking hand) from the Ten to the Ace; for example, a **10♠-J♠-Q♠-K♠-A♠**.

RUN UP A HAND
An on-the-spot manufacture of what would be a *cold deck* had the cards been arranged in advance. This is done by a skillful card manipulator (cheat) who takes cards from the discards and arranges them according to where he is seated in relation to the other players and is able to assure himself (or a *confederate*) of a very good hand when it's his turn to deal.

RUN YOU DOWN
Chase you.

RUNNING PAIR
Two cards of the same denomination (such as two Sevens) that fall consecutively on Fourth and Fifth Streets in Hold 'em.

RUSH
A rapid succession of winning hands. Also known as "winning streak".

SANDBAG
Checking the probable best hand with the intention of raising.

SANDWICH
Two players (Bettors) having another player in the middle during the action.

SCOOP
Win both (High and Low) ends of a High-Low Split pot.

SCORED PAIR
A Pair *In the Pocket* in Hold 'em.

SCREWED DOWN
A player who's playing very tight is said to be *Screwed Down*.

SEAT POSITION
The **actual** seat a player has — not to be confused with his *position* in the pot.

SECOND BUTTON
See *Second Pair.*

SECOND DEALER
A card manipulator (Cheat) who can deal **Seconds**.

SECOND (or THIRD) NUTS
The second (or third) best possible hand.

SECOND PAIR (or SECOND BUTTON)
A Pair made with the second highest card on the *Board* in Hold 'em.

SECONDS (or SECOND CARD)
The second card from the top of the deck that's dealt by a card cheat when he wants to save the top card for himself (or a *Confederate*). Also see *Mechanic*.

SELLING A HAND
1. Getting your opponent to call your bet.
2. The art of making a bet that's not too big since it might discourage your opponent from calling, yet not too small so that you don't *sell your hand* too cheaply...but the perfect size (amount) so that you can extract the maximum value out of your hand.

SEMI-BLUFFING
Bluffing with an *Out*.

SEND IT AROUND
To *slow play* a big hand in an early position hoping another player behind you will raise so that you can re-raise when the action gets back to you.

SET
A term used to describe *Trips* or *Fours* (Four-of-a-kind), as in a *Set of Trips*.

SET HIM ALL-IN (or MOVE HIM ALL-IN)
In a No-Limit game, making a bet so big that it would force another player to commit all his chips to the pot.

SEVENS RULE
A rule used in Draw Lowball (especially in the Gardena, California Poker clubs) that states a player **must** bet his hand if it's a "Seven" (or better). If the player breaks this rule by **not** betting a Seven he **cannot** participate in any further profits from the pot.

SHILL
A House player who's paid by a Casino to stimulate action and encourage other players to join in the game, and one who plays with House money and has no real stake in the game.

SHOOT IT UP
Raise.

SHORT
See *Shy.*

SHORT CALL
To Call a bet with an insufficient amount of money in a No-Limit (or even in a Limit) game when the amount of the Call is all the money that the player has left on the table.

SHORT CARDS
Any game played with cards besides Poker. For example, Gin Rummy, Bridge, etc.

SHORT-HANDED GAME
A Poker game that is **not** full — one that has many seats open. (The opposite of *Ring Game.)*

SHORT MONEY
An amount of money less than what a player would normally *Buy-In* for in a particular game.

SHORTS
Any Pair **less than** Jacks in a Draw Poker game that requires Jacks-or-better to open.

SHOWDOWN
See *Hot and Cold.*

SHUT OUT
You can get *shut out* of a pot when an opponent in a No-Limit game makes a bet bigger than you can legitimately call. Similarly, you can *shut out* your opponents.

SHY

To owe money in the pot.

SIDECARD

See *Kicker*.

SIMULTANEOUS DECLARATION

A form of High-Low Poker in which the players simultaneously declare whether they will play their hand for High, Low, or both High and Low. The way the players declare is usually with a chip or chips concealed in their hand. That is, when a player opens his hand and there is **no** chip in it, he has declared for *Low*. When he has **one** chip in his hand, he has declared for *High*. When he has **two** chips in his hand, he has declared for **both** *High* and *Low*.

SIXTH STREET

The sixth card dealt each active player in Stud Poker.

SLOW GAME

See *Pace*.

SLOW-PLAY

To play a strong hand weakly, that is, let your opponents take the lead in the betting.

SMOOTH

See *Rough*.

SMOOTH CALL

When someone slow-plays a hand or makes a difficult call. Also, an expression used when a player calls anticipating a raise by a player behind him.

SNAPPED OFF

To get called when a person is bluffing.

SNATCH GAME

A game in which the dealer is raking an excessive amount of money out of the pot.

SNOW HAND

In Draw games when a player stands pat on worthless hands and bets at the pot hoping his bet, rather than his hand, will win the pot.

SOUP

See *Lay-Down*.

SPEEDING AROUND
A player who plays real *loose* with no definable pattern is said to be *Speeding Around*.

SPIKE
See *Nail*.

SPLIT OPENERS
In Draw Poker, a strategic play made by the Opener who discards one or more of the cards necessary to open the pot in order to draw to a hand that's more likely to win. For example, a player opens the pot with a Pair of Jacks and then declares that he's *splitting openers*. He may want to, for example, draw to a Straight or a Flush. He segregates the part of his hand that he's splitting and withholds it from the other discards to **prove** his openers at the end of the hand.

SPLIT PAIR
A Pair in Seven-Card Stud Poker in which one of the cards is face-up and one is face-down.

SPLIT POT
A pot in which two or more players have hands with equal value and, therefore, split the money in the pot. (This is **not** the same as a split pot in High-Low Split.)

SQUEEZE (or "SWEAT")
To look at your cards by spreading them apart so that their value will be revealed to you as slowly as possible.

SQUEEZE BET OR RAISE
A technique or strategy used in all forms of Poker, but especially in High-Low Split, to extract additional money from a player not likely to win (share) the pot.

STAY
To continue as an active player by calling a bet or raise.

STEAL (or STEAL A POT)
To win a pot on a bluff.

STEAL POSITION
1. Next-to-last *Baby* card in Low Poker.
2. Next-to-last *High* card in High Poker.

STEAM
See *On Tilt*.

STRADDLE
See *Big Blind*.

STRAGGLERS

Players who *limp* in from early positions.

STRAIGHT

Five cards in sequence such as a 7-8-9-10-J (mixed suits).

STRAIGHT-FLUSH

Five cards in **sequence** and in the **same** suit such as 5♡-6♡-7♡-8♡-9♡.

STRANGER

1. An unfamiliar player in the game. Also called *Drop-In*.
2. A card that was received on the draw and is therefore new and unfamiliar.

STRATEGIC BLUFF

The opposite of *automatic bluff* — one that's clearly thought out and planned.

STRETCH

A hand that won't *Stretch* is one that **can't** make a Straight.

STRING BET

A way of betting that's generally considered illegal in most Poker games, especially public games. It's a bet that's not made with a continuous action, that is, part of the bet is made, then the player hesitates, and then he completes the remainder of the bet. The hesitation in the betting action is the "illegal" part of the move. It's considered to be "illegal" because during the period of hesitation, the player making the string bet can possibly observe the reaction(s) of anyone already in the pot and especially the reaction(s) of active players behind him.

STRIKING

See *Rush*.

STUCK

When a player's losing, he's said to be *Stuck*.

SUCKER

A player who thinks he knows how to play, but really has no chance of winning (consistently) because of his ineptitude.

SUITED

A term often used to describe the first two cards in Hold 'em that are of the same suit.

SWING HAND

A hand in High-Low Split that has a chance to win **both** the High and Low ends of the pot.

Tab 551

TAB

An expression indigenous to the South and Southwestern part of the United States that is synonymous with "Credit".

TAKE-OUT

See *Buy–In.*

TAKING A TURN

Trying to catch a card (or cards).

TAP

To go *all–in.*

TAKING INSURANCE

A way to protect your investment in the pot by allowing an "Insurance Man" to lay you a price on your hand when you have the hand with the best winning potential. The price that you'll be getting is always considerably less than the true price that your hand is worth. The difference between the true price and the actual price the Insurance Man is willing to lay is his *Vigorish.* Also see *Insurance.*

TAP-CITY

A slang term to signify that a player went completely broke, that is, he went to *Tap–City.*

TAP-OUT (or TAPPED-OUT)

See *Tap–City.*

TELL

An habitual mannerism of a player in a particular situation that gives you an indication of the strength of his hand or whether or not he's bluffing.

THIRD STREET

In Stud Poker, the third card dealt to each player.

THREE-OF-A-KIND

Three cards of the same rank and two side cards, such as K–K–K–6–9.

THREES

See *Trips.*

THROW A PARTY

A Sucker who is literally giving his money away in the game is said to be *Throwing a Party.*

TICKET

A slang term for a card as in "give me a *ticket*".

TIED-ON

When your hand is so good that you must play it until all the cards are out, you're said to be *Tied-On* to it.

TIGHT HOLD 'EM

See *Omaha.*

TIGHT PLAYER

A player who tends to play only very strong hands and gets involved in very few pots.

TIME

The amount of money collected by the House from each player at specific *time* periods to pay for the use of the table. Also see *Rake.*

TIP YOUR DUKE

To reveal the quality of your hand.

TOKE

A Gratuity. Commonly used in gambling circles instead of the word "Tip". The derivation of the term is not known, but it may stand for "Token of Appreciation".

TOP KICKER

The highest (or higher) side card when two or more players have identical hands and that card is used to determine the winner of the pot.

TOP PAIR

Pairing one of your hole cards with the highest card on the *Board* in Hold 'em.

TRAIL A HAND AROUND

Slow-play a hand in an early position.

TRAP

See *Check-Raise* and *Sandbagging.*

TREY

Slang for Three. A Three-spot.

TRIPLETS

See *Trips.*

TRIPS

Slang for Three-of-a-kind.

TUNA (FISH)

See *Sucker.*

TURKEY
>See *Sucker*.

TURN
> 1. In Hold 'em, a word often used by Texans (and players from the South and Southwestern part of the United States) instead of the word *Flop*.
> 2. In addition to the above meaning, this term is also used to describe the Fourth card placed on the *Board* in Hold 'em.

TURN ONE
>An expression often used by the last player to act during a Hold 'em hand when all the other active players before him have checked. The expression means that he has also checked.

TUSH HOG
>A very tough player.

TWO-PAIR
>Two separate sets of two cards of the same rank and a side card, such as K-K-5-5-7.

UNDERBET
>To make a smaller bet than you normally would. This is done (usually) to entice a raise.

UNDERDOG
>See *Dog*.

UNDERFULL
>Any Full House in Hold 'em less than the *Big Full*.

UNDER THE GUN
>The first player to act in a Poker pot.

UNGLUED
>See *On Tilt*.

UP-CARD(S)
>The exposed (open) card(s) in a Stud Poker game.

UPHILL
>To go *uphill* is to have the worst hand and *chase* a better hand.

VIGORISH
>A percentage extracted by the House (Casino) to enable it to make a profit on the game.

WALK
>Letting the *Blind* win unchallenged.

WASHED (or WASH-OUT)

A term sometimes used to indicate that a player, after a period of time, broke approximately even during the time he played.

WHEEL

See *Bicycle.*

WHEEL LOWBALL

See *California Lowball.*

WHEN ALL THE CARDS ARE OUT

The point when there are no more cards to be dealt.

WHIPSAW

To be the caller between two players who are both raising.

WHITE MEAT

The sophisticated parts of a Poker discussion.

WINDOW CARD

A card held on the bottom of a playing hand in Draw Poker which is either deliberately or involuntarily exposed.

WIRED

See *Wired Pair.*

WIRED PAIR

A Pair on the first two cards in any Poker game.

SUPER/SYSTEM's
POKER
STATISTICS

A TOUR OF THE TABLES

*The text and tables that follow are by *"Crazy Mike"* **Caro.**

No sooner had I tapped my friend on the shoulder than he shook his head miserably and shoved $300 in chips across the table. The other player had just spread J♥-J◇-9♥-7◇-3♣ and since this was an Ace-to-Five Lowball game, I naturally became curious.

"What was that?" I asked when my friend turned toward me.

"Two red Jacks. I'm laying him $300 to $2 he can't get both red Jacks before the draw."

"That's 150 to one," I said, trying not to sound incredulous. *"Are you sure` of the odds?"*

He quickly raised a finger to his lips, fearing I would wise up the **Sucker** who was still stacking the $300.

"Get up—I need to talk to you," I said.

Away from the table, he lamented, *"That guy's killing me. For two weeks he's been beating me at the same proposition. Do you suppose he's holding out a red Jack?"*

"The odds are 136.8 to one," I told him.

"What?" He paused, his mind whizzing over the problem. He is a mathematician of the highest order, and we've often exchanged Poker information. But in this case he was **wrong**. *"No!"* he decided. *"The odds are 191 to one. I'm the favorite."*

"Friendly bet," I suggested. *"Here's a hundred that you're wrong."*

"All right, 'Crazy Mike'," said he, emphasizing the word **"Crazy"**. *"I call that obvious bluff!"* He extracted a hundred dollar bill from his wallet.

We went for coffee.

He stated his case first. *"There are 89,760 ways to get a Pair of Jacks,"* He began, writing on a napkin to accentuate his argument. *"We know this from the DISTRIBUTION OF HANDS Tables we've worked up independently. You agree? Okay, now there are six types of Pair-partners that make up two Jacks— Jack of Diamonds with Jack of Clubs, Jack of Clubs with Jack of Spades, and so forth. One of these is the Jack of Diamonds with the Jack of Hearts, the* **two red** *ones. So exactly one-sixth of the 89,760 are two red Jacks. There, that's 14,960."* He underlined the answer on the napkin. *"So we divide that into 2,869,685— the total number of possible hands—and we get...191.8. It's 190.8 to one, just like I said."*

It was my turn. *"You're overlooking the obvious. That answer is right if the guy holds* **exactly** *two Jacks. But he can have four Jacks, a Full House, three Jacks or two Pair and still have a hand which* **includes both red Jacks.** *Here's the easiest way to get the answer. Since there are 53 cards, you get five shots out of 53 to come up with the Jack of Diamonds.. When that happens, there are four chances remaining out of 52 that the Jack of Hearts is present. One chance in 10.6 for the Jack of Diamonds. Then one chance in 13 for the Jack of Hearts. Multiplied together, that's 137.8, and the price is 136.8 to one."*

He nodded dismally and said, *"Sometimes a person's mind gets jammed in a certain mode of thinking and he keeps making the same kindergarten mistake over and over."*

I sympathized, accepted his $100 and paid for his coffee.

Even mathematicians make mistakes dealing with **elementary** Poker probability, like the Red-Jacks problem. When you consider situations hundreds of times more complicated, it's understandable why so many existing Poker books are packed with wrong information.

The following tables were done by me personally, and they are accurate beyond question (I hope) . . .

TABLE I

THE PROBABILITY OF BEING DEALT SPECIFIC HANDS BEFORE THE DRAW

(53-card deck — including Joker)

The probability of being dealt. . . (before the draw)	Expressed in percent (%) is. . .	The odds against it are. . .	Number of possible Combinations
5-ACES	**0.00***	**2,869,684 to 1**	**1**
STRAIGHT-FLUSH	**0.01**	**14,066 to 1**	**204**
Royal Flush	0.00**	119,569 to 1	24
Other Straight-Flush	0.01	15,942 to 1	180
FOUR-OF-A-KIND	**0.03**	**3,465 to 1**	**828**
FULL HOUSE	**0.15**	**656 to 1**	**4,368**
FLUSH	**0.27**	**367 to 1**	**7,804**
STRAIGHT	**0.71**	**139 to 1**	**20,532**
THREE-OF-A-KIND	**2.21**	**44.3 to 1**	**63,360**
3-Aces	0.37	271 to 1	10,560
Three-of-a-kind (Large: K's — 8's)	0.92	108 to 1	26,400
Three-of-a-kind (Small: 7's — 2's)	0.92	108 to 1	26,400
TWO-PAIR	**4.83**	**19.7 to 1**	**138,600**
Aces-up	1.10	89.6 to 1	31,680
K-up,Q-up,J-up	1.69	58.0 to 1	48,600
Small Two-Pair (Tens-up and under)	2.03	48.2 to 1	58,320
ONE PAIR	**42.34**	**1.36 to 1**	**1,215,024**
PAIR OF A,K,Q,J (Openers)	14.19	6.05 to 1	407,184
Aces	4.81	19.8 to 1	137,904
Kings	3.13	31.0 to 1	89,760
Queens	3.13	31.0 to 1	89,760
Jacks	3.13	31.0 to 1	89,760
SHORTS	**28.15**	**2.55 to 1**	**807,840**
Shorts (Large: 10's — 7's)	12.51	6.99 to 1	359,040
Shorts (Small: 6's — 2's)	15.64	5.39 to 1	448,800

* Actually 0.000035% ** Actually 0.000836%

TABLE II

THE PROBABILITY OF BEING DEALT SPECIFIC HANDS <u>OR BETTER</u> BEFORE THE DRAW

(53-card deck — including Joker)

The probability of being dealt . . . (before the draw)	Expressed in percent (%) is. . .	The odds against it are. . .	Number of possible combinations
5-ACES	0.00*	2,869,684 to 1	1
STRAIGHT-FLUSH ■	0.01	13,997 to 1	205
Royal Flush ■	0.00**	114,786 to 1	25
Other Straight-Flush ■	0.01	13,997 to 1	205
FOUR-OF-A-KIND ■	0.04	2,777 to 1	1,033
FULL HOUSE ■	0.19	530 to 1	5,401
FLUSH ■	0.46	216 to 1	13,205
STRAIGHT ■	1.18	84.1 to 1	33,737
THREE-OF-A-KIND ■	3.38	28.6 to 1	97,097
3-Aces ■	1.54	63.8 to 1	44,297
Three-of-a-kind ■ (Large: K's — 8's)	2.46	39.6 to 1	70,697
Three-of-a-kind ■ (Small: 7's — 2's)	3.38	28.6 to 1	97,097
TWO-PAIR ■	8.21	11.2 to 1	235,697
Aces-up ■	4.49	21.3 to 1	128,777
K-up,Q-up,J-up ■	6.18	15.2 to 1	177,377
Small Two-Pair ■ (Tens-up and under)	8.21	11.2 to 1	235,697
ONE PAIR ■	50.55	0.98 to 1	1,450,721
PAIR OF A,K,Q,J ■ (Openers)	22.40	3.46 to 1	642,881
Aces ■	13.02	6.68 to 1	373,601
Kings ■	16.15	5.19 to 1	463,361
Queens ■	19.27	4.19 to 1	553,121
Jacks ■	22.40	3.46 to 1	642,881
SHORTS ■	50.55	0.98 to 1	1,450,721
Shorts ■ (Large: 10's — 7's)	34.91	1.86 to 1	1,001,921
Shorts ■ (Small: 6's — 2's)	50.55	0.98 to 1	1,450,721

* Actually 0.000035%   ** Actually 0.000871%   ■ OR BETTER

TABLE III

BASIC ONE—CARD HIGH DRAWING CHANCES
(53-card deck — including Joker)

You're drawing one card to. . .	Probability of making a complete hand expressed in percent (%), is. . .	Odds against making a complete hand are. . .
8♠-7♠-6♠-Joker (22-way hand)	45.83	1.18 to 1
9♡-7♡-6♡-Joker (19-way hand)	39.58	1.53 to 1
6♣-5♠-4◇-Joker or 6◇-9◇-10◇-Joker or J♠-10♠-9♠-8♠ (16-way hands)	33.33	2 to 1
K♣-J♣-10♣-9♣ (13-way hand)	27.08	2.69 to 1
6◇-5♣-3♠-Joker (12-way Straight)	25.00	3 to 1
K♡-8♡-7♡-4♡ (Flush)	20.83	3.8 to 1
9◇-8♣-7♠-6◇ (Open-end Straight)	18.75	4.33 to 1
J♠-10♠-8◇-7◇ (Inside Straight)	10.42	8.6 to 1
A◇-A♡-7♣-7♠ (Aces-up)	10.42	8.6 to 1
7◇-7♣-4♠-4◇ (Small Two-Pair)*	8.33	11 to 1
A◇-A♡-A♠-4◇ (Three Aces with kicker)*	10.42	8.6 to 1
8♣-8♡-8♠-A◇ (Trips with Ace kicker)*	10.42	8.6 to 1

*Four-of-a-kind counts as a complete hand

Let's look at **Table I** and **Table II.** Get used to those little black boxes. Although every culture, no matter how remote or unstudied, recognizes the small solid-black box as a symbol for Universal Disease Prevention, the nice folks at **B & G Publishing** are using it to indicate that the data given applies to a certain hand **or better. Table II,** for instance, shows that the odds against being dealt any Straight **or better** before the draw (53-card deck, with Joker) are 84.1 to 1. The odds against getting **exactly** a Straight, though, are shown on **Table I** (139 to 1).

Table I also shows that you'll get a Pat Royal Flush 24 times for every one time you'll be dealt 5-Aces pat. You can see a big difference in the frequency you can expect a Straight and the frequency you can expect a Flush. There's a big difference between how often you'll get a Flush and a Full House, too, but the most startling comparison is between a Full House and Four-of-a-kind.

You'll get a lone Pair of Openers once every 7 deals.

Table II shows that you'll receive a hand as good as Openers (Jacks-or-better) 22.4% of the time (about two out of nine hands). You'll get **any Pair or better** slightly more than half the time. It's 21.3 to 1 against getting a hand as good as Aces-up (the minimum raising standard for most pleasure players).

How you'll fare drawing one card is shown in **Table III**. You can expect to make the best possible Come hand (22-way) 46% of the time. When you draw to a Flush, you'll connect 21% of the time. The figures 10.42% and 8.6 to 1 occur four times on this table. There's nothing wrong with our typographer. It's just that hitting an inside Straight, making a Full House drawing to Aces-up, making at least a Full House drawing to 3-Aces with a kicker, and ending up with a Full House or better drawing to Trips with an Ace kicker all have the same probability.

If you're drawing down to Trips less than Aces (53-card deck), **Table IV** and **Table V** list the odds against making Four-of-a-kind at 23 to 1 and the odds against making a Full House or better at 8.64 to 1. About 90% of the time, you won't help.

With 3-Aces, you'll help more often. You'll make either 4-Aces or 5-Aces one out of 12 tries, and you'll make Aces-Full or better about once in seven tries.

Table VI and **Table VII** tell us that it's 96 to 1 against making a Full House when you draw three to a Pair of Kings. It's 7 to 1 against making Trips or better, and it's 5 to 2 against helping.

The next four tables, **VIII, IX, X** and **XI**, give the breakdown on a very elaborate Draw Poker comparison. When the Joker is part of your hand, decisions of this type

TABLE IV

DRAWING TWO
TO THREE-OF-A-KIND
Making Specific Hands

(53-card deck — including Joker)

A) You draw two to K♠-K♣-K♢, discarding 3♢-2♡. . .

The probability that you will make. . .	Expressed in percent (%) is. . .	The odds against it are. . .	Number of possible combinations
4-Kings	4.17	23 to 1	47
Kings-Full..............	6.21	15.1 to 1	70

B) You draw two to A♣-A♡-A♠, discarding 3♢-2♣. . .

The probability that you will make. . .	Expressed in percent (%) is. . .	The odds against it are. . .	Number of possible combinations
5-Aces	0.09	1,127 to 1	1
4-Aces	8.16	11.3 to 1	92
Aces-Full	5.85	16.1 to 1	66

Number of possible outcomes: 1,128

can be difficult. If you hold **A♣-Joker-K♣-9♠-6♠**, should you draw **two** cards or **three** cards? Your chances of improving are better if you draw **two**. Your chances of making 3-Aces or better are more favorable drawing **three**, but only slightly. Your chances of beating a Pat hand are **much** better drawing **two**.

With **Table XII** and **Table XIII**, we're dealing with a 52-card deck (no Joker). It's a lot harder to get a Pat Straight-Flush than it was with a 53-card deck. It was 14,000 to 1 then, and it's 65,000 to 1 now. As you'd expect, it's quite a bit harder to get Pat Straights and Flushes, but it's actually **easier to be dealt a Pat Full House.** Whereas you got a Pair or better slightly more than half the time when the

TABLE V

DRAWING TWO
TO THREE-OF-A-KIND
Making Specific Hands or Better

(53-card deck — including Joker)

A) You draw two to K♠-K♣-K◇, discarding 3◇-2♡. . .

The probability that you will make. . .	Expressed in percent (%) is. . .	The odds against it are. . .	Number of possible combinations
4-Kings	4.17	23 to 1	47
Kings Full ■	10.37	8.64 to 1	117
No Help	89.63	0.12 to 1	1,011

B) You draw two to A♣-A♡-A♠, discarding 3◇-2♣. . .

The probability that you will make. . .	Expressed in percent (%) is. . .	The odds against it are. . .	Number of possible combinations
5-Aces	0.09	1,127 to 1	1
4-Aces ■..............	8.24	11.1 to 1	93
Aces Full ■	14.10	6.09 to 1	159
No Help	85.90	0.16 to 1	969

Number of possible outcomes: 1,128   **■ OR BETTER**

Joker was included, you now get a Pair or better slightly **less** than half the time.

Table XIV shows that if you draw one card to an Open-end Straight-Flush, your best Come shot in Draw with the 52-card deck, you'll make at least a Straight 32% of the time—not nearly as good as the best Come hand using a 53-card deck (including the Joker). When you draw down to Trips, you'll improve 10.4% of the time, about the same as with the Joker included, according to **Table XV**.

Tables **XVI** and **XVII** show what happens, using the standard 52-card deck, when you draw three to a Pair. You'll

(Text continues on page 566)

TABLE VI

DRAWING THREE
TO A PAIR
Making Specific Hands
(53-card deck — including Joker)

You draw three to K◇-K♣, discarding 4◇-3♣-2♠. . .

The probability that you will make. . .	Expressed in percent (%) is. . .	The odds against it are. . .	Number of possible combinations
4-Kings	0.27	375 to 1	46
Full House	1.03	95.6 to 1	179
3-Kings	11.19	7.93 to 1	1,936
Aces-up	2.37	41.2 to 1	410
Kings-up	13.89	6.20 to 1	2,403

Number of possible outcomes: 17,296

TABLE VIII

DRAW POKER COMPARISON
(53-card deck — including Joker)

You have A♣-Joker-K♣-9♠-6♠ *(Draw either two or three)*
If you draw three, discarding K♣-9♠-6♠. . .

The probability that you will make. . .	Expressed in percent (%) is. . .	The odds against it are. . .	Number of possible combinations
5-Aces	0.01	17,295 to 1	1
Straight-Flush	0.03	3,458 to 1	5
4-Aces	0.78	127 to 1	135
Aces-Full	1.09	90.5 to 1	189
Other Full.	0.23	442 to 1	39
Flush	0.93	107 to 1	160
Straight	2.65	36.7 to 1	459
3-Aces	16.08	5.22 to 1	2,781
Aces-up	14.99	5.67 to 1	2,592

Number of possible outcomes: 17,296

TABLE VII

DRAWING THREE
TO A PAIR
Making Specific Hands or Better

(53-card deck — including Joker)

You draw three to K◇-K♣, discarding 4◇-3♣-2♠. . .

The probability that you will make. . .	Expressed in percent (%) is. . .	The odds against it are. . .	Number of possible combinations
4-Kings	0.27	375 to 1	46
Full House ■..........	1.30	75.9 to 1	225
3-Kings ■..............	12.49	7.00 to 1	2,161
Aces-up ■	14.86	5.73 to 1	2,571
Kings-up ■.............	28.76	2.48 to 1	4,974
No Help	71.24	0.40 to 1	12,322

Number of possible outcomes: 17,296   ■ OR BETTER

TABLE IX

DRAW POKER COMPARISON

(53-card deck — including Joker)

You have A♣-Joker-K♣-9♠-6♠ *(Draw either two or three)*
If you draw three, discarding K♣-9♠-6♠. . .

The probability that you will make. . .	Expressed in percent (%) is. . .	The odds against it are. . .	Number of possible combinations
5-Aces	0.01	17,295 to 1	1
Straight-Flush ■........	0.03	2,882 to 1	6
4-Aces ■..............	0.82	122 to 1	141
Aces-Full ■	1.91	51.4 to 1	330
Other Full ■	2.13	45.9 to 1	369
Flush ■	3.06	31.7 to 1	529
Straight ■..............	5.71	16.5 to 1	988
3-Aces ■..............	21.79	3.59 to 1	3,769
Aces-up ■	36.78	1.72 to 1	6,361
No Help	63.22	0.58 to 1	10,935

Number of possible outcomes: 17,296   ■ OR BETTER

TABLE X

DRAW POKER COMPARISON

(53-card deck — including Joker)

You have A♣-Joker-K♣-9♠-6♠ *(Draw either two or three)*
If you draw two, discarding 9♠-6♠. . .

The probability that you will make. . .	Expressed in percent (%) is. . .	The odds against it are. . .	Number of possible combinations
5-Aces	--	--	0
Straight-Flush	0.27	375 to 1	3
4-Aces	0.27	375 to 1	3
Aces-Full	0.80	124 to 1	9
Kings-Full	0.27	375 to 1	3
Flush	4.61	20.7 to 1	52
Straight	3.99	24.1 to 1	45
3-Aces	11.17	7.95 to 1	126
Aces-up	16.49	5.06 to 1	186

Number of possible outcomes: 1,128

help almost 29% of the time, not much different from drawing to a Pair **other than Aces** with the Joker added.

Beginning with **Table XVIII,** we're dealing with Hold 'em. This first table tells you that it's 220 to 1 against holding a Pair of Aces before the Flop. It's harder than that, even, to hold King-Queen of the same suit (331 to 1). You will begin with suited cards 23.5% of the time.

When you begin with Ace–King suited, **Table XIX** gives you an idea what sort of Flops you can expect. Once every 20,000 times you will have a Royal Flush after the Flop. It's more than 2 to 1 **against** an Ace or a King flopping. **(Not shown: If you begin with Ace–King and stay through** *seven cards* **there's a 49% chance of at least one other Ace or King turning up.)** When you begin with a Pair of Kings, according to **Table XX,** two more Kings will flop (giving you 4–Kings), once in about 400 times. You can expect any Flop that includes a King 12% of the time. What you definitely do not

TABLE XI

DRAW POKER COMPARISON

(53-card deck — including Joker)

You have A♣-Joker-K♣-9♠-6♠ *(Draw either two or three)*
If you draw two, discarding 9♠-6♠. . .

The probability that you will make. . .	Expressed in percent (%) is. . .	The odds against it are. . .	Number of possible combinations
5-Aces	--	--	0
Straight-Flush ■........	0.27	375 to 1	3
4-Aces ■..............	0.53	187 to 1	6
Aces-Full ■	1.33	74.2 to 1	15
Kings-Full ■	1.60	61.7 to 1	18
Flush ■	6.21	15.1 to 1	70
Straight ■.............	10.20	8.81 to 1	115
3-Aces ■..............	21.37	3.68 to 1	241
Aces-up ■	37.85	1.64 to 1	427
No Help	62.15	0.61 to 1	701

Number of possible outcomes: 1,128   ■ OR BETTER

want to see is a Flop consisting of **one** Ace and **no** King — but that will happen 19% of the time. **(Not shown: If you begin with two Queens,** *at least* **one Ace or King,** *but no Queen,* **will flop 38% of the time.)**

When you begin with an inferior hand like **Q♠-J◇** *(Pinochle),* **Table XXI,** it's 100 to 1 against you flopping a Straight. More than two out of three times the Flop will **not** include a Queen or a Jack.

If you hold Aces and four parts of a Straight **after** the Flop, 41.4% of the time you will not improve, according to **Table XXII. Table XXIII** shows what can be expected if you hold four cards to a Flush with no Pair after the Flop. About 35% of the time, you'll make the Flush.

Table XXIV tells you that in a 10-handed Hold 'em game, there's better than a 13% chance that **no one** will hold an Ace before the Flop. If you're against nine opponents and

TABLE XII

THE PROBABILITY OF BEING DEALT SPECIFIC HANDS BEFORE THE DRAW

(52-card deck — without Joker)

The probability of being dealt. . . (before the draw)	Expressed in percent (%) is. . .	The odds against it are. . .	Number of possible combinations
Straight-Flush	0.00*	64,973 to 1	40
Four-of-a-kind..........	0.02	4,164 to 1	624
Full House	0.14	693 to 1	3,744
Flush	0.20	508 to 1	5,108
Straight	0.39	254 to 1	10,200
Three-of-a-kind	2.11	46.3 to 1	54,912
Two-Pair	4.75	20.0 to 1	123,552
Pair of A,K,Q,J (Openers)	13.00	6.69 to 1	337,920
Shorts (10's-2's)	29.25	2.42 to 1	760,320

Total Hands: 2,598,960
*Actually 0.0015%

you hold Ace-Jack, there's better than one chance in four that no **other** player holds an Ace. If you're in a 10-handed game with King-Queen, there's a 15.6% chance that no opponent has you high-carded. In a four-handed game, it's better than even money that no one will be dealt an Ace before the Flop.

Table XXV provides you with **basic** facts about Hold 'em. It's 16 to 1 against holding a Pair before the Flop. It's 13 to 4 that you will **not** begin with suited cards. You will hold one Ace or two Aces before the Flop 15% of the time. If you have Trips after the Flop, you'll end up with a Full House or better about a third of the time. If you begin with a Pair, it's 15 to 2 against another card of **that kind** flopping. If you begin with a Pair and stay through Seven cards, 19% of the time you'll see the third card **of your kind** turn-up.

TABLE XIII

THE PROBABILITY OF BEING DEALT SPECIFIC HANDS <u>OR BETTER</u> BEFORE THE DRAW

(52-card deck — without Joker)

The probability of being dealt. . . (before the draw)	Expressed in percent (%) is. . .	The odds against it are. . .	Number of possible combinations
Straight-Flush	0.00*	64,973 to 1	40
Four-of-a-kind ■	0.03	3,913 to 1	664
Full House ■..........	0.17	589 to 1	4,408
Flush ■	0.37	272 to 1	9,516
Straight ■.............	0.76	131 to 1	19,716
Three-of-a-kind ■	2.87	33.8 to 1	74,628
Two-Pair ■............	7.63	12.1 to 1	198,180
Pair of A,K,Q,J (Openers) ■..........	20.63	3.85 to 1	536,100
Shorts (10's-2's) ■	49.88	1.00 to 1	1,296,420

Total Hands: 2,598,960   ■ OR BETTER

*Actually, 0.0015%

Table XXVI deals with long shots. When you begin suited, it's 118 to 1 against flopping a Flush. If you begin with 9-8 suited, it's about 5,000 to 1 against flopping a Straight-Flush.

Now let's look at Seven-Stud. It's over 5,500 to 1 against having 3-Aces rolled up, according to **Table XXVII**. It's 424 to 1 against having **any** Trips rolled up. Here, when you see **"Three Parts of Other Straight"**, that figure deals with **any** Straight (other than a Straight-Flush), even **7-5-3**. And "Three parts of a Straight-Flush" includes **4♣-6♣-8♣** and **8◊-9◊-10◊**. It's almost 5 to 1 against having any Pair on the first three cards.

Table XXVIII says that if you begin with 3-Aces, you can expect to make a Full House less than one out of three

(Text continues on page 576)

TABLE XIV

BASIC ONE-CARD HIGH DRAWING CHANCES

(52-card deck — without Joker)

If you're drawing one card to. . .	The probability of making a complete hand expressed in percent (%). . .	The odds against making complete hand are. . .
Open-end Straight-Flush	31.91	2.13 to 1
Inside Straight-Flush	25.53	2.92 to 1
Two-Pair	8.51	10.75 to 1
Trips with a kicker*	8.51	10.75 to 1
Flush	19.15	4.22 to 1
Open-end Straight	17.02	4.88 to 1
Inside Straight	8.51	10.75 to 1

*Four-of-a-kind counts as a complete hand

TABLE XVI

DRAWING THREE TO A PAIR
Making Specific Hands

(52-card deck — without Joker)

You draw three to A◇-A♡, discarding 4♣-3♠-2◇. . .

The probability that you will make. . .	Expressed in percent (%) is. . .	The odds against it are. . .	Number of possible combinations
4-Aces	0.28	359 to 1	45
Full House	1.02	97.3 to 1	165
3-Aces	11.43	7.75 to 1	1,854
Aces-up	15.99	5.26 to 1	2,592

Number of possible outcomes: 16,215

TABLE XV

DRAWING TWO
TO THREE-OF-A-KIND
Making Specific Hands and
Specific Hands or Better

(52-card deck — without Joker)

(Example: You have K♡-K◇-K♣, discarding 3♠-2♡). . .

The probability that you will make. . .	Expressed in percent (%) is. . .	The odds against it are. . .	Number of possible combinations
4-Kings Exactly	4.26	22.5 to 1	46
Kings-Full Exactly	6.11	15.4 to 1	66
Kings-Full ■	10.36	8.65 to 1	112
No Help	89.64	0.12 to 1	969

Number of possible outcomes: 1,081   ■ **OR BETTER**

TABLE XVII

DRAWING THREE
TO A PAIR
Making Specific Hands or Better

(52-card deck — without Joker)

You draw three to A♣-A◇, discarding 4◇-3♣-2♡. . .

The probability that you will make. . .	Expressed in percent (%) is. . .	The odds against it are. . .	Number of possible combinations
4-Aces	0.28	359 to 1	45
Full House ■..........	1.30	76.2 to 1	210
3-Aces ■..............	12.73	6.86 to 1	2,064
Aces-up ■	28.71	2.48 to 1	4,656
No Help	71.29	0.40 to 1	11,559

Number of possible outcomes: 16,215   ■ **OR BETTER**

TABLE XVIII

THE PROBABILITY OF BEING DEALT SPECIFIC HOLD 'EM HANDS BEFORE THE FLOP

The probability being dealt. . .	Expressed in percent (%) is...	The odds against it are. . .
2-Aces	0.45	220 to 1
2-Kings through 2-Jacks	1.36	72.7 to 1
2-Tens through 2-Sixes	2.26	43.2 to 1
2-Fives through 2-Deuces	1.81	54.3 to 1
Ace-King suited	0.30	331 to 1
Ace-King offsuit......................	0.90	110 to 1
Ace-Queen or Ace-Jack suited	0.60	165 to 1
Ace-Queen or Ace-Jack offsuit......	1.81	54.3 to 1
King-Queen suited	0.30	331 to 1
King-Queen offsuit	0.90	110 to 1
Ace with less than Jack, suited	2.71	35.8 to 1
Ace with less than Jack, offsuit	8.14	11.3 to 1
ANY Pair	5.88	16 to 1
ANY two cards suited	23.53	3.25 to 1
ANY two cards adjacent and suited with *maximum stretch**	2.11	46.4 to 1
ANY two cards adjacent and offsuit with *maximum stretch**	6.33	14.8 to 1
ANY hand with a Pair or an Ace	20.36	3.91 to 1

Total Hands: 1,326

*Two cards in order, allowing the maximum chance at a Straight. The lowest eligible combination is 5-4. The highest eligible combination is Jack-10.

TABLE XIX

FLOPS FOR SELECTED HOLD 'EM HANDS

Selection A) YOU HOLD A◊-K◊:

The probability that the Flop will be. . .	Expressed in percent (%) is. . .	The odds against it are. . .	Note
Q◊-J◊-10◊	0.01	19,599 to 1	*Makes Royal Flush
A-A-A or K-K-K	0.01	9,799 to 1	*Makes 4-Aces or 4-Kings
A-A-K or K-K-A	0.09	1,088 to 1	*Makes Aces Full or Kings Full
Three Diamonds **other than** Q-J-10	0.84	119 to 1	*Makes Flush
Two Diamonds with an Ace or King	1.68	58.4 to 1	*Makes Aces or Kings with four-Flush or four parts of Straight-Flush
Two Diamonds with a Pair of 2's-Q's	1.68	58.4 to 1	*Four parts of Flush or Straight-Flush, the Pair is unfavorable
Two Diamonds, **not** with a Pair of 2's-Q's and **not** Q-J-10	7.53	12.3 to 1	*Four parts of Flush or Straight-Flush
Q-J-10 (not all Diamonds)	0.32	310 to 1	*Makes Straight
Pair less than Kings, with one or no Diamonds	11.79	7.48 to 1	*Unfavorable
Three of another suit	4.38	21.8 to 1	*Danger, even if Q-J-10
Ace-King and smaller card	2.02	48.5 to 1	*Makes Aces **and** Kings
Three-of-a-kind 2's-Q's	0.22	444 to 1	*Unfavorable unless no one holds Fourth one or Pair
ANY Flop which includes an Ace or King	32.43	2.08 to 1	*Makes **key** Pair or better
ANY two Diamonds	10.94	8.14 to 1	*Four parts of a Flush or Straight-Flush
A-A with 2-Q or K-K with a 2-Q	1.35	73.2 to 1	*Makes **key** Three-of-a-kind

Number of possible Flops 19,600

TABLE XX

FLOPS FOR SELECTED HOLD 'EM HANDS

Selection B) YOU HOLD A PAIR OF KINGS: K♣-K♠:

The probability that the Flop will be. . .	Expressed in percent (%) is. . .	The odds against it are. . .	Note
K-K and card other than King	0.24	407 to 1	*Makes 4-Kings
King and 2-Aces	0.06	1,632 to 1	*Kings Full
Ace-King and smaller card	1.80	54.7 to 1	*3-Kings, possible trouble trouble if 2nd Ace falls
King and smaller Pair	0.67	147 to 1	*Makes Kings Full
King and un-paired smaller cards	8.98	10.1 to 1	*Makes 3-Kings
A-A-A	0.02	4,899 to 1	*Makes Aces Full, but you lose if someone has the last Ace
2-Aces and other, 2-Q	1.35	73.2 to 1	*Dangerous
Three-of-a-kind, 2's-Q's	0.22	444 to 1	*Dangerous
Three suited cards, Clubs or Spades	2.24	43.5 to 1	*Four parts of a Flush, much better if it includes Ace
Three suited cards, Diamonds or Hearts	2.92	33.3 to 1	*Unfavorable
Q-J-10, other than all three Spades or three Clubs	0.32	315 to 1	*Open-end Straight (probable trouble)
Pair of 2's-Q's, and another card (But not King)	14.82	5.75 to 1	*Kings-up and trouble
Q-J-10, Clubs or Spades	0.01	9,799 to 1	*Open-end Straight Flush
ANY Flop including at least 1 King	11.76	7.51 to 1	*Generally very favorable
1 Ace and two cards, 2-Q, (including a Pair of 2's-Q's)	19.31	4.18 to 1	*Bad news
1 Ace and two cards, 2-Q, **excluding** a Pair	17.96	4.57 to 1	*Unfavorable

Number of possible Flops: 19,600

TABLE XXI

FLOPS FOR SELECTED
HOLD 'EM HANDS

Selection C) YOU HOLD Q♠-J◇ (For related Flops, see Selection A)

The probability that the Flop will be. . .	Expressed in percent (%) is. . .	The odds against it are. . .	Note
Q-Q-Q or J-J-J	0.01	9,799 to 1	*Makes 4-Queens or 4-Jacks
Q-Q-J or J-J-Q	0.09	1,088 to 1	*Full House: Q-Q-J is better (2,177 to 1)
A-K-10	0.33	305 to 1	*Makes Ace-high Straight--3.13% of these will also be four parts of a Straight-Flush
K-10-9 or 10-9-8	0.65	152 to 1	*Makes Straight--3.13% of these will also be four parts of a Straight-Flush
ANY Straight when combined with your hand	0.98	101 to 1	*A-K-10, K-10,9 or 10-9-8
K-10 and any other card, or 10-9 and any other card (No Straight)	6.04	15.6 to 1	*Open-end Straight--16.22% of these include a Pair of Jacks or Queens, 8.11% include a cold Pair
Three suited cards (your suits)	2.24	43.5 to 1	*Four parts of a Flush or Straight-Flush--0.03% of these already make Straights, 25% include a Pair of Queens or Jacks
Q-Q-Other, or J-J-Other, (not Full House)	1.35	73.2 to 1	*Makes Three-of-a-kind
ANY Flop without an Ace or King	58.57	0.71 to 1	*Sometimes helpful, but often hopeless
ANY Flop without an Ace	77.45	0.29 to 1	*Generally helpful
Queens or Jack with smaller Pair	1.65	59.5 to 1	*Queens-up or Jacks-up
ANY Flop without a Queen or Jack	67.57	0.48 to 1	*Not good unless a Straight, four-Straight or four-Flush
A-A or K-K with a Queen or Jack	0.37	271 to 1	*Makes a very unfavorable Aces-up or Kings-up

Number of possible Flops: 19,600

TABLE XXII

HOLD 'EM — FROM FLOP TO FINISH

Selection A) YOU HOLD A♠-A◇, & THE FLOP IS K♣-Q♠-J◇:

The probabllity that the final strength of your hand will be. . .	Expressed In percent (%) Is. . .	The odds against It are. . .	Note
4-Aces	0.09	1,080 to 1	*Lock
Aces Full	1.67	59.1 to 1	*Could lose to 4-Kings, 4-Queens, or 4-Jacks (whichever Pair is on the Board)
Other Full	0.83	119 to 1	*A player holding the 4th Jack, Queen or King wins, otherwise you have a lock (could tie)
Straight	16.47	5.07 to 1	*Okay, but a tie is threatened and opponent could have a Flush if the three on the Board are suited--or Full House if a a Pair is on the Board
3-Aces	5.92	15.9 to 1	*Very favorable (Unless all three Board cards are suited, you can only lose to a Straight)
Aces-up	33.58	1.98 to 1	*You're better off without the 'ups' on the Board
Aces	41.44	1.41 to 1	*Might win

times. (You can expect to improve 41% of the time.) Beginning with 2-Aces, it's more than 12 to 1 against finishing with a Full House. (You'll improve 62% of the time.) When you start with 10♣-J♣-Q♣, it's 66 to 1 against catching a Straight-Flush. (You'll make at least Two-Pair 55% of the time.)

Table XXIX. When you have Two-Pair after four cards, it's 10 to 3 against making a Full House. (You'll improve 24% of the time.) If you have J♠-J♣-Q♣-K♣-10◇, it's more than 500 to 1 against making the Straight-Flush. (Expect to improve 72% of the time.)

TABLE XXIII

HOLD 'EM — FROM FLOP TO FINISH

Selection B) YOU HOLD A◇-Q◇, AND THE FLOP IS 7◇-4◇-2♣:

The probability that the final strength of your hand will be. . .	Expressed in percent (%) is. . .	The odds against it are. . .	Note
Flush	34.97	1.86 to 1	*The last two cards will both be Diamonds 3.33% of the time
3-Aces or 3-Queens	0.56	179 to 1	*Strong
Aces over Queens	0.83	119 to 1	*Strong
Aces over Sevens, Fours or Deuces	2.22	44.0 to 1	*Dangerous
Queens over Sevens, Fours or Deuces	2.22	44.0 to 1	*Dangerous
Aces or Queens	13.32	6.51 to 1	*Might win
Three-of-a-kind on Board (No Flush)	0.65	153 to 1	*Slight chances

Number of possible Outcomes: 1,081

Your short-range improvement chances are given on **Table XXX.** If you have **three** Pair after six cards, you're going to fill up 13% of the time. If you hold two red Jacks and a possible Straight-Flush in Clubs, you'll only make 3-Jacks once in 46 times, since the J♣ will give you a Flush. Three top-notch Poker players questioned that statistic before it occurred to them that the J♣ did **not** make three Jacks. If intelligent people can overlook something that obvious — dealing with just one card to come — you can imagine why so many mistakes are published elsewhere dealing with much more complex problems. If you have Trips and an Open-end Straight-Flush after six cards, you'll **make** a Straight-Flush one out of 23 tries. (About 54% of the time, you'll end up with **at least** a Straight.) Additionally, if you have three parts of a Flush after four cards, you'll make a Flush 10.6% of the time. If you have three parts of a Flush after five cards, you'll make a Flush 4.2% of the time.

(Text continues on page 586)

TABLE XXIV

HOLD 'EM — ABSENCE OF ACES BEFORE FLOP, BY NUMBER OF PLAYERS

Number of Players	The probability that no player has an Ace, (including yourself), expressed in percent (%)...	If you have one Ace, the probability that no other player has an Ace, expressed in percent (%)...	If you have no Ace the probability that no other player has an Ace, expressed in percent (%)...
2	71.87	88.24	84.49
3	60.28	77.45	70.86
4	50.14	67.57	58.95
5	41.34	58.57	48.60
6	33.76	50.41	39.68
7	27.27	43.04	32.05
8	21.76	36.43	25.58
9	17.13	30.53	20.14
10	13.28	25.31	15.61
11	10.12	20.71	11.90
12	7.56	16.71	8.89
15	2.70	7.86	3.18
20	0.18	1.12	0.21

NOTE: Your hand will have no Ace 85.07% of the time.

TABLE XXV

HOLD 'EM — BASIC DATA

The probability that. . .	Expressed in percent (%). . .	The odds against it are. . .
You will hold a **Pair** before the Flop	5.88	16 to 1
You will hold **suited cards** before the Flop	23.53	3.25 to 1
You will hold 2 **Kings** or 2 **Aces** before the Flop	0.90	110 to 1
You will hold **Ace-King** before the Flop	1.21	81.9 to 1
You will hold *at least* **1 Ace** before the Flop	14.93	5.70 to 1
If you have four parts of a **Flush** after the Flop, you will make it	34.97	1.86 to 1
If you have four parts of an Open-end Straight-Flush after the Flop, you will make a **Straight-Flush**	8.42	10.9 to 1
If you have four parts of an Open-end Straight-Flush after the Flop, you will make *at least* a **Straight**	54.12	0.85 to 1
If you have Two-Pair after the Flop, you will make a **Full House or better***	16.74	4.97 to 1
If you have Three-of-a-kind after the Flop, you will make a **Full House or better***	33.40	1.99 to 1
If you have a Pair after the Flop at least one more of that kind will turn up (on the last two cards)	8.42	10.9 to 1
If you hold a Pair, at least one more of that kind will Flop	11.76	7.51 to 1
If you hold no Pair, you will **pair** at least one of your cards on the Flop	32.43	2.08 to 1
If you hold two suited cards, two or more of that suit will Flop	11.79	7.48 to 1
If you begin suited and stay through seven cards, three more *(But not four or five more!)* of your suit will turn up	5.77	16.3 to 1
If you begin paired and stay through seven cards, *at least* one more of your kind will turn up	19.18	4.21 to 1

*Includes unfavorable Full Houses.

TABLE XXVI

HOLD 'EM — LONG SHOTS

The probability that. . .	Expressed in percent (%) is.	The odds against it are. . .
If you hold suited cards, a Flush will Flop	0.84	118 to 1
If you hold a Pair, Four-of-a-kind will Flop	0.24	407 to 1
If you hold 6-5 offsuit, a Straight will Flop	1.31	75.6 to 1
If you hold 7-5 offsuit, a Straight will Flop	0.98	101 to 1
If you hold 8-5 offsuit, a Straight will Flop	0.65	152 to 1
If you hold 9-5 offsuit, a Straight will Flop	0.33	305 to 1
If you hold 9-8 suited, a Straight-Flush will Flop	0.02	4,899 to 1
If you hold 9-7 suited, a Straight-Flush will Flop	0.02	6,532 to 1
If you hold 9-6 suited, a Straight-Flush will Flop	0.01	9,799 to 1
If you hold 9-5 suited, a Straight-Flush will Flop	0.01	19,599 to 1
No one hold an Ace or King in a 10-handed game	1.40	70.5 to 1
Heads-up Hold 'em, both players hold paired Aces	0.00*	270,724 to 1
You will not hold a Pair or an Ace before the Flop for the next 20 hands	1.05	94.0 to 1
You will not hold a Pair or an Ace before the Flop for the next 50 hands	0.00**	87,897 to 1
You will hold a Pair of Aces before the Flop each of the next four hands	0.00***	{ 2,385,443, 280 to 1 }

*Actually 0.00037%
**Actually 0.0011%
***Actually 0.00000004%

TABLE XXVII

THE PROBABILITY OF BEING DEALT SEVEN-STUD STARTING HANDS
(First three cards)

The probability that you will be dealt this on the first three cards. . .	Expressed in percent (%) is. . .	The odds against it are. . .	Number of possible combinations
3-Aces	0.02	5,524 to 1	4
3-Jacks through 3-Kings	0.05	1,841 to 1	12
3-Sixes through 3-Tens	0.09	1,104 to 1	20
3-Two's through 3-Fives	0.07	1,380 to 1	16
2-Aces	1.30	75.7 to 1	288
2-Jacks through 2-Kings	3.91	24.6 to 1	864
2-Sixes through 2-Tens	6.52	14.3 to 1	1,440
2-Two's through 2-Fives	5.21	18.2 to 1	1,152
Three Parts of a Straight-Flush	1.16	85.3 to 1	256
Three Parts of Other Flush	4.02	23.9 to 1	888
Three Parts of Other Straight	17.38	4.76 to 1	3,840
ANY Three-of-a-kind . . .	0.24	424 to 1	52
ANY Pair	16.94	4.90 to 1	3,744

There are 22,100 possible combinations

TABLE XXVIII

CHANCE OF IMPROVEMENT FOR VARIOUS SEVEN-STUD HANDS LONG RANGE

(You hold three cards)

IF YOU HAVE A♡-A◇-A♣:

The probability that the final strength of your hand after seven cards will be. . .	Expressed in in percent (%)	The odds against it are. . .
Straight-Flush	0.00*	35,312 to 1
Four-of-a-kind	8.17	11.2 to 1
Full House	32.02	2.12 to 1
Flush	0.70	142 to 1
Straight	0.24	418 to 1
Three-of-a-kind......................	--	---
Two-Pair	--	---

*Actually 0.0028%

IF YOU HAVE A♣-A◇-9♡:

The probability that the final strength of your hand after seven cards will be. . .	Expressed in percent (%)	The odds against it are. . .
Straight-Flush	0.00**	23,541 to 1
Four-of-a-kind	0.54	185 to 1
Full House	7.57	12.2 to 1
Flush	0.70	143 to 1
Straight	0.84	118 to 1
Three-of-a-kind......................	9,89	9.11 to 1
Two-Pair	42.05	1.38 to 1

**Actually 0.0042%

(continued)

(continued)

IF YOU HAVE 10♣-J♣-Q♣:

The probability that the final strength of your hand after seven cards will be. . .	Expressed in percent (%)	The odds against it are. . .
Straight-Flush	1.49	66.2 to 1
Four-of-a-kind	0.07	1,431 to 1
Full House	1.50	65.9 to 1
Flush	16.56	5.04 to 1
Straight	14.91	5.71 to 1
Three-of-a-kind	3.19	30.3 to 1
Two-Pair	17.33	4.77 to 1

NOTE: This chart assumes no knowledge of exposed cards in other hands.
For each three-card hand, there are 211,876 possible hands you can end up with after receiving the next four cards.

TABLE XXIX

CHANCE OF IMPROVEMENT FOR VARIOUS SEVEN-STUD HANDS MIDDLE RANGE

(You hold four or five cards)

IF YOU HAVE 8♣-8◇-4♠-4♡:

The probability that the final strength of your hand after seven cards will be. . .	Expressed in percent (%)	The odds against it are. . .
Straight-Flush	--	---
Four-of-a-kind	0.53	187 to 1
Full House	23.15	3.32 to 1
Flush	--	---
Straight	0.37	269 to 1
Three-of-a-kind	--	---
Two-Pair	---	---

(continued)

TABLE XXIX

CHANCE OF IMPROVEMENT FOR VARIOUS SEVEN-STUD HANDS MIDDLE RANGE

(You hold four or five cards)

(*continued*)

IF YOU HAVE J♠-J♣-Q♣-K♣-10◇:

The probability that the final strength of your hand after seven cards will be. . .	Expressed in percent (%)	The odds against it are. . .
Straight-Flush	0.19	540 to 1
Four-of-a-kind	0.09	1,080 to 1
Full House	2.50	39.0 to 1
Flush	3.98	24.1 to 1
Straight	30.99	2.23 to 1
Three-of-a-kind	5.18	18.3 to 1
Two-Pair	29.05	2.44 to 1

IF YOU HAVE A♡-A♣-K♣-9♣-2♡:

The probability that the final strength of your hand after seven cards will be. . .	Expressed in percent (%)	The odds against it are. . .
Straight-Flush	--	---
Four-of-a-kind	0.09	1,080 to 1
Full House	2.50	39.0 to 1
Flush	4.16	23.0 to 1
Straight	--	---
Three-of-a-kind	6.66	14.0 to 1
Two-Pair	36.63	1.73

NOTE: This chart assumes no knowledge of exposed cards in other hands.

For each four-card hand there are 17,296 possible combinations when receiving the next three cards.

For each five-card hand there are 1,081 possible combinations when receiving the next two cards.

TABLE XXX

CHANCE OF IMPROVEMENT FOR VARIOUS SEVEN-STUD HANDS SHORT RANGE

(You hold six cards)

YOU HAVE A-A-9-9-2-2

The probability that the final strength of your hand after seven cards will be. . .	Expressed in percent (%)	The odds against it are. . .
Straight-Flush	--	---
Four-of-a-kind	--	---
Full House	13.04	6.67 to 1
Flush	--	---
Straight	--	---
Three-of-a-kind	--	---
Two-Pair	--	---

IF YOU HAVE J◇-J♡-6♣-4♣-3♣-2♣:

The probability that the final strength of your hand after seven cards will be. . .	Expressed in percent (%)	The odds against it are. . .
Straight-Flush	2.17	45 to 1
Four-of-a-kind	--	---
Full House	--	---
Flush	17.39	4.75 to 1
Straight	6.52	14.3 to 1
Three-of-a-kind	2.17	45 to 1
Two-Pair	26.09	2.83 to 1

(continued)

CHANCE OF IMPROVEMENT FOR VARIOUS SEVEN-STUD HANDS SHORT RANGE

(continued)

IF YOU HAVE 10♡-10♣-10♠-9♠-8♠-7♠:

The probability that the final strength of your hand after seven cards will be. . .	Expressed in percent (%)	The odds against it are. . .
Straight-Flush	4.35	22 to 1
Four-of-a-kind	2.17	45 to 1
Full House	19.57	4.11 to 1
Flush	15.22	5.57 to 1
Straight	13.04	6.67 to 1
Three-of-a-kind	--	---
Two-Pair	--	---

This chart assumes no knowledge of exposed cards in other hands. For each six-card hand there are 46 outcomes on the seventh card.

BASIC SEVEN-STUD PROBABILITIES

If you have a *four-Flush* with *three cards to come*, the **probability of making a Flush is 47.16%** (1.12 to 1 against), assuming no knowledge of exposed cards in other hands.

With *two cards to come*, it's **34.97%** (1.86 to 1 against).
With *one card to come*, it's **19.57%** (4.11 to 1 against).

If you have an *Open-end Straight* with *three cards to come*, the **probability of making a Straight is 42.88%** (1.33 to 1 against).

With *two cards to come* it's **31.45%** (2.18 to 1 against).
With *one card to come* it's **17.39%** (4.75 to 1 against).

If you have a *Gut-shot Straight* with *three cards to come*, the **probability of making a Straight is 23.43%** (3.27 to 1 against).

With *two cards to come*, it's **16.47%** (5.07 to 1 against).
With *one card to come*, it's **8.70%** (10.5 to 1 against).

If you have *Three-Sixes* rolled up, the **probability of making either Four-of-a-kind or a Full House is 40.19%** (1.49 to 1 against). The **probability of making Four-of-a-kind is 8.17%** (11.2 to 1 against). With *three cards to come*, the **probability of making** either a

Full House or Four-of-a-kind is 39.00% (1.56 to 1 against). The probability of making Four-of-a-kind is 6.26% (14.99 to 1 against).

With *two cards to come*, it's **33.40%** (1.99 to 1 against), for either a Full House or Four-of-a-kind. Four-of-a-kind is 4.26% (22.5 to 1 against).

With *one card to come*, it's **21.74%** (3.6 to 1 against), for either a Full House or Four-of-a-kind. Four-of-a-kind is 2.17% (45 to 1 against.

Next we'll visit the Lowball tables. **Tables XXXI** and **XXXII** break down the chances of having hands dealt before the draw in Ace-to-Five when the Joker is included in the deck. **Notice that it's harder to get a Six-Four Pat than a Bicycle** (1,245 to 1 against the Bike and 1,400 to 1 against the **6-4-3-2-A.** That last figure applies to a Seven-Four, Eight-Four, etc. — you'll get a Pat Wheel more often than a pat **8-7-3-2-A**). Expect a Pat Seven or better *(those little black boxes again)* once every 94 deals. Notice that **(Table XXXII)** more than half of your Pat Bicycles include the Joker.

Table XXXIII shows you what your prospects are when you draw one-card to various Low hands, using the 53-card deck. See how much **better** your chances are when you hold the Joker than when you don't, especially when you're trying for very good hands. **Table XXXIV** lists your two-card drawing chances. If you draw two to **6-A-Joker**, the odds are about 11 to 1 against making a Six. **Table XXXIII** and **Table XXXIV** do **more** than tell you what the chances are of making a specific hand drawn to (and this is true of **any** of the other Lowball draw improvement tables). When you draw to an Eight-high with the Joker, it's 1.4 to 1 against making the Eight. But that same figure applies to making an **Eight or better** drawing to **4-3-2-Joker**. Likewise, when you draw to a Seven-high and you don't hold the Joker, you'll connect 27.08% of the time. That figure is the **same** if you draw to **6-5-4-A** and are interested in your **chances** of making a Seven **or better**.

Tables **XXXV** and **XXXVI** give you your chances of receiving various Pat hands before the draw using a 52-card

(Text continues on page 590)

TABLE XXXI

THE PROBABILITY OF BEING DEALT SPECIFIC ACE-TO-FIVE LOW HANDS BEFORE THE DRAW

(53-card deck — including Joker)

The probability of being dealt. . . (Before the Draw)	Expressed in percent (%) is. . .	The odds against it are. . .	Number of possible combinations
Bicycle (5-4-3-2-A)	**0.08**	**1,245 to 1**	**2,304**
Six-high	**0.27**	**373 to 1**	**7,680**
6-4	0.07	1,400 to 1	2,048
6-5	0.12	509 to 1	5,632
Seven-high	**0.71**	**139 to 1**	**20,480**
7-4	0.07	1,400 to 1	2,048
7-5	0.12	509 to 1	5,632
7-6	0.45	223 to 1	12,800
Eight-high	**1.56**	**63.1 to 1**	**44,800**
8-4	0.07	1,400 to 1	2,048
8-5	0.12	509 to 1	5,632
8-6	0.45	223 to 1	12,800
8-7	0.85	117 to 1	24,320
Nine-high	**3.00**	**32.4 to 1**	**86,016**
9-4	0.07	1,400 to 1	2,048
9-5	0.12	509 to 1	5,632
9-6	0.45	223 to 1	12,800
9-7	0.85	117 to 1	24,320
9-8	1.43	68.6 to 1	41,216

TOTAL HANDS: 2,869,685 possible with 53-card deck.

TABLE XXXII

THE PROBABILITY OF BEING DEALT SPECIFIC ACE-TO-FIVE LOW HANDS <u>OR BETTER</u> BEFORE THE DRAW

(53-card deck — including Joker)

The probability of being dealt the following hand OR BETTER (Before the Draw)	Expressed in percent (%) is. . .	The odds against it are. . .	Number of possible combinations	Number of possible combinations (with Joker)	Number of possible combinations (Without Joker)
Bicycle (5-4-3-2-A)	0.08	1,245 to 1	2,304	1,280	1,024
Six-High ■	0.35	286 to 1	9,984	3,840	6,144
6-4 ■ ..	0.15	658 to 1	4,352	2,304	2,048
6-5 ■ ..	0.35	286 to 1	9,984	3,840	6,144
Seven-High ■	1.06	93.2 to 1	30,464	8,960	21,504
7-4 ■ ..	0.42	238 to 1	12,032	4,864	7,168
7-5 ■ ..	0.62	161 to 1	17,664	6,400	11,264
7-6 ■ ..	1.06	93.2 to 1	30,464	8,960	21,504
Eight-High ■	2.62	37.1 to 1	75,264	17,920	57,344
8-4 ■ ..	1.13	87.3 to 1	32,512	9,984	22,528
8-5 ■ .,	1.33	74.2 to 1	38,144	11,520	26,624
8-6 ■ ..	1.78	55.3 to 1	50,994	14,080	36,864
8-7 ■ ..	2.62	37.1 to 1	75,264	17,920	57,344
Nine-High ■	5.62	16.8 to 1	161,280	32,256	129,024
9-4 ■ ..	2.69	36.1 to 1	77,312	18,944	58,368
9-5 ■ ..	2.89	33.6 to 1	82,944	20,480	62,464
9-6 ■ ..	3.34	29.0 to 1	95,744	23,040	72,704
9-7 ■ ..	4.18	22.9 to 1	120,064	26,880	93,184
9-8 ■ ..	5.62	16.8 to 1	161,280	32,256	129,024

TOTAL HANDS: 2,869,685 possible with 53-card deck. ■ OR BETTER

TABLE XXXIII

BASIC ONE-CARD DRAWING CHANCES FOR ACE-TO-FIVE LOW

(53-card deck — including Joker)

If you're drawing one card to. . .	Probability of making exact hand express'd in percent (%)	The odds against it are. . .
"Bicycle" Five-high *(you hold Joker)* ..	16.67	5 to 1
"Bicycle" Five-high *(you **don't** hold Joker)*	10.42	8.6 to 1
Six-high *(you hold the Joker)*	25.00	3 to 1
Six-high *(you **don't** hold the Joker)* ...	18.75	.4.33 to 1
Seven-high *(you hold the Joker)*	33.33	2 to 1
Seven-high *(you **don't** hold the Joker)*	27.08	2.69 to 1
Eight-high *(you hold the Joker)*	41.67	1.4 to 1
Eight-high *(you **don't** hold the Joker)*.	35.42	1.82 to 1
Nine-high *(you hold the Joker)*	50.00	1 to 1
Nine-high *(you **don't** hold the Joker)* .	43.75	1.29 to 1
Ten-high *(you hold the Joker)*	58.33	0.71 to 1
Ten-high *(you **don't** hold the Joker)* ..	52.08	0.92 to 1

deck (no Joker included). It's more than twice as hard to get a Pat Bicycle as it is **with** the Joker included. And **without** the Joker, you'll only get a Pat Seven or better once every 121 deals (as compared to once every 94 deals **with** the Joker).

Table XXXVII and Table XXXVIII give you your drawing chances when you play Ace-to-Five **without** the Joker. If you draw to a Bicycle it's almost 11 to 1 against connecting. Two cards to a Bike is a 67 to 1 shot.

Table XXXIX and Table XL show you what the probabilities are of receiving Pat hands in Deuce-to-Seven Lowball. It's more than 600 to 1 against being dealt a Pat Seven, and it's 20 to 1 against getting a Pat hand as good as a Ten.

TABLE XXXIV

BASIC TWO-CARD DRAWING CHANCES FOR ACE-TO-FIVE LOW

(53-card deck — including Joker)

If you're drawing two cards to...	Probability of making exact hand express'd in percent (%)	The odds against it are...
"Bicycle" Five-high *(you hold Joker)*..	4.26	22.5 to 1
"Bicycle" Five-high *(you **don't** hold Joker)*	2.13	46 to 1
Six-high *(you hold the Joker)*	8.51	10.8 to 1
Six-high *(you **don't** hold the Joker)* ...	5.32	17.8 to 1
Seven-high *(you hold the Joker)*......	14.18	6.05 to 1
Seven-high *(you **don't** hold the Joker)*	9.93	9.07 to 1
Eight-high *(you hold the Joker)*	21.28	3.7 to 1
Eight-high *(you **don't** hold the Joker)*.	15.96	5.27 to 1

NOTE: The assumption for tables 33 and 34 is that all one-card draws have discarded a King, all two-card draws have discarded a King and a Queen. There are 48 possible one-card draws and 1,128 possible two-card draws.

Your Deuce-to-Seven drawing chances are spelled out in **Table XLI** and **Table XLII**. Notice the difference between drawing to hands where Straights and Flushes are possible and **much better hands where Straights and Flushes are impossible.**

Table XLIII compares hands **by their ranks** in the games of Ace-to-Five and Deuce-to-Seven. The 21st ranking Ace-to-Five hand is a Straight Seven, but the 21st ranking Deuce-to-Seven hand is **9-6-5-3-2.**

But just because two hands have the same rank, doesn't mean that they will occur just as often. **Table XLIV** shows that you'll get a Pat **7-6-5-4-A** in Ace-to-Five and a Pat **9-7-5-3-2** in Deuce-to-Seven at **about** the same frequencies. However the comparison of ranks (**Table XLIII**) was **19th** for

(Text continues on page 595)

TABLE XXXV

THE PROBABILITY OF BEING DEALT SPECIFIC ACE-TO-FIVE LOW HANDS BEFORE THE DRAW

(52-card deck — without Joker)

The probability of being dealt. . . (Before the Draw)	Expressed in percent (%) is	The odds against it are. . .
Bicycle (5-4-3-2-A)	**0.04**	**2,537 to 1**
Six-high............................	**0.20**	**507 to 1**
6-4	0.04	2,537 to 1
6-5................................	0.16	634 to 1
Seven-high	**0.59**	**168 to 1**
7-4................................	0.04	2,537 to 1
7-5................................	0.16	634 to 1
7-6................................	0.39	253 to 1
Eight-high..........................	**1.38**	**71.5 to 1**
8-4................................	0.04	2,537 to 1
8-5................................	0.16	634 to 1
8-6................................	0.39	253 to 1
8-7................................	0.79	126 to 1
Nine-high	**2.76**	**35.3 to 1**
9-4................................	0.04	2,537 to 1
9-5................................	0.16	634 to 1
9-6................................	0.39	253 to 1
9-7................................	0.79	126 to 1
9-8................................	1.38	71.5 to 1

TOTAL HANDS: 2,598,960 possible with 52-card deck.

TABLE XXXVI

THE PROBABILTIY OF BEING DEALT SPECIFIC ACE-TO-FIVE LOW HANDS *OR BETTER* BEFORE THE DRAW

(52-card deck — without Joker)

The probability of being dealt. . . (Before the Draw)	Expressed in percent (%) is. . .	The odds against it are. . .
Bicycle ■ (5-4-3-2-A)	0.04	2,537 to 1
Six-high ■	0.24	422 to 1
6-4 ■	0.08	1,268 to 1
6-5 ■	0.24	422 to 1
Seven-high ■.......................	0.83	120 to 1
7-4 ■	0.28	362 to 1
7-5 ■	0.43	230 to 1
7-6 ■	0.83	120 to 1
Eight-high ■	2.21	44.3 to 1
8-4 ■	0.87	114 to 1
8-5 ■	1.02	96.6 to 1
8-6 ■	1.42	69.5 to 1
8-7 ■	2.21	44.3 to 1
Nine-high ■	4.96	19.1 to 1
9-4 ■	2.25	43.5 to 1
9-5 ■	2.40	40.6 to 1
9-6 ■	2.80	34.7 to 1
9-7 ■	3.59	26.9 to 1
9-8 ■	4.96	19.1 to 1

TOTAL HANDS: 2,598,960 possible with 52-card deck. ■ OR BETTER

TABLE XXXVII

BASIC ONE-CARD DRAWING CHANCES ACE-TO-FIVE LOW

(52-card deck — without Joker)

If you're drawing one card to. . .	Probability of making exact hand express'd in percent (%)	The odds against it are. . .
Bicycle (Five-high)	8.51	10.75 to 1
Six-high.............................	17.02	4.88 to 1
Seven-high	25.53	2.92 to 1
Eight-high..........................	34.04	1.94 to 1
Nine-high	42.55	1.35 to 1
Ten-high	51.06	0.96 to 1
Jack-high	59.57	0.68 to 1

TABLE XXXVIII

BASIC TWO-CARD DRAWING CHANCES FOR ACE-TO-FIVE LOW

(52-card deck — without Joker)

If you're drawing two cards to. . .	Probability of making exact hand express'd in percent (%)	The odds against it are. . .
Bicycle (Five-high)	1.48	66.6 to 1
Six-high.............................	4.44	21.5 to 1
Seven-high	8.88	10.3 to 1
Eight-high..........................	14.80	5.76 to 1
Nine-high	22.20	3.50 to 1

NOTE: The assumption for tables 37 and 38 is that all one-card draws have discarded a King, all two-card draws have discarded a King and a Queen. There are 47 possible one-card draws and 1,081 possible two-card draws.

7-6-5-4-A in Ace-to-Five and **25th** for 9-7-5-3-2 in Deuce-to-Seven.

Table **XLV** deals with the first three starting cards in Seven-Card Low (Razz). It's 9 to 1 against starting with **7-6-5** or lower. The *ABC* hand (**3-2-A**) will only occur once in 345 deals.

Table **XLVI** provides your chance of improvement from various stages in Razz. If you begin **3-2-A**, it's 13 to 1 against making a Bicycle—providing you'll stay through Seven cards. If you begin with **2-A-K**, you'll only make a Bicycle once in 80 tries. If you have **3-2-A-K-Q** after five cards, expect to make an Eight-high or better about 15% of the time.

Naturally, you **don't** need **perfect** cards for **Table XLVI** to be useful. If instead of the **4♣-3♡-2♣-A♢-K♢** listed, you have **4♣-3♠-8♠-2♡-K♣**, your chances of making an Eight-high **or better** remain the same (57%). Your chances of making any hand better than the Eight, though, are the same as if your **8♠** were the **Q♠**—so see **3♢-2♣-A♡-Q♠-K♡** (4.4% to make a six or better).

It's been argued that Poker is **more complex than chess.** That's probably **true.** Not only must you deal wisely with limitless probabilities, you need to understand people. When a grandmaster at chess challenges an average player to a game, he's almost certain of victory. But when a World Class Poker player locks up with an average gambler for a few hours, there's a possibility of an upset. That's because *chance* is a part of Poker. In chess, you maneuver to make exactly definable gains, like winning a piece or checkmating your opponent. If you outplay him, you'll win. When you outplay an opponent at Poker, though, you only gain an edge, you're winning a **theoretical percentage,** but you might lose the

(Text continues on page 602)

TABLE XXXIX

THE PROBABILITY OF BEING DEALT SPECIFIC DEUCE-TO-SEVEN LOW HANDS
Before the Draw

The probability of being dealt. . . (Before the Draw)	Expressed in percent (%). . .	The odds against it are. . .	Number of possible combinations
Seven-High	**0.16**	**636 to 1**	**4,080**
7-5-4-3-2	0.04	2,547 to 1	1,020
7-6	0.12	848 to 1	3,060
Eight-High	**0.55**	**181 to 1**	**14,280**
8-5	0.04	2,547 to 1	1,020
8-6	0.16	636 to 1	4,080
8-7	0.35	282 to 1	9,180
Nine-High	**1.33**	**73.9 to 1**	**34,680**
9-5	0.04	2,547 to 1	1,020
9-6	0.16	636 to 1	4,080
9-7	0.39	254 to 1	10,200
9-8	0.75	133 to 1	19,380
Ten-High	**2.71**	**35.9 to 1**	**70,380**
10-5	0.04	2,547 to 1	1,020
10-6	0.16	636 to 1	4,080
10-7	0.39	254 to 1	10,200
10-8	0.78	126 to 1	20,400
10-9	1.33	73.9 to 1	34,680

NOTE: For each specific hand in 52-card Deuce-to-Seven Low (excluding hands with Pairs), the Pat-hand probability is identical. As an example, a Pat 7-5-4-3-2 and a Pat 9-8-7-4-3 have equal probabilities. There are 1,020 possible ways to be dealt a hand of given rank less than a Pair of Two's. This is out of 2,598,960 possible five-card combinations. The probability of any specific non-Pair Pat low hand is 0.04%. The odds against are 2,547 to 1.

TABLE XL

THE PROBABILITY OF BEING DEALT SPECIFIC DEUCE-TO-SEVEN LOW HANDS <u>OR BETTER</u>
Before the Draw

The probability of being dealt this hand or better (Before the Draw)	Expressed in percent (%)...	The odds against it are...	Number of possible combinations
Seven-High	**0.16**	**636 to 1**	**4,080**
7-5-4-3-2	0.04	2,547 to 1	1,020
7-6 ■	0.16	636 to 1	4,080
Eight-High ■	**0.71**	**141 to 1**	**18,360**
8-5 ■	0.20	509 to 1	5,100
8-6 ■	0.35	282 to 1	9,180
8-7 ■	0.71	141 to 1	18,360
Nine-High ■	**2.04**	**48 to 1**	**53,040**
9-5 ■	0.75	133 to 1	19,380
9-6 ■	0.90	110 to 1	23,460
9-7 ■	1.30	76.2 to 1	33,660
9-8 ■	2.04	48 to 1	53,040
Ten-High ■	**4.75**	**20.1 to 1**	**123,420**
10-5 ■	2.08	47.1 to 1	54,060
10-6 ■	2.24	43.7 to 1	58,140
10-7 ■	2.63	37.0 to 1	68,340
10-8 ■	3.41	28.3 to 1	88,740
10-9 ■	4.75	20.1 to 1	123,420

■ OR BETTER

TABLE XLI

BASIC ONE-CARD DRAWING CHANCES FOR DEUCE-TO-SEVEN LOW

If you're drawing one card to. . .	Probability of making exact hand express'd in percent (%)	The odds against it are. . .
Seven-high *(Best: offsuit, no Straight possible)*	17.02	4.88 to 1
Seven-high *(Worst: 7-6-5-4, suited)* ...	6.38	14.7 to 1
Eight-high *(Best: offsuit, no Straight possible)*	25.53	2.92 to 1
Eight-high *(Worst: 8-7-6-5, suited)*	12.77	6.83 to 1
Nine-high *(Best: offsuit, no Straight possible)*	34.04	1.94 to 1
Nine-high *(Worst: 9-8-7-6, suited)*	19.15	4.22 to 1
Ten-high *(Best: offsuit, no Straight possible)*	42.55	1.35 to 1
Ten-high *(Worst: 10-9-8-7, suited)*	25.53	2.92 to 1

NOTE: The assumption is that all one-card draws have discarded a King.

TABLE XLII

BASIC TWO-CARD DRAWING CHANCES FOR DEUCE-TO-SEVEN LOW

If you're drawing two cards to. . .	Probability of making exact hand express'd in percent (%)	The odds against it are. . .
Seven-high *(Best: offsuit no Straight possible)*	4.44	21.5 to 1
Seven-high *(Worst: 7-6-5, suited)*	2.78	35.0 to 1
Eight-high *(Best: offsuit, no Straight possible)*	8.88	10.3 to 1
Eight-high *(Worst: 8-7-6, suited)*	6.94	13.4 to 1
Nine-high *(Best: offsuit, no Straight possible)*	14.80	5.76 to 1
Nine-high *(Worst: 9-8-7, suited)*	12.49	7.01 to 1

NOTE: The assumption for tables 41 and 42 is that all one-card draws have discarded a King, all two-card draws a King and a Queen. There are 47 possible one-card draws and 1,081 possible two-card draws.

TABLE XLIII

Ace-to-Five — Deuce-to-Seven

Rank Comparison Chart*

Rank of Hand	Ace-to-Five	Deuce-to-Seven	Rank of Hand	Ace-to-Five	Deuce-to-Seven
1	5432A	75432	37	**8732A**	98543
2	**6432A**	76432	38	8742A	98632
3	**6532A**	76532	39	**8743A**	98642
4	**6542A**	76542	40	**87432**	98643
5	**6543A**	**85432**	41	**8752A**	98652
6	**65432**	**86432**	42	**8753A**	98653
7	7432A	**86532**	43	**87532**	98654
8	7532A	**86542**	44	**8754A**	98732
9	7542A	**86543**	45	**87542**	98742
10	7543A	**87432**	46	**87543**	98743
11	75432	**87532**	47	**8762A**	98752
12	7632A	**87542**	48	**8763A**	98753
13	7642A	**87543**	49	**87632**	98754
14	7643A	**87632**	50	**8764A**	98762
15	76432	**87642**	51	**87642**	98763
16	7652A	**87643**	52	**87643**	98764
17	7653A	**87652**	53	**8765A**	**10-5432**
18	76532	**87653**	54	**87652**	**10-6432**
19	7654A	95432	55	**87653**	**10-6532**
20	76542	96432	56	**87654**	**10-6542**
21	76543	96532	57	9432A	**10-6543**
22	**8432A**	96542	58	9532A	**10-7432**
23	**8532A**	96543	59	9542A	**10-7532**
24	**8542A**	97432	60	9543A	**10-7542**
25	**8543A**	97532	61	95432	**10-7543**
26	**85432**	97542	62	9632A	**10-7632**
27	**8632A**	97543	63	9642A	**10-7642**
28	**8642A**	97632	64	9643A	**10-7643**
29	**8643A**	97642	65	96432	**10-7652**
30	**86432**	97643	66	9652A	**10-7653**
31	**8652A**	97652	67	9653A	10-7654
32	**8653A**	97653	68	96532	**10-8432**
33	**86532**	97654	69	9654A	**10-8532**
34	**8654A**	98432	70	96542	**10-8542**
35	**86542**	98532	71	96543	**10-8543**
36	**86543**	98542	72	9732A	**10-8632**

(continued)

TABLE XLIII

Ace-to-Five — Deuce-to-Seven
Rank Comparison Chart*
(continued)

Rank of Hand	Ace-to-Five	Deuce-to-Seven	Rank of Hand	Ace-to-Five	Deuce-to-Seven
73	9742A	10-8642	100	98542	10-9743
74	9743A	10-8643	101	98543	10-9752
75	97432	10-8652	102	9862A	10-9753
76	9752A	10-8653	103	9863A	10-9754
77	9753A	10-8654	104	98632	10-9762
78	97532	10-8732	105	9864A	10-9763
79	9754A	10-8742	106	98642	10-9764
80	97542	10-8753	107	98643	10-9765
81	97543	10-8752	108	9865A	10-9832
82	9762A	10-8753	109	98652	10-9842
83	9763A	10-8754	110	98653	10-9843
84	97632	10-8762	111	98654	10-9852
85	9764A	10-8763	112	9872A	10-9853
86	97642	10-8764	113	9873A	10-9854
87	97643	10-8765	114	98732	10-9862
88	9765A	10-9432	115	9874A	10-9863
89	97652	10-9532	116	98742	10-9864
90	97653	10-9542	117	98743	10-9865
91	97654	10-9543	118	9875A	10-9872
92	9832A	10-9632	119	98752	10-9873
93	9842A	10-9642	120	98753	10-9874
94	9843A	10-9643	121	98754	10-9875
95	98432	10-9652	122	9876A	J-5432
96	9852A	10-9653	123	98762	J-6432
97	9853A	10-9654	124	98763	J-6532
98	98532	10-9732	125	98764	J-6542
99	9854A	10-9742	126	98765	J-6543

*This chart compares hands by rank, **not** by frequency of distribution.

TABLE XLIV

ACE-TO-FIVE (with Joker) — DEUCE-TO-SEVEN (without Joker) APPROXIMATE* FREQUENCY OF DISTRIBUTION COMPARISION

You will be dealt this Pat hand or better in Ace-to-Five (with Joker). . .	or. . .	This Pat hand or better in Deuce-to-Seven (without Joker). . .	About this often. . .
5-4-3-2-A		7-6-4-3-2	One time in 1,250
6-5-3-2-A		8-5-4-3-2	One time in 500
6-5-4-3-2		8-6-5-4-3	One time in 285
7-5-4-3-2		8-7-6-4-3	One time in 160
7-6-5-4-A		9-7-5-3-2	One time in 100
8-5-4-3-2		9-8-4-3-2	One time in 75
8-7-5-2-A		9-8-7-6-3	One time in 50
9-6-5-4-3		10-8-7-6-3	One time in 30
9-8-6-5-3		J-7-5-3-2	One time in 20

*The frequencies of these hands do not coincide exactly. They are the closest pairing possible.

TABLE XLV

THE PROBABILITY OF BEING DEALT SPECIFIC SEVEN-CARD LOW (RAZZ) STARTING HANDS
(1st three cards)

The probability that you will be dealt this on the first three cards. . .	Expressed in percent (%) is	The odds against it are. . .	Number of possible combinations
3-2-A (Lowest possible)	0.29	344 to 1	64
Four-High or lower	1.16	85.3 to 1	256
Five-High or lower	2.90	33.5 to 1	640
Six-High or lower	5.79	16.3 to 1	1,280
Seven-High or lower ..	10.14	8.87 to 1	2,240
Eight-High or lower ...	16.22	5.17 to 1	3,584
Nine-High or lower	24.33	3.11 to. 1	5,376
Two parts of a Five-High or lower* .	13.76	6.27 to 1	3,040
Two parts of a Six-High or lower* ..	20.63	3.85 to 1	4,560
Two parts of a Seven-High or lower*	28.89	2.46 to 1	6,384
Two parts of an Eight-High or lower*	38.52	1.60 to 1	8,512

*These starting hands either include at 10-J-Q or K **or** a Pair.

pot. In chess you **cannot** do the right thing and lose, but in Poker you **can.**

Sometimes it takes time for the percentages to guarantee you a profit. You need to search for tiny advantages, and these tables were designed to help you find them.

TABLE XLVI

CHANCE OF IMPROVEMENT FOR VARIOUS SEVEN-CARD LOW (RAZZ) HANDS

IF YOU HAVE 3♡-2♣-A◇:

The probability that the final strength of your hand after seven cards will be...	Expressed in percent (%) is	The odds against it are...
Bicycle (5-4-3-2-A)	7.15	13.0 to 1
Six-High	11.80	7.48 to 1
Six-High ■	18.95	4.28 to 1
Seven-High	14.30	5.99 to 1
Seven-High ■	33.25	2.01 to 1
Eight-High	15.02	5.66 to 1
Eight-High ■	48.27	1.07 to 1

IF YOU HAVE 2♠-A♡-K◇:

The probability that the final strength of your hand after seven cards will be...	Expressed in percent (%) is	The odds against it are...
Bicycle (5-4-3-2-A)	1.25	78.8 to 1
Six-High	3.40	28.4 to 1
Six-High ■	4.65	20.5 to 1
Seven-High	6.07	15.5 to 1
Seven-High ■	10.73	8.33 to 1
Eight-High	8.91	10.22 to 1
Eight-High ■	19.63	4.09 to 1

IF YOU HAVE A◇-Q♣-K◇:

The probability that the final strength of your hand after seven cards will be...	Expressed in percent (%) is	The odds against it are...
Bicycle (5-4-3-2-A)	0.12	827 to 1
Six-High	0.48	206 to 1
Six-High ■	0.60	165 to 1
Seven-High	1.21	81.8 to 1
Seven-High ■	1.81	54.2 to 1
Eight-High	2.42	40.4 to 1
Eight-High ■	4.23	22.6 to 1

(continued)

(continued)

CHANCE OF IMPROVEMENT FOR VARIOUS SEVEN-CARD LOW (RAZZ) HANDS

IF YOU HAVE 4♣-3♠-2♠-A♣:

The probability that the final strength of your hand after seven cards will be. . .	Expressed in percent (%) is	The odds against it are. . .
Bicycle (5-4-3-2-A)	23.43	3.27 to 1
Six-High	19.45	4.14 to 1
Six-High ■	42.88	1.33 to 1
Seven-High	15.84	5.31 to 1
Seven-High ■	58.72	0.70 to 1
Eight-High	12.60	6.93 to 1
Eight-High ■	71.32	0.40 to 1

IF YOU HAVE 3◇-2◇-A♣-K◇:

The probability that the final strength of your hand after seven cards will be. . .	Expressed in percent (%) is	The odds against it are. . .
Bicycle (5-4-3-2-A)	3.98	24.1 to 1
Six-High	7.22	12.9 to 1
Six-High ■	11.19	7.93 to 1
Seven-High	9.71	9.30 to 1
Seven-High ■	20.90	3.78 to 1
Eight-High	11.47	7.72 to 1
Eight-High ■	32.38	2.09 to 1

IF YOU HAVE 2♣-A♡-Q♣-K◇:

The probability that the final strength of your hand after seven cards will be. . .	Expressed in percent (%) is	The odds against it are. . .
Bicycle (5-4-3-2-A)	0.37	269 to 1
Six-High	1.11	89.1 to 1
Six-High ■	1.48	66.6 to 1
Seven-High	2.22	44.0 to 1
Seven-High ■	3.70	26.0 to 1
Eight-High	3.70	26.0 to 1
Eight-High ■	7.40	12.5 to 1

(continued)

IF YOU HAVE 4♣-3♡-2♣-A♢-K♢:

The probability that the final strength of your hand after seven cards will be. . .	Expressed in percent (%) is	The odds against it are. . .
Bicycle (5-4-3-2-A)	16.47	5.07 to 1
Six-High	14.99	5.67 to 1
Six-High ■	31.45	2.18 to 1
Seven-High	13.51	6.40 to 1
Seven-High ■	44.96	1.22 to 1
Eight-High	12.03	7.32 to 1
Eight-High ■	56.98	0.75 to 1

IF YOU HAVE 3♢-2♣-A♡-Q♠-K♡:

The probability that the final strength of your hand after seven cards will be. . .	Expressed in percent (%) is	The odds against it are. . .
Bicycle (5-4-3-2-A)	1.48	66.6 to 1
Six-High	2.96	32.8 to 1
Six-High ■	4.44	21.5 to 1
Seven-High	4.44	21.5 to 1
Seven-High ■	8.88	10.3 to 1
Eight-High	5.92	15.9 to 1
Eight-High ■	14.80	5.76 to 1

IF YOU HAVE 4♣-3♣-2♡-A♣-K♢-Q♠:

The probability that the final strength of your hand after seven cards will be. . .	Expressed in percent (%) is	The odds against it are. . .
Bicycle (5-4-3-2-A)	8.70	10.5 to 1
Six-High	8.70	10.5 to 1
Six-High ■	17.39	4.75 to 1
Seven-High	8.70	10.5 to 1
Seven-High ■	26.09	2.83 to 1
Eight-High	8.70	10.5 to 1
Eight-High ■	34.78	1.88 to 1

With four cards to come, there are 211,876 possible outcomes. With three cards to come, there are 17,296 possible outcomes. With two cards to come, there are 1,081 possible outcomes. With one card to come, there are 46 possible outcomes.

NOTE: This chart assumes no knowledge of exposed cards in other hands.

■ OR BETTER

*There are 656 pages in *Super/System*, both numbered and unnumbered.

GREAT CARDOZA BOOKS
ORDER TOLL-FREE 1-800-577-WINS

• MIKE CARO •

CARO'S MOST PROFITABLE HOLD'EM ADVICE by Mike Caro. The "Mad Genius of Poker" has influenced just about every professional player and world champion alive. You'll journey far beyond the traditional tactical tools offered in most poker books and for the first time, have access to the entire missing arsenal of strategies left out of everything you've ever seen or experienced. Caro's first major work in two decades is packed with hundreds of powerful ideas, concepts, and strategies. This book represents Caro's lifelong research into beating the game of hold'em. 408 pages, $24.95.

MASTERING HOLD'EM AND OMAHA by Mike Caro and Mike Cappelletti. Learn the professional secrets to mastering the two most popular games of big-money poker. This book is packed with ideas, with the focus on making you a winning player. You'll learn everything from the strategies for play on the preflop, flop, turn and river, to image control and taking advantage of players stuck in losing patterns. You'll also learn how to create consistent winning patterns, use perception to gain an edge, avoid common errors, go after and win default pots, recognize and use the various types of raises, play marginal hands for profit, and Cappelletti's unique point count system for Omaha. 328 pages, $19.95.

CARO'S GUIDE TO DOYLE BRUNSON'S SUPER SYSTEM - Working with World Champion Doyle Brunson, the legendary Mike Caro has created a fresh look to the "Bible" of all poker books, adding new and personal insights that help you understand the original work. Caro breaks 36 concepts into either "Analysis, Commentary, Concept, Mission, Play-By-Play, Psychology, Statistics, Story or Strategy. Lots of illustrations and winning concepts give even more value to this great work. 86 pages, 8 1/2 x 11, stapled. $19.95.

CARO'S BOOK OF TELLS (THE BODY LANGUAGE OF POKER) - Finally! Mike Caro's classic book is now revised and back in print! This long-awaited revision takes a detailed look at the art and science of tells, the physical mannerisms which give away a player's hand. Featuring photos of poker players in action along with explanations about when players are bluffing and when they're not, these powerful ideas can give you the decisive edge! This invaluable book should be in every player's library! 352 pages! $24.95.

CARO'S FUNDAMENTAL SECRETS OF WINNING POKER - The world's foremost poker theoretician and strategist presents the essential strategies, concepts, and secret winning plays that comprise the very foundation of winning poker play. Shows how to win more from weak players, equalize stronger players, bluff a bluffer, win big pots, where to sit against weak players, the six factors of strategic table image. Includes selected tips on hold 'em, 7 stud, draw, lowball, tournaments, more. 160 Pages, $12.95.

• DOYLE BRUNSON •

SUPER SYSTEM by Doyle Brunson - This classic book is considered by the pros to be the best book ever written on poker! Jam-packed with advanced strategies, theories, tactics and money-making techniques—no serious poker player can afford to be without this hard-hitting information. Includes fifty pages of the most precise poker statistics ever published. Features chapters written by poker's biggest superstars, such as Dave Sklansky, Mike Caro, Chip Reese, Bobby Baldwin, and Doyle—two world champions and three master theorists. This is a must-read. 605 pages. $29.95.

SUPER SYSTEM 2 by Doyle Brunson - The most anticipated poker book ever, SS2 expands upon the original with more games and professional secrets from the best in the world. Superstar contributors include Daniel Negreanu, Lyle Berman, Bobby Baldwin, Johnny Chan, Mike Caro, Jennifer Harman, Todd Brunson, and Crandell Addington. 672 pages. $34.95.

ACCORDING TO DOYLE by Doyle Brunson - Learn what it takes to be a great poker player by climbing inside the mind of poker's most famous champion. Fascinating anecdotes and adventures from Doyle's early career playing poker in roadhouses and with other great champions are interspersed with lessons one can learn from the champion who has made more money at poker than anyone else in the history of the game. Readers learn what makes a great player tick, how he approaches the game, and receive candid, powerful advice from the legend himself. The Mad Genius of poker, Mike Caro, says, "Brunson is the greatest poker player who ever lived. This book shows why." 208 pgs. $14.95.

POWERFUL POKER SIMULATIONS

A MUST FOR SERIOUS PLAYERS WITH A COMPUTER!
IBM compatibles CD ROM Windows 3.1, 95, and 98 - Full Color Graphics

Play interactive poker against these **incredible** full color poker simulation programs - they're the absolute **best** method to improve game. *Computer players act like real players.* All games let you set the limits and rake, have fully programmable players, adjustable lineup, stat tracking, and Hand Analyzer for starting hands. MIke Caro, the world's foremost poker theoretician says, *"Amazing...A steal for under $500...get it, it's great."* Includes *free telephone support.* **New Feature!** - "Smart advisor" gives expert advice for *every* play in *every* game!

NEW!
Windows Versions
More Features!

1. TURBO TEXAS HOLD'EM FOR WINDOWS - $89.95 - Choose which players, how many, 2-10, you want to play, create loose/tight game, control check-raising, bluffing, position, sensitivity to pot odds, more! Also, instant replay, pop-up odds, Professional Advisor, keeps track of play statistics. Free bonus: *Hold'em Hand Analyzer* analyzes all 169 pocket hands in detail, their win rates under any conditions you set. Caro says this *"hold'em software is the most powerful ever created."* Great product!

2. TURBO SEVEN-CARD STUD FOR WINDOWS - $89.95 - *Create any conditions of play*; choose number of players (2-8), bet amounts, fixed or spread limit, bring-in method, tight/loose conditions, position, reaction to board, number of dead cards, stack deck to create special conditions, instant replay. Terrific stat reporting includes analysis of starting cards, 3-D bar charts, graphs. Play interactively, run high speed simulation to test strategies. *Hand Analyzer* analyzes starting hands in detail. Wow!

3. TURBO OMAHA HIGH-LOW SPLIT FOR WINDOWS - $89.95 -Specify any playing conditions; betting limits, number of raises, blind structures, button position, aggressiveness/passiveness of opponents, number of players (2-10), types of hands dealt, blinds, position, board reaction, specify flop, turn, river cards! Choose opponents, use provided point count or create your own. Statistical reporting, instant replay, pop-up odds, high speed simulation to test strategies, amazing Hand Analyzer, much more!

4. TURBO OMAHA HIGH FOR WINDOWS - $89.95 - Same features as above, but tailored for the Omaha High-only game. Caro says program is *"an electrifying research tool...it can clearly be worth thousands of dollars to any serious player.* A must for Omaha High players.

5. TURBO 7 STUD 8 OR BETTER - $89.95 - Brand new with all the features you expect from the Wilson Turbo products: the latest artificial intelligence, instant advice and exact odds, play versus 2-7 opponents, enhanced data charts that can be exported or printed, the ability to fold out of turn and immediately go to the next hand, ability to peek at opponents hand, optional warning mode that warns you if a play disagrees with the advisor, and automatic testing mode that can run up to 50 tests unattended. Challenge tough computer players who vary their styles for a truly great poker game.

---

6. TOURNAMENT TEXAS HOLD'EM - $59.95

Set-up for tournament practice and play, this realistic simulation pits you against celebrity look-alikes. Tons of options let you control tournament size with 10 to 300 entrants, select limits, ante, rake, blind structures, freezeouts, number of rebuys and competition level of opponents - average, tough, or toughest. Pop-up status report shows how you're doing vs. the competition. Save tournaments in progress to play again later. Additional feature allows you to quickly finish a folded hand and go on to the next.